Management of
MIGRATORY SHORE AND
UPLAND GAME BIRDS
in North America

Management of MIGRATORY SHORE AND UPLAND GAME BIRDS in North America

Edited By
GLEN C. SANDERSON

University of Nebraska Press
Lincoln and London

CONTRIBUTORS

Administrators and biologists in the International Association of Fish and Wildlife Agencies, and the Fish and Wildlife Service, U.S. Department of the Interior, have joined forces in a unique effort to provide this book. The work of more than 50 contributing authors from most of the states and provinces in the United States and Canada has been augmented by advice and counsel from many others. Further, the information provided by scientists in previously published records has been of immeasurable value in preparation of this material and in the collective advancement of our knowledge of migratory shore and upland birds.

First Bison Book printing: 1980

Most recent printing indicated by first digit below:
1   2   3   4   5   6   7   8   9   10

Library of Congress Cataloging in Publication Data

Main entry under title:

Management of migratory shore and upland game birds in North America.

   Originally produced through the cooperation of the International Association of Fish and Wildlife Agencies, and the U.S. Fish and Wildlife Service.
   Reprint of the 1977 ed. published by the International Association of Fish and Wildlife Agencies, Washington.
   Includes index.
   1. Game bird management—North America.   I.   Sanderson, Glen C.   II.   International Association of Fish and Wildlife Agencies.   III.   United States. Fish and Wildlife Service.
SK361.M33   1977   639'.97'8297   79–23802

ISBN 0–8032–9117–5 (paper)

First published in 1977 by the International Association of Fish and Wildlife Agencies in cooperation with the Fish and Wildlife Service, U.S. Department of the Interior.

Manufactured in the United States of America

About the Book

Wildlife is becoming more commonly defined as all the wild or nondomesticated animals and plants on our earth. An awesome number of creatures and components of their environment are involved, and the charge to preserve, protect, enhance, and manage these is a challenging, difficult, and complicated responsibility.

Awareness of the broad picture is important for evaluating total wildlife needs, but accomplishments are most likely to occur when attention is given to the individual species or wildlife groups having similarities in management problems. Emphasis in this direction is now occurring with endangered and threatened wildlife, as has been the case with game species of major human interest through the years.

This book has singled out a group of migratory game birds that has received relatively less attention than more popular species, although they have provided outstanding human enjoyment and benefits for centuries. The group includes migratory shore and upland species, often referred to as "webless" migratory birds.

Accelerated research and management for these species were stimulated through urging by state and federal organizations and citizens groups as early as the 1950's. These efforts resulted in the dedication of special funds, starting in 1967, to gather information needed for more effective management of migratory shore and upland game birds. These funds stimulated and augmented work throughout the United States.

Information in this book shows what has been accomplished, what needs to be done, and what action is required to implement programs necessary to maintain shore and upland bird populations and realize their many benefits. The printed text is complemented by attractive and informative artwork and photographs. Collectively this publication advances information and awareness of needs for migratory shore and upland birds a great step beyond that available before. It is a valuable guide for helping all of us meet our collective responsibilities to this outstanding wildlife resource.

Lynn A. Greenwalt, Director
U.S. Fish and Wildlife Service

Foreword

It is difficult to predict the results of a particular action, how far the "ripples" will go, or in which direction. Some actions produce no results, others produce results well beyond anything anticipated. This publication is a case in point.

In September 1967, the International Association of Fish and Wildlife Agencies, through its (then) President, Melvin O. Steen, created a National Program Planning Committee for Migratory Shore and Upland Game Birds. Few would have guessed that the book you are about to read would result from that action. Although the International Association recognized the need to upgrade research and management efforts directed toward these species, they could hardly have anticipated as thorough a planning job as is presented here. The Steering Committee and the Species Committees have done their work well.

Perhaps as a holdover from an earlier era, the major effort directed toward migratory game bird research and management by state and federal agencies has been, and still is, for ducks and geese. The other migratory game birds — mourning doves, white-winged doves, woodcock, snipe, rails and gallinules, band-tailed pigeons, coots, and sandhill cranes — have indeed been neglected species. This neglect is totally unrealistic in view of the present and future recreational opportunities they provide. Mourning doves alone stimulate an estimated 11.4 million hunting trips in the United States annually. This number represents more trips than are made for either ducks or geese, and almost as many as for ducks and geese *combined*.

The authors and the Committee have documened, to the extent possible, the present status of these resources and have presented programs and financing needed to bring their management into the 20th century. The International Association of Fish and Wildlife Agencies commends its earlier members and the National Program Planning Committee for the farsightedness of the former and the effective presentation of the problems and their solution by the latter.

I wish to recognize the support that this project has received from other presidents of the International Association: Carl N. Crouse, Kenneth H. Doan, John E. Phelps, and Charles D. Kelley, who have served during the development of materials for this book.

Completion of the programs presented in the following pages will require that the International Association and its regional associations join with other national conservation organizations to press for early adoption and adequate funding of these programs.

O. Earle Frye, Jr., President, 1973-74
International Association of
Fish and Wildlife Agencies
Tallahassee, Florida
23 March 1976

Preface

An annual charge to the National Program Planning Group of the International Association of Fish and Wildlife Agencies has been the solicitation, screening, and selection of accelerated research projects for migratory shore and upland game birds. Many significant studies have been completed or are under way. A prevailing primary concern is that of funding many of the worthwhile projects proposed. Because funding is limited, administrative units comprised of groups of states must annually establish project priority and thus award contracts for only a portion of the projects requested. Several approaches to providing additional monies and more realistic funding sources have been unsuccessful.

The planning group has recognized that most successful nationwide programs are based on adequate preliminary planning, including clear identification of resource needs. Those responsible for overall funding support have stated that they have not been provided with sufficient background data and clear identification of needs from which to most effectively develop budget requests and provide appropriate funds. Recognition of this fact prompted the development of a National Plan for management of migratory shore and upland game birds.

Obtaining and organizing basic scientific data of a diversified nature obviously required the assistance of the best talent in the business. Initial assistance with organization and format was given by Dr. Lee E. Yeager. As this book relates, nine species committee chairmen or cochairmen were selected by a Steering Committee. These chairmen, in turn, worked with shore and upland bird technical committees within administrative units in the recruitment of more than 50 scientists from throughout the United States and Canada. The scientists recruited provided basic information and developed recommendations for species within their area of responsibility. Their reports have been complemented by the work of steering committee members through the amalgamation of information from species plans into overall appraisals and conclusions. Of foremost importance, and a major requisite for the successful completion of this plan has been the approval given by administrators in many agencies, institutions, and organizations for the volunteer service of their employees. This volunteer work, which has necessitated hundreds of hours of time, some travel, and many miscellaneous expenses, has been of immeasurable value.

Success in preparing material and in printing the resulting book also has been dependent upon financial support provided by the U.S. Fish and Wildlife Service through dedication of part of the funds earmarked for the Accelerated Research Program. Substantial allocations have been made during fiscal years 1973 through 1976. Fant W. Martin and Judith Bladen represented the U.S. Fish and Wildlife Service in liaison with the International Association of Fish and Wildlife Agencies in the publication of this book. Richard A. Coon, U.S. Fish and Wildlife Service, assisted with the preparation of the final manuscript.

Generous financial assistance has also been given by the National Audubon Society, who supported the outstanding contribution of Karl Badgley in preparing the artwork for the frontispiece and for the introduction to each species plan. Karl Badgley is Assistant Art Director, WKYC-TV, Cleveland, and is a free-lance wildlife artist in his spare time.

Additional illustrations were graciously provided through the interest and talent of Beverley C. Sanderson.

Glenn D. Chambers and Charles W. Schwartz, Missouri Department of Conservation, provided the spectacular photographs of sandhill cranes and mourning doves, respectively, for the end sheets of this book.

John S. Gottschalk, Executive Director of the International Association of Fish and Wildlife Agencies, reviewed the manuscript and offered important suggestions for improvement. His liaison work with the United States Fish and Wildlife Service, the Editor, and the Steering Committee in preparation of the printing contract and in effecting final publication also is gratefully acknowledged.

Glen C. Sanderson, Head, Section of Wildlife Research, Illinois Natural History Survey, Urbana, assisted by Ruth Stillwell and Helen C. Schultz, edited the book. Laurie Sanderson checked the references and read proof and Beverley C. Sanderson was called on to assist with virtually all phases of the work. The following employees of the Illinois Natural History Survey assisted as indicated: Eleanore Wilson and Elizabeth McConaha typed the manuscript, Lloyd LeMere drew the maps and graphs, and Larry Farlow made prints of many negatives submitted by authors and photographed the maps and graphs.

Administration of the Accelerated Research funds utilized in completing this book has involved the cooperative efforts of the Migratory Bird and Habitat Research Laboratory of the U.S. Fish and Wildlife Service and the Missouri Department of Conservation.

Steering Committee of the National Program Planning Group for Migratory Shore and Upland Game Birds:

Wayne W. Sandfort, Assistant Director, Resources, Colorado Division of Wildlife, Denver, *Chairman.*

Spencer R. Amend, Energy Activities Leader, Office of Biological Services, U.S. Fish and Wildlife Service, Portland, Oregon.

George A. Ammann, Former Wildlife Biologist, Michigan Department of Natural Resources, Lansing.

John M. Anderson, Director Sanctuary Department, National Audubon Society, Sharon, Connecticut.

Harold T. Harper, Upland Game Coordinator, California Department of Fish and Game, Sacramento.

Fant W. Martin, Director, Migratory Bird and Habitat Research Laboratory, U.S. Fish and Wildlife Service, Laurel, Maryland.

James M. Ruckel, Assistant Chief, In Charge of Game Management, Division of Wildlife Resources, West Virginia Department of Natural Resources, Charleston.

Kenneth C. Sadler, Research Supervisor, Wildlife Research Section, Missouri Department of Conservation, Columbia.

Contents

1 Introduction   1
Wayne W. Sandfort

2 Sandhill Crane   5
James C. Lewis
Chairman of the Species Committee

3 Rails and Gallinules   45
Dan C. Holliman
Chairman of the Species Committee

4 American Coot   123
Leigh H. Frederickson
Chairman of the Species Committee

5 American Woodcock   149
Ray B. Owen, Jr.
Chairman of the Species Committee

6 Common Snipe 189

Michael J. Fogarty and Keith A. Arnold
Cochairmen of the Species Committee

7 Band-Tailed Pigeon 211

Robert G. Jeffrey
Chairman of the Species Committee

8 White-Winged Dove 247

David E. Brown
Chairman of the Species Committee

9 Mourning Dove 275

James E. Keeler
Chairman of the Species Committee

10 Shorebirds 301

Ronald M. Jurek and Howard R. Leach
Cochairmen of the Species Committee

11 The Resources and Their Values 323

Wayne W. Sandfort
Chairman of the Steering Committee

Index 351

1

Introduction

Wayne W. Sandfort, Assistant Director, Resources, Colorado Division of Wildlife, Denver.

Wildlife management at its inception was primarily game management, and big game, small game, and waterfowl held major management interests. On the other hand, migratory shore and upland game birds — doves (*Zenaida macroura, Z. asiatica*), woodcock (*Philohela minor = Scolopax minor* of Edwards 1974), band-tailed pigeon (*Columba fasciata*), American coot (*Fulica americana*), common snipe (*Capella gallinago = Gallinago gallinago* of Edwards 1974), sandhill crane (*Grus canadensis*), and others of this resource category — although having dedicated hunter and other followings, generally took a back seat to the game species more popular with sport hunters. For this reason, research and management programs have lagged for migratory shore and upland birds, and the collection of basic data on populations, habitat needs, use potentials, and effective management programs has received too little attention.

In recent years, however, there have been some changes, both in public attitudes toward all wildlife — including the less popular and less abundant game species and nongame wildlife — and in the interests and concerns of wildlife biologists and administrators. In the mid-1960's, primarily through the impetus and interest of the Southeastern Association of Game and Fish Commissioners, the then United States Bureau of Sport Fisheries and Wildlife, the Wildlife Management Institute, the National Audubon Society, and other agencies and organizations, successful efforts were made to obtain earmarked federal funds for new and accelerated studies of migratory shore and upland game birds. The late Thomas R. Evans, Illinois Department of Conservation, was appointed as Chairman of National Program Planning Committee to represent the International Association of Fish and Wildlife Agencies in the new Accelerated Research Program. Duncan MacDonald administered the program for the Bureau of Sport Fisheries and Wildlife.

Original plans called for an annual budget of $450,000, including $250,000 for state projects and $200,000 to supplement Bureau funds. It was requested that appropriations be increased in the second and third years to attain a stable annual funding level of $1,296,000. Of this amount, $500,000 was to be used for work performed by states under contract with the Bureau of Sport Fisheries and Wildlife, $596,000 for operating funds for the Bureau, and $200,000 for special studies to be conducted by the Bureau.

The initial appropriation in July 1967, for fiscal year 1968, was $250,000. Of this amount, $175,000 was allocated for state projects, $50,000 for two Bureau projects, and $25,000 for administration of the program by the Bureau. Subsequent annual appropriations remained at $250,000 for fiscal years 1969 through 1975, and thus the hoped-for appropriations of $1,296,000 annually were not attained.

Despite shortages of funds, much significant research work on migratory shore and upland game birds has been accomplished during the time the Accelerated Research Program has been in effect. Through contracts with 40 states, 67 projects related to nine species or groups of species were conducted through FY 75. Types of studies included banding, randomization of census routes, telemetry, habitat evaluation, parasite research, general ecology, call-count evaluation, and general census and inventory.

Work conducted under the accelerated research programs has been rewarding and has resulted not only in benefits to various species but in the realization of the great recreational potential offered by migratory shore and upland birds. Studies thus far have given initial insight into the management complexities of the problems associated with the many species involved. They also have provided preliminary information on the amount of support, in terms of finances, man power, studies, land acquisitions, and similar concerns, that must be authorized if full public benefits from these species are to be realized.

To identify additional needed actions, technical committee chairmen in each of five administrative units — Southeast, Northeast, Central, Midwest, and Western — assisted the Steering Committee in developing this plan by selecting a chairman and committee members for each of nine Species Committees. The species represented included the mourning dove, sandhill crane, woodcock, white-winged dove, band-tailed pigeon, American coot, common snipe, rails and gallinules, and shore and upland birds — general. Most Species Committees worked with an individual bird, but the committee with the responsibility for rails and gallinules was concerned with eight species. The Committee on Shore and Upland Birds — General, considered 64 species of which all but the common snipe and American woodcock are not hunted.

Working under the general auspices of the International Association of Fish and Wildlife Agencies, the editor, Species Committees, and the Steering Committee have assembled this comprehensive treatise on migratory shore and upland game bird resources. Detailed results are presented in sections covering individual species or groups of species. These sections are followed by an overall view that indicates: (1) *Distribution and Abundance,* prepared by James M. Ruckel and Kenneth C. Sadler; (2) *Management Approaches and Benefits,* written by Harold T. Harper and Kenneth C. Sadler; (3) *Manage-*

ment Needs — Now and in the Future, authored by George A. Ammann and Fant W. Martin; and (4) *Financing — Past, Present, and Future,* assembled by Spencer R. Amend, Fant W. Martin, and Wayne W. Sandfort.

Although data support a solid recommendation for action and related funding, it is recognized that budget developments may result in less available money than that amount suggested here for documented needs of species and optimum management programs. It should also be recognized that continuing study and knowledge could result in modification of the recommendations outlined. It is important to note that all individuals, agencies, and organizations that have contributed to this book do not necessarily support or endorse all of the recommendations and suggestions made in all accounts.

As the material in this report is reviewed and appraised, the great present and future recreational potential of the so-called "minor" migratory game bird resources should become apparent. It is hoped that the evaluation and recommendations contained here will assist all those involved in wildlife management to tap this potential, not only for the benefit of migratory shore and upland game birds but for all who appreciate them as a valuable resource.

LITERATURE CITED

Edwards, Ernest P. 1974. A coded list of birds of the world. Ernest P. Edwards, Sweet Briar, Va. 174pp.

2

Sandhill Crane
(Grus canadensis)

James C. Lewis, Assistant Unit Leader, Oklahoma Cooperative Wildlife Research Unit, Oklahoma State University, Stillwater, *Chairman.*

George W. Archibald, Director, International Crane Foundation, Barbaboo, Wisconsin.

Roderick C. Drewien, Research Associate, Idaho Cooperative Wildlife Research Unit, College of Forestry, Wildlife and Range Sciences, University of Idaho, Moscow.

Charles R. Frith, Supervisory Environmental Resources Specialist, Army Corps of Engineers, Omaha, Nebraska.

Ernest A. Gluesing, Department of Wildlife Sciences, Utah State University, Logan.

Ronald D. Klataske, Regional Representative, National Audubon Society, 813 Juniper Drive, Manhattan, Kansas.

Carroll D. Littlefield, Biologist, Malheur National Wildlife Refuge, Burns, Oregon.

James Sands, Co-Project Leader, Game Bird Studies, New Mexico Department of Game & Fish, Albuquerque.

W. J. D. Stephen, Research Manager (Migratory Birds), Canadian Wildlife Service, Edmonton, Alberta.

Lovett E. Williams, Jr., Wildlife Biologist, Florida Game and Fresh Water Fish Commission, Gainesville.

SUMMARY

Three subspecies of sandhill cranes are still threatened: the Cuban (*G. c. nesiotes*), the Florida (*G. c. pratensis*), and the Mississippi (*G. c. pulla*). There are now an estimated 22,000 to 26,000 greater (*G. c. tabida*), 220,000 (minimum) lesser (*G. c. canadensis*) and Canadian (*G. c. rowani*), 4,000 to 6,000 Florida, and 30 to 45 Mississippi sandhill cranes, and an unknown but small number of Cuban cranes. In recent decades, populations of all subspecies, except the Mississippi, have increased. Despite this encouraging trend, we do not know the population trends of the two most abundant subspecies (lesser and Canadian) in the decade since hunting was legalized. Accurate harvest data are not presently available; however, the annual harvest may exceed 15,000 cranes of the lesser and Canadian subspecies. This harvest is large enough possibly to jeopardize some subpopulations, and emphasizes the need to initiate good harvest surveys and studies of age ratios and to improve the accuracy of censuses. Utilization of the crane resource by bird watchers and naturalists far exceeds the use by hunters, and these nonconsumptive uses continue to increase. Managers should take steps to insure that the public is aware of cranes and has opportunities to enjoy them. Major management needs include purchase of land where key habitat is threatened, expanded banding programs, harvest surveys, and annual population surveys. High-priority research needs include (1) development of an improved technique for censusing cranes along the Platte River in Nebraska, (2) harvest surveys in Mexico and Siberia and improvement of harvest surveys in the United States and Canada, (3) an inventory and classification of nesting and wintering habitat of lessers, Canadians, and some greaters, and (4) surveys of how people want to use the crane resource.

DESCRIPTION

Sandhill cranes, in the family Gruidae, are, with the exception of those that nest in Siberia and Cuba, restricted to North America. Cranes have long legs, necks, and bills (Fig. 2-1) and adults weigh from 2.72 to 5.44 kg (6.0 to 12.0 lb). Adults have dark red papillose skin on the crown; immatures have rusty brown plummage on the crown until the postjuvenile molt is complete. The body plummage of adults is slate gray except when stained a rusty brown in summer by ferric oxide when the cranes preen themselves with marsh debris.

Six subspecies are presently known. The lesser nests in tundra and boreal

Fig. 2-1. Sandhill cranes, some dancing, on a secondary roost near the Platte River, Nebraska. (Photo by James C. Lewis.)

forests of Siberia, Alaska, and Canada; the Canadian nests in central Canada; and the greater nests in the Lake States, the northwestern United States, and the extreme southern edge of Canada. These three subspecies are migratory. The other three subspecies are sedentary: the Mississippi in Jackson County, Mississippi; the Florida (Fig. 2-2) in Florida and extreme southwestern Georgia; and the Cuban in Cuba.

Size, head profile, and coloration are used to distinguish subspecies. There is disagreement over the validity of the Canadian subspecies (Stephen et al. 1966, Johnson and Stewart 1973, Walkinshaw 1973a:81). There is considerable overlap in body measurements and coloration of lesser and Canadian and between Canadian and greater sandhills (Walkinshaw 1949:6-20, 1965a; Aldrich 1972).

LIFE HISTORY

Breeding pairs select tundra, dunes, shallow-water marshes or bogs for nesting. Territory size varies; one pair may defend 405 hectares (1,000 acres of marsh), whereas another pair may defend only 2.5 hectares (6.2 acres). Requirements of nesting habitat (Fig. 2-3A) are (1) water (nests are located in or close to shallow water), (2) a feeding area (meadow, cultivated field, or open wood-

Fig. 2-2. Florida sandhill cranes. (Photo by Lovett E. Williams, Jr.)

Fig. 2-3. A. Nesting habitat of the Florida sand-hill crane. (Photo by Lovett E. Williams, Jr.)

Fig. 2-3. B. Nest of the Florida sandhill crane (Photo by Lovett E. Williams, Jr.)

land), and (3) privacy (cranes will desert nests and territories if unduly disturbed by man).

Pairs become aggressive toward their young of the previous year at the beginning of the breeding season. They proclaim their territories with loud, synchronized unison calls (Walkinshaw 1973a:115-116). Nests may be established on dry-land sites with almost no nest material but are more often in water on piles of emergent aquatic plants, sticks, grass, mud, and sphagnum.

Clutches contain usually two, occasionally one, or rarely three ovate eggs (Fig. 2-3B). Incubation begins after the first egg is laid. Additional eggs may be laid at 24- to 48-hour intervals. After 28 to 31 days of incubation, eggs hatch asynchronously.

Hatching takes 24 to 36 hours. The colt is dry a few hours later and is walking the next day. After the colt or colts hatch, the family moves to open uplands or meadows for feeding. The family returns to the marsh each night to roost, and it may return to the nest or the parents may build a platform for roosting. The colts' diet during the preflight period appears to be almost exclusively animal food, but young feed readily on agricultural grains in autumn.

Mississippi sandhills in captivity have laid eggs in their second year. Immature greaters group together during their second year. Some color-marked greaters in Idaho successfully nested in their third year. Florida sandhills at the Patuxent Wildlife Research Center of the United States Fish and Wildlife Service at Laurel, Maryland, begin to nest at the age of 3 years. We assume from records for captive birds that 20 to 30 years is the potential life-span. Lovett Williams reported banded wild cranes now living that are more than 9 years old and Roderick Drewien annually observed greater sandhill cranes on their breeding grounds in northern Rocky Mountain states that were color-marked 11 to 14 years earlier (Huey 1965).

HISTORICAL REVIEW

In the early 1800's, the migratory subspecies of sandhill cranes nested in wetland habitats over much of eastern Siberia, Alaska, Canada, and the northern United States as far south as northeastern California, northern Arizona, Utah, western Colorado, central Nebraska, northern and eastern Iowa, southern Illinois, central Indiana and Ohio, and the southern borders of Lake St. Clair and Lake Erie. In addition, the nonmigratory subspecies nested in Alabama, Georgia, Florida, Louisiana, Mississippi, Cuba, and the Isle of Pines. Cranes disappeared from many nesting areas as a consequence of shooting for food, drainage of wetlands, settlement, and general disturbance by man. The decline in their populations was most rapid between 1870 and 1915 (Walkinshaw 1949: 130). Cranes are no longer found nesting in Alabama, Ohio, Indiana, Illinois, Iowa, Louisiana, Nebraska, the Dakotas, Washington, Arizona, and most of the southern portions of the Canadian provinces that border the United States.

Crane hunting was outlawed in the United States and Canada by the Migratory Bird Treaty Act in 1916. Populations of Canadian, greater, Florida, and lesser cranes have increased in recent years as a result of protection of the birds and their habitat. In the 1930's there were only a few dozen nesting pairs in southern Michigan and Wisconsin (Henika 1936, Walkinshaw 1949: 134) in contrast to today's population of more than 700 pairs. The Rocky Mountain population of greater, the lesser, and the Florida subspecies have also increased markedly. The greater subspecies was removed in 1973 from the United States Fish and Wildlife Service's list of rare and endangered wildilfe of the United States. The Florida and Mississippi subspecies are still considered threatened (Office of Endangered Species and International Activities 1973).

Increasing populations and crop depredations led to open hunting seasons on lesser and Canadian subspecies in the United States in 1960 and in Canada in 1964. Cranes are presently hunted as game in nine states of the United States, two Canadian provinces, and in Mexico and Russia. Under proper management, some populations can continue to increase and efforts can be made to reestablish cranes in nesting habitat now unoccupied.

DISTRIBUTION AND DENSITY

Greater Subspecies

Four populations of greaters are (1) the *eastern,* nesting in Minnesota, Michigan, and Wisconsin and possibly in central Manitoba and western Ontario; (2) the *Rocky Mountain,* nesting from northwestern Colorado and northeastern Utah northward through eastern Idaho, western Wyoming, and southwestern

Montana; (3) the *Colorado River Valley,* nesting in northeastern Nevada and probably central and southwestern Idaho; and (4) the *Central Valley,* nesting in south central and southeastern Oregon and northeastern California (Fig. 2-4).

Eastern Population. — Nesting habitat of the eastern population consists of isolated, irregularly shaped open marshes or bogs, surrounded by shrubs and

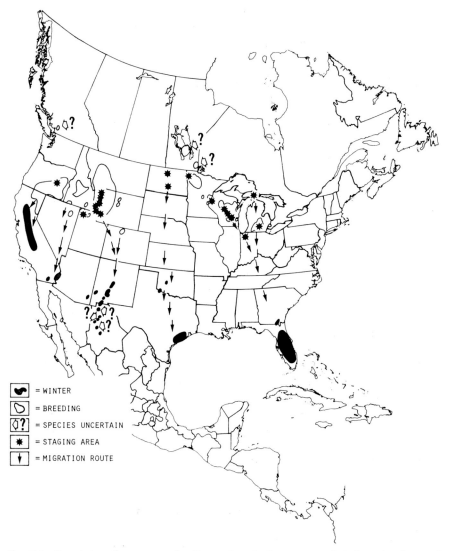

Fig. 2-4. Occupied nesting range, migration routes, staging areas used during migration, and winter areas for the greater sandhill crane.

forests (Hamerstrom 1938, Walkinshaw 1950, 1973a:116, 1973b). Nesting occurs in northern and southern Michigan, central and northwestern Wisconsin, northern Minnesota, Ontario, and probably southeastern Manitoba (Table 2-1) (Lumsden 1971, Walkinshaw 1973a:123-127, Gluesing 1974, Jon Johnson, personal communication).

Cranes of this population migrate through Illinois, Indiana, Ohio, Tennessee, Kentucky, and Georgia (Walkinshaw 1960, Williams and Phillips 1972, L. E. Williams, Jr., unpublished banding data). The Jasper-Pulaski Game Preserve in northern Indiana is the major spring and fall concentration area for eastern greaters (Table 2-2).

Easterns winter in Alabama, Georgia, and Florida (Table 2-3). Five to nine thousand winter in the same habitat with the resident Florida subspecies but do not go as far south, in significant numbers, as the Everglades, where a few Floridas reside.

Rocky Mountain Populations. — Cranes of the Rocky Mountain population nest in isolated, well-watered river valleys, marshes, and meadows, mainly above 1.5 km (0.93 mile) elevation. Largest concentrations are located from northwestern Colorado northward along the Utah-Wyoming and Idaho-Wyoming borders to southwestern Montana (Drewien 1973, Drewien and Bizeau 1974) (Table 2-2). Parts of Idaho, northern Nevada, western Montana and Wyoming, and possibly western Colorado were formerly occupied and still appear suitable for nesting, but they are presently unoccupied or used by only a few cranes.

The major concentration area in spring is along the Bear River in Lincoln County, Wyoming (Drewien 1973), and adjacent Rich County, Utah, where peak populations of 2,000 to 3,000 are found. The largest concentrations in fall occur at Gray's Lake and Teton Basin in Idaho (Table 2-2) (Drewien and Bizeau 1974). They feed in grainfields, mainly barley (*Hordeum* spp.), and crop depredations occur. Depredation complaints received by the Idaho Fish and Game Department have been increasing. Cranes concentrate both spring and fall in the San Luis Valley, Colorado; 8,000 have been seen at Monte Vista National Wildlife Refuge and vicinity.

Cranes of this population winter in the middle and lower Rio Grande valley of New Mexico, mainly at Bosque del Apache National Wildlife Refuge and nearby Bernardo and La Joya state management areas (Table 2-3). Smaller flocks winter in scattered locales in southwestern New Mexico, southeastern Arizona, and northern Mexico (Fig. 2-4). In New Mexico, agriculture is primarily livestock farming with irrigated pasture, cotton farming, and truck gardening. In the Rio Grande valley, the acreage of corn and small grains has decreased in the past 5 years, causing cranes to concentrate on refuges and on dairy farms where grains are raised. Wetlands are scarce because of drainage projects carried out by the Bureau of Reclamation.

Table 2-1. Populations of greaters on breeding grounds, based on 1970–73 data.

Location	Number of Cranes	Source
ROCKY MOUNTAIN POPULATION		
Idaho		
Gray's Lake NWR and vicinity	588	R. C. Drewien
Blackfoot River — Caribou Co.	270	R. C. Drewien
Bear River Valley — Caribou and Bear Lake Cos.	41	R. C. Drewien
Bear Lake NWR and vicinity	193	R. C. Drewien
Henry's Fork and Snake River — Fremont Co.	412	R. C. Drewien
Teton Basin	50	R. C. Drewien
Camas NWR	18	R. Twist
Wyoming		
Bear River — Lincoln Co.	214	R. C. Drewien
Salt River — Lincoln Co.	102	R. C. Drewien
Green River — Sublette Co.	61	R. C. Drewien
South Fork and Snake River — Teton Co.	22	L. Serdiuk
Montana		
Red Rock Lakes NWR and vicinity	164	R. C. Drewien
Utah		
Rich Co.	113	J. Nagel
Cache Co.	9	J. Nagel
Box Elder Co.	4	J. Nagel
Colorado		
Routt Co.	70	C. Hurd, R. J. Tully
COLORADO RIVER VALLEY POPULATION		
Nevada		
Ruby Valley — Elko and White Pine Cos.	60	R. C. Drewien
Other locations in Elko Co.	118	R. J. Oakleaf and U. S. Fish & Wildlife Service
Idaho		
Camas, Custer, Elmore, and Valley Cos.	94	R. C. Drewien
Bruneau River — Owyhee Co.	12	R. C. Drewien
CENTRAL VALLEY POPULATION		
Oregon		
Malheur NWR	550	C. D. Littlefield
Sycan Marsh	105	C. D. Littlefield
Alvord Valley	40	C. D. Littlefield
Harney Valley	125	C. D. Littlefield
Chewaucan Valley	75	C. D. Littlefield
Warner Valley	100	C. D. Littlefield
California		
Surprise Valley	100	C. D. Littlefield
Big Valley	80	C. D. Littlefield

(Continued)

(Table 2-1. Continued.)

Location	Number of Cranes	Source
EASTERN POPULATION		
Wisconsin		
32 counties	850	E. A. Gluesing, G. W. Archibald
Minnesota		
12 counties	unknown	Walkinshaw 1973a, Jon Johnson
Michigan		
Lower Peninsula (18-20 counties)	480	L. H. Walkinshaw, R. Hoffman
Upper Peninsula (6-8 counties)	800-1,100	W. E. Taylor, L. H. Walkinshaw
Canada		
Southern Manitoba	unknown	Walkinshaw 1973a
OTHER POPULATION(S)		
Canada		
Saskatchewan	unknown	L. H. Walkinshaw
Alberta	unknown	L. H. Walkinshaw
British Columbia	unknown	L. H. Walkinshaw

Surveys during 1971 and 1973 in Chihuahua and during 1973 in Durango (Drewien and Bizeau, unpublished data) showed that small numbers of greaters occur in mixed flocks with lessers (Table 2-3).

The future of the Rocky Mountain population appears secure because considerable portions of the nesting grounds are in publicly owned national forests, parks, and wildlife refuges. Proper management of such areas will insure survival of these groups.

Colorado River Valley Population. — The cranes in the Colorado River valley population nest in northeastern Nevada and probably in south central and southwestern Idaho. Hundreds of cranes, apparently associated with this population, concentrate each spring and fall near Luno, Nevada. Approximately 200 congregate during spring and fall near Fairfield, Camas County, Idaho. They winter principally in the Colorado River valley of Arizona (Table 2-3).

Their nesting and winter habitats are similar to those of the Rocky Mountain population. The future of this population seems secure because considerable portions of its nesting grounds are publicly owned.

Central Valley Population. — Cranes of the Central Valley population nest in flooded meadows and marshes in the Great Basin and in the southern Cascade Mountains of Oregon and California (Table 2-1) (Littlefield and Ryder 1968). Greaters formerly nested east and west of the Cascades in Washington, but few records exist for recent years. The last known nesting occurred in 1941. Approximately 70 percent of the nesting habitat in Oregon and northeastern California is privately owned.

Table 2-2. Peak sandhill crane populations at fall concentration areas in Canada and the United States.

Location	Peak Populations	Subspecies[a]	Source
PACIFIC FLYWAY			
Canada			
Peace River district — British Columbia and Alberta	5,000	Unknown	W. J. D. Stephen
Oregon			
Malheur NWR	3,000	Greater (CV)	C. D. Littlefield
Idaho			
Gray's Lake NWR	1,450	Greater (RM)	R. C. Drewien
Teton Basin	1,650	Greater (RM)	R. C. Drewien
Bear River valley	450	Greater (RM)	R. C. Drewien
Blackfoot Reservoir	600	Greater (RM)	R. C. Drewien
Henry's Lake outlet	450	Greater (RM)	R. C. Drewien
Camas Prairie	200	Greater (CRV)	R. C. Drewien
Utah			
Bear River valley	842	Greater (RM)	J. Nagel
CENTRAL FLYWAY			
Canada			
East central Alberta and West central Saskatchewan	40,000	Unknown	W. J. D. Stephen
Central Saskatchewan	30,000	Unknown	W. J. D. Stephen
Big Grass Marsh — Manitoba	5,000	Unknown	W. J. D. Stephen
Montana			
Bowdoin NWR — Phillips Co.	5,000	Lesser and Canadian	Johnson and Stewart 1973
Medicine Lake NWR — Sheridan County	10,000	Unknown	Buller 1967
Wyoming			
Southeast Co.	25,000-30,000	Unknown	Buller 1967
Keyhole Reservoir — Crook Co.	4,000	Unknown	G. F. Wrakestraw
Bear River Valley	1,200	Greater (RM)	R. C. Drewien
North Dakota			
McLean County	7,000	Lesser and Canadian	Johnson and Stewart 1973
Kidder and Stutsman cos.	16,000	Lesser, Canadian, and greater	Johnson and Stewart 1973
Kidder and Pierce cos.	10,000	Canadian, lesser, and greater	Buller 1967
South Dakota			
Pollack-Mobridge Area	12,000–18,000	Lesser and Canadian	Buller 1967, D. Fisher
Colorado			
Arkansas Valley	10,000	Unknown	Tully 1974
South Platte	50,000	Unknown	Tully 1974
San Luis Valley	8,000	Greater (RM)	R. C. Drewien
Kansas			
Quivira NWR	4,100	Greater and Canadian	J. C. Lewis
Kirwin NWR	500	?	J. C. Lewis

(Continued)

(Table 2-2. Continued.)

Location	Peak Populations	Subspecies[a]	Source
Oklahoma			
Washita NWR	2,000–15,000	Greater, lesser, and Canadian	J. C. Lewis
Salt Plains NWR	7,900	Greater and Lesser	Buller 1967, J. C. Lewis
Tillman County	1,500	Lesser and Canadian	J. C. Lewis
Jackson County	7,000	Greater, lesser, and Canadian	J. C. Lewis
MISSISSIPPI FLYWAY			
Wisconsin			
White River Marsh — Green Lake Co.	413	Greater (E)	J. Weber
Necadah NWR — Juneau Co.	400+	Greater (E)	G. Updike
Burnett Co.	200+	Greater (E)	N. Stone
Dike 17 — Jackson Co.	225	Greater (E)	E. Kohlmeyer
Minnesota			
Kittson Co.	1,800	Greater (E)	Johnson and Stewart 1973
	1,200	Canadian	Johnson and Stewart 1973
Indiana			
Jasper-Pulaski Fish and Wildlife Area	8,000	Greater (E)	D. L. Shroufe
Michigan			
Haehnle Sanctuary — Jackson Co.	700	Greater (E)	H. Wing
Fibre — Chippewa Co.	200+	Greater (E)	L. H. Walkinshaw, W. E. Taylor

[a] RM = Rocky Mountain, E = Eastern, CRV = Colorado River Valley, and CV = Central Valley.

This population migrates from September through November southwestward to the Central Valley of California. Winter concentrations occur from Chico southward to Delano, with the highest density northwest of Lodi, near Thornton (Table 2-3). They occur where shallow water provides loafing and roosting sites and farmlands provide food — primarily cereal grains such as rice (*Oryza sativa*), sorghum (*Sorghum* spp.), barley, and corn (*Zea mays*).

There has been a high degree of land disturbance, primarily for agricultural purposes, on winter areas. Most loafing and roosting sites are on private land; exceptions are Gray Lodge Wildlife Area, near Yuba City, and Merced National Wildlife Refuge, near Merced. Feeding areas, other than grainfields, include flooded meadows, stands of salt grass, and pastureland.

Lesser and Canadian Subspecies

The breeding range of sandhill cranes in Canada is not well known (Fig. 2-5) because cranes occupy remote areas. The nesting range of Canadians and lessers includes five habitat types. The Canadian prairies and transition zone, the cordillera and West Coast, and the boreal forest portion of the Canadian Shield are

Table 2-3. Wintering populations of Canadian, Florida, greater, and lesser subspecies.

Location	Number of Cranes	Subspecies[a]	Source
ALABAMA			
Baldwin Co.	50	Greater (E)	T. A. Imhof
GEORGIA AND FLORIDA			
Okefenokee Swamp	1,200	Greater (E)	J. R. Eadie
Okefenokee Swamp	200	Florida	J. R. Eadie
FLORIDA			
Florida Peninsula	5,000	Greater (E)	L. E. Willimas, Jr.
Florida Peninsula	5,000	Florida	L. E. Williams, Jr.
Madison Co.	100	Greater (E)	L. E. Williams, Jr.
Apalachicola National Forest	10	Florida	L. E. Williams, Jr.
OKLAHOMA			
Jackson Co.	2,000+	Greater, Canadian, Lesser	Lewis 1974
Washita NWR	1,500	Greater, Canadian, Lesser	Lewis 1974
TEXAS			
Muleshoe NWR and vicinity	90,000-140,000	Lesser and Canadian	Buller 1967
Central Texas	?	?	
Coastal Texas	23,000	Greater, Canadian, Lesser	Guthery 1972, Lewis 1974
NEW MEXICO			
Bernardo and La Joya State refuges	3,500+	Greater (RM) and Lesser	R. C. Drewien
Bosque del Apache NWR	12,500+	Greater (RM) and Lesser	R. Rigby, R. C. Drewien
Gila River valley near Cliff	150	Greater (RM)	R. C. Drewien
Columbus — Las Palomas — Mexico	3,500	Greater (RM)	R. C. Drewien
Columbus — Las Palomas — Mexico	4,000	Lesser	R. C. Drewien
Las Vegas	200	Greater (RM) and Lesser	J. L. Sands, R. C. Drewien
Bitter Lakes–Portales–Artesia	12,000-15,000	Lesser	J. L. Sands
Dell City — Texas area	2,000+	Lesser	J. L. Sands
Elephant Butte–Caballo Lake	400	Greater and Lesser	R. C. Drewien
Uvas Valley	350	Greater and Lesser	R. C. Drewien
MEXICO			
Chihuahua			
Janos-Ascension Area	350	Greater (RM) and Lesser	R. C. Drewien
Galeana	400	Greater and Lesser	R. C. Drewien
Zaragosa–Tres Castillos	85	Unknown	R. C. Drewien
Laguna de Babicora	15,000+	Greater and Lesser	R. C. Drewien
Lago de Los Mexicanos	3,500	Greater (RM) and Lesser	R. C. Drewien
Laguna Bustillos	100	Unknown	R. C. Drewien
Ciudad Guerrero	480	Unknown	R. C. Drewien
Lago Toronto	58	Unknown	R. C. Derwien

(Continued)

(Table 2-3. Continued.)

Location	Number of Cranes	Subspecies[a]	Source
Durango			
Laguna de Santiaguillo	60	Greater and Lesser	R. C. Drewien, E. G. Bizeau
Puebla			
Carmen Marshes	230	Lesser	Boeker and Baer 1963
ARIZONA			
Gila River near Buckeye	50	Greater (CRV)	C. D. Littlefield
Colorado River Indian Reservation	800	Greater (CRV)	C. D. Littlefield, W. H. Mullins
S.E. of Brawley — Calif.	50	Greater (CRV)	C. D. Littlefield
Willcox Playa	400	Greater (RM)	R. C. Drewien
Willcox Playa	700+	Lesser	R. C. Drewien
CALIFORNIA			
Yuba City	800	Greater (CV)	C. D. Littlefield
Modesto	400	Greater (CV)	C. D. Littlefield
Modesto	3,000	Lesser	C. D. Littlefield
Handord	300	Lesser	C. D. Littlefield
Delano	70	Greater (CV)	C. D. Littlefield
Simmler	1,500-3,000	Lesser	C. D. Littlefield
Goose Lake	400	Lesser	C. D. Littlefield
Merced	110	Greater (CV)	C. D. Littlefield
Merced	12,000	Lesser	C. D. Littlefield
Lodi	3,000	Lesser	C. D. Littlefield
Lodi	1,000	Greater (CV)	C. D. Littlefield
Chico	800	Greater (CV)	C. D. Littlefield
Red Bluff	900	Lesser	C. D. Littlefield

[a] RM = Rocky Mountain, CRV = Colorado River Valley, E = Eastern, and CV = Central Valley.

probably of least value as breeding habitat. They have limitations due to industrial and agricultural development, rock outcrops, and deep, steep-shored wetlands and lakes. The best habitat is believed to be tundra and boreal and mixed forest on plains south of the Canadian Shield and in the Mackenzie Valley lowlands.

Maximum densities of breeding pairs in the best northern range are estimated to be less than two per 1.6 km² (0.6 mile²) (T. W. Barry, personal communication). Large areas are unoccupied (Parmelee and MacDonald 1960, Manning and MacPherson 1961) ; some are clearly unsuitable as crane habitat, but failure of cranes to occupy other areas is not fully understood.

The estimated population on the Adelaide Peninsula was 800 adults, of which 750 nested on coastal till (MacPherson and Manning 1959:23). Pairs, presumably nesting, were common at Perry River in the Queen Maud Gulf lowlands and were widely scattered over tundra of the coastal plain (Hanson et al. 1956:68). Manning et al. (1956:56) estimated the population on Bank's Island to be 3,000. Cranes on this island apparently prefer to nest in broad

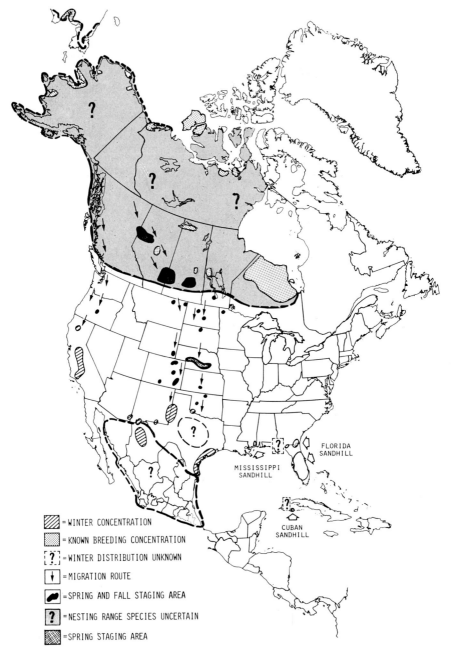

Fig. 2-5. Occupied nesting range, migration routes, and staging areas used during migration; winter areas for lesser or Canadian subspecies, or both; and occupied range of Cuban, Florida, and Mississippi races.

flat valleys cut through hilly country or sheltered on the north by long scarps;
they avoid most of the low, level western coast and rolling hills of the eastern
DeSalis Bay region. The large inland distribution on Bank's Island contrasts
with the small coastal distribution reported for Adelaide Peninsula and has
been attributed to snow conditions when the cranes initiated nesting.

Cranes are uncommon in the southeastern part of Victoria Island, where a
few widely scattered pairs breed (Parmelee et al. 1967:79). Snyder (1957:124)
indicated that nesting occurs only on the northwest corner. Small numbers
nest in the vicinity of Nipawin, Saskatchewan; the south shore of Lake Athabasca; and near Fawcett, Alberta (Houston and Street 1959:78-79, Nero 1963,
Salt and Wilk 1966).

Nesting is usually in progress in Alaska by the last week in May. An esti-
mated 70,000 lessers nest from the Alaska Peninsula west and north to the
Bering Sea and Arctic Ocean (Daniel Timm, personal communication). Con-
centrations occur along the Kuskokwim, Yukon (Leopold and Leonard 1966),
Noatak, Meade, and Colville rivers; on Norton Sound and Kuskokwim and
Hooper bays; in the vicinity of Point Barrow; inland from Fairbanks and Circle
north to the Arctic coast and east to the Canadian border; and on Nunivak
Island in the Bering Sea (Swarth 1934). Cranes nest on St. Lawrence Island
(Sauer and Urban 1964). A small population, subspecies status unknown, nests
in southeast Alaska on islands near Wrangell and Petersburg (Webster 1950).

Because of its remoteness and inaccessibility, most nesting habitat in Alaska
and northern Canada does not seem in immediate danger. However, with
increasing interest in oil exploration, problems may develop. Losses could occur
through habitat destruction and human disturbance in many major nesting
localities. Drilling sites, vehicular traffic, pipelines, and low-flying aircraft
would presumably be detrimental to nesting cranes in these remote areas.

Lessers nest in Siberia, but little information about them is available. Lessers
winter in New Mexico (Huey 1965), California, Texas, and Mexico. Daniel
Timm (personal communication) reports that between 70,000 and 100,000,
some presumably migrating from Siberia, passed over Tok, Alaska, on 16 September 1972. In late August, lessers begin migrating from Siberia, western
Alaska, and northern Canada, and most have usually left Alaska by early
October. The majority migrate southeast toward southern Canada and the
north central states.

Distribution of lesser and Canadian cranes in Canada during the autumn
migration is known only generally because a census is not regularly or systematically taken. There are two major concentration areas and two minor
ones (Table 2-2). Smaller numbers occur in scattered locations across the
four western provinces. These locations include the general vicinity of White-
water Lake in Manitoba and the Caribou Parklands of interior British Columbia. In general, the spring staging areas are the same locations used during the

fall migration, but little is known about the numbers of cranes stopping at staging areas in Canada during the spring.

During the fall migration, cranes concentrate briefly in many parts of the Central Flyway in the United States. Buller and Boeker (1965), Buller (1967), Johnson and Stewart (1973), Tully (1974), and Lewis (1974:37-76, 84-95) have described locations and phenology of migration. The concentration areas contain shallow reservoirs, marshes, or river borders for roosting habitat. Isolation from disturbance is provided by landownership or difficult terrain. Small grains grown in the vicinity provide an abundance of food. In many cases, the composition of subspecies using specific areas is still unknown (Table 2-2).

Lesser and Canadian sandhills winter in the southwestern United States and in Mexico (Table 2-3). In general, lessers are more prevalent than Canadian subspecies in the southernmost winter areas. In Texas and Oklahoma, numbers peak in November–December and decline until late February, when the spring migration begins (Lewis 1970, Guthery 1972:65). The largest concentration occurs around Muleshoe National Wildlife Refuge in Texas, where the cranes roost at alkaline lakes and feed in nearby grainfields. Crop depredations have been a problem there. In general, winter habitat is similar to that utilized during migration. Most winter habitat is not presently threatened.

Saunders (in Allen 1952:37-38) reported that most cranes wintering in Mexico enter on a broad front between El Paso, Texas, and Columbus, New Mexico. Wintering flocks are widely scattered in Mexico (Fig. 2-5). Most cranes probably winter in northern Mexico, but they are found south to Sinaloa and Nayarit on the West Coast (G. H. Jensen, personal communication; Walkinshaw 1949:113); to Jalisco, Michoacan, San Luis Potosi, Guanajuato, and Puebla in the interior (Cooke 1914:10, Bent 1926:251, Ridgway and Friedman 1941:20, Walkinshaw 1949:114, Friedmann et al. 1950:82, Leopold 1959:281), and south to the Yucatan Peninsula on the east coast (Friedmann et al. 1959: 82, Leopold 1959:281). The principal wintering area in Mexico is probably in Chihuahua, encompassed by Laguna de Guzman on the north, Laguna de Bavicora on the west, and Laguna Bustillos on the south (Saunders in Allen 1952:38; Boeker and Baer 1962, 1963).

Little is known about the distribution of subspecies or numbers in the various wintering flocks in Mexico. The only surveys made specifically for cranes were conducted by Boeker and Baer (1962, 1963) and Drewien and Bizeau (unpublished), and their efforts were concentrated mainly in northern Mexico (Table 2-3). G. H. Jensen (personal communication) reports that small flocks, usually fewer than 200 to 300, are scattered along the West Coast from southern Sonora to northern Nayarit, most frequently in the vicinities of Huatabampo in Sonora, Topolobampo and El Dorado in Sinaloa, and the Marismas region of southern Sinaloa and northern Nayarit.

Survey data are probably of little value in showing trends in winter numbers. Fluctuations in numbers most likely reflect changes in habitat conditions

throughout the wintering range, date of census, and weather. Wintering populations of greater, lesser, and Canadian subspecies seem fairly mobile, and
birds move as necessary in response to weather and local food supplies (Lewis
1970, Guthery 1972:42). Residents at Laguna de Santiguillo, Durango, Mexico,
stated that in most years cranes are abundant and are regularly hunted for
food; yet few cranes were counted on surveys made in 1962–63 and 1973, when
drought conditions prevailed in this region (Boeker and Baer 1962, 1963;
Drewien and Bizeau, unpublished data).

In recent years, few records have been kept for Baja California, and we
assume that cranes no longer occur there in significant numbers. Birds that
formerly wintered in this region may be shortstopped on the Colorado River
near Parker, Arizona, by recent agricultural developments.

There do not appear to be important concentration areas for sandhill cranes
in the Dakotas, Kansas, Montana, Oklahoma, Texas, or eastern Wyoming during the spring migration. Cranes apparently leave wintering areas and fly
directly to the Platte River in Nebraska, with only brief stops along the way.
On the Platte they utilize three types of habitat: (1) shallowly submerged
sandbars (Fig. 2-6) in broad stretches of river as roosting sites (Wheeler and
Lewis 1972); (2) wet meadows, particularly those near roosting areas, for

Fig. 2-6. Sandhill cranes along the Platte River, Nebraska. (Photo by Glenn D. Chambers, Missouri
Department of Conservation.)

feeding and loafing, and as secondary roosts (Frith unpublished data); and
(3) corn stubble, alfalfa (*Medicago sativa*), and meadows as feeding sites.

Various factors have altered and are affecting habitat in Nebraska. The
construction and use of Interstate Highway 80 north of the Platte River between Lexington and Grand Island have greatly reduced the use of nearby
meadows and fields by cranes (personal communication from landowners and
Loren J. Bonde). Many wet meadows have been cultivated in recent years,
particularly in the area between Gibbon and Kearney. Development of drainage
ditches and blockages of existing drainage patterns by the construction of road-
ways and railroad beds have stimulated cultivation of former wetlands. Farm
development subsidies (cost-sharing programs) and price supports on crops
raised on new lands have helped make such land-use changes economical. In
addition, diversions and other water development projects upstream have
altered seasonal rates of water flow and reduced total flow in the Platte. A
dramatic change in the river has resulted over the past 3 decades — stretches
that were broad and open, with shallow water and submerged sandbars, have
been filled by willows (*Salix* spp.) and other vegetation. Cranes seem to be
shifting to parts of the river that have remained relatively open, for example,
the area from Grand Island to 21 km (13.0 mi) west. Additional diversion
schemes, such as the Mid-State Reclamation Project, threaten to accelerate
the succession of open sandbars to rank willow thickets.

Florida Subspecies

The Florida subspecies is restricted to Florida and the adjacent Okefenokee
Swamp, in Charlton and Ware counties, Georgia (Table 2-3, Fig. 2-5).

Approximately 4,000 to 6,000 reside in the peninsula of Florida and nest
in open wet areas from Alachua, Putnam, and St. Johns counties (Williams
and Phillips 1972, Walkinshaw 1973a:130) into the edge of the Everglades
(Thompson 1970). Typical habitat contains small, shallow lakes with sparse
emergent vegetation, surrounded by prairies or improved cattle pastures, or
both. Florida cranes avoid densely wooded areas, brackish and saltwater
marshes, urban situations, and marshes with dense vegetation such as cattail
(*Typha* sp.) or saw grass (*Cladium* sp.). The landscape and visibility in the
peninsula are similar to those on crane habitat in Mississippi and northern
Florida, but habitat there is distinctly more open and often drier except in
ponds and marshes.

Extensive drainage projects and real estate development have destroyed or
threatened much of the habitat. Examples are the recent channelization of the
Kissimmee River by the United States Army Corps of Engineers, an operation
that probably destroyed 20 percent of the year-round range, and construction
of Disney World near Orlando, which is causing a great amount of real estate
development in the heart of the Florida crane habitat.

Cranes readily use improved pastures and grazing is a major beneficial land-use practice that continues to increase in Florida. It is difficult to assess accurately the offsetting effects of beneficial land clearings for improved pastures versus the destructive drainage of marshes and ponds, but it seems that one may be counterbalancing the other at this time.

Mississippi Subspecies
The Mississippi race occurs only in Jackson County, Mississippi (Fig. 2-5). Habitat is open flatwoods savannah containing slash pine (*Pinus caribaea*) and longleaf pine (*P. palustris*) and moist, meadowlike ground cover (Valentine and Noble 1970, Walkinshaw 1973a:137-138). Similar areas, presumably offering potential habitat, exist along the northern Gulf coast from Texas into the Panhandle of Florida, especially from the Louisiana-Mississippi line to the Apalachicola River Swamp in Florida.

Cuban Subspecies
The Cuban subspecies is restricted to western Cuba and the Isle of Pines (Fig. 2-5). Large savannahs are used for feeding, roosting, nesting, and rearing of young in foothills or pine flats, usually near streams (Walkinshaw 1949:100, 1953). Most nests are on high, dry land, but some nests have been found in small pools of water during the rainy season. Walkinshaw (1953) estimated that 200 were still living in Cuba. The present population is unknown, but a letter to L. H. Walkinshaw from Abelando Moreno indicates that the numbers of this race are increasing.

CENSUS PROCEDURES AND POPULATION TRENDS
Sandhill cranes have been censused on some breeding grounds, wintering areas, and concentration areas during migration. Counting methods vary, the methods used depending upon agency needs and economic considerations. Censuses may be taken from fixed-wing aircraft along transects in specific areas (Wheeler and Lewis 1972) or during aerial surveys for waterfowl. All aerial surveys are subject to much error. The use of different observers from year to year, difficulties in estimating accurately numbers in large flocks while observers are traveling at high speeds, the weather, and the time of day affect reliability of the censuses. Counts made primarily for waterfowl frequently do not sample adequately concentration areas of cranes.

In some circumstances, helicopters are superior to fixed-wing aircraft for counting cranes and locating nests (Valentine and Noble 1970, Williams and Phillips 1972). The use of helicopters for general survey work probably will not become routine, however, because of the high expense. Nest counts along transect lines are being tested as an index to resident crane populations in Florida. In northern Michigan, cranes build their nests on the ground among trees. In such circumstances, nests are easily overlooked, even from a helicopter. Walkinshaw (personal communication) found that considerable ground work, in combination with a survey from a helicopter, was required to locate all nests at Betchler Lake in northern Michigan. Counts of cranes leaving and entering roosts in early morning and late evening are commonly used and are as reliable as aerial censuses when only a few thousand cranes use the site. Larger populations on roosts can probably be counted more accurately from aircraft.

The Mississippi and Florida races and some of the greater subspecies nest or winter in relatively well-defined areas where they can easily be censused. In contrast, the Canadian and lesser subspecies winter and nest sparsely in habitat where access is difficult or expensive, or both. They migrate in fall along a wide pathway through western Canada and the western United States. On winter areas, the population is in a state of flux (Guthery 1972:42), moving further south during severe weather (December to mid-February) and then northward (mid-February to mid-April) as spring approaches (Drewien, unpublished data; Lewis, unpublished data). These habits of lessers, Canadians, and some greaters make them difficult to census. Presumably the entire continental population of the lesser and Canadian subspecies, with the exception of 20,000 lessers wintering in California, stage annually in March and April along the Platte River in Nebraska. At this time they are concentrated and census becomes practical. However, there is no time when the total population is in Nebraska. Some cranes are as far south as Texas and northern Mexico at the time when others have moved on to the Dakotas. Weather has sometimes delayed the survey until several days after the population reached its estimated peak numbers and declined as some cranes migrated northward. Such a census underestimates the continental population of lesser and Canadian subspecies. The technique also has some inherent inaccuracies of aerial censuses. Thus, the counts made along the Platte River provide only minimum population figures, but this census is being improved by simultaneous counts in states north and south of Nebraska.

Counts on the Platte have varied as much as 93,000 birds from one year to the next (Wheeler and Lewis 1972). So large a variation must be caused, at least in part, by limitations of the census technique. No clear-cut trends have been evident since 1957. In the past 3 years (1971–73) the average count has been approximately 195,500 cranes.

To increase the accuracy of the census along the Platte, the United States Fish and Wildlife Service recently tested a technique that utilized aerial photographs taken of cranes at roosts at dawn. Many cranes, however, leave the roost soon after daybreak (Lewis 1974:119) and are not counted by daylight photography. Thermal imagery mapping of roosts at night should be tested in the future.

The minimum continental population of the lesser and Canadian subspecies is estimated to be between 220,000 and 290,000 (Table 2-4), including the

Table 2-4. Population estimates of subspecies of sandhill cranes.

Subspecies	Population Estimates (1973)	Trend Over Past Decade	Source
GREATER			
Central Valley Population	3,200	Stable	C. D. Littlefield
Colorado River Valley Population	1,000	Unknown	C. D. Littlefield, R. C. Drewien
Rocky Mountain Population	10,000-15,000	Increasing	R. C. Drewien
Eastern Population	8,000-10,000	Increasing	J. R. Eadie, T. A. Imhof, D, L. Shroufe, L. H. Walkinshaw, L. E. Williams, Jr.
Greaters in Western Canada	Unknown	Unknown	
LESSER AND CANADIAN			
Platte River, Nebraska	200,000-270,000[a]	Unknown	Fish and Wildlife Service data
Lesser (winter in California)	20,000	Stable	Fish and Wildlife Service data
FLORIDA	4,000-6,000	Increasing	L. E. Williams, Jr., L. H. Walkinshaw, and others
MISSISSIPPI	30-45	Stable to Decreasing	J. M. Valentine, Jr.
CUBAN	Unknown	Increasing	Abelando Moreno

[a] Minimum estimate; see discussion in text.

20,000 lessers that winter in California. The population wintering in California has remained constant in numbers for 20 years (U.S. Fish and Wildlife Service Narrative Reports).

Greaters have increased considerably (Table 2-4) since 1944, when Walkinshaw (1949:134) estimated the total population to be between 1,339 and 1,836. Full protection and the development of refuges and management areas throughout their range have enhanced their status.

Little is known about populations of greaters in Canada, not only those in the northern segment of the eastern population, but also those in the western provinces. This lack of information explains part of the wide range in population estimates for the eastern population. L. H. Walkinshaw (personal communication) estimates that 8,000 to 10,000 migrate southeastward from the Lake States. Lovett E. Williams, Jr. (personal communication) and others estimate 6,250 greaters on wintering areas in Florida and southern Georgia. The discrepancy in these estimates indicates a need for a systematic census of this population.

HARVEST AND HUNTING PRESSURE

Harvest of cranes by Eskimos and Indians in Canada is not believed to be large. The wariness of cranes and their relative scarcity on the nesting grounds makes colonial-nesting species easier quarry for the few people who still hunt and trap for their livelihood. Cranes are shot by Eskimos during the spring in Alaska; 1,000 were taken in 1 year on the Yukon-Kuskokwim Delta (Klein 1966:330). The total harvest by natives in spring in Alaska probably does not exceed 2,000 cranes (Klein, personal communication). Crane hunting has been legal during the spring in Siberia for several years, but information on hunting pressure and harvest there is not available.

After the migratory bird convention in 1916, sandhill cranes were protected in the United States and Canada, but in 1961 the hunting of cranes was permitted in Alaska, New Mexico, and Texas. Since 1967, seasons have opened in six other states (Table 2-5). In Alaska, bag limits have always been two daily and four in possession. In the Central Flyway, the limits were the same as in Alaska until 1967, but at that time they were increased to three daily and six in possession.

A hunting season in Canada for cranes was first set in Saskatchewan and Manitoba in 1964. An estimated 3,000 cranes have since been harvested annually there (1964–72), 75 percent in Saskatchewan. Data were obtained from bag checks in 1965 (Hatfield 1966) and from mail questionnaires from 1967 through 1972. The latter technique was designed to determine waterfowl har-

Table 2-5. Estimated hunting pressure on and harvest of cranes in Canada and the United States, 1961–72.

Year	Manitoba and Saskatchewan		New Mexico		Texas	Other States	Totals[a]	
	Hunters	Harvest	Hunters	Harvest	Harvest	Harvest	Hunters	Harvest
1961[b]			1,146	542			3,286	3,146
1961[c]			1,385	1,014	1,200	2,633[d]	3,346	2,847
1962			1,161	1,224	1,230[e]	2,633[d]	5,294	5,087
1963			1,064	1,042	1,230[e]	2,633[d]	5,197	4,905
1964	2,058	3,124	1,133	1,246	1,260	2,633[d]	7,356	8,263
1965	1,075	625	652	631	1,350	2,633[d]	5,989	5,239
1966	964	531	689	514	890	2,633[d]	5,423	4,568
1967	1,469	3,604	842	697	1,070	2,635[f]	6,275	8,006
1968	1,409	4,837	1,093	1,076	1,339	2,705[g]	6,829	9,957
1969	1,586	4,444	979	1,212	991	2,980[h]	6,814	9,627
1970	1,171	5,344	2,574	1,805	2,213	3,185[g]	9,521	12,547
1971	1,049	2,943	1,241	2,183	3,076	2,588[g]	8,350	10,790
1972	999	2,143	927	780	ND	3,055[i]	8,486	9,054

[a] Includes assumptions described in text, but does not include an estimate of harvest by Indians and Eskimos in Canada in the spring.
[b] 1–30 January 1961.
[c] Fall 1961.
[d] Alaska only; estimated as described in text.
[e] Texas, estimated as described in text.
[f] Colorado (Tully 1974) and Alaska.
[g] Alaska, Colorado (Tully 1974), North and South Dakota, and Oklahoma.
[h] Alaska, Colorado (Tully 1974), North Dakota, and Oklahoma.
[i] Colorado (Tully 1974), North and South Dakota, Oklahoma, Alaska, Montana, and Wyoming.

vest throughout Canada and the sample size was inadequate for estimating accurately the harvest of lightly hunted species like cranes; the harvest figures are believed to be inflated. Hunters surveyed in Saskatchewan indicated that they had a higher preference for hunting geese, ducks, or upland game (Schweitzer et al. 1973) than for hunting sandhill cranes.

Hunting is generally pass shooting as cranes leave or arrive at roosts or feeding fields. A few hunters use decoys and calls. Interest in crane hunting has been less than expected by game managers in some states. Some hunters equate cranes with herons or fish-eating birds and assume that they are neither sporting nor edible. Hunters who have hunted cranes find them wary, similar to geese in sporting quality, and good to eat.

One problem in setting seasons and harvest boundaries for sandhill cranes is their similarity in appearance to the endangered whooping crane (*G. americana*). Peak migration periods and routes for the lesser and Canadian subspecies coincide with migration dates and pathways for whooping cranes in central Canada and the United States (Allen 1952:87-103, Buller 1967). Thus, crane-hunting seasons in the Dakotas, Oklahoma, and the eastern Panhandle of Texas open after the peak of migration of sandhills to minimize the chance that whooping cranes might accidentally be shot. Future recommendations for changes in hunting regulations will undoubtedly fail if they threaten the status of whooping cranes.

New Mexico and North Dakota are the only states that obtain estimates of harvest from questionnaires mailed to hunters (Raymond J. Buller, personal communication). Alaska initiated a harvest survey in 1972. Other states make estimates of harvest and hunting pressure or have no data.

In recent years, hunters in New Mexico have averaged 3.6–4.0 trips per season. In states such as the Dakotas, where opportunities to hunt exist for only a brief period, the average number of hunting trips per season would obviously be less. In Canada and the United States, two trips per hunter is probably a conservative estimate. On this basis, the hunting seasons for sandhill cranes provided recreation for hunters taking 23,000 hunting trips in 1972.

During the past two seasons, the harvest in Alaska has been 502 and 765 cranes by 228 and 260 successful hunters, respectively. There was no harvest in the Dakotas in 1971 because the cranes migrated from there before the opening date of the hunting season. In 1969, the season in South Dakota was closed because a whooping crane was seen in the hunting area just before the opening date. Harvest and hunting pressure in Oklahoma have been only 12 to 24 hunters and harvested cranes each season. Data on the harvest and hunting effort are not available for 1960–70 in Alaska, and 1962–63 in Texas. In addition, information on hunting pressure is not available for 1967–72 in North Dakota, and for 1972 in Montana and Wyoming. Crane hunting is legal in Mexico. Much of the harvest occurs in Chihuahua, and Kenard Baer reports that hunting is increasing because there are more hunters, better access roads to wintering areas, more hunting clubs now active in the area, and some hunters are using decoys and thereby increasing the kill. To offset this increased kill, the Mexican government shortened the crane-hunting season in 1971 and 1972. Baer estimated that the annual harvest in Mexico was 500 to 1,000, of which slightly over 10 percent were greaters. In a sample of 46 cranes taken by hunters in western Chihuahua in 1970, Drewien found 42 were lessers and 4 were greaters. Drewien was told by employees of one of the largest hunting clubs that 800 were harvested at the club in 1969.

To provide an estimate of trends in harvest and hunting effort the following assumptions were made: (1) the annual harvest in Alaska was an average of the 1971 and 1972 harvests plus an annual average of 2,000 harvested in spring; (2) the annual harvest in Texas from 1962 to 1963 was an average of the 1961 and 1964 harvest figures; (3) the number of hunters per crane harvested in Alaska, Colorado, the Dakotas, Montana, Oklahoma, Texas, and Wyoming was the same as the number of hunters per crane harvested in New Mexico from 1960 to 1972 (1.07); and (4) the harvest in Texas in 1972 was the same as that experienced in 1971. There are obvious inadequacies in such assumptions, but they provide a rough estimate of harvest and hunting pressure (Table 2-5).

Boeker et al. (1962) reported crippling losses were 15.9 percent in Texas and 14.6 percent in New Mexico. If we add crippling losses, harvest in Siberia and Mexico, and harvest by natives in Canada in spring to the estimates in Table 2-5, we see that the annual mortality caused by hunters may approach 15,000 cranes.

POTENTIAL HARVEST

Some concern has been expressed that present harvest levels may be excessive (Sherwood 1971, Miller et al. 1972:43, Miller 1974). Although the continental population of lesser and Canadian subspecies may not be threatened, some flocks or subpopulations may be subject to excessive harvest from a combination of harvests during the hunting season in Siberia in spring, by Indians and Eskimos during spring and summer in Alaska, during fall migration in Canada and the United States, and on wintering areas in the United States and Mexico.

Although banding of cranes has been limited, work in several locations has provided some insight concerning shooting pressure exerted on hunted populations of the Canadian and lesser subspecies. In western Texas, 134 were banded during winters from 1959 to 1969. No recoveries were reported from shooting in the first complete hunting season after banding (first-year recoveries) and only 4 birds (3.0 percent) had been recovered by the end of 1972. In Nebraska, 542 wintering cranes were banded along the Platte River between 1965 and 1968; 9 (1.7 percent) were first-year recoveries and 19 (3.5 percent) had been reported by hunters by the end of 1972. Finally, the first-year recovery rate was 1.5 percent for 236 cranes banded in eastern New Mexico during the winters of 1960–72. These band-recovery rates do not suggest high hunting mortality of sandhill cranes; however, there is an obvious need for increased banding effort, especially for the subspecies that are hunted.

It would be unwise at present to increase harvest and hunting effort beyond those already existing for most of the continental population of lesser and Canadian subspecies (Table 2-6). Hunting of these two subspecies should be re-evaluated using more adequate census and banding programs.

Many of the lessers wintering in California intermingle with flocks of greaters of the Central Valley population. The Central Valley population has been only maintaining itself and should not be subjected to hunting pressure. The few lessers wintering separately from greaters would provide little hunting.

Obviously, the endangered Cuban and Mississippi subspecies should not be hunted. The Florida subspecies is increasing, but hunting would be unwise in view of continuing habitat losses. The eastern population of greaters is increasing, but anticipated losses of nesting grounds make it unwise to hunt this

Table 2-6. Current and potential harvest for sandhill cranes.

State or Province Where Substantial Numbers Occur	Hunting Allowed in 1973
Alaska	Yes
Arizona	No
California	No
Colorado	Yes
Florida	No
Georgia	No
Idaho	No
Indiana	No
Kansas	No
Michigan	No
Minnesota	No
Montana	Yes
Nebraska	No
New Mexico	Yes
North Dakota	Yes
Oklahoma	Yes
Oregon	No
South Dakota	Yes
Texas	Yes
Utah	No
Washington	No
Wisconsin	No
Wyoming	Yes
Alberta	No
British Columbia	No
Manitoba	Yes
Saskatchewan	Yes

Note: An extension of the harvest is not recommended until we have a better estimate of total populations.

population. Populations of Rocky Mountain greaters are increasing and are the only population of greaters that might eventually provide limited hunting.

SPECIES NEEDS

The most important need of cranes throughout North America is habitat preservation adequate to hold populations at least at their present levels. The nesting habitat in southern Michigan is in the greatest danger of being destroyed by urban and industrial expansion. In Lower Michigan, only 33 percent of the marshes used by cranes are owned by the state or the Audubon Society (Ron Hoffman, personal communication). We do not know how long existing marshes will be preserved under private ownership, but these are generally shallow marshes that could be easily drained. Drainage programs may be accelerated as a result of the current emphasis on agricultural production. Unless an adequate refuge system is established, the long-range prognosis for cranes in southern Michigan is not bright.

Preservation of Mississippi sandhills also depends upon measures to protect their habitat from disturbance. L. H. Walkinshaw (personal communication) indicates that the International Crane Committee of the International Union for the Conservation of Nature is planning a refuge in Jackson County, Mississippi. A refuge for this subspecies should be a top priority.

The Florida race is probably secure at present population levels as long as current land-use practices continue; such a continuance, however, is not likely. About 80 percent of the Florida's nesting habitat is privately owned. Purchase of land or some other means of preserving habitat is probably the only long-range solution. Habitat in central Florida is selling for $1,000 per acre and will be much more expensive by the time any can be purchased for cranes.

The greatest need for cranes in the Central Flyway is protection of the Platte River habitat, especially by insuring adequate water flow. We need to acquire key habitat, particularly roosting areas and wet meadows for feeding. Ideally, a management unit should include at least one large area and additional satellite areas along the river. Large units are needed to include all habitat types. Small satellite units are necessary to protect scattered roosting areas and to help disperse cranes in groups of 10,000 to 30,000 (Klataske 1972). The danger of a single refuge site rather than several is obvious — an environmental threat would be more critical and diseases could become disastrous. To offset these dangers, the National Audubon Society has acquired some land along the Platte River, and the United States Fish and Wildlife Service is planning a refuge in the area.

Cranes wintering near Thornton, California, may eventually be affected by urban expansion of Sacramento. A new refuge should be established in the Modesto area. Suitable habitat exists near the confluence of the Stanislaus and San Joaquin rivers. With additional habitat improvement, a large percentage of the Central Valley population of greater sandhill cranes would no doubt winter in this area. The total cost would be between $600,000 and $750,000.

PUBLIC NEEDS

Cranes are stately and photogenic, and they attract much attention. Nature enthusiasts travel hundreds of kilometers to see concentrations of sandhill cranes, and in many areas birders make annual trips to observe their rituals. Increased public interest in and concern for wildlife of all kinds are demonstrated by the environmental movement of recent years and are reflected by the growth in membership of citizen environmental groups, by increased activity of these groups, and by greater visitation to wildlife areas. This increasing public demand for opportunities to observe wildlife will probably continue and should be encouraged.

In Saskatchewan, 87 percent of the citizens surveyed expressed an interest in watching birds and 34 percent expressed an interest in studying birds (Schweitzer et al. 1973). The number of persons looking for opportunities to observe wildlife has recently increased considerably at many of the national refuges. Seventy-five percent of the visitors at Malheur National Wildlife Refuge in Oregon ask about sandhill cranes.

In Nebraska, most land used by cranes is privately owned and posted against trespass. Thus, the general public is largely restricted to public roads for observing or photographing cranes. Problems of access illustrate the need for areas where the public can observe cranes. However, wildlife enthusiasts can create problems for cranes. Persons who go too near to roosts, disregarding the nervous nature of cranes, can disrupt their activities and frighten them away. Establishing observation blinds or towers in a federal refuge or in areas owned by the Nebraska Game and Parks Commission and private organizations could provide the solution. Florida recently purchased the 12,000-acre (4,856-ha) Payne's Prairie, not only to provide a wintering ground for the greaters and year-round habitat for Florida cranes, but also to give the public an opportunity to observe cranes.

MANAGEMENT NEEDS

Production studies (annual recruitment data) and accurate estimates of total populations, both migratory and resident, with measured confidence limits, are needed to detect trends in populations. Productivity must be equal to or greater than mortality rates; some population units may not be achieving this survival rate. Suitable censuses should be designed and conducted regularly.

An inventory and a classification of habitat are needed. We know little about the principal nesting areas of lesser and Canadian subspecies, of parts of the eastern population of greaters, or of the Florida subspecies. Likewise, there are gaps in our knowledge of winter habitat in Florida, Mexico, and central Texas. We do not know specific locations of key nesting and winter habitats nor precisely what characterizes these habitat types. We need to develop a means of classifying such habitats for all subspecies so that we can judge with greater accuracy the importance of various areas. Only in this way can we insure the preservation of key areas and learn to recognize optimum habitat.

Inadequacies in our knowledge of harvest have already been discussed. We need to improve the accuracy of harvest surveys where they are already being made and initiate them where they are lacking.

A better knowledge of various population units, especially of their wintering and nesting habitats and their migration pathways, is needed and can be achieved by banding programs. Banding would also provide mortality data. Harvest regulations should be reevaluated several years after the banding program is initiated. Management should be directed toward populations of cranes using specific geographic areas. Thus, populations or flocks, rather than subspecies, should be the basic management unit as they are for Canada geese (*Branta canadensis*). Banding is needed along the Platte River in Nebraska and on wintering areas in Texas and New Mexico. We also need to determine where the greater sandhills that nest in Minnesota spend the winter. This information could be determined by banding and color-marking cranes.

The need to purchase lands to preserve some key habitat for cranes was discussed previously. Much habitat will necessarily remain in private ownership and will play an important role in meeting the habitat needs of sandhill cranes. However, certain key habitat must be acquired to insure its preservation.

Severe crop damage by cranes occurs locally in Idaho and Canada. These depredations have resulted in considerable illegal shooting by farmers in Idaho. Depredation problems can be partially alleviated by planting lure crops near traditional gathering sites or by some form of crop-sharing with local farmers. In the traditional problem areas, fields of small grains, planted for the cranes, would solve most of the depredation problems (Stephen 1967:42-45). Refinements in technique indicate fields smaller than 40 hectares (98.8 acres) are most effective and the costs of the operation can be met by harvesting a portion of the grain (W. J. D. Stephen, personal communication).

RESEARCH NEEDS

In compiling the following list of subject areas for concentrated research, we assumed that the major management goal is to maintain or increase crane populations in as near the natural state as possible in the same range that cranes now occupy, or possibly to expand the occupied range into areas of unoccupied suitable habitat that contained cranes in the 19th and early 20th centuries.

One of the highest-priority needs is refinement of the annual census on the Platte River. Such a study should include nighttime observations of roosting cranes to determine the best time for census, and testing of thermal imagery mapping techniques from aircraft at night. Research is also needed to devise a census technique for the eastern population of greaters. The Jasper-Pulaski Game Preserve and other staging areas used in the fall might provide the focal points for this census.

We need accurate information on the extent of harvest of cranes in Mexico. Such a harvest survey is considered research because the basic technique for acquiring the harvest data will require investigative work.

To help us define management goals and costs, we need studies of how people want to use the crane resource. Is there or will there be a strong demand for opportunities to hunt cranes or do people want only to look at them? Does the public want unoccupied crane habitat restocked? Questionnaires sent to the general public could answer these questions.

We need to know how much disturbance cranes will accept without abandoning nests or leaving local habitat. Acquiring this knowledge has become imperative with the increase in exploration for oil and gas, in mining coal and oil-bearing shale, and in expansion of suburban areas.

To maintain habitat in some areas, we need to learn how to retain vegetation in successional stages attractive to cranes. One area where such information is needed is along the Platte River in Nebraska, where habitat is rapidly being altered by man's activities. Such techniques as manipulating water level, mowing, grazing, burning, and discing should be tested.

Research is needed to develop techniques for restocking habitats that were occupied in the 19th and early 20th centuries. Two separate jobs are proposed. One would develop techniques for establishing greaters in nesting habitat in states such as Washington and North Dakota. The other would investigate techniques for reintroducing cranes into the coastal wetlands of Alabama, Louisiana, western Florida, and Mississippi.

We need to refine a technique for determining sex by external examination. This technique is needed for use in banding programs designed to further our understanding of population dynamics and to assist in evaluation of the differential vulnerability of males and females to harvest. The technique used by Blackman (1971) on brogla cranes (*Grus rubicunda*) appears to be accurate only for sexually mature sandhill cranes (Lewis 1974:158-162).

Taxonomic questions need solving. Can other races be recognized that would make population or flock management easier? Is the Canadian race valid? Banding, chemical analysis of feathers, and basic taxonomic criteria might be used in this proposed study.

We know very little about parasites and diseases. At the present time, neither parasites nor diseases seem to be major limiting factors, but substantial losses to disease may be occurring without our knowledge. Surveys should eventually be made for parasites, and blood should be tested for antibodies to important diseases.

Recommendations for corrective action to meet management and research needs are summarized in Table 2-7.

Table 2-7. Budget requirements for a 10-year sandhill crane management plan.

Major Programs, Subspecies, and Season or Location	Research or Management (R or M)	Job Priority	Estimated Cost of Jobs for Each Fiscal Year (in thousands of dollars)										Total Cost per Job (thousands)	Continuing Job
			1	2	3	4	5	6	7	8	9	10		
CENSUS														
Florida Subspecies Summer	M	1	15	0	15	0	15	0	15	0	15	0	$ 75	Yes
Greater Subspecies, Eastern Population, Jasper-Pulaski, fall	M	1			3.5	3.5	3.5	3.5	3.5	3.5	3.5	3.5	28	Yes
Greater Subspecies, Central Valley	M	2						10	10	10	10	10	50	Yes
Greater Subspecies, Rocky Mountain and Colorado River Valley Population	M	2						2.5	2.5	2.5	2.5	2.5	12.5	Yes
Canadian and Lesser Subspecies, Platte River	M	1			4	4	4	4	4	4	4	4	32	Yes
Program Cost			15	0	22.5	7.5	22.5	20.0	35.0	20.0	35.0	20.0	197.5	
DEVELOPING CENSUS TECHNIQUES														
Greater Subspecies, Eastern Population	R	1	3.5	3.5									7	No
Canadian and Lesser, Subspecies, Platte River	R	1	8	8									16	No
Program Cost			11.5	11.5									23	
HABITAT SURVEYS														
Florida Subspecies	M	1	10	10	10	10							40	No

Program Area	Type	No.											Total	Completed
Greater Subspecies, Eastern Population														
Nesting	M			20	20	20							60	No
Lesser and Canadian Subspecies														
Nesting	M	1	20	20	20	20	20	20					120	Unknown
Winter Habitat														
West-Central Texas	M	1	10	10									20	No
Mexico	M	1	20	20	20								60	No
Program Cost			30	80	80	70	20	20					300	
HARVEST SURVEYS														
Hunting States and Provinces	M	1	20	20	20	20	20	20	20	20	20	20	200	Yes
Mexico	R		7	7									14	
Program Cost			27	27	20	20	20	20	20	20	20	20	214	
SURVEY OF PUBLIC NEEDS														
Continent Wide in Specific Areas	R	1	20	20									40	No
BANDING														
Platte River Nebraska	R & M	1	10	10	10	10	10	10	10	10	10	10	100	Yes
Wintering Areas New Mexico and Texas	M	1	20	20	20	20	20	20	20	20	20	20	200	Yes
Greater Subspecies Indiana, Minnesota, and Wisconsin	R	2						10	10	10	10	10	50	No
Greaters Wintering in Florida	R				3	3	3						9	Unknown
Program Cost			30	30	33	33	33	40	40	40	40	40	359	

(Continued)

(Table 2-7. Continued.)

Major Programs, Subspecies, and Season or Location	Research or Management (R or M)	Job Priority	Estimated Cost of Jobs for Each Fiscal Year (in thousands of dollars)										Total Cost per Job (thousands)	Continuing Job
			1	2	3	4	5	6	7	8	9	10		
EFFECTS OF MAN'S ACTIVITIES ON CRANES														
Oil and Gas Industry														
Nesting	R	1		7	7	7	7						28	No
Coal and Oil Shale Industry														
Nesting	R	1		7	7	7	7						28	No
Effects of Highways and Urbanization	R	1		7	7	7	7	7					35	Unknown
Program Cost				21	21	21	21	7					91	
HABITAT MANAGEMENT TECHNIQUES														
Nebraska	R	2						30	30	30	30	30	150	No
Florida	R	2						20	20	20	20	20	100	No
Program Cost								50	50	50	50	50	250	
RESTOCKING NESTING HABITAT														
Eastern Gulf Coast	R & M	2						25	25	25	25	25	125	Unknown
Western Greaters	R & M	2						25	25	15	15	15	95	
Program Cost								50	50	40	40	40	220	
DEPREDATION CONTROL														
As needed in Specific Locales	M	2			20	20	20	20	20	20	20	20	160	Yes

													Total	
SEX DETERMINATION TECHNIQUES	R	3								10	10	10	30	No
TAXONOMIC INVESTIGATIONS	R	3							20	20	20		60	Unknown
TECHNIQUE FOR DETERMINING YEAR CLASSES	R	3									7	7	14	No
PARASITES AND DISEASES	R	3									10	10	20	Unknown
Total Cost of Research and Management			113.5	189.5	216.5	171.5	136.5	227.0	215.0	220.0	252.0	237.0	1,978.5	
HABITAT ACQUISITION														
Nebraska	M	1	500	500									1,000	Unknown
Michigan	M	1			200								200	Unknown
Florida	M	2				500	500						1,000	Unknown
California	M	2						500	250				750	Unknown
Program Cost			500	500	200	500	500	500	250				2,950	

Table 2-8. Occurrence and status of sandhill cranes in the contiguous United States.

Name of State	Common	Peripheral	Uncommon	Endangered
Alabama			X	
Alaska	X			
Arizona	X			
California	X			
Colorado	X			
Florida	X			
Georgia			X	
Idaho	X			
Illinois			X	
Indiana	X			
Kansas	X			
Kentucky			X	
Michigan	X			
Minnesota		X		
Mississippi				X
Missouri		X		
Montana	X			
Nebraska	X			
Nevada		X		
New Mexico	X			
North Dakota	X			
Ohio			X	
Oklahoma	X			
Oregon	X			
South Dakota	X			
Tennessee			X	
Texas	X			
Utah			X	
Washington	X			
Wisconsin	X			
Wyoming	X			

Note: Absent in states not listed.

RECOMMENDATIONS

This review of the status of sandhill crane populations and their management has revealed two main problems: (1) a large number of actual and potential users of the resource but a shortage of information on the extent of their demand, and (2) a dangerous shortage of biological information, particularly on hunted migratory populations.

Some data on harvest are required to manage migratory crane populations. If cooperation from wildlife management agencies in Canada, Mexico, and Siberia can be secured, then research and management proposals outlined in detail in this report can be implemented.

Our committee has described the current state of knowledge on the status of sandhill cranes and related research and management needs. We believe that the following list of management needs should be met within the next decade. These are immediate needs and are basic to any good management plan.

1. Population inventories of all subspecies should be taken regularly.
2. Key habitat that is jeopardized by changes in land use should be acquired.
3. The harvest of cranes should be surveyed annually.
4. Banding studies should be conducted to determine mortality rates and movement patterns and to define distinct population units.
5. Nesting and wintering habitats in specific areas should be surveyed to determine their importance.
6. Problems of crop depredation should be alleviated by using lure crops or other management techniques.

The following research needs should be met within the next decade:

1. Existing census techniques should be refined and better techniques developed.
2. Techniques should be developed for harvest surveys in Mexico.
3. How the public wants to use the crane resource should be determined.
4. The impact on cranes of extractive industries and urban development in or near nesting habitat should be evaluated.
5. Techniques should be developed for maintaining successional stages of vegetation attractive to cranes.
6. Techniques should be developed for restocking unoccupied nesting habitat with cranes.

Other research needs, with lower priority, that should be met in the next decade if possible are the following:

1. A method of determining sex by external examination should be developed.
2. The number of valid subspecies of sandhill cranes should be determined.
3. A technique for determining year classes of sandhill cranes should be developed.
4. The importance of parasites and diseases to crane populations should be investigated.

ACKNOWLEDGMENTS

Following is a list of persons who contributed data for this report: John W. Aldrich, Edward G. Bizeau, Loren J. Bonde, Raymond J. Buller, D. W. Fisher, Henry A. Hansen, J. Harmon, Lynn C. Howard, G. H. Jensen, David R. Klein, R. W. Rigby, Charles E. Scheffe, Robert E. Stewart, R. Twist, and G. Updike, all with the United States Fish and Wildlife Service; Howard D. Funk, C. Hurd, Thomas Kuck, J. Nagel, R. J. Oakleaf, Charles H. Schroader, Leonard Serdiuk, D. L. Shroufe, Norman R. Stone, Daniel Timm, Robert J. Tully, J. Weber, Robert L. West, H. Wing, Dale Witt, and George F. Wrakestraw, all with state fish and wildlife agencies; and Thomas W. Barry, with the Canadian Wildlife Service. Other contributors were J. R. Eadie, A. H. Grewe, Ronald Hoffman, T. A. Imhof, Jon Johnson, Abelando Moreno, William H.

Mullins, Stephen A. Nesbitt, William E. Taylor, William H. Turcotte, Jacob M. Valentine, Jr., and Lawrence H. Walkinshaw.

LITERATURE CITED

Aldrich, John. 1972. A new subspecies of sandhill crane from Mississippi. Proceedings of the Biological Society of Washington 85(5):63-70.

Allen, Robert P. 1952. The whooping crane. National Audubon Society Research Report 3. 246pp.

Bent, Arthur C. 1926. Life histories of North American marsh birds. U.S. National Museum Bulletin 135. 490pp.

Blackman, J. G. 1971. Sex determination of Australian cranes (Gruidae). Queensland Journal Agriculture and Animal Science 28(4):281-286.

Boeker, Erwin L., and Kenard P. Baer. 1962. Study of wintering distribution of sandhill cranes in southwestern United States and Mexico. Annual Progress Report, Bureau of Sport Fisheries and Wildlife, Denver Wildlife Research Center. 7pp.

———, and ———. 1963. Study of wintering distribution of sandhill cranes in southwestern United States and Mexico. Annual Progress Report, Bureau of Sport Fisheries and Wildlife, Denver Wildlife Research Center. 6pp.

———, William S. Huey, and Pierce B. Uzzell. 1962. Study of Texas–New Mexico lesser sandhill crane hunting seasons — November 4–December 3, 1961. United States Fish and Wildlife Service. 11pp. (Mimeo.)

Buller, Raymond J. 1967. Sandhill crane study in the Central Flyway. United States Fish and Wildlife Service Special Scientific Report Wildlife 113. 17pp.

———, and Erwin L. Boeker. 1965. Coordinated sandhill crane study in the Central Flyway. Transactions North American Wildlife and Natural Resources Conference 30:100-113.

Cooke, Wells W. 1914. Distribution and migration of North American rails and their allies. United States Department Agriculture Bulletin 128. 50pp.

Drewien, Roderick C. 1973. The sandhill crane in Wyoming. Wyoming Wildlife 37(7):20-25.

———, and Elwood G. Bizeau. 1974. Status and distribution of Rocky Mountain greater sandhill cranes. Journal Wildlife Management 38(4):720-742.

Friedmann, Herbert, Ludlow Griscom, and Robert T. Moore. 1950. Distributional check-list of the birds of Mexico. Part I. Pacific Coast Avifauna 29. 202pp.

Gluesing, Ernest A. 1974. Distribution and status of the greater sandhill crane in Wisconsin. M. S. Thesis. University of Wisconsin, Stevens Point. 85pp.

Guthery, Frederick S. 1972. Food habits, habitat, distribution, numbers, and subspecies of sandhill cranes wintering in southern Texas. M. S. Thesis. Texas A&M University. College Station. 80pp.

Hamerstrom, Frederick M., Jr. 1938. Central Wisconsin crane study. Wilson Bulletin 50(3):175-184.

Hanson, H. C., P. Queneau, and P. Scott. 1956. The geography, birds and mammals of the Perry River region. Arctic Institute of North America. Special Report No. 3. 96pp.

Hatfield, John P. 1966. Evaluation of the 1965 sandhill crane hunting season in Saskatchewan and Manitoba. Project p1-4-2, Progress Report 1965. Canadian Wildlife Service. Edmonton Library Catalogue No. 18-65.

Henika, Franklin S. 1936. Sandhill cranes in Wisconsin and other lake states. Proceedings North American Wildlife Conference 1:644-646.

Houston, C. Stuart, and Maurice G. Street. 1959. The birds of the Saskatchewan River. Saskatchewan Natural History Society, Special Publication No. 2. 205pp.

Huey, William S. 1965. Sight records of color-marked sandhill cranes. Auk 82(4):640-643.

Johnson, Douglas H., and Robert E. Stewart. 1973. Racial composition of migrant populations of sandhill cranes in the northern plains states. Wilson Bulletin 85(2): 148-162.

Klataske, Ronald. 1972. Wings across the Platte. National Wildlife 10(5):44-47.

Klein, David R. 1966. Waterfowl in the economy of the Eskimos on the Yukon-Kuskokwim Delta, Alaska. Journal Arctic Institute of North America 19(4):319-336.

Leopold, A. Starker. 1959. Wildlife of Mexico. University of California Press, Berkeley. 568pp.

——, and Justin W. Leonard. 1966. Effects of the proposed Rampart Dam on wildlife and fisheries. Transactions North American Wildlife and Natural Resources Conference 31:454-459.

Lewis, James C. 1970. Sandhill cranes wintering in Jackson County, Oklahoma. Bulletin Oklahoma Ornithological Society 3(1):1-4.

——. 1974. Ecology of the sandhill crane in the southeastern central flyway. Ph.D. dissertation. Oklahoma State University, Stillwater. 204pp.

Linnaeus, Carl. 1758. Systema Naturae 10(1):141.

Littlefield, Carroll D., and Ronald A. Ryder. 1968. Breeding biology of the greater sandhill crane on Malheur National Wildlife Refuge, Oregon. Transactions North American Wildlife and Natural Resources Conference 33:444-454.

Lumsden, Harry G. 1971. The status of the sandhill crane in northern Ontario. The Canadian Field–Naturalist 85:285-293.

MacPherson, A. H., and T. H. Manning. 1959. The birds and mammals of Adelaide Peninsula, N.W.T. National Museum Canada Bulletin 161. Queen's Printer, Ottawa. 63pp.

Manning, T. H., E. O. Höhn, and A. H. MacPherson. 1956. The birds of Banks Island. National Museum Canada Bulletin 143, Biological Series 48. Queen's Printer, Ottawa. 144pp.

——, and A. H. MacPherson. 1961. A biological investigation of Prince of Wales Island, N.W.T. Transactions Royal Canadian Institute 33:Part 2:116-239.

Miller, Richard S. 1974. The programmed extinction of the sandhill crane. Natural History (February):62-69.

——, George S. Hochbaum, and Daniel B. Botkin. 1972. A simulation model for the management of sandhill cranes. Yale University: School of Forestry and Environmental Studies, Bulletin 80. 49pp.

Nero, Robert W. 1963. Birds of the Lake Athabasca region, Saskatchewan. Saskatchewan Natural History Society, Regina. Special Publication 5. 143pp.

Office of Endangered Species and International Activities. 1973. Threatened wildlife of the United States. United States Bureau Sport Fisheries and Wildlife. Resource Publication 114. 289pp.

Parmelee, David F., and S. D. MacDonald. 1960. The birds of west-central Ellesmere

Island and adjacent areas. National Museum Canada, Bulletin 169. Queen's Printer, Ottawa. 103pp.

——, H. A. Stephens, and Richard H. Schmidt. 1967. The birds of southeastern Victoria Island and adjacent small islands. National Museum Canada, Bulletin 222. Queen's Printer, Ottawa. 229pp.

Peters, James L. 1925. Notes on the taxonomy of *Ardea canadensis* Linné. Auk 42:120-122.

Ridgway, Robert, and Herbert Friedmann. 1941. The birds of North and Middle America. Part IX. Smithsonian Institute, United States National Museum Bulletin 50. 254pp.

Salt, W. R., and A. L. Wilk. 1966. The birds of Alberta. Queen's Printer, Edmonton. 2nd edition. 511pp.

Sauer, E. G. F., and E. K. Urban. 1964. Bird notes from St. Lawrence Island, Alaska. Bonner Zoologische Beitr. 1/2:45-48.

Schweitzer, Douglas H., David A. Scott, Arthur W. Blue, and Jonathan P. Secter. 1973. Recreational preferences for birds in Saskatchewan. Transactions North American Wildlife and Natural Resources Conference 38:205-212.

Sherwood, Glen. 1971. If its big and flies — shoot it. Audubon Magazine 73(November):72-99.

Snyder, L. L. 1957. Arctic birds of Canada. University Toronto Press. 310pp.

Stephen, W. J. Douglas. 1967. Bionomics of the sandhill crane. Canadian Wildlife Service Report Series 2. 48pp.

——, Richard S. Miller, and John P. Hatfield. 1966. Demographic factors affecting management of sandhill cranes. Journal Wildlife Management 30(3):581-589.

Swarth, Harry Schelwaldt. 1934. Birds of Nunivak Island, Alaska. Pacific Coast Avifauna 22. Cooper Ornithological Club, Los Angeles. 64pp.

Taylor, William E. n.d. Do not fold spindle or shoot. Hiawatha National Forest, Eastern Region, Forest Service, United States Department of Agriculture. 7pp.

Thompson, Richard L. 1970. Florida sandhill crane nesting on the Loxahatchee National Wildlife Refuge. Auk 87(3):492-502.

Tully, Robert J. 1974. Brief notes on the little brown crane. Central Flyway Technical Council Meeting, March 11–13, Denver, Colorado. Multilithed Report. 6pp.

Valentine, Jacob M., Jr., and Robert E. Noble. 1970. A colony of sandhill cranes in Mississippi. Journal Wildlife Management 34(4):761-768.

Walkinshaw, Lawrence H. 1949. The sandhill cranes. Cranbrook Institute of Science Bulletin 29, Bloomfield Hills, Michigan. 202pp.

——. 1950. The sandhill crane in the Bernard W. Baker Sanctuary, Michigan. Auk 67(1):38-51.

——. 1953. Nesting and abundance of the Cuban sandhill crane on the Isle of Pines. Auk 70(1):1-10.

——. 1960. Migration of the sandhill crane east of the Mississippi River. Wilson Bulletin 72(4):358-384.

——. 1965a. A new sandhill crane from central Canada. Canadian Field Naturalist 79(3):181-184.

——. 1965b. One hundred thirty-three Michigan sandhill crane nests. The Jack-Pine Warbler 43(3):136-143.

——. 1973a. Cranes of the world. Winchester Press, New York. 370pp.

————. 1973*b*. A history of sandhill cranes on the Haehnle Sanctuary, Michigan. The Jack-Pine Warbler 51(2):54-74.

————, W. Powell Cottrille, and Betty D. Cottrille. 1960. Southern Michigan sandhill crane survey, 1952–1958. The Jack-Pine Warbler 38(1):25-28.

————, and Ronald Hoffman. 1972. Sandhill cranes have excellent increase. Michigan Audubon News Letter 20(5):1-3.

Webster, J. Dan. 1950. Notes on the birds of Wrangell and vicinity, southeastern Alaska. Condor 52(1):32-38.

Wheeler, Robert H., and James C. Lewis. 1972. Trapping techniques for sandhill crane studies in the Platte River Valley. United States Bureau Sport Fisheries and Wildlife. Resource Publication 107. 19pp.

Williams, Lovett E., Jr., and Robert W. Phillips. 1972. North Florida sandhill crane populations. Auk 89(3):541-548.

3

Rails and Gallinules

Dan C. Holliman, Professor of Biology, Birmingham-Southern College, Birmingham, Alabama, *Chairman*.

John M. Anderson, Director, Sanctuary Department, National Audubon Society, Sharon, Connecticut.

Hugh A. Bateman, Jr., Biologist, Louisiana Wildlife and Fisheries Commission, Baton Rouge.

Robert E. Mangold, New Jersey Division of Fish, Game and Shellfishes, Trenton.

Ron R. Odom, Biologist, Georgia Department of Natural Resources, Social Circle.

David L. Strohmeyer, Associate Professor of Biology, Wisconsin State University, Oshkosh.

Richard L. Todd, Wildlife Specialist, Arizona Game and Fish Department, Phoenix.

John L. Zimmerman, Associate Professor, Ecology and Systematics, Kansas State University, Manhattan.

Virginia Rail
(Rallus limicola)

John L. Zimmerman, Associate Professor, Ecology and Systematics, Kansas State University, Mahattan.

SUMMARY

The Virginia rail breeds across North America from approximately 35°N to 50°N and winters along the Pacific coast from Washington southward through Mexico to northern Central America and along the Atlantic coast from North Carolina southward. It inhabits both salt- and freshwater marshes, occurring in the shallower sedge (*Carex*), cattail (*Typha*), and salt-marsh grass (*Spartina alterniflora*) belts, where it builds its nest over the water. Nesting begins in late April to mid-June, and the incubation period is reported to be about 18 to 20 days. Clutch size ranges from 6 to 13 eggs. Fifty to 78 percent of the nests produce young. Predation by mammals and flooding are thought to be the major causes of nest loss. The young are precocial and are capable of flight at an age of 6 to 7 weeks. The birds are completely flightless during the postnuptial molt but begin their fall migration in September and October. They are primarily secondary and tertiary consumers in the marsh ecosystem. Little is known of their population densities across the entirety of their range, but local studies indicate a range of densities from 0.6 to 4.0 pairs per hectare (0.2 to 1.6 pairs per acre). There are no objective measurements of current population trends, but the species appears to be stable in the Central Plains and decreasing in the Midwest (Ohio and Indiana). The Virginia rail is not an important game species, and as a result game managers generally show little interest in directing efforts toward basic research and management studies. With bird watchers, on the other hand, the species is popular, and as a recreational resource in this context, the species deserves further study.

DESCRIPTION

The upperparts of the adult are fuscous or black, the feathers bordered by pale grayish brown, the wing coverts rufous, the lores whitish, the cheeks gray, the throat white, the rest of the underparts cinnamon rufous, and the flanks and undertail coverts barred or spotted with black and white. The long bill of the Virginia rail separates it from the similarly sized sora (*Porzana carolina*), and the gray cheeks distinguish it from the larger but similarly patterned king rail (*Rallus elegans*). The downy young are glossy black (Chapman 1912:233).

Only one subspecies, *R. l. limicola,* occurs in North America. There is another population in South America that ranges from Ecuador to the Straits of Magellan.

LIFE HISTORY

The Virginia rail does not appear to be territorial (Tanner and Hendrickson 1954), and the species is considered to be monogamous, although there is no information reported on pair-bond relationships. The species nests in the sedge and cattail borders of freshwater marshes (Billard 1947, Pospichal 1952, Tanner 1952, Tanner and Hendrickson 1954, Weller and Spatcher 1965), and in salt-marsh grass in saltwater marshes (Post and Enders 1970). The nest is constructed out of the immediately available vegetation. There is one report of the Virginia rail using low bushes as a substrate (Burtch 1917), but typically the substrate is the characteristic plant of the habitat. The nest is placed from 5 to 13 cm (2 to 5 inches) above the water level (Berger 1951) at sites where the water depth is from 8 to 25 cm (3 to 10 inches) (Bent 1926:293, Walkinshaw 1937, Billard 1947, Pospichal 1952). Nest construction takes from 3 to 4 days (Pospichal 1952), but material is still added to the nest after incubation begins (Bent 1926:294).

Clutch size ranges from 6 to 13 eggs (Gillette 1897, McLean 1916, Bent 1926:294, Walkinshaw 1937, Trautman 1940:230, Billard 1947, Pospichal 1952, Tanner and Hendrickson 1954). Most clutches are completed between late April and mid-June (McLean 1916, Walkinshaw 1937, Trautman 1940:230, Billard 1947, Berger 1951, Pospichal 1952, Tanner 1952), but Walkinshaw (1937) reported one as late as 31 July in Michigan. One egg is laid each day, usually in the early morning (Pospichal 1952). Pospichal (1952) also suggested that a second nesting can occur after the successful completion of the first. On the basis of total available habitat, Pospichal (1952) found that annual production was from 1.1 to 2.4 young Virginia rails per acre (2.7 to 5.9 per ha).

Incubation begins on either the day before or the day when the last egg is laid (Walkinshaw 1937). The incubation period is reported to range from 13 days (Pospichal 1952) to as long as 22 days (Tanner and Hendrickson 1954), but most investigators report lengths of 18, 19, and 20 days (McLean 1916, Walkinshaw 1937, Wood 1937, Mousley 1940, Billard 1947).

The young are precocial and leave the nest before the down is dry. Some young leave the nest before the last egg hatches (Bent 1926:294). Newly hatched young can readily swim, run, jump, and dive (Burtch 1917, Walkinshaw 1937, Trautman 1940:230). Young feed with parental assistance the first day, but by the end of the first week they can feed themselves without assistance (Pospichal 1952). Burtch (1917) provides a photograph of an adult carrying a newly hatched young in its bill. Nesting successes of 50 percent (Pospichal 1952), 68 percent (Billard 1947), 75 percent Tanner and Hendrickson 1954), and 78 percent (Tanner 1952) have been reported. Mammalian predators appear to be the most important cause of nesting failure (Pospichal 1952), but flooding also is important in some cases (Tanner 1952).

The postnatal molt occurs in the second week, and the full juvenile plumage is attained by the sixth week (Pospichal 1952). Billard (1947) observed that the young are capable of flight at 6 to 7 weeks of age. The postjuvenile molt begins when the birds are 12 to 14 weeks of age (Pospichal 1952). Adult birds lose all their flight feathers simultaneously during the postnuptial molt and are incapable of flight at this time. In Connecticut, the postnuptial molt lasts from the last week of July to the first of September (Billard 1947).

Virginia rails probe for food rather than pick it off the surface (Peterson 1952). Horak (1970) reported that animal food is most important, mainly Coleoptera, particularly adult and larval Hydrophilidae and Dytiscidae, but also larval Diptera and snails. Virginia rails feed on duckweed (*Lemna* sp.) but seldom on seeds.

HISTORICAL REVIEW

As early as 1840, John James Audubon described the courtship behavior of the Virginia rail in his *Birds of America* (Bent 1926:293). Although there have been subsequent descriptions of the behavior of this species (Weber 1909, Pospichal and Marshall 1954, Sibley 1955, Wiens 1966), most writers deal only with its distribution.

Several graduate students have undertaken research studies that have made important contributions to the understanding of the ecology of the Virginia rail (Billard 1947, Pospichal 1952, Tanner 1953, Horak 1964). Other references to its life history and ecology are included elsewhere in this report. Two bibliographies on the Virginia rail have been compiled (Smyth 1933; J. F. Glahn 1968, Literature related to Virginia and sora rails, unpublished manuscript, Colorado State University).

DISTRIBUTION AND DENSITY

The summer and winter ranges as delineated by the American Ornithologists' Union (1957:155) are shown in Figure 3-1. In addition, there is a breeding record (three nests) collected from 8 to 10 July at 8,600 feet (2,621 m) elevation near Lema, Distrito Federal, Mexico (Goldman 1908). The Virginia rail is most common as a breeding species around Puget Sound; in the interior valleys of California; on the high plains at the base of the Rockies in Colorado and Wyoming; in eastern South Dakota; in southern Minnesota; in northern Iowa; around Green Bay, Wisconsin; in northeastern Illinois; in both the upper and lower peninsulas of Michigan; in northeastern Ohio; throughout New York, Connecticut, and Massachusetts; and in southern Maine (Robbins 1949).

There are scattered winter observations of the species north of its regular winter range — in Maine (Robbins 1949, Beston 1954, Werner 1955), Massachusetts (Teel 1920, 1924), Connecticut (J. M. Anderson, personal communication), New York (Gokay 1961), New Jersey (Stone 1937), Kentucky

(Schneider 1962), Tennessee (Mayfield 1966), Michigan (Brocke 1958), Wisconsin (Degner 1963, Dunwiddle 1963), Minnesota (Tanner and Hendrickson 1954, Glassel 1959), Kansas (M. D. Schwilling, personal communication), and Oklahoma (Sutton 1967:159).

The occurrence of the species throughout its range is clumped, being dependent upon the distribution of wetlands. Throughout much of its breeding

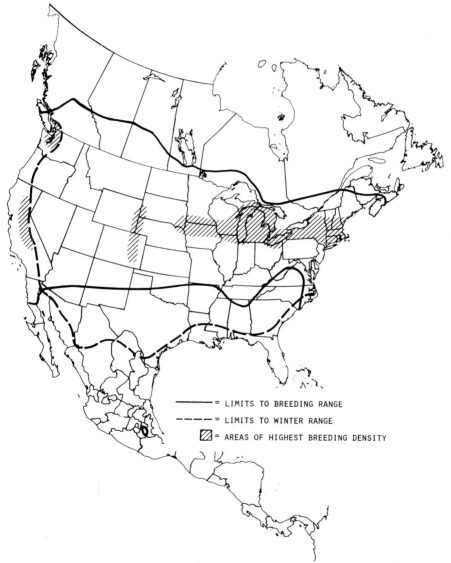

= LIMITS TO BREEDING RANGE
= LIMITS TO WINTER RANGE
= AREAS OF HIGHEST BREEDING DENSITY

Fig. 3-1. Winter and breeding ranges of the Virginia rail and areas of highest breeding density. The dashed line indicates the northern or eastern limits of the winter range.

range it is associated with freshwater marshes (Bent 1926:298-299) and is limited to the sedge edge and shallow cattail belts (Weller and Spatcher 1965). In coastal regions, it utilizes the upper reaches of salt marshes (Bent 1926:293, Post and Enders 1970).

In winter, the species is regularly found in both fresh and salt marshes, being considered common along the Gulf coast (H. A. Bateman, D. C. Holliman, and R. R. Odum, personal communications). It is considered rare to accidental in Cuba (Bond 1947:242). Eisenmann (1955:27) states that it winters south to Guatemala.

Reported breeding densities are 1.2 pairs per hectare (0.5 pair per acre) at Fossel Creek Reservoir, Larimer County, Colorado (R. J. Tully, personal communication), 1.2 pairs per hectare in New York (Post and Enders 1970), 0.6 pair per hectare (0.24 pair per acre) in Minnesota (Pospichal 1952), and 4.0 pairs per hectare (1.6 pairs per acre) in Michigan (Berger 1951).

Spring migration is in March and April and reaches the northern limit of the breeding range in May (Bent 1926:299-300). Peak migration in central Ohio (Trautman 1940:137) and southern Michigan (Walkinshaw 1937) is from late April to early May. Prior to the fall departure, Virginia rails concentrate in large marsh areas in August (Pospichal 1952) and leave during September and October, and as late as November in the southerly regions of their breeding range (Bent 1926:300-301). Trautman (1940:137) reports that the fall migration peak for central Ohio is from mid-September to mid-October.

CENSUS PROCEDURES AND POPULATION TRENDS

No regular, systematic censuses are conducted on Virginia rails. There have been some exploratory investigations, however, to develop field techniques for systematic censusing. In Colorado, J. F. Glahn (personal communication) used recordings of the *grunt* call. He played 5 to 10 calls with 20 to 30 seconds between calls at regular stops along a transect. This technique was used throughout the day and night, but best results were obtained in the early morning and late evening hours during the first few weeks of the breeding season. This technique was believed to detect birds up to 100 yards (R. J. Tully, personal communication). Pospichal (1952) found drive-trapping and overnight-trapping sets to be effective in obtaining birds for banding. Horak (1964) also used drive-trapping, and Labisky (1959) successfully used night-lighting in connection with mist nets. Tanner (1952:2), using cloverleaf traps with 25-foot (7.6 m) leads, captured 277 Virginia rails and soras over a 2-year period.

No data on population trends are available, but a few subjective opinions have been obtained. The population of the species is considered stable in Michigan (G. A. Ammann, personal communication), Wisconsin (S. Robbins, personal communication), and Colorado (R. J. Tully, personal communication). In Kansas, it is thought to be stable and perhaps increasing (M. D. Schwilling, personal communication). In both Indiana (R. E. Mumford, personal communication) and Ohio (M. B. Trautman, personal communication), however, it is believed that the population is decreasing. The following comments from M. B. Trautman (personal communication) are significant:

> Before 1940, this (the Virginia Rail) was the most common nesting rail in the State of Ohio. At Buckeye Lake I averaged 5 nesting pairs per year for 12 years between 1922–34, during migration in the period I averaged 5-16 birds daily and a maximum of over 100 individuals per day. I have not flushed a Virginia Rail for the past 5 years at Buckeye Lake. Between 1929–32 a companion and I, dragging a rope in order to flush nesting ducks in the Lake Erie Marshes of southwestern Lake Erie, found 5-30 Virginia Rail nests in a day during the incubation period. Last year I saw two Virginia Rails in the State of Ohio. This year I have seen none, despite my usual intensive tramping of marshes. The species appears to be on the verge of extirpation in Ohio.

Overall population trends are a function of the presence of available habitat, but Trautman again comments that "there still appears to be several hundreds of acres of nesting habitat in Ohio which to me appears to be very similar to that in which the species formerly nested." In New Mexico, reclamation projects have eliminated much rail habitat (J. L. Sands, personal communication). Similarly, ditching for mosquito control has adversely affected the density of this species (Post and Enders 1970). R. E. Mumford (personal communication) suggests drainage as the cause of decreasing populations in Indiana.

CURRENT AND POTENTIAL HARVEST

Of the states and provinces where substantial numbers of Virginia rails occur, hunting is allowed in all except California, Illinois, South Carolina, South Dakota, Virginia, and Washington. Respondents in 13 of the 48 contiguous states indicated that their states had no substantial populations of Virginia rails. Only from Alabama, Iowa, Maryland, Ontario, Rhode Island, South Dakota, and Texas was additional hunting potential for this species reported.

In states where the species is a game animal, the taking of Virginia rails is incidental to the quest for other game by hunters. Thus, the number of hunters and the kill of Virginia rails are both unknown. In Colorado, it is estimated that there are fewer than 500 hunters shooting Virginia rails and that fewer than 1,000 birds were killed (R. J. Tully, personal communication). In New Jersey, harvest estimates range from several hundred to a few thousand (R. E. Mangold, personal communication). In all other states, hunting pressure is reported to be either nil or very low.

Because population data are not available, it is difficult to estimate the potential harvest for this species. Where the Virginia rail occurs more commonly — for example in Colorado, Iowa, and Kansas — the potential is considered high. Elsewhere, the potential is considered to be quite low.

SPECIES NEEDS

The availability of wetlands with sufficient sedge and cattail edge is essential. It does not appear that such areas need to be large. For example, Berger (1951) found a high density in a half-acre (0.2 ha) marsh.

Pospichal (1952) reported few adverse effects from fluctuations of water levels, but Gillette (1897), Post and Enders (1970), and Tanner (1952) noted that nests were flooded by high water. The lowering of water levels appears to be more detrimental than flooding, and it is believed that the species does best under wet marsh conditions (Weller and Spatcher 1965). Yet Walkinshaw (1937) observed adults adding nest material as water levels rose and also noted that nests were not deserted when water completely receded from around them.

PUBLIC NEEDS

There is agreement that the major public need is education toward the realization of the Virginia rail's potential as a game species. Because of its generally low densities, its secretive behavior, its unwillingness to flush, and the fact that it is not an unusually challenging target when it flushes, the Virginia rail's popularity as a game animal will probably never be high. On the other hand, the popularity of rails among bird watchers (who outnumber hunters in the United States) is high because of the rail's reclusive habits. Thus, access to marsh areas is a need for this growing segment of the public.

MANAGEMENT AND RESEARCH NEEDS AND COSTS

Because there is little basic research information upon which to base management techniques, any statement of management needs is premature. Furthermore, game managers see little need for information on the Virginia rail because of its lack of importance as a game species and because there is little interest in it as a nonconsumptive, esthetic resource. Good techniques of marsh management for the more important game birds and mammals will be beneficial to the Virginia rail. The protection of existing wetlands and the restoration of marshes are essential.

If effort is to be expended for the Virginia rail, obtaining basic information on its population ecology should be the primary goal. In most situations, research on this species would be more efficient if coupled with work on the other species of rails that commonly share the same habitat, such as the sora and the king rail.

First in importance is the identification of breeding sites, the development of censusing techniques, the measurement of population densities on the breeding grounds, and an estimate of annual productivity. A careful description of habitat requirements would be part of a basic investigation. Because of its importance to the hunting season and hunting pressure, such a preliminary study should continue into the autumn to measure the time course and intensity of the fall migration. A study of this type would be best handled on a state-by-

Table 3-1. Budget requirements for a 10-year Virginia rail management plan.

Major Program or Area for Funding	Specific Jobs Within Each Program	Research or Management (R or M)	Job Priority	Estimated Cost of Jobs for Each Fiscal Year (in thousands of dollars)										Total Cost by Job[a] (thousands)	Continuing Job
				1	2	3	4	5	6	7	8	9	10		
Local Population Ecology[b]	Identify breeding sites														No
	Measure population densities														No
	Measure annual productivity														No
Total Cost of Program per Fiscal Year		R	1	10	10	10								$ 30[c]	
Comparative Population Ecology[d]	Identify limiting factors														No
Total Cost of Program per Fiscal Year		R	2				15	15	15	15	15			75[d]	
Effects of Hunting[e]	Measure effects of hunting on breeding and wintering populations														Yes
Total Cost of Program per Fiscal Year		M	3								10	10	10	30[e]	
Grand Total Cost of All Programs by Fiscal Year Period				10	10	10	15	15	15	15	25	10	10	135[f]	

[a] All figures exclude salary of principal investigator.
[b] Local population ecology study would be done by states and provinces. Suggested states and provinces are California, Colorado, Connecticut, Delaware, Iowa, Kansas, Minnesota, Michigan, Massachusetts, Nebraska, New Jersey, New York, Ontario, Pennsylvania, Rhode Island, Washington, Wisconsin, and Wyoming.
[c] Per state; $540,000 total if all suggested states are involved.
[d] By regions; cost figures are per region — $375,000 if all five regions are involved.
[e] To be done by individual states; cost figures are per state — $900,000 if an estimated 30 states are involved.
[f] Per state or region — $1,815,000 total if all states are involved.

state basis and would involve a 2- to 3-year investigation costing approximately $10,000 annually for each state in addition to the salary of the principal investigator (Table 3-1). One principal investigator for each state would be sufficient.

The second level of investigation would involve comparisons of population densities and productivity between habitat types and across biomes. Such studies would attempt to identify the density-dependent and density-independent factors that affect population size. Vegetative structure, water levels, pair-bond relationships, and the postfledging mortality of the young appear to be the most important parameters to consider. These studies should be conducted at least on the regional level over a 4- to 5-year period at a cost of about $15,000 per year in addition to the salary for the principal investigator (Table 3-1). A cooperative study involving several co-principal investigators across the geographic range covered by the study would appear to be the most economical approach.

With this basic informational background, it appears feasible to investigate effects of hunting pressure by permit-type hunting on study populations at different hunter densities over different weeks in the fall. This investigation would be conducted on a state-by-state basis over a 3-year period at an estimated cost of $10,000 per year in each state in addition to the salary of the principal investigator (Table 3-1).

RECOMMENDATIONS

The recommendations of the Species Committee on Rails and Gallinules for the Virginia rail are as follows:

Protect existing wetlands.

Restore marsh habitat throughout the breeding and wintering ranges as rapidly as possible.

Implement studies of population ecology in individual states to determine breeding sites, develop censusing techniques, measure population densities, estimate annual productivity, and determine habitat requirements. These initial studies should also include the definition of the time course and intensity of the fall migration, because this information is essential for setting hunting seasons.

Implement comparative population studies on a regional basis in order to define limiting factors; suggested parameters are itemized in this report.

Measure hunting pressure by permit-type hunting, using different hunter densities and different weeks in the fall as treatments.

If it is concluded that the Virginia rail can be maintained as a huntable resource with a minimum of effort, a program of education should be started to make hunters aware of this resource.

Ongoing management is dependent on the information that will be provided by the research on the population ecology of the Virginia rail. In the absence of this information, it is suggested that good management for the marsh will probably be good management for the Virginia rail.

LITERATURE CITED

American Ornithologists' Union. 1957. Check-list of North American birds. 5th ed. The Lord Baltimore Press, Inc., Baltimore. 691pp.

Bent, Arthur C. 1926. Life histories of North American marsh birds. United States National Museum, Bulletin No. 135. 490pp.

Berger, Andrew J. 1951. Nesting density of Virginia and sora rails in Michigan. Condor 53(4):202.

Beston, Henry. 1954. Virginia rail captured at Nobleboro. Bulletin Maine Audubon Society 10(2):31.

Billard, R. S. 1947. An ecological study of the Virginia rail (*Rallus limicola*) and the sora (*Porzana carolina*) in some Connecticut swamps. M.S. Thesis. Iowa State College, Ames. 84pp.

Bond, James. 1947. Field guide to birds of the West Indies. Macmillan Co., New York. 257pp.

Brocke, Rainer H. 1958. A Virginia rail defies a record winter. Jack-Pine Warbler 36(2):100.

Burtch, V. 1917. The summer life of the Virginia rail. Bird Lore 19:243-248.

Chapman, Frank M. 1912. Handbook of birds of eastern North America. D. Appleton and Co., New York. 530pp.

Degner, Elizabeth. 1963. The sad tale of the rails. Passenger Pigeon 25(3):106.

Dunwiddie, Alan. 1963. Another note on wintering rails. Passenger Pigeon 25(3):107.

Eisenmann, E. 1955. The species of middle American birds. Transactions Linnean Society of New York 7:1-128.

Gillette, Dana C. 1897. Notes on the Virginia and sora rails. Oologist 14(2):21-23.

Glassel, Raymond A. 1959. Wintering Virginia rails in Minnesota. Flicker 31(1):23.

Gokay, A. 1961. Virginia rails in winter in Columbia County. Kingbird 11:29-30.

Goldman, E. A. 1908. The Virginia rail (*Rallus virginianus*) breeding in Mexico. Condor 10(4):181.

Horak, G. J. 1964. A comparative study of Virginia and sora rails with emphasis on foods. M.S. Thesis. Iowa State University, Ames. 73pp.

————. 1970. A comparative study of the foods of the sora and Virginia rail. Wilson Bulletin 82(2):206-213.

Labisky, R. F. 1959. Night-lighting: A technique for capturing birds and mammals. Illinois Natural History Survey Biological Notes. No. 40. 11pp.

Mayfield, G. R., Jr. 1966. Virginia rail at Arrow Lake in January. Migrant 37(1):11.

McLean, Donald D. 1916. Nesting habits of the Virginia rail in Mariposa County, California. Condor 18(5):229.

Mousley, Henry. 1940. Further notes on the nesting habits of the Virginia rail. Wilson Bulletin 52(2):87-90.

Peterson, A. 1952. Virginia rail and sora. South Dakota Bird Notes 4:43-44.

Pospichal, L. B. 1952. A field study of sora rail (*Porzana carolina*) and Virginia rail (*Rallus limicola*) populations in central Minnesota. M.S. Thesis. University of Minnesota, St. Paul. 80pp.

————, and William H. Marshall. 1954. A field study of sora rail and Virginia rail in central Minnesota. Flicker 26(1):2-32.

Post, W., and F. Enders. 1970. Notes on a salt marsh Virginia rail population. Kingbird 20:61-67.

Robbins, C., Jr. 1967. Virginia rail on Christmas count. Maine Field Naturalist 23(1): 13.

Schneider, Evelyn. 1962. Virginia rail at Mammoth Cave. Kentucky Warbler 38(3): 54.

Sibley, Charles G. 1955. The responses of salt-marsh birds to extremely high tides. Condor 57(4):241-242.

Smyth, J. A. 1933. The literature of the Virginia rail. M.S. Thesis. Cornell University, Ithaca, New York. 122pp.

Stone, Witmer. 1937. Bird studies at Old Cape May. Delaware Valley Ornithological Club. 941pp.

Sutton, George M. 1967. Oklahoma birds. University of Oklahoma Press, Norman. 674pp.

Tanner, Ward D. 1952. Rail production in northwest Iowa. Midwest Wildlife Conference 14. 3pp (mimeo).

————. 1953. Ecology of the Virginia and king rails and the sora in Clay County, Iowa. Ph.D. Thesis. Iowa State College, Ames. 154pp.

————, and George O. Hendrickson. 1954. Ecology of the Virginia rail in Clay County, Iowa. Iowa Bird Life 24(4):65-70.

Teel, George M. 1920. A Virginia rail at Salem, Mass., January 1920. Bulletin Essex Co. Ornithology Club 2(1):40.

————. 1924. A December Virginia rail. Bulletin Essex Co. Ornithology Club 6(1):43.

Trautman, Milton B. 1940. The birds of Buckeye Lake, Ohio. Miscellaneous Publication, Museum of Zoology, University of Michigan, No. 44. 466pp.

Walkinshaw, Lawrence H. 1937. The Virginia rail in Michigan. Auk 54(4):464-475.

Weber, J. A. 1909. The Virginia and sora rails nesting in New York City. Auk 26(1): 19-22.

Weller, M. W., and C. S. Spatcher. 1965. Role of habitat in the distribution and abundance of marsh birds. Agriculture and Home Economics Experiment Station, Iowa State University. Special Report No. 43. 31pp.

Werner, I. A. 1955. Virginia rail winter record. Bulletin Maine Audubon Society 11(2):30.

Wiens, J. A. 1966. Notes on the distraction display of the Virginia rail. Wilson Bulletin 78(2):229-231.

Wood, Harold B. 1937. Incubation period of Virginia rail. Auk 54(4):535-536.

Sora
(Porzana carolina)

Ron R. Odom, Biologist, Georgia Department of Natural Resources, Social Circle.

SUMMARY

The sora rail appears to be common throughout the United States; it is perhaps more popular with nonconsumptive users than with sportsmen. Although the potential harvest may be high, current figures show that the actual harvest is insignificant or low; most soras appear to be taken incidentally to other kinds of hunting. Although sora populations seem to be in good shape, the future may not be so bright. Intensive development of our country's wetlands is gradually reducing the principal habitat of the sora. Draining and filling of these wetland areas clearly are the number one problem facing us with regard to this species. Preservation of wetland habitat is essential if sora numbers are to be maintained at a healthy level. Information regarding census, populations, current harvest, hunting pressure, and potential harvest is nearly nonexistent. The bulk of information contained in this report is based on educated opinion, which, in effect, reflects the lack of interest and knowledge quite well. Increasing pressures on other, more popular species, however, may soon bring about changes in this attitude of indifference that has characterized many game managers and administrators in past years. Management and research needs of the species are great, underscoring the need for a long-range, comprehensive program. Initiation of a long-range program, including studies of populations and habitat, combined with an educational effort, will insure the maximum utilization of this resource when the demand arrives — without endangering the resource.

DESCRIPTION

The sora or Carolina rail is a small, plump, gray-brown bird of the marsh, with a black patch on the face and throat and a short yellow bill. The female strongly resembles the male except that in the female the black on the head is duller and more restricted, the mantle is usually more spotted with white, and colors in general are less intense. The immature bird lacks the black throat patch and is buffy brown (Peterson 1947:81). The young are nearly all black except for a small tuft of stiff, curly, chrome-colored hairs under the chin (Bent 1926:307).

LIFE HISTORY

The sora is undoubtedly the most common rail of North America (Pough 1951: 200), although its popularity as a game bird has declined over the years. During part of the year, it is fairly common almost anywhere on the North American continent. The sora is a bird of the wet, soggy marshes, thriving in areas that, until recently, no one else would have.

Although freshwater marshes are their preferred habitat, many thousands of soras use the brackish and salt-marsh areas also, particularly during migration. Nesting usually occurs in the fresh marshes. The nests, well hidden among the vegetation, resemble baskets suspended inches above the water level. The average nest contains 10 to 12 eggs, although extremes of 6 to 18 eggs have been noted. The oval eggs are yellowish buff, with numerous dull brown spots (Bent 1926:305). Incubation lasts about 14 days, with both sexes sharing the responsibilities. Nests are seldom left unoccupied, even when partially submerged. According to Gibbs (1899), partially submerged eggs often produce young.

Small mollusks and insects are the primary food items, except in fall, when soras rely heavily on seeds such as wild rice (*Zizania aquatica*). Rice comprised 74.6 percent of the volume of sora stomach contents in fall collections (Meanly 1960). Webster (1964) found that plant seeds made up 98 percent of the diet of soras from fresh marshes, whereas insects comprised 91 percent of the diet of soras from brackish waters. In Maryland (Maryland Game and Inland Fish Commission 1955), soras have been observed feeding on fish. Often, huge numbers of soras will congregate in areas having extensive beds of wild rice.

In marsh areas, soras often are difficult to flush, usually getting up at the last minute underfoot. The flight is slow, short, and labored, usually just high enough to clear the marsh vegetation. What the sora lacks in flight, however, it makes up in its ability to maneuver on foot through the marsh. If necessary, it does not hesitate to take to the water or even dive, both of which it does well.

According to Pough (1951:201), the sora's spring call is "a clear, plaintive, quail-like, ascending 'ker-wee' that in the distance sounds like a spring peeper. ... Its most characteristic call is its 'whinny,' a rapid series of a dozen or more clear, pleasing notes run together on a descending scale, becoming weaker as it slows down and levels off in a pitch at the end." In late summer and early fall, soras begin to concentrate in the rice fields and other seed-producing areas, prior to their southern migration, initiated by cold weather. Great distances are covered during migration, a fact that is difficult to believe after one has observed a sora flush from the marsh. Starrett (1947) recorded a sora's landing on a ship 190 miles northeast of Abaco Island in the Bahamas.

HISTORICAL REVIEW

The sora was described in detail by Audubon in *Birds of America* (Bent 1926: 304). Although a number of subsequent publications report on its life history, most are brief and not comprehensive (Brewer 1874, Gibbs 1899, Barger 1958, Meanley 1960).

Walkinshaw (1940) provided an excellent review of the summer life of the sora in Michigan. Other references to this species are provided in other sections of the present report. The most recent work on soras deals with their behavior and ecology (mostly of captive birds) in northwest Iowa and central Minnesota (J. Kaufman, personal communication, 1973).

L. C. Sanford provided a descriptive account of a sora hunt near the turn of the century (Bent 1926:312). Since those early days, the popularity of the sora as a game bird has declined.

DISTRIBUTION AND DENSITY

The sora breeds from Nova Scotia, southern Quebec, northern Ontario, southern Mackenzie, and central British Columbia south to Maryland, southern Ohio, southern Illinois, Kansas, Utah, and northern Lower California (Fig. 3-2). It winters from northern Florida, the Gulf Coast, Texas, Arizona, and California south to Venezuela and Peru (Pough 1951:201). Few data exist on population density and distribution other than general descriptions and opinions. At the Fossil Creek Reservoir in Larimer County, Colorado, where the sora is a common local breeding resident, the breeding-population density is thought to be 12 birds per acre (30 per ha) Colorado Division of Wildlife, personal communication, 1973). In Iowa, Tanner and Hendrickson (1956) reported a breeding density of 35 nests in 107 acres (43 ha) and a hatch of 1.7 birds per acre (4.2 per ha) on an 81-acre (33-ha) study area.

The sora presently occupies most of the potential range throughout the country. Wetlands, the sora's principal habitat, are being eliminated rather than created in most parts of its range.

CENSUS PROCEDURES AND POPULATION TRENDS

Census procedures appear to be nonexistent, with the exception of one or two isolated attempts at census on small study areas. Most information from states on population trends is in the form of opinions and is general. In some states, populations are believed to have declined over the years (New Jersey), whereas, in other states, populations have remained stable (Louisiana, Colorado) or are possibly increasing (Kansas).

CURRENT AND POTENTIAL HARVEST

No accurate harvest figures are available for soras. A few estimates were obtained through correspondence with state agencies and knowledgeable individuals. The available information summarized in Table 3-2 clearly illustrates the need for data on this species.

Nebraska was the only state with a firm estimate. All other harvest estimates were general and were presented in the form of opinions. Harvest figures from Nebraska are assumed to represent mainly soras. Most available data from mail surveys lump all species of rails and do not attempt to break the figures down by individual species. It appears from these reported harvest figures that the number of soras harvested annually is insignificant. In most states, soras are shot incidentally to other forms of hunting.

Throughout many areas of the country, the potential sora harvest is high. The low harvest figures indicate a lack of interest in and knowledge about the species rather than a lack of abundance. This lack of interest is caused in many areas by the difficulty of hunting the species. Hunters are reluctant to make the effort required to hunt soras. With heavy pressure currently being

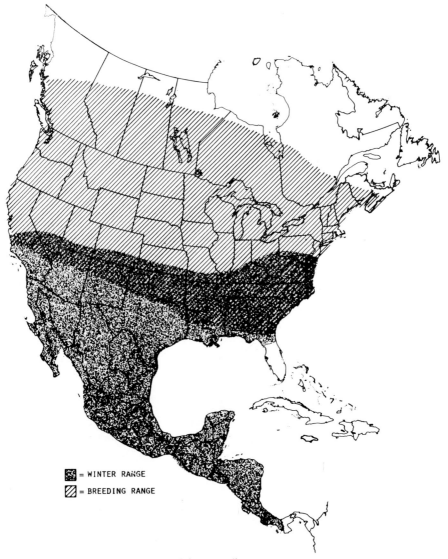

= WINTER RANGE
= BREEDING RANGE

Fig. 3-2. Winter and breeding ranges of the sora rail.

Table 3-2. Current and potential harvest of the sora in states where hunting was allowed in 1973.

State[a]	Estimated Number of Hunters	Number Harvested	Additional Hunting Potential
Colorado	<50	<150	Yes
Georgia	Low	Low	Yes
Kansas	Low	Light	Yes
Louisiana	Low	Low	Yes
Nebraska	ND	5,680 (1971)	Yes
New Jersey	Moderate	Moderate	No
North Carolina	Low	Low	ND
North Dakota[b]	0	0	No
Ohio	<50	<150	ND
South Carolina	Low	Low	ND
Virginia	Low	ND	ND
Wyoming	Low	Low	No

Note: This table is based on information provided by responding state agencies or knowledgeable individuals, or both.

[a] Includes all where substantial numbers occur.

[b] Other than North Dakota, which reported none, all states reported unknown for the number of days each hunter hunted and for the total number of days hunted.

exerted on many other species of game, however, and with even heavier pressures expected in the future, soras could become increasingly important to hunters. The potential of migratory webless birds for helping to meet the recreational demands of North American hunters is now being recognized by many (MacDonald and Evans 1970).

SPECIES NEEDS

The most critical need of the sora at this time is the preservation of wetland habitat. Land reclamation, in the form of drainage and filling, has ruined vast amounts of high-quality wetlands and is an even greater threat for future years. Some of the country's prime wetland areas are continually under the watchful eye of the speculator, who sees them as sites for future development. Additional legislation that will protect our wetlands from indiscriminate filling and draining is desperately needed in many states. Some states have created marshland protection agencies to oversee projects or proposals that would in any way alter the marsh ecology. Other needs, as expressed by respondents from individual states but applicable to all, are summarized in Table 3-3.

PUBLIC NEEDS

Public needs, particularly those of the sora hunter, differ somewhat from those connected with more sought-after species. Some of these needs and suggested methods of satisfying them are presented here.

Table 3-3. Budget requirements for a 10-year sora management plan.

Major Program or Area for Funding	Specific Jobs Within Each Program	Research or Management (R or M)	Job Priority	Estimated Cost of Jobs for Each Fiscal Year (in thousands of dollars)										Total Cost by Job (thousands)	Continuing Job
				1	2	3	4	5	6	7	8	9	10		
Population Studies	Determine distribution and densities at various seasons (migration patterns)	R	1	40	40	40	40	40						$ 200	No
	Develop reliable census techniques (direct and indirect)	R	2	30	30	30	30	30						150	No
	Measure sex and age compositions of selected populations through trapping and banding, collecting, and bag checks	R	3			100	100	100	100	100				500	No
	Develop trapping, aging, and sexing techniques	R	4	20	20	20								60	No
	Determine the effects of hunting on the population — measure harvest rates and hunting pressure	M	5						25	20	10	10	10	75	No
	Determine breeding and nesting chronology	R	6	20	15	10								45	No
	Survey productivity	M	7	25	25	10	10	10	10	10	10	10	10	130	Yes
	Study life history	R	8	20	20	20	20	20	20	20	20	20	20	200	Yes
	Determine the influence of hunting regulations on hunter success, harvest, and hunter distribution	R	9							25	20	10		55	No
	Study competition between sora and blackbirds for available foods	R	10	10	10	10								30	No
Total Cost of Program per Fiscal Year				165	160	240	200	200	155	175	60	50	40	1,445	

	Code	No.	1	2	3	4	5	6	7	8	9	10	Total	
Habitat Studies														
Determine seasonal habitat preferences	R	11	50	50	50	50	50						250	No
Determine effects of drainage, agriculture, pesticides, and heavy metals	R	12	50	25	10	10	10						105	No
Improve habitat for production and increasing harvest	M	14			20	20	10	10					60	No
Inventory habitat	M	15			125	125	125						375	No
Total Cost of Program per Fiscal Year			100	75	205	205	195	10					790	
Public Education														
Assist public with identifying and realizing its value as a game bird	M	16	25	25	25	10							85	No
Expand educational efforts related to the preservation, management, and improvement of wetland habitat	M	17	25	25	25	10							85	No
Total Cost of Program per Fiscal Year			50	50	50	20							170	
Grand Total Cost of All Programs by Fiscal Year for 10-Year Period			315	285	495	425	395	165	175	60	50	40	2,405	
Habitat Acquisition	M	13	100	100	100	100	100	100	100				700	

Classes in species identification are needed for the average rail hunter, in addition to information on life history, habits, and similar subjects.

Some public and private lands are closed to the public, both hunters and nonhunters. Because of limited interest, there is no access problem at present, but should interest grow, access could become a problem. Nonconsumptive users probably outnumber the hunting segment with regard to popularity of the rail family. Because of their secretive ways, rails rank high on the bird watcher's desirability list and will become even more popular as the nature movement expands.

The public should be made aware of the problems of drainage and destruction of wetlands. Educational efforts should be expanded in this direction.

Concentrating soras on various state and federally managed wildlife areas would benefit the hunter, the nonconsumptive observer, and the sora.

MANAGEMENT AND RESEARCH NEEDS AND COSTS

Management and research needs and costs are summarized in Table 3-3.

RECOMMENDATIONS

Keeping in mind the paucity of information on soras, we make the following recommendations on the management of this potentially valuable resource over the next 10 years.

Every effort should be made to promote preservation of our country's wetlands. This preservation surely is the most critical need of the species, since without habitat we will not have a resource to manage. Draining and filling operations and proposals must be critically reviewed to determine which are absolutely necessary. The committee should continue to seek to establish a National Migratory Webless Bird Conservation Stamp to identify the hunting segment and to provide support for management programs.

Basic information on life history should be obtained so that this resource can be managed intelligently. This effort is needed now, while pressures on the species are light, rather than later, when pressures could become critical.

Before we can expect the public to recognize and utilize the sora as a game bird, biologists, game managers, and administrators must recognize its potential. An educational effort should be directed toward the various state and federal agencies to stimulate awareness of and interest in what could be an important game-bird resource in future years. Although the sora may not appeal to most hunters now, present hunting trends suggest that it will be more in demand in the future.

Federal support should be made available to those states willing to engage in sora management and research. With sufficient financial incentive, state departments would be more likely to initiate such activities.

If these recommendations are accepted and acted on over the next 10 years, we will have made great strides, for we will have reversed a trend of indifference toward a potentially high-value game-bird resource. This attitude of indifference must be reversed before we can even consider management of this species.

ACKNOWLEDGMENTS
The following individuals and agencies contributed to this report: G. A. Ammann, John M. Anderson, Hugh A. Bateman, Jr., Richard A. Bishop, Warren Blandin, California Department of Natural Resources, W. B. Conrad, Jr., John J. Craighead, E. Dale Crider, Jack Dermid, David M. Donaldson, Jack Donnelly, Frederick Ferrigno, Michael J. Fogarty, C. P. Gilchrist, Richard Hamilton, Dan C. Holliman, Roger M. Holmes, Robert W. Johnson, Jerry Kaufman, Chester Kebbe, Robert E. Mangold, Marine Environmental Sciences Consortium, Mrs. Carl Masters, J. A. Morrison, Russell E. Mumford, Richard Norell, Ron R. Odom, Porter Reed, Carroll A. Rieck, Sam Robbins, George J. Schildman, Charles H. Schroeder, M. D. Schwilling, Walter A. Snyder, David Strohmeyer, Ward D. Tanner, Jr., Richard Todd, Roy E. Tomlinson, Milton B. Trautman, Robert J. Tully, Utah Department of Natural Resources, Milton W. Weller, George F. Wrakestraw, and John L. Zimmerman.

LITERATURE CITED
Barger, N. R. 1958. Sora rail. Wisconsin Conservation Bulletin 23(3):35.

Bent, Arthur C. 1926. Life histories of North American marsh birds. United States National Museum, Bulletin No. 135. 490pp.

Brewer, T. M. 1874. Breeding grounds of the sora rail. American Sportsman 4(22):339.

Gibbs, M. 1899. The sora. Oologist 16(10):151-153.

MacDonald, Duncan, and Thomas R. Evans. 1970. Accelerated research on migratory webless game birds. Transactions North American Wildlife and Natural Resources Conference 35:149-156.

Maryland Game and Inland Fish Commission. 1955. Sora. Maryland Conservationist 32(1):30.

Meanly, Brooke. 1960. Fall food of the sora rail in the Arkansas rice fields. Journal Wildlife Management 24(3):339.

Peterson, Roger T. 1947. A field guide to the birds. Houghton Mifflin Co., Boston. 290pp.

Pough, Richard H. 1951. Audubon water bird guide. Doubleday and Company, Inc., Garden City, New York. 353pp.

Starrett, William C. 1947. Sora rail at sea. Wilson Bulletin 59(1):37.

Tanner, Ward D., Jr., and George O. Hendrickson. 1956. Ecology of the sora in Clay County, Iowa. Iowa Bird Life 26(4):78-81.

Walkinshaw, Lawrence H. 1940. Summer life of the sora rail. Auk 57(2):153-168.

Webster, Clark G. 1964. Fall foods of soras from two habitats in Connecticut. Journal Wildlife Management 28(1):163-165.

Yellow Rail
(Coturnicops noveboracensis)

John M. Anderson, Director, Sanctuary Department, National Audubon Society, Sharon, Connecticut.

SUMMARY

Because of its secretive habits, the yellow rail is probably more abundant throughout its wide range than is commonly supposed. Lack of interest by hunters is such that few, if any, wildlife administrators feel justified in spending money for research or management. The destruction of wetlands appears to be the greatest threat to the species. The development of census techniques should receive high priority in research.

DESCRIPTION

The yellow rail (Fig. 3-3) is small (total length is 5 inches — 12.7 cm) and extremely secretive in habits. It has yellow plumage except for a dark crown,

Fig. 3-3. Yellow rail, Champaign, Illinois. (Photo by William E. Clark, Illinois Natural History Survey.)

dark brown stripes on the back, white wing patches, and lightly barred flanks. The bill is small and yellow.

LIFE HISTORY

Data on nesting, migration, and wintering habits are limited. Spring migrants reach the northern tier of states and southern Canada in April or May. Nesting apparently begins in late May or June in that latitude. Nests containing from 7 to 10 eggs have been found (Devitt 1939, Walkinshaw 1939), but data are too limited to provide average clutch size.

The incubation period of the sora (*Porzana carolina*) is about 16 to 20 days, and it is presumed that the incubation period for the yellow rail is roughly the same. Whether both sexes participate in incubating and brood rearing is not known. The average fall departure from the nesting range in southern Canada and the northern tier of states occurs in late September and early October.

HISTORICAL REVIEW

Because of their extremely secretive habits and small size, yellow rails attracted little attention from early settlers and market gunners. Similarly, research and management efforts are nonexistent. Ornithologists have spent many hours attempting to observe this species and searching for its nests. These efforts have established the relatively wide range of the species and the suspicion that it is more abundant than sight records indicate. In general, museum specimens are few.

DISTRIBUTION AND DENSITY

Although the species is widely distributed (Fig. 3-4), it can hardly be said to be plentiful anywhere. There is scattered evidence that because of its extremely secretive habits it may be much more abundant than is generally supposed. There are a few nesting records for east central California (Mono County), but the yellow rail appears to be rare or casual in the other western states. The species is common throughout North Dakota during the summer. Walkinshaw (1939) found it nesting in the Upper Peninsula of Michigan and considered it more common there than other rails. Devitt (1939) noted its distribution throughout Ontario during the summer months in favorable habitat from Lake St. Clair to James Bay. Scattered breeding records also occur in Minnesota, Wisconsin, Illinois, Ohio, Massachusetts, Maine, Nova Scotia, central Quebec, Manitoba, and Saskatchewan.

The yellow rail seems to prefer the high margins of marshes and grassy or sedge meadows. The species winters in central California and along the Gulf of Mexico from eastern Texas to Florida, and north along the coast to North Carolina. In the coastal marshes, it appears to prefer the drier portions of wire-grass (*Spartina patens*) marshes.

CENSUS PROCEDURES, POPULATION TRENDS, AND CURRENT AND POTENTIAL HARVEST

No satisfactory census procedures or methods for measuring population trends are known, and there are no estimates available from any state or province.

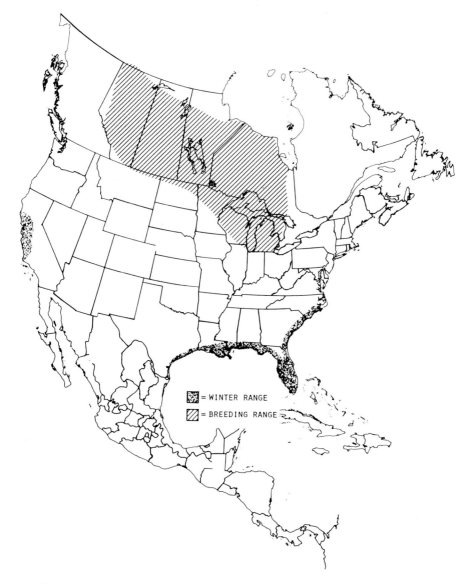

Fig. 3-4. Winter and breeding ranges of the yellow rail.

SPECIES NEEDS
To insure the future of the yellow rail, drainage of wetlands throughout North America must be curtailed. Hunting is not permitted and no threats, other than habitat destruction, are known.

PUBLIC NEEDS
The species is eagerly sought, but seldom found, by bird watchers. A marsh buggy in Louisiana's brackish marshes has proven quite effective in flushing wintering birds. It is possible that state, federal, and private refuges might gain additional support for their maintenance if they could devise means of showing the public more yellow rails.

MANAGEMENT AND RESEARCH NEEDS AND ESTIMATED COST
At present, no state or province feels justified in devoting management efforts to the yellow rail. The species undoubtedly benefits indirectly from habitat management for waterfowl and for clapper (*Rallus longirostris*), king (*R. elegans*), and sora rails.

Preservation of the nation's freshwater marshes and estuaries constitutes the only practical management effort for this species. The costs of stopping stream channelization, wetland drainage, and the destruction of salt marshes are constantly changing and cannot be estimated.

At present, no research is in progress except an occasional search for nests by private individuals. Deliberate attempts to census breeding birds are few. There is a general consensus that the species is much more abundant than sight records indicate, but techniques for gathering quantitative data are lacking. Census of breeding birds by call counts seems to offer the most promise.

Federal and state wildlife agencies can hardly justify research on a species that is neither on the game list nor on the endangered list. For the foreseeable future, graduate students and both professional and amateur ornithologists must be called upon to develop census techniques, habitat inventory and evaluation, and food-habits studies. Underwriting such programs would cost from $5,000 to $10,000 per year for 10 years under present (1974) economic conditions.

RECOMMENDATIONS
An education program to develop wider interest in the species among hunters and nonhunters could lead to support for habitat preservation and is strongly recommended. Since the bird calls persistently on the breeding grounds, the possibility of using a call-count census method should be explored. Where feasible, refuge managers should conduct field trips, especially on the wintering grounds using marsh buggies, to acquaint visitors with the yellow rail. Such a

program could lead to broader support for the overall refuge program. A hunting stamp for rails as a means of developing a sampling frame for measuring the harvest of hunted species is recommended.

LITERATURE CITED

Devitt, Otto E. 1939. The yellow rail breeding in Ontario. Auk 56(3):238-243.
Walkinshaw, Lawrence H. 1939. The yellow rail in Michigan. Auk 56(3):227-237.

Black Rail, Little Black Rail, Black Crake, Farallon Rail
(Laterallus jamaicensis)

Richard L. Todd, Wildlife Specialist, Arizona Game and Fish Department, Phoenix.

SUMMARY

The black rail is a seldom-detected small rail, whose population dynamics, including migration patterns and food habits, have not been investigated to any significant extent. Its annual population densities are virtually unknown for most states within its hypothetical range. Its life history is so poorly known that only a calculated guess can be made regarding the overall population trend, but the estimate is that black rails have declined nearly everywhere because of habitat loss. In some parts of the country, the populations may be critically low. Only a small segment of the American public has any esthetic or economic interest in the black rail, but to that minority the black rail is indeed important. The chief positive economic importance of the black rail is associated with the funds these people will expend to find or preserve this bird of mystery. An inventory and preservation program should be considered by wildlife agencies in states with populations of black rails.

DESCRIPTION

The total length of the adult bird is 5 to 6 inches (12.7 to 15.2 cm), the wingspread is 10 to 11 inches (25.4 to 27.9 cm) (Howell 1932:208), the blackish bill is approximately 0.6 inch (1.5 cm) in length, and the dull blackish chocolate-colored tarsus (Meanley and Stewart 1960) is approximately 0.8 inch (2.0 cm) long. The head, breast, and upper belly are slate colored; the lower belly and wings are brownish black, barred or spotted with white; and the nape is dark reddish brown (Chapman 1895:256-257). A description (Grinnel et al. 1918:304, Dawson 1923:1549) of the California black rail (*L. j. coturniculus*) notes that the blackish slate color of the foreparts of the body is darkest on top of the head, and the dark chestnut of the back and hind neck is brightest on the hind neck and deepens to black on the rump and tail. Small dots and short, irregular crossbars of white speckle the middle of the back, the rump, the tail, and the outer surface of the closed wing. The slaty brown flanks are barred narrowly with white, and the pale slate belly has whitish barring. The adult bird has a red eye. Feathered juvenile birds have generally lighter plumage than the adults.

LIFE HISTORY

Though the natural history of the black rail is little known, it seems evident that it is a bird of the wet meadows. Along the ocean, these may be salt-hay (*Spartina patens*) meadows or pickleweed (*Salicornia* spp.) flats located on the highest parts of the coastal marshes, where only the highest tides reach them (Pough 1951:202). Inland, black rails frequent marshes occupied by several species of rushes, sedges, or grasses, but the typical niche consists of a dense, though not necessarily tall, growth form of the dominant plants and a wet ground surface. Rank old marsh growth is apparently preferred to disturbed areas. Marsh growth that is typically semiflooded with several centimeters of water does not seem to be black rail habitat. Black rails utilize grainfields and hay meadows to some extent; there are numerous records of black rails being killed by scythes and mowing machinery (Howell 1932:209).

Before the late 1960's, summer-resident populations of California black rails in the United States seemed to be identified only in coastal salt marshes. Their habitat there seemed to be old clumps of pickleweed (Ingersoll 1909:124), presumably in situations seldom reached by high tides.

In 1969, black rails — presumably California black rails — were found along the lower Colorado River east of Yuma, Arizona (Snider 1969). Though marsh plant associations and their average heights differed, two constants seemed to hold: three-square bulrush (*Scirpus americanus*) was always an important constituent, and the black rail niche bordered the uplands rather than the open water (Richard L. Todd, 1971, Arizona Game and Fish Department, P-R Project W-53-21; 1972, Arizona Game and Fish Department, P-R Project W-53-22).

Nesting in the northern and central states seems to extend from May to August (Howell 1932:209). In the more southern latitudes, the nesting probably commences earlier and may end earlier. An egg collector (Huey 1916) interested in the California black rail recorded nesting dates from 24 March to 25 May over a 3-year time span. In Florida, Howell (1932:208) noted evidence of nesting from 11 May (adult and small young) to July (nest with eggs). It is possible that there are two breeding efforts in a season in the more southern latitudes of the United States.

Huey (1916:59) described the nests of California black rails as follows: "Sometimes the nests are raised well off the ground, but this is unusual. The more typical ground nests are greatly affected by the tides. Some that I have seen were fully five inches [12.7 cm] thick, with as many as three distinct layers, showing how often reconstruction had been necessary." Sometimes high tides left black rail eggs scattered about the marsh as flotsam. Clark (1884:394) noted that a nest site he observed near the mouth of the Connecticut River was in a moist meadow often overflowed by spring tides. He said that the nest resembled that of the eastern meadowlark (*Sturnella magna*), also nesting in the area, and that it consisted of "fine meadow grasses loosely put together, with a covering of one side." Dawson (1923:1551) stated that on the West Coast the nests are "hidden in the depths of the salicornia." They are cushions of broken bits of pickleweed placed either on the ground or on "convenient shelves of matted vegetation. The eggs are invisibly concealed from above by overarching foliage . . . ."

Approximately 6 to 10 of the inch-long (2.54 cm) whitish eggs are laid. There is not enough information for confident estimation of an overall average. They may be laid over a period of several days, but the hatching and the departure from the nest seem to take place on the same day (Heaton 1937*b*).

Black rails apparently leave most of their breeding range in the United States during migration. Those that remain in the United States seem to winter principally in the vicinity of the Gulf of Mexico, from southern Louisiana eastward through southern Georgia to Florida (Fig. 3-5) (American Ornithologists' Union 1961:158, Robbins et al. 1966:102). Significant numbers, however, may cross the Gulf of Mexico to South and Central America. Published *late dates* (Bent 1926:332) indicate that the birds depart from the northern half of the United States by mid-October. The bulk of them probably return to their summer abodes between mid-April and early May. Howell (1932:208) noted a record of apparent migration as early as 10 March. He mentioned fatalities at a lighthouse that indicated a departure in April or early May. Much of the black rail's migration occurs at night.

In the West, there is a fair amount of evidence showing migration or wandering activity by California black rails (Cohen 1901, Emerson 1904, Brewster 1907, Wall 1919, Gander 1930). Though these birds have seemed to be the California black rail, there now seems to be some mystery about where the remaining birds of this subspecies breed. Most of the sightings of this subspecies in recent years (away from the lower Colorado River) seem to have occurred in the fall and winter.

Little information is available on the food habits of the black rail. One bird exhibited insectivorous tendencies during its brief existence in captivity (Cobb 1906). Huey (1916) also had a captive that apparently accepted invertebrates ("bugs"), as well as bread crumbs. He had a "small series" of stomachs analyzed from birds collected in the autumn and found that they contained an isopod crustacean (*Alloniscus mirabilis*) abundant on the marshes. The black rails possibly feed mostly on invertebrates. The importance to them of plant material has yet to be determined. Gosse and Hill (1847:376) said, "The gizzard of the one that I examined, contained a few hard seeds." Scarcely any other references to the black rail's diet seem to be available.

DISTRIBUTION AND DENSITY

Records of the black rail indicate its range to be most of the eastern and central United States, generally south of the Great Lakes but also as far northeast as Connecticut and perhaps even farther north. The black rail also occurs on or within 50 miles of the coast of California, from the San Francisco area southward to (and within) Baja California, and for a distance of approximately 20 miles in disjunct localities along the lower Colorado River. There is a year-round population at the latter locality.

The approximate occurrence of the black rail in the United States is shown in Figure 3-5. It has been found breeding in Connecticut, Delaware, Florida, Illinois, Indiana, Kansas, Massachusetts, New Jersey, New York, North Carolina, Ohio, South Carolina, and Virginia (American Ornithologists' Union 1961:158). The distribution and suspected density of black rails, as reported

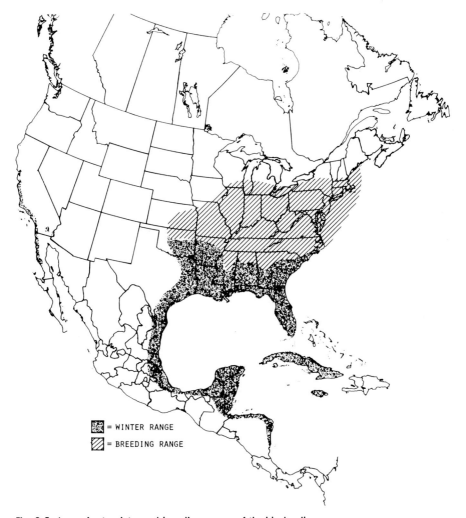

= WINTER RANGE

= BREEDING RANGE

Fig. 3-5. Approximate winter and breeding ranges of the black rail.

by other members of the Rail and Gallinule Technical Committee and as derived from the literature, are shown in Table 3-4.

The black rail is not limited to the United States. An old account of its occurrence in Jamaica (Gosse and Hill 1847:376) indicates that it once was

Table 3-4. Occurrence of the black rail in the United States.

Section and State	Occurrence[a]	Section and State	Occurrence
NORTHEAST		**EASTERN NORTH CENTRAL**	
Connecticut	4	Kentucky	7
Maine	5	Michigan	4
Massachusetts	4	Ohio	6
New Hampshire	5	Wisconsin	5
Rhode Island	4		
Vermont	7	**CENTRAL NORTH CENTRAL**	
		Iowa	5, ?[c]
EAST COAST		Kansas	4
Delaware	7	Minnesota	6, ?[d]
Maryland	1, 3[b]	Missouri	4a, ?[c]
New Jersey	4	Nebraska	6
New York	3 or 4	North Dakota	6
North Carolina	3	South Dakota	7
Pennsylvania	7		
South Carolina	4	**WESTERN NORTH CENTRAL**	
Virginia	7, probably 4[c]	Colorado	6
West Virginia	7	Idaho	7
		Montana	7
SOUTHEAST		Wyoming	7
Alabama	3a		
Florida	3a	**SOUTH CENTRAL**	
Georgia	4a	Arkansas	7
Mississippi	3a	Louisiana	4a
Tennessee	7	Oklahoma	4a, ?[c]
		Texas	4a[e]
EASTERN NORTH CENTRAL			
Illinois	was 4[c], probably 5	**WEST COAST**	
Indiana	4[c] or 5	California	4
		Oregon	6, 7, ?
SOUTHWEST		Washington	6, 7, ?
Arizona	4		
Nevada	7		
New Mexico	7		
Utah	7		

[a] 1 = Common in some tidewater marshes, 2 = common in local situations, 3 = uncommon and local, 3a = uncommon and local — augmented by winter residents, 4 = rare and local or regionally restricted, 4a = residency in summer not established — uncommon and regionally restricted or local in winter, 5 = very rare or accidental — residency not established, 6 = accidental — probably migrant or wandered, and 7 = no data obtained to date (or no occurrence records).
[b] Stewart and Robbins (1958:130-131).
[c] American Ornithologists' Union (1961:158).
[d] Roberts (1932:450).
[e] Peterson (1963:86).

resident there. It probably is severely reduced or near extermination there now, perhaps because the mongoose (*Herpestes javanicus*) was introduced (Coale 1923). The status of the black rail in Mexico and the rest of Middle America is not assignable because too little information is available. There may be small and local resident populations augmented by winter visitors from the United States. These may consist predominantly of winter visitors, or they may consist predominantly of local residents with minor augmentation by winter migrants. In British Honduras, Russell (1966) located an apparently resident population of black rails. Both Dickerman (1971) and Russell thought that they had probably found the eastern subspecies (*L. j. jamaicensis*) in Central America, though neither believed that any character other than the bill safely separated their birds from *L. j. coturniculus*. The total *extralimital* (outside the United States) range of the black rail is "not well known" (Davis 1972:38), to put it conservatively. The species is thought to occur, as a resident, in Peru, Chile, western Argentina, and possibly Colombia (De Schauensee 1966:79).

Traditionally, the black rail has been given the designation of "rare," especially "rare and local" (American Ornithologists' Union 1961:158), throughout much of its range, but because of its secretive habits, some ornithologists have thought that it is not as rare as it seems (Bent 1926:326, Howell 1932: 209, Forbush and May 1939:165), at least in the eastern United States. In some eastern localities it has even been considered "fairly common locally in tidewater areas . . . ." (Stewart and Robbins 1958:130). Inland, it appears to be an event to discover the location of black rails that are apparently nesting (for example, Kellogg 1962). None of the state respondents to questionnaires on the species now seem to consider the black rail to be common, and a few expressed concern for its status. The United States Department of the Interior lists the California black rail as threatened (U.S. Office of Endangered Species 1973:146).

On the lower Colorado River, the highest densities of black rails seem to be in marshes composed of very dense (high stem count) stands of some vegetation like common three-square bulrush, where there is a wet substrate to a depth of 1 to 3 inches (2.54 to 7.6 cm) of water.

CENSUS PROCEDURES AND POPULATION TRENDS

It seems that the use of tape recorder playbacks is the most promising technique for investigating the occurrence of black rails. It has worked well on the lower Colorado River in spring and early summer. Fall and winter trials with this technique have been less successful.

In most areas of the United States, counts have been obtained in the spring on birds that were calling on their own volition (Stewart and Robbins 1958: 131, also information relayed by R. E. Mangold for New Jersey). Unusual high-water conditions, especially extra-high tides, which force the birds into relatively open situations, constitute another opportunity to estimate approximate numbers. High tides can be accurately predicted and an investigation can be prepared to take advantage of any unusual weather conditions that exaggerate the tidal effect.

For the most part, there seems to be no information available on population trends. The California black rail, however, is believed to have disappeared from virtually all its former salt-marsh breeding grounds on the west coast of the United States.

CURRENT HARVEST, HUNTING PRESSURE, AND POTENTIAL HARVEST

There have been no open seasons on black rails in recent years and, consequently, no harvest estimates. Dogs accompanying waterfowl hunters may account for a few birds being accidentally taken. No estimate of the potential harvest can be made.

SPECIES NEEDS

Wetland meadows and marshes where the bird occurs must be preserved from drainage. Heavy human utilization of the sites (such as excessive livestock grazing or high-intensity mowing operations) should be decreased because of the impact upon the vegetative cover.

The highest numbers of black rails are found in coastal marshes, and, on both the east and west coasts, marshes and estuaries are habitat types that are disappearing. Disappearance of coastal marshes is a particularly acute problem on the West Coast, where there were far fewer suitable salt marshes to begin with and only a few of those had records of breeding populations. The possibility exists that during the breeding season there are now virtually no black rails in west coast salt marshes north of Baja California (personal communications from various knowledgeable workers in the San Diego area).

Many campaigns for preservation of estuaries seem to have emphasized the importance of estuaries to marine life and water birds, with habitat for the clapper rail (*Rallus longirostris*) often getting much attention. It may be that black rail habitat — whether next to fresh- or saltwater — is even more vulnerable than clapper habitat, because habitat for the black rail is in a situation more favorable to human exploitation. Agricultural operations and livestock grazing, as well as landfill by refuse or for development, may be significant threats in freshwater areas.

PUBLIC NEEDS

The public at large and most hunters have virtually no knowledge of the black rail and little interest in it. Among bird watchers, the black rail is highly valued. The American Birding Association (1971) rated the black rail as number three among the 40 birds that bird watchers most wanted to see. Since the first two species on this list — Bachman's warbler (*Vermivora bachmanii*) and the ivory-billed woodpecker (*Campephilus principalis*) — have virtually no probability of being located, the black rail, in effect, becomes the number one desire of bird watchers.

This information suggests services that the states can perform for members of the public interested in observing wildlife. Areas inhabited by black rails can be preserved, and their locations can be publicized. The first suggestion would be commendable, the second debatable. A number of workers have commented on the inclination of California black rails to desert their nests when disturbed (Huey 1916, Dawson 1923:1552, Heaton 1937*b*). This disturbance, plus the trampling of the habitat, which in turn encourages exploration by mammalian predators, including domestic dogs, perhaps makes it unwise to encourage public visits to black rail sites, though supervised guidance of the visitors onto an established path or road would probably reduce these dangers.

MANAGEMENT NEEDS AND COSTS

Much of the management need is self-evident from the foregoing discussion. Areas presently identified as black rail habitat need to be totally or partially protected from human disturbances, including drainage, livestock grazing, agricultural operations, fires, and any other heavy and prolonged disturbance by people, their machines, and their domesticated predators. All these are believed to have some influence, though of course they are not all equal in their effects. Some alterations of marshes for waterfowl management — such as changing water levels over prolonged periods and growing farm grains — may not be compatible with management for rails. Building structures for manipulation of water levels and perhaps control of woody plants may be instrumental in perpetuating the necessary sere for black rail habitat in some localities, particularly on inland sites. The cost of black rail management would be contingent upon a state's policy decisions regarding priorities. Should a state decide that the black rail deserves priority consideration in selected areas, other tactics come to mind. For instance, is it possible to pass legislation regulating ownership or stewardship of wetlands? It might be feasible to establish statewide systems of *natural heritage sites,* which would include black rail marshes.

The cost of black rail management in the future may consist chiefly of the price of acquiring privately owned habitat, or perhaps remuneration to private landowners to encourage improvement in land-use practices for the sake of preserving optimum habitat for black rails. Another cost voluntarily borne by the state could be the construction of fences to exclude livestock partially or totally from marshland.

A state should probably have between $10,000 and $30,000 per year available for building water-control structures and fences, posting, and disseminating interpretative literature on the black rail. An additional fund of at least $200,000 should be gradually established for emergency or opportune purchase of key areas.

NEEDED RESEARCH AND ESTIMATED COSTS

The outstanding research need for the black rail is possibly an investigation into the status of the western populations of *Laterallus jamaicensis coturniculus*. This subspecies may be in danger of extinction in the United States.

Although not apparently in similar danger, *L. j. jamaicensis* in the East has probably disappeared from enough localities to merit concern and investigation in its established breeding range. New Jersey, for instance, lists it "unofficially as rare and endangered" (personal communication, R. E. Mangold).

What is most immediately needed is an assessment of the known and potential habitats of black rails and an estimate of their populations. Tape recorders will probably work as well at eliciting responses in known habitats in the East as they have on the lower Colorado River. Evaluation of the niche most frequented by black rails should be concomitant with such an inventory.

A banding project on the black rail would probably not be worthwhile in determining migration patterns because there seems to be no probability of recovery away from the banding site. Yet should a banding program be successful and compatible with the bird's reproductive activities, it could determine whether individuals return to the same marsh and indicate the rate of population turnover.

It would be desirable to identify positively the regions that are important to birds that migrate. Some form of biotelemetry or isotope marking may be usable. The limited transmittal range of a device small enough not to be a hindrance to a black rail's flight would seem to necessitate use of an aircraft and nocturnal monitoring. We believe this, however, to be research of an advanced nature in terms of committed personnel, sophisticated procedures, available funding, and interstate or even international cooperation. In the meantime, it may serve just as well for states that locate black rail populations to take action to preserve the sites on which they are found, regardless of the summer status of the birds.

Equipping one researcher with a suitable vehicle, a portable boat with a small engine (and occasional use of more powerful boats), audio equipment, and binoculars would probably enable him to make adequate inspection of potential black rail habitat over a 3- to 5-year period in most states. Such a project would involve an outlay of from $25,000 to $55,000 per year, or perhaps only half this amount if most of the work were done on a seasonal contract basis with college personnel (Table 3-5). It may be feasible to combine the black rail objectives with a project on the yellow rail (*Coturnicops noveboracensis*), since habitat requirements of the two have some similarity.

Table 3-5. Budget requirements for a 10-year black rail management plan.

Major Program or Area for Funding	Specific Jobs Within Each Program	Research or Management (R or M)	Job Priority	Estimated Cost of Jobs for Each Fiscal Year (in thousands of dollars)										Total Cost by Job (thousands)	Continuing Job
				1	2	3	4	5	6	7	8	9	10		
Population Studies	Conduct singing-ground survey of California black rail	R & M	1	50	30	15	5	5	3	5	2	2	10	$ 127	Yes
	Conduct singing-ground survey of all other black rails	R & M	4	100	400	100	50	20	10	10	10	10	20	730	Yes
	Test efficiency of electronic aids in censusing for all seasons	R	6	30	30	30								90	No
	Monitor pesticide effects and pollution effects	R	8	20	20	10	10	10	5	5	5	10	10	105	Yes
	Investigate trapping, banding, and telemetry techniques	R	10	50	50	50	50	50	50	10	10	5	5	330	No
	Study reproduction (annual increment)	R	11	5	30	50	15	5						105	No
	Determine population turnover (mortality)	R	12	5	20	30	15	5						75	No
	Study food habits	R	13		10	20	5							35	No
	Study migration: establish departure and arrival periods, initiate trapping and banding (or isotope marking) techniques	R	14	10	20	10	15	200	100	100	80	70	65	670	No
	Develop other direct and indirect methods of population enumeration (contingent upon success of electronically based techniques)	R	17			10	30	30	30	10	5	5	5	125	No
Total Cost of Program per Fiscal Year				270	610	325	195	325	198	140	112	102	115	2,392	

Habitat program			1	2	3	4	5	6	7	8	9	10	Total	
Habitat Studies														
Determine breeding, migration, and winter habitat preferences	R	2	50	20	20								90	No
Inventory habitat, both known and potential sites; study historical occurrence	R	5	300	100	50								450	No
Evaluate effects of land-use practices on habitat quantity and quality	R	7	20	30	40	50	30	5	5	5	5	20	210	Yes
Manage habitat using known techniques	M	15	5	15	50	50	100	100	100	100	100	100	720	Yes
Develop and evaluate habitat management techniques on selected demonstration areas	R	16	20	30	30	50	50	50	30	30	30	50	370	No
Total Cost of Program per Fiscal Year			395	195	190	150	180	155	135	135	135	170	1,840	
Grand Total Cost of All Programs by Fiscal Year for 10-Year Period			665	805	515	345	505	368	295	247	237	250	4,232	
Habitat Acquisition														
Acquire habitat	M	9	50	100	500	500	500	500	300	300	50	50	2,850	No
Preserve habitat for California black rail; acquire habitat (in part contingent upon findings of job with priority 1)	M	3		100	300	500	300			500			1,700	Yes
Total Cost of Habitat Acquisition			50	200	800	1,000	800	500	300	800	50	50	4,550	

RECOMMENDATIONS

The status of the California black rail should be investigated and established as soon as possible. The threats to known sites of occurrence are critical.

Steps should be taken to preserve black rail habitat where possible until an adequate inventory has been made.

If the interest, recent occurrence of the species, need for information, and funding exist, the populations of black rails and the trends of their habitats should be determined and evaluated.

Migration patterns and winter quarters should be adequately assessed.

Such life-history studies as are possible should be undertaken on reproduction, population turnover, limiting factors, causes of mortality, food habits, and characteristics of the various types of wetlands inhabited.

Several more specific suggestions for managing marshes for black rails should be considered: (a) inhibit pesticide applications on the marsh or adjacent watersheds; (b) protect the area from widespread fire (old plant growth should be present on some or most of an area for black rails); (c) protect the area from fire during the suspected breeding season; (d) protect the area from most levels of livestock grazing (light grazing by cattle may be acceptable and should be assessed more fully); (e) restrict agricultural operations on those portions of marsh meadow frequented by black rails; (f) oppose the establishment of public campgrounds or play areas, boat-launching sites, and roads through or near black-rail marshes; (g) discourage heavy visitation by humans and domestic predators to the marshes used by rails during the breeding season; and (h) oppose running telephone lines or other cables through marsh habitat if alternative routing is feasible.

LITERATURE CITED

American Ornithologists' Union. 1961. Check-list of North American birds. 5th edition. Port City Press, Baltimore. 691pp.

Bent, Arthur C. 1926. Life histories of North American marsh birds. [Reprint 1963.] Dover Publications, New York. 392pp.

Brewster, William. 1901. An ornithological mystery. Auk 18(4):321-328.

———. 1907. Notes on the black rail of California. Auk 24(2):205-210.

Chapman, Frank M. 1895. Handbook of birds of eastern North America. [Reprint 1966.] Dover Publications, New York. 581pp.

Clark, John N. 1884. Nesting of the little black rail in Connecticut. Auk 1(4):393-394.

Coale, Henry K. 1923. A new subspecies of the little black rail. Auk 40(1):88-90.

Cobb, Stanley. 1906. A little black rail in Massachusetts. Bird-Lore 8(4):136-137.

Cohen, Donald A. 1901. Notes from Almeda, California. Condor 3(6):185-186.

Davis, L. Irby. 1972. A field guide to the birds of Mexico and Central America. University of Texas Press, Austin and London. 282pp.

Dawson, William L. 1923. The birds of California: South Moulton Co., San Diego, Los Angeles, and San Francisco. Vol. 4:1549-2121.

De Schauensee, Rodolphe M. 1966. The species of birds of South America and their distribution. The Academy of Natural Sciences of Philadelphia. 577pp.

Dickerman, Robert W. 1971. Notes on various rails in Mexico. Wilson Bulletin 83(1): 49-56.

Emerson, W. Otto. 1904. Destruction of birds by wires. Condor 6(2):37-38.

Forbush, Edward H., and John B. May. 1939. A natural history of American birds of eastern and central North America. Houghton Mifflin Co., Boston. 553pp.

Gander, Frank F. 1930. A black rail leaves the salt marsh. Condor 32(4):211.

Gosse, Philip H., and Richard Hill. 1847. The birds of Jamaica. John Van Vorst, London. 447pp.

Grinnell, Joseph, Harold C. Bryant, and Tracy I. Storer. 1918. The game birds of California. University of California Press, Berkeley. 642pp.

Heaton, Harry L. 1937a. Disproving the rule. The Farallon rail. Oologist 54(3):30-31.

———. 1937b. Baby Farallon rails. Oologist 54(9):102-103.

Howell, Arthur H. 1932. Florida bird life. Florida Department of Game and Fresh Water Fish in cooperation with U.S. Bureau of Biological Survey. New York. 519pp.

Huey, Laurence M. 1916. The Farallon rails of San Diego County. Condor 18(2):58-62.

Ingersoll, A. M. 1909. The only known breeding ground of Creciscus coturniculus. Condor 11(4):123-127.

Kellogg, Peter P. 1962. Vocalizations of the black rail (Laterallus jamaicensis) and the yellow rail (Coturnicops noveboracensis). Auk 79(4):698-701.

Meanley, Brooke, and Robert E. Stewart. 1960. Color of the tarsi and toes of the black rail. Auk 77(1):83-84.

Peterson, Roger T. 1963. A field guide to the birds of Texas and adjacent states. Houghton Mifflin Co., Boston. 304pp.

Pough, Richard H. 1951. Audubon water bird guide. Eastern and central North America from southern Texas to central Greenland. Doubleday and Co., Garden City, New York. 352pp.

Robbins, Chandler S., Bertel Bruun, and Herbert S. Zimm. 1966. Birds of North America. Golden Press, New York. 340pp.

Roberts, Thomas S. 1932. The Birds of Minnesota, Volume 1. University of Minnesota Press, Minneapolis. 691pp.

Russell, Stephen M. 1966. Status of the black rail and the gray-breasted crake in British Honduras. Condor 68(1):105-107.

Snider, Patricia R. 1969. Southwest region regional reports. The nesting season June 1, 1969–August 15, 1969. Audubon Field Notes 23(5):680-683.

Stewart, Robert E., and Chandler S. Robbins. 1958. Birds of Maryland and the District of Columbia. North American Fauna, No. 62. U.S. Government Printing Office, Washington, D.C. 401pp.

Stoddard, H. L. 1916. The black rail (Creciscus jamaicensis) at Chicago, Ill. Auk. 33(4):433-434.

U.S. Office of Endangered Species and International Activities. 1973. Threatened wildlife of the United States. Bureau of Sport Fisheries and Wildlife, Resource Publication 114. 289pp.

Wall, Edward. 1919. California black rail at San Bernardino, California. Condor 21(6):238.

Clapper Rail
(Rallus longirostris)

Robert E. Mangold, New Jersey Division of Fish, Game and Shellfishes, Trenton.

SUMMARY
The clapper rail, in one or more of its subspecific forms, breeds along coastal salt marshes from Maine to California, and one form is found in fresh marshes along the Colorado River. Most subspecies appear to be nonmigratory, but two races migrate from mid-Atlantic states to South Atlantic states. The migratory forms leave their breeding marshes between August and November and return in April. Apparently clappers are monogamous and, in three subspecies at least, have been found to be multibrooded. Nesting activities appear to begin in April and end in August. The number of eggs laid ranges between 5 and 14, with a mean of about 9. Hatchability is high. Most losses are caused by storm tides, but there is predation of significance in some locations. Densities of breeding birds range from a reported 0.9 to 3.4 per acre (2.2 to 8.4 per ha) of prime habitat; census methods vary with habitat, but calling is used to determine both numbers and trends. Another useful method is locating all nests on a given area. Reported annual harvests on a statewide basis have ranged from 500 to 85,000, with potential harvests usually much higher. Needs include population enumeration, habitat protection, harvest data, basic life-history studies, habitat inventory, survival information, and study of pesticide effects. Suggested costs over a 10-year period total more than $5.3 million.

DESCRIPTION
The clapper rail is a large grayish, gray-brown, or tan rail, with a short neck and slightly downcurved bill (Fig. 3-6A). The flanks are barred with white, and the short tail is cocked upward, displaying a white patch. The grayer cheeks and grayer back distinguish this bird from the king rail (*R. elegans*).

LIFE HISTORY
The clapper rail prefers a tidal marsh bordered by shallow bodies of salt or brackish water (Stone 1937:335). Dense growths of cordgrass (*Spartina* sp.) or needlerush (*Juncus* sp.), with deep, soft soils, characterize its habitat (Fig. 3-6B). Normally, this rail keeps well hidden in the thick vegetation unless flushed from its protective cover. At dawn and at dusk, it may venture out to feed along tidal flats and muddy shores of bayous and tidal creeks. The elevated nest is constructed of the surrounding vegetation and situated near water (Fig. 3-6C). The nest may be arched over with marsh grass for concealment. There are 4 to 14 (Fig. 3-6D) pale lavender eggs spotted with brown in a clutch (Kozicky and Schmidt 1949:358). The young are black (Fig. 3-6E).

Fig. 3-6. A. The northern clapper rail is found in the salt marsh, nearly always associated with saltmarsh cordgrass. Note young.

Fig. 3-6. B. The nest of the northern clapper rail is usually found in the taller stands of cordgrass, within a short distance of water.

Fig. 3-6. C. A typical location for the nest of the northern clapper rail in New Jersey.

Fig. 3-6. D. The clutch of the northern clapper rail in New Jersey averages between eight and nine eggs.

Fig. 3-6. E. A clutch of clappers beginning to hatch. The chicks are completely black except for feet and bill.

Fig. 3-6. F. The northern clapper rail occasionally attempts to overwinter in New Jersey, usually with poor success. (All photos in Fig. 3-6 by R. E. Mangold.)

The main food consists of small crabs, other custaceans, snails, and shellfish, but small fish, clam worms, and aquatic insects are occasionally eaten (Bateman 1965:99). Seeds constitute only a small part of the diet. In some locations, up to 90 percent of the diet may consist of only one food, such as fiddler crabs (*Uca* sp.).

The clapper rail apparently is monogamous and has been reported to be multibrooded in South Carolina (Blandin 1963:67), California, and New Jersey (Schmidt and McLain 1951:4). The incubation period has been reported as 18 to 22 days for the eastern subspecies and 23 to 29 days for at least one western subspecies. It has been reported to cross successfully with the king rail where the clapper's salt-marsh habitat and the king's fresh-marsh habitat intermingle (Meanley 1969:6). Although most nest losses are associated with storm tides, predators such as raccoons (*Procyon lotor*), crows (*Corvus* spp.), and gulls (*Larus* spp.) take eggs, chicks, and adult rails.

HISTORICAL REVIEW

The best historical account of the clappers is provided by Bent (1926:266-292), who discusses eight rails that are presently considered subspecies of *Rallus longirostris* and does not mention one, the mangrove clapper (*R. l. insularum*), also present in the continental United States. The clapper on the eastern seaboard was numerous and heavily hunted, as reported by Audubon (in Bent 1926:281), as was the California clapper (*R. l. obsoletus*), as reported by Grinnell et al. (in Bent 1926:270-271). Much interesting natural history is presented by Bent.

A revision of clapper rails is provided by Oberholser (1937), who comments on 25 subspecies, 8 of which occur in the United States.

DISTRIBUTION AND DENSITY

The clapper rail and its eight subspecies or races (Fig. 3-7) are principally found in the coastal salt marsh from New Jersey and rarely north as far as southern Maine (northern clapper rail, *R. l. crepitans*), down the Atlantic coast (Wayne clapper rail, *R. l. waynei*), across the Gulf Coast (Florida clapper rail, *R. l. scottii,* and Louisiana clapper rail, *R. l. saturatus*), and up part of the California coast (light-footed clapper rail, *R. l. levipes,* and California clapper rail), wherever cordgrass (*Spartina alterniflora*) marshes are found (Table 3-6). It is also found in freshwater locations in at least two southwestern states, for example, the Yuma clapper rail (*R. l. yumanensis*) along the Colorado River between Arizona and California (Dickey 1923:93). Three subspecies are listed as endangered by the United States Department of the Interior. These are the California, light-footed, and Yuma clapper rails.

Density of the clapper in prime habitat, as measured by breeding birds, ranges from 0.9 to 1.9 rails per acre (2.2 to 4.7 per ha) in Georgia (Oney 1954:32) to 1.3 (3.2 per ha) in New Jersey and 3.4 (8.4 per ha) in Virginia. Chick production ranges from a high of 11.2 and 6.9 per acre (27.7 and 17.0 per ha) in South Carolina to 5.3 and 0.9 (13.1 and 2.2 per ha) in New Jersey.

The northern clapper rail (found from perhaps Virginia to Maine) is migratory, wintering between Charleston, South Carolina, and Jacksonville, Florida (Stewart 1951:429). Other races or subspecies either do not migrate or move very little (Adams and Quay 1958:154).

CENSUS PROCEDURES AND POPULATION TRENDS

Several census methods have been used, with varying success; counting active nests per area annually yields an index of abundance in some states and is of little value in others. Brood counts have been used in South Carolina. In some cases, eliciting calls by playing taped calls has met with success, as with the

Fig. 3-7. Distribution of the clapper rail. The northern clapper rail is migratory, wintering between Charleston, South Carolina, and Jacksonville, Florida; other races either do not migrate or move very little.

Table 3-6. Current and potential harvest of the clapper rail.

State	Hunting Allowed in 1973	Estimated Hunters (thousands)	Estimated Total Hunting Days (thousands)	Estimated Harvest (thousands)	Additional Hunting Potential
SUBSTANTIAL NUMBERS PRESENT					
Alabama	Yes				
Delaware	Yes	very few			No
Florida	Yes				Yes
Georgia	Yes	4		50-75	Yes
Louisiana	Yes				Yes
Maryland	Yes				
Mississippi	Yes				
New Jersey	Yes	3-5[a]	15-25	15-25	Yes
North Carolina	Yes			0.5	
South Carolina	Yes	2-4		14-74	Yes
Texas	Yes				
Virginia	Yes				No
LESSER NUMBERS PRESENT					
California	No				No
Connecticut	Yes				No
Maine	No				No
Massachusetts	No				No
New Hampshire	No				No
New York	No				No
Rhode Island	Yes				No

[a] Each hunter hunted an estimated 5 days.

Yuma clapper rail. Recently in New Jersey, experiments with call counts have had some success (Mangold 1973).

Population trends in those southern states where rails apparently do not migrate are unknown or appear to be stable. Western states, northeastern states, and Florida have lost significant amounts of habitat. Connecticut, for example, reported in 1950 that the clapper had formerly been a rather rare summer resident but that, beginning about 1931, it increased in abundance. By 1944 it was considered exceedingly common in suitable habitat (Saunders 1950). Since 1944, however, the clapper has been declining, and it is now (1973) considered a rare summer resident again. In New Jersey, breeding populations have fluctuated but are now increasing. In California, habitat loss seems to be the major problem. In 1956, Georgia estimated a population of 282,000.

CURRENT AND POTENTIAL HARVEST

Few states have quantitative data on harvests. In recent years, estimates for New Jersey indicate about 3,000 hunters with a seasonal bag of about 15,000 clapper rails. In 1947, the last year in which hunters were allowed to use motors, about 85,000 clappers were harvested in Georgia; in 1948 and 1956, the harvests were about 25,000 and 52,000, respectively. In 1972, about 4,000 hunters bagged from 50,000 to 75,000 clappers. In South Carolina, a 1966 estimate indicated that 5,775 hunters harvested nearly 74,000 clapper rails; in recent years, the total bag has been estimated as probably less than 14,000. North Carolina estimates that lack of huntable territory has reduced the current harvest to less than 500.

The potential harvest in the Atlantic seaboard states may be greater, but until more is known about components of the fall population, it may not be wise to change the current regulations to any great extent. For example, in New Jersey most of the adult birds and many of the young birds migrate south before 1 September, the opening day of the hunting season. At the same time, some hunters in several southeastern states desire the relaxation of the ban on the use of powerboats for hunting. Along the Gulf Coast, hunting pressure apparently is relatively low. The potential harvest may be much larger than the present harvest.

SPECIES NEEDS

The most important species need, as indicated by respondents from the several states, is habitat protection. A need for research on the essential requirements of the species and ways of providing for those needs were also suggested.

PUBLIC NEEDS

The most frequent suggestion on public needs made by respondents from the southeastern states was a relaxation of the ban against powerboating. Also suggested were access to marshland and information and education on hunting potential; in some cases, guide service was listed as a need.

MANAGEMENT AND RESEARCH NEEDS AND COSTS

Probably the greatest need is for research projects. The rail up to now has principally been managed by no management. Little rangewide information is currently available on populations, trends, harvest, potential harvest, or even basic life history. In the 18 years from 1955 to 1972, fewer than 4,000 clapper rails were banded, and more than 2,500 of those were banded in one state alone. Banding should be given high priority in any research program. Through banding, New Jersey has found that few of the adult birds banded on the breeding grounds are shot in New Jersey but that most recoveries of shot birds come from Virginia, South Carolina, Georgia, and northeastern Florida; however, large numbers return each spring to help form breeding populations. Georgia has just begun banding and in 1973 banded more than 600 clapper rails. Habitat inventory is another aspect of management that has hardly been investigated.

Estimated costs for management needs are mere guesses and may range from a few thousand dollars per state to higher figures, depending on whether such items as land acquisition are included. It is difficult to distinguish between management and research because so much of management work has been loosely termed research. Basic life-history studies on the clapper rail are not plentiful; many management plans must be based on less than adequate information. For example, there are great regional differences in foods eaten. We do not know what proportions of the rail harvest are made up of the various subspecies or races. It is a revelation to some that clappers may be multibrooded, that they are monogamous, and that some are migratory and others may be nonmigratory. We need data on the effects of the various pesticides and heavy metals on rails. Although we can sex adult northern clappers by external characteristics, methods are needed for sexing young birds and other subspecies; aging techniques are also needed. Costs of management and research are suggested in Table 3-7 and total over $5.3 million.

RECOMMENDATIONS

Recommendations are listed in the general order of priority.

Banding of clappers on breeding grounds, as well as on winter grounds, should be encouraged on a continuing basis.

Census techniques already developed should be used, or modified, or both, for use throughout the range of the species in the United States.

An inventory of habitat should be undertaken in each state where significant numbers of clappers are present.

This inventory of habitat should be the basis of a continuing and meaningful habitat-acquisition program. Habitat acquired could be under federal or state ownership, or both, and could be used as public hunting areas.

Annual harvest surveys should be specific to the clapper rail, as well as to other species of rails.

Basic life-history studies of the various subspecies are essential to intelligent management and should be undertaken.

Annual productivity studies should form part of the basis for annual harvest rates.

Survival rates, especially of young-of-the-year, are practically unknown and are also essential to management. Regional studies of this phase of the life of the clapper should be made.

Disease and pollution studies should be undertaken by a central laboratory with regional input.

LITERATURE CITED

Adams, David A., and Thomas L. Quay. 1958. Ecology of the clapper rail in southeastern North Carolina. Journal Wildlife Management 22(2):149-156.

Bateman, Hugh A., Jr. 1965. Clapper rail (*Rallus longirostris*) studies on Grand Terre

Table 3-7. Budget requirements for a 10-year clapper rail management plan.

Major Program or Area for Funding	Specific Jobs Within Each Program	Research or Management (R or M)	Job Priority	Estimated Cost of Jobs for Each Fiscal Year (in thousands of dollars)										Total Cost by Job (thousands)	Continuing Job
				1	2	3	4	5	6	7	8	9	10		
Population Studies	Conduct banding	M	1	25	25	25	25	25	25	25	25	25	25	$ 250	Yes
	Enumerate population by indirect methods	M	2	70	20	20	20	20	20	20	20	20	20	250	Yes
	Survey harvest	M	5	10	10	10	10	10	10	10	10	10	10	100	Yes
	Study basic life history	R	6	30	30	30	30	30						150	No
	Study productivity	M	7	30	30	30	30	30	30	30	30	30	30	300	Yes
	Study survival	R	8		25	25	25				25	25	25	150	No
	Study disease and pollution	R	9	10	10	10	10	10						50	No
Total Cost of Program per Fiscal Year				175	150	150	150	125	85	85	110	110	110	1,250	
Habitat Studies	Inventory habitat	R	3		50	50	50							150	No
Total Cost of Program per Fiscal Year					50	50	50							150	
Grand Total Cost of All by Fiscal Year for 10-Year Period				175	200	200	200	125	85	85	110	110	110	1,400	
Habitat Acquisition and Preservation		M	4		500	500	500	500	500	500	500	500		4,000	

Island, Jefferson Parish, Louisiana. M.S. Thesis. Louisiana State University, Baton Rouge. 145pp.

Bent, Arthur C. 1926. Life histories of North American marsh birds. United States National Museum, Bulletin No. 135. 490pp.

Blandin, Warren W. 1963. Renesting and multiple brooding studies of marked clapper rails. Proceedings Annual Conference Southeastern Association Game and Fish Commissioners 17:60-68.

Dickey, Donald B. 1923. Description of a new clapper rail from the Colorado River valley. Auk 40(1):90-94.

Kozicky, Edward L., and Francis V. Schmidt. 1949. Nesting habits of the clapper rail in New Jersey. Auk 66(4):355-364.

Mangold, Robert E. 1973. Clapper rail studies in New Jersey under the accelerated research program. Proceedings Northeastern Fish and Wildlife Conference 30. 8pp.

Meanley, Brooke. 1969. Natural history of the king rail. United States Fish and Wildlife Service. North American Fauna, No. 67. 108pp.

Oberholser, Harry C. 1937. A revision of the clapper rails (*Rallus longirostris* Boddaert). Proceedings United States National Museum 84(3018):313-354.

Oney, John. 1954. Final report, clapper rail survey and investigation study. Georgia Game and Fish Commission. 50pp.

Saunders, Aretas A. 1950. Changes in status of Connecticut birds. Auk 67(2):253-255.

Schmidt, F. V., and P. D. McLain. 1951. The clapper rail in New Jersey. Proceedings Northeastern Fish and Wildlife Conference 7. 9pp.

Stewart, Robert E. 1951. Clapper rail populations of the middle Atlantic states. Transactions North American Wildlife Conference 16:421-430.

Stone, Witmer. 1937. Bird studies at Old Cape May. Vol. 1. [Reprint 1965.] Dover Publications Inc., New York. 484pp.

King Rail
(Rallus elegans)

Hugh A. Bateman, Jr., Biologist, Louisiana Wildlife and Fisheries Commission, Baton Rouge.

SUMMARY

The king rail is the largest member of the rail family. Its breeding range and distribution in North America are restricted to the humid, freshwater regions of the eastern United States from the Canadian border south to the Gulf coast and from the 100th meridian east to the Atlantic coast. The species is migratory over most of its geographic range and winters primarily along the coastal plain and marshes of the South Atlantic and Gulf Coasts. The two major migration periods are April and May in the spring and August and September in the fall. The Atlantic coastal plain and the Mississippi River valley are accepted as the two primary migration routes for king rails. Sexes are alike in plumage, but the male averages larger than the female. Young-of-the-year can be distinguished from adults for several months by color of the soft parts. The molt of the king rail is not clearly understood. Nesting activity for king rails extends from March to September in southern latitudes. In more northern climates, the nesting season spans about 3 or 4 months. Clutch size is 10 or 11 eggs on the average, and incubation requires 21 to 23 days. Both sexes share in incubation and care of young. The young king rail has obtained its juvenile plumage by 60 days after hatching and is capable of flight at 9 weeks. The king rail's distribution covers a wider range of habitat types than does that of other members of the rail family. Water-oriented animal foods, particularly crustaceans, make up a major part of the king rail's diet, and plant material is used sparingly. The bulk of the mortality among king rail populations probably results from aerial collisions, predation, severe weather, disease, and parasites. Loss caused by pesticides has not been researched and is not understood. The king rail, like other members of the rail family, is not a heavily hunted game bird anywhere within its range. As of 1972, king rails were hunted in only 11 states, all in the East or Southeast. The species is most often incidental in the bag of hunters seeking other rails, bobwhites (*Colinus virginianus*), woodcock (*Philohela minor = Scolopax minor* of Edwards 1974), or waterfowl. The nongregarious nature of the species, its secretiveness, and the inaccessibility of its habitat, all contribute towards the lack of interest by the public in the king rail. The basic life history of the king rail is well documented by Meanley (1969), but information on available habitat, population density, migration, hunting harvest, and pesticide relationships is lacking.

DESCRIPTION

The king rail is the largest of all North American rails (Fig. 3-8). It is a large, long-billed, reddish-brown bird that resembles the clapper rail (*Rallus longirostris*) (Fig. 3-6A) of saltwater habitats in size and plumage. The king rail is more prominently barred, however, and possesses more of a reddish cast than the clapper. The king rail is characteristically a drab-colored, secretive bird of marshy, freshwater habitats in the eastern half of the United States. There are no apparent differences in plumage between the male and the female.

The ranges of king and clapper rails frequently overlap, and the two species are separated by only slight differences in size, color of plumage, and vocal characteristics. Much debate still lingers on the proper *specific* alignment of

Fig. 3-8. King rail in a Louisiana marsh. (Photo by J. L. Herring, Louisiana Wild Life and Fisheries Commission.)

these two rails, and some ornithologists believe that the two may be simply ecological representatives of the same species (Lowery 1955:227).

The king rail, like all other rails and gallinules, has been a game bird of very localized and limited interest in spite of historically liberal hunting regulations. Likewise, the species has stimulated only sporadic study by individuals, and there has been no cooperative, comprehensive research on a broad basis among states within its range.

Meanley (1969), research biologist with the then United States Bureau of Sport Fisheries and Wildlife, published an excellent report as a result of his personal interest in these birds. His report is the most detailed compilation of research information available for any of the North American rails or gallinules. Most of the present report is based on Meanley's publication.

The three North American species of the genus *Rallus* — the king rail, the clapper rail, and the Virginia rail (*R. limicola*) — have laterally compressed bodies that facilitate passage through dense marsh vegetation. They also have long, slender, and slightly curved bills that are as long as or longer than the tarsi and longer than the heads; large, strong legs; long, slender, unwebbed toes; short, rounded wings (with vestigial claws) ; short, tipped-up, pointed tails less than half as long as the wings; flanks conspicuously barred with white; olive or grayish dorsal regions striped with black or dusty markings; and buffy or rufescent breasts. The king rail is larger than the Virginia rail, which it resembles in color; it is more rufescent than races of the clapper rail but is about the same size as that species.

Two races of the king rail are generally recognized: *R. e. elegans* of North America and *R. e. ramsdeni,* the Cuban form. Apparently a third form, *R. e. tenuirostris,* occurs in the freshwater marshes of the Valley of Mexico.

LIFE HISTORY

Details on the life history of the king rail are presented by Meanley (1969: 96-97).

> King Rail sexes appear to be alike in plumage. The male averages larger than the female. Immature birds apparently can be externally distinguished from adults during the first autumn by the color of the soft parts. Most rails in juvenal and first-winter (Immature) plumage have some white barring on the wing coverts. This is also true of some adults. The light-phase adult plumage described by Ridgway and Friedmann (1941) is probably typical of hybrids. The small sample of weights and measurements given in this report indicated that the King Rail averages slightly larger than the Clapper Rail.

> Molt is not well understood. Apparently all individuals molt after the nesting season, but some also molt during it.

> King Rails are known to return to the same section of the same marsh

for several consecutive years to breed. Territories are established and maintained by aggressive behavior, primarily that of the male. The mating call,
given by the male, presumably serves the same purpose as the song of a
passerine bird on its territory, namely to attract a mate and to repel other
birds of the same sex (but also, in the case of the King Rail, to maintain
contact after pairing).

The display of the male during prenuptial courtship consists mostly in
walking about with tail uplifted and white undertail coverts extended.
After pairing, other forms of display and a repertoire of subdued calls are
used to maintain the pair bond.

Copulation takes place near the nest site, before and during egg laying.

The incubation period for king rails will range between 21 and 23 days.
Both sexes help incubate the clutch.

The nesting season of the King Rail is one of the longest among birds
in the South. In Florida, there is evidence of nesting from January to
July; and in Louisiana, from March to September. In the middle and
northern latitudes the nesting season is usually about 3 to 4 months long.

Since the Clapper Rail in South Carolina is known to be double-brooded,
it is possible that the King Rail in the southern part of its range may also
have more than one successful brood; however, this has not yet been
established.

Clutch size is large, averaging 10 to 11 eggs. There appears to be no
geographic variation in clutch size.

Nesting success appears to be high in most areas. In one Arkansas sample, success was 75 percent; and in one Iowa sample it was 67 percent.
Such success is probably due in some measure to the incubating birds'
pugnacity toward would-be offenders. Survival of young until 2 weeks of
age was about 50 percent in the Arkansas rice belt.

Downy young of the King Rail are black. A change from the downy
plumage begins at about 1 month. Juvenal plumage is obtained in about
60 days, and wings are developed enough for short flights after the ninth
week.

Usually chicks are more than 1 hour old before they can go over the
nest and return. During the first month six different calls were recorded.

The King Rail occurs in a wider range of habitats and feeds on a greater
variety of foods than most other North American rallids. Aquatic animals,
particularly crustaceans, are its main food. Plant food items are taken
more under emergency conditions. When the King Rail occurs in the same
environment as the Clapper Rail, it may subsist mostly on a 1-item diet
like that species.

In most areas King Rails feed mainly in shallow water where the depth
is usually 2 or 3 inches. In Delaware Bay marshes, King Rail fed almost

entirely on mud flats, exposed at low tide, on the Arkansas Grand Prairie, in summer, they fed almost exclusively in rice fields.

HISTORICAL REVIEW

The literature provides numerous accounts of basic life history, including physical descriptions, distribution, nesting, food habits, predation, and accounts of past and present hunting methods. Meanley (1969) offers thorough coverage of the available information on the king rail.

DISTRIBUTION AND DENSITY

According to Meanley (1969:10), the king rail's breeding range extends northward to southern Canada, eastward to the Atlantic coast, westward to the eastern Great Plains (about the 100th meridian), and southward to the Gulf of Mexico (Fig. 3-9). Meanley defines the northern edge of its winter range as extending from New York City on the East Coast to southeast Missouri in the Mississippi River valley. The southern extreme of its winter range is reported to extend from the lower Rio Grande valley eastward along the Gulf Coast to Florida.

The density of king rail populations throughout their range is unknown. Meanley (1969:12) concluded that the greatest densities are found in the coastal populations from the Delaware valley to southeastern Georgia, southward into Florida, and then westward through the Gulf Coast marshes and the rice (*Oryza sativa*) belts of Louisiana, Arkansas, and Texas. He mentions only two inland concentration areas for king rails, the Lake Erie marshes in Ohio and the St. Clair Flats on Lake Michigan.

The distribution and density of king rails, based on the information available, is shown in Tables 3-8 and 3-9. There are two important migration areas for the king rail. One is along the Atlantic coastal plain and the other is through the Mississippi River valley (Meanley 1969:12). Fall migration probably occurs from August in the north to October in the south; spring migrants are moving primarily during March and April.

CENSUS PROCEDURES AND POPULATION TRENDS

Meanley (1969:19) suggests that call counts or nest counts could be used to determine nesting density in various habitat types. He also used roadside counts to estimate relative abundance of king rails in Arkansas, Louisiana, and Florida during fall and winter. A sampling procedure was set up in South Carolina to census king rails during the nesting season. Call counts conducted between 0500 and 0800 hours or between 1700 and 1900 hours at randomly selected stations were used in a 3,000-acre (1,214-ha) marsh and the results were considered satisfactory.

Population trends of king rails are unknown, but, like all species associated with and dependent on wetlands, these rails are probably decreasing in total numbers. Losses of wetlands in the interior portions of the king rail's range and along the North Atlantic coast have been locally severe. Coastal habitats have remained more stable in most South Atlantic states and along the Gulf Coast (Fig. 3-10B). Florida has probably suffered the greatest total loss of king rail habitat.

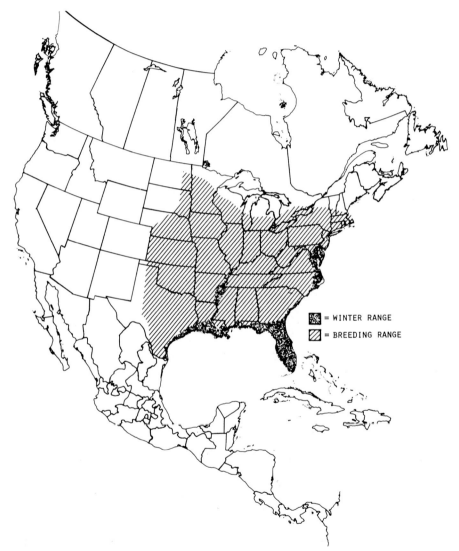

= WINTER RANGE

= BREEDING RANGE

Fig. 3-9. Approximate breeding range and principal distribution of the king rail in North America (Meanley 1969).

Table 3-8. King rail abundance by habitat types.

State	Habitat Type	Estimated Number	Area Censused
South Carolina	Tidal river marsh	25	100 acres (40.5 ha)
		14	13 acres (5.3 ha)
Florida	Inland fresh marsh	30	100 acres (40.5 ha)
Arkansas	Rice field	22	6-mile route (9.6 km)
Louisiana	Coastal fresh marsh	19	1-mile route (1.6 km)
		24	1-mile route
		20	1-mile route

Source: Meanley (1969:19).

Table 3-9. Major habitat types important to king rails, estimated existing acreage, and expected trends.

Habitat Type	Estimated Acreage[a]	Trend
Costal Fresh Marsh	3,820,000 (1,545,933 ha)	Gradual decrease
Inland Fresh Marsh	6,067,000 (2,455,281 ha)	Rapid decrease
Agricultural (rice)	1,500,000 (607,042 ha)	Stable
Total or Trend	11,387,000 (4,608,256 ha)	Decrease

[a] Estimates from Shaw and Fredine (1956:32), Harmon et al. (1960:153), and Meanley (1969:16).

Prospects for maintaining substantial amounts of coastal wetlands, especially along the Gulf Coast, are reasonably encouraging, whereas losses inland and along the Upper Atlantic coast can be expected to continue. Thus, king rail populations in the Atlantic and Gulf coast marshes should remain at a comparatively high level, at least for the near future.

CURRENT AND POTENTIAL HARVEST

There are no measurements presently available to calculate specifically the harvest of king rails in the United States. A few state kill surveys reflect the number of rail hunters and perhaps their kill but give no indication of species. Meanley (1969:90) reported that he believed the king rail is lightly harvested even in southern rice fields, where hunting pressure is probably heaviest. King rails are most often taken incidentally by hunters in pursuit of sora rails (*Porzana carolina*), clapper rails, bobwhites, and woodcock. Meanley believed that probably less than 1 percent of any local king rail population is ever taken by hunters.

A certain consensus of professional opinions would portray total hunting pressure on the king rail population as insignificant and perhaps even nonexistent. In spite of a tradition of liberal hunting regulations, all of the available

Fig. 3-10. A. Habitat of king rail on Elliott Island, Maryland.

Fig. 3-10. B. King rail habitat, Cameron Parish, Louisiana.

Fig. 3-10. C. King rail wading toward nest on dike, Stuttgart, Arkansas.

Fig. 3-10. D. King rail nest in roadside ditch near Stuttgart, Arkansas.

Fig. 3-10. E. King rail on nest in roadside ditch, Arkansas Grand Prairie.

Fig. 3-10. F. Hunting rails in Patuxent River wild marshes Maryland. The skiff is poled through marshes at flood tide. (All photos in Fig. 3-10 by Brooke Meanley, U.S. Fish and Wildlife Service.)

information points toward a consistently low interest in king rails among hunters. Except in some traditional hunting areas along the Middle Atlantic coast (Fig. 3-10F) and in certain rice fields in the South, the species is of little consequence as a game bird. Apparently, closing the hunting season for king rails in midwestern states, where populations were probably never large, is unnecessary. For example, the Cheyenne Bottoms in Kansas apparently support a locally abundant rail population including king rails. Provisions should be made to allow for some hunting opportunity on these birds.

The potential harvest is unknown, but, if the popular concept that the species is lightly hunted is correct, many additional king rails could no doubt be taken by hunters. The hunter's lack of interest in the king rail is easily understood because of what Meanley (1969:90) calls "the difficulty of maneuvering in its habitat, and the unlikelihood of finding concentrated numbers." Because rail-hunting regulations have been very liberal historically, any additional harvest of king rails seems unlikely. As long as the more popular waterfowl and upland game birds remain plentiful, king rails will continue to be lightly regarded as game birds.

SPECIES NEEDS

The king rail can adapt to a wide variety of habitat types as long as the terrain supports a reasonable amount of vegetation and is frequently wet. But man continues to destroy the wetlands; therefore, habitat protection is the king rail's greatest need. There is also a need for better information on the effects of pesticides on aquatic animals, especially insects and crustaceans, which are the major food of king rails.

The needs of king rails will no doubt continue to have low priority in private, state, and federal wildlife conservation programs. However, the king rail will benefit from efforts to protect the wetland habitats of ducks and geese in the eastern half of the United States.

PUBLIC NEEDS

At present there are open hunting seasons on the king rail in the states where it is most abundant. Hunting opportunity has been adequate; however, the character of the species and the methods required to hunt it successfully severely limit hunter interest. Additionally, these birds are not well known among the nonconsumptive public, for rails are not spectacular in coloration, do not concentrate in large numbers, are extremely secretive, and occupy habitats not readily accessible to the average person. They are, however, prized by ardent bird watching enthusiasts because of their secretive habits and their relative scarcity in the fringe areas of their range.

Unless the present professional interest in rails takes a dramatic upturn or competition for public use of this resource increases, or both, there is little urgency so far as public needs are concerned. A continuing education and publicity program, together with attractive hunting opportunities, appears to be the only practical approach toward stimulating more recreational use of the king rail resource.

There is perhaps some merit in aligning hunting seasons for king rails with those for more popular species, especially waterfowl, so that rails will be available during periods of peak hunting activity. To accomplish this alignment, the days allowed for rail hunting should be increased and options for split seasons should be included in the framework.

MANAGEMENT AND RESEARCH NEEDS AND COSTS

Present management of king rail populations consists simply of setting hunting regulations that allow a legal harvest and provide recreational opportunity. Beyond this, some initial attempts are being made to measure populations and harvests for rails in general. Until banding data, population densities, mortality rates, harvest figures, and other information are available over a large part of its range, any further management of the species remains impossible. As long as king rail populations command no great interest among most wildlife managers or public users, intensive management of these populations will remain unnecessary.

Meanley (1969) has reported on the basic life history of the king rail. The important areas of population densities, productivity, mortality rates, banding data, and pesticide relationships are key fields for research. Future proposals for research on king rails will probably enjoy better acceptance and results if they are directed toward coastal states where rails and their habitat are still abundant and secure for the near future.

There is no realistic timetable for scheduling needed rail research because research will continue to be regulated by local urgency and available funds (Table 3-10). Using graduate students on research projects in cooperation with state conservation agencies is probably the most practical approach. Standard budgets for the student research projects will range from $5,000 to $6,000 per year now (1974) and can be expected to increase sharply.

RECOMMENDATIONS

A state-by-state inventory of king rail habitat should be initiated to determine the quality and quantity of wetlands presently available for this species.

Studies should be conducted to determine king rail population densities and productivity in each major habitat type.

Only 11 states presently permit hunting of king rails. A harvest survey should be developed to provide a reliable measure of the king rail harvest in each of these states.

A determination should be made on pesticide-residue levels in king rails, especially in the rice-field habitat and in areas where efforts to control mosquitoes are significant.

With the exception of harvest surveys, all of the suggested research jobs or additional life-history studies on king rails can be conducted at the graduate student level, and this approach is strongly recommended.

If funds are made available for king rail studies, these studies should be car-

Table 3-10. Budget requirements for a 10-year king rail management plan.

Major Program or Area for Funding	Specific Jobs Within Each Program	Research or Management (R or M)	Job Priority	Estimated Cost of Jobs for Each Fiscal Year (in thousands of dollars)										Total Cost by Job (thousands)	Continuing Job
				1	2	3	4	5	6	7	8	9	10		
Population Studies	Evaluate and survey habitat (by state)	M	1	20	20	20								$ 60	No
	Study population density, productivity, and distribution (by habitat types)	R	2	30	30	30								90	No
	Survey harvest (by state)	M	3	50	50	50	50	50	50	50	50	50	50	500	Yes
	Study pesticide relationships	R	4	10	10									20	No
Total Cost of Program per Fiscal Year				110	110	100	50	50	50	50	50	50	50	670	

ried out in states where hunting is permitted, so that local interest and support may be stimulated.

LITERATURE CITED

Edwards, Ernest P. 1974. A coded list of birds of the world. Ernest P. Edwards, Sweet Briar, Va. 174pp.

Harmon, B. G., Carl H. Thomas, and L. Glasgow. 1960. Waterfowl foods in Louisiana rice fields. Transactions North American Wildlife and Natural Resources Conference 25:153-161.

Lowery, George H., Jr. 1955. Louisiana birds. Louisiana Wildlife and Fisheries Commission. Louisiana State University Press, Baton Rouge. 556pp.

Meanley, Brooke. 1969. Natural history of the king rail. United States Bureau of Sport Fisheries and Wildlife. North American Fauna No. 67. 108pp.

Shaw, S. P., and C. G. Fredine. 1956. Wetlands of the United States, their extent and their value to waterfowl and other wildlife. United States Department of the Interior, Fish and Wildlife Service. Circular No. 39. 67pp.

Purple Gallinule
(Porphyrula martinica)

Dan C. Holliman, Professor of Biology, Birmingham-Southern College, Birmingham, Alabama.

SUMMARY

Probably the purple gallinule will never assume the status of a game bird highly prized by the hunter. Its fate as a game bird, in terms of huntable numbers, will largely be determined by the viability of the ecosystem in which it lives. Therefore, it would be wise to make a strong effort to maintain its habitat. Research endeavors should involve studies of distribution, the life cycle, and the effects of pesticides and heavy metals. For the sake of economy, it may be wise to combine studies of this bird with studies of the common gallinule (*Gallinula chloropus*) because of the general similarity of their habitat requirements. If limited research funds are available, modest grants to graduate schools may be a sound investment in the training of young biologists in marshland ecology while adding to the knowledge of this bird.

DESCRIPTION

The purple gallinule is a brightly colored bird with a bluish purple neck and underparts and bronzy green back. The frontal shield is light blue and there is a white patch beneath the tail. There are no apparent differences between the sexes in plumage. The young bird has a head scantily covered with black and silvery white down on the crown, cheeks, and throat. The remainder of the body is thickly covered with long, black, glossy down on the back and sooty-black down on the venter. "The base of the bill is yellowish, the outer half black, with a white nail . . . ." (Bent 1926:342).

This gallinule is characteristically a bird of marshy habitat, ranging from the lowland swamps of Florida and Texas north to South Carolina and Tennessee. It frequently wanders even farther north. It winters along the coast from Florida to south Texas.

Although the purple gallinule and the common gallinule are approximately the same size, the deep purple underparts and the blue frontal shield of the former distinguish it from the latter. The purple gallinule does not subspeciate. A henlike, cackling call, *kek, kek, kek,* and dangling bright yellow legs are excellent field characteristics. The two gallinules are found in the same habitat and are affected by similar ecological parameters.

Traditionally, the purple gallinule has not been highly sought after as a game bird in spite of liberal hunting regulations. There has been no organized, cooperative research on a rangewide basis. Most of the contributions to the literature have been in the form of sight records and scattered nesting records.

LIFE HISTORY

Bent (1926:339) describes the life history of the purple gallinule. The molt is variable in its progress, or much prolonged, for various stages of it can be seen all through the fall and winter. The juvenile plumage is replaced on the head and breast by purple feathers tipped with white. New plumage on the back is glossy green, resembling that of the adult. Evidences of immaturity persist through the spring, such as brown feathers on the head and neck, with some whitish feathers on the throat. The first postnuptial molt produces the adult plumage.

This bird prefers freshwater marshes and is common along the reedy edges of ponds and lakes. It will frequent deep water that maintains growths of water lilies (*Nymphae* sp. and *Nelumbo* sp.). It is adapted for swimming as well as for walking across lily pads. Usually the nest is constructed over the water at a height of several feet (1 or 2 m). It is well concealed and contains 6 to 10 off-white eggs thinly spotted with lavender. This bird feeds on the seeds of wild rice (*Zizania aquatica*), duckweed (*Lemna* spp.), wild millet (*Echinochola crusgalli*), and other aquatic plants. Aquatic insects and small animals supplement its diet (Imhof 1962:213). There are numerous recorded observations that describe unusual predatory habits.

HISTORICAL REVIEW

The available literature describes records of occurrence and breeding and various facets of the natural history of the purple gallinule. Bent (1926:339) and Gross and Van Tyne (1929) provide detailed life-history data.

DISTRIBUTION AND DENSITY

This gallinule occurs in the lowlands from western Tennessee, central Alabama, and South Carolina (Fig. 3-11) through Central America and the West Indies to northern Argentina and Peru. It winters as far north as Florida and Louisiana (American Ornithologists' Union 1961). During migration it occurs rarely in almost all of the northeastern United States and in southeastern Canadian provinces.

CENSUS PROCEDURES AND POPULATION TRENDS

There are no known methods that effectively assay population trends. Louisiana is the only state that has estimated that the purple gallinule is common during the nesting season (Louisiana Wildlife and Fisheries Commission 1973). Lack of hard data makes it impossible to determine population trends.

CURRENT AND POTENTIAL HARVEST

Louisiana is again the only state with quantitative data on harvest. In the 1971–72 season for license holders in this state, there were 6,106 gallinule hunters, and in the 1972–73 season, there was a slight increase to 6,125. There was no attempt to separate hunters pursuing the two species of gallinules (Louisiana Wildlife and Fisheries Commission 1973). The potential harvest within the range of this bird may be greater than is realized. However, the purple gallinule has never been subjected to significant hunting pressure. At the present time, there is no effective way to determine harvest on a statewide basis.

Fig. 3-11. The winter and breeding ranges of the purple gallinule.

SPECIES AND PUBLIC NEEDS

As is true with the other members of this group, the single most pressing need is for habitat identification and acquisition. Until the potential harvest is known and the interests of hunters can be determined, public needs can hardly be formulated. Conservation education is probably the greatest vacuity in this area.

MANAGEMENT AND RESEARCH NEEDS AND ESTIMATED COSTS

Like the clapper rail (*Rallus longirostris*), which is the most heavily harvested bird in the rail family, the gallinules have been managed by no management. More information on population trends and life cycles is needed before any realistic plan can be made and long-range costs estimated (Table 3-11).

Basic research should focus on life-history studies, food habits, distribution, aging and sexing techniques, and the effects of the various pesticides and heavy metals on the ecosystem. Long-range costs at this point cannot be realistically predicted. Priority for any available research funds, however, should be given to habitat preservation and acquisition and to ecosystem studies.

RECOMMENDATIONS

The recommendations for the purple gallinule are not listed in order of priority.

Research should be on a rangewide basis rather than being confined by state boundaries.

Existing and potential habitat should be acquired.

Hunter harvest as well as seasonal population data should be gathered.

Life-history studies on reproduction, population dynamics, migration, limiting factors, food habits, and pollutants should be undertaken.

A conservation education program should be mounted to alert the general public to the importance of rails and gallinules in a marsh ecosystem.

More specific considerations should include opposing pesticide application on the marsh and adjacent watersheds, setting aside *mini* refuges wherever pockets of available habitat exist, and educating landowners as to the importance of maintaining the water-holding capacity of their marshlands.

LITERATURE CITED

American Ornithologists' Union. 1961. Check-list of North American birds. 5th edition. Port City Press, Baltimore. 691pp.

Bent, Arthur C. 1926. Life histories of North American marsh birds. United States National Museum, Bulletin 135. 490pp.

Gross, A. O., and Josselyn Van Tyne. 1929. The purple gallinule (*Ionornis martinicus*) of Barro Colorado Island, Canal Zone. Auk 46(4):431-446.

Imhof, T. A. 1962. Alabama birds. University of Alabama Press, University. 591pp.

Louisiana Wildlife and Fisheries Commission. 1973. Small Game Survey 1971–1972 and 1972–1973 Season. Louisiana Wildlife and Fisheries Commisson, Baton Rouge.

Table 3-11. Budget requirements for a 10-year purple gallinule management plan.

Major Program or Area for Funding	Specific Jobs Within Each Program	Research or Management (R or M)	Job Priority	Estimated Cost of Jobs for Each Fiscal Year (in thousands of dollars)										Total Cost by Job (thousands)	Continuing Job
				1	2	3	4	5	6	7	8	9	10		
Habitat Studies	Identify breeding, migration, and wintering preferences	R	5	100	100	100	100	100						$ 500	No
Total Cost of Program per Fiscal Year				100	100	100	100	100						500	No
Population Studies	Develop and conduct harvest survey	M	2	5	5	5	5	5	5	5	5	5	5	50	Yes
	Develop census technique	M	3	5	5	5	5	5	5	5	5	5	5	50	?
	Conduct life-history studies	R	4	20	20	20	20	20	20	20	20	20	20	200	Yes
Total Cost of Program per Fiscal Year				30	30	30	30	30	30	30	30	30	30	300	
Grand Total Cost of All Research and Management Programs by Fiscal Year for 10-Year Period				130	130	130	130	130	30	30	30	30	30	800	
Habitat Acquisition		M	1	100	100	100	100	100	100	100	100	100	100	1,000	Yes

Common Gallinule
(Gallinula chloropus)

David L. Strohmeyer, Associate Professor of Biology, Wisconsin State University, Oshkosh.

SUMMARY

The common gallinule is a large rail with a wide distribution in the United States. It does not appear to be especially abundant anywhere within its range and this scarcity, in combination with its secretive habitation of marshes, makes it an infrequently observed species. It is likewise seldom hunted. Little study has therefore been made of it and specific information about its population levels and management needs is lacking. General opinions are that the species' numbers are decreasing, probably as a result of habitat loss. The main needs of this species seem to be more complete study of population dynamics and preservation of habitat.

DESCRIPTION

The common gallinule has the body form of a small coot (*Fulica americana*) but the gallinule's red bill and the white line on each side of the body distinguish it from its larger relative. Its secretive behavior and choice of vegetated areas, rather than open water, are more like the behavior of the smaller members of the Rallidae than like that of the coot and make the common gallinule difficult to observe casually in the field. No obvious visible dimorphism exists between the sexes, but vocal tones differ.

LIFE HISTORY

Two recent studies (Fredrickson 1971, Krauth 1972) have summarized the life history of the common gallinule. The following account is taken largely from these studies.

The common gallinule arrives on the breeding range at about the same time as the coot (late April in Iowa and Wisconsin) but begins breeding activity sooner than the coot. Courtship likely begins during migration and continues in the breeding habitat as is shown by the establishment of a territory and the performance of sexual displays. Howard (1940:18-37) has described and named these activities and Fredrickson has filmed and analyzed a few sequences.

Nesting begins in early May, but nests are initiated into early June. The last nests initiated are possibly either first attempts by young birds or renests. The nests are built of dead vegetation, which is carried to the nest site by both sexes. Krauth (1972) found nests in all types of emergent vegetation and concluded that cover was used in proportion to its occurrence. The nests are built primarily from emergent vegetation. They are well concealed within the stand, usually in areas with 1 to 3 feet (0.3 to 0.9 m) of water. The nest is provided with a ramp and a canopy.

The hen lays one egg daily and both sexes incubate from about the time the fifth egg is laid (Krauth 1972). Exchanges are made on the nest from three to seven times a day (Perkins 1922, Fredrickson 1971, Krauth 1972), but the hen seems to perform the greater share of incubation duties. Reports of clutch size vary from 2 to 17 eggs, but the studies with most data (Harlow 1918, Cottam and Glazener 1959, Causey et al. 1968, Fredrickson 1971, Krauth 1972) suggest an average of 8 to 10 eggs with a slight possibility of larger clutches in the northern portions of the range.

The required time for incubation is poorly reported, perhaps because it varies for eggs within a clutch. Krauth (1972) reported that a seven-egg clutch re- quired 4 days from the first pipping to the emergence of the last chick. Thus, hatching time is influenced by the initiation of incubation behavior when the clutch is about half complete.

After hatching the young are brooded on platforms built by the adults or by coots or muskrats (*Ondatra zibethicus*). Both sexes share the duties of brood- ing and feeding the young birds.

Full growth seems to be attained by 10 weeks. During this time the broods are not readily seen in the emergent cover, which is now fully grown. No infor- mation is given on early flight activity, but fall migration appears to be an early occurrence.

DISTRIBUTION AND DENSITY

The common gallinule seems to be distributed throughout the United States except in mountainous areas and the western high plains (Fig. 3-12). Nowhere within this range does this rail appear to be even a common resident, but it is uncertain whether this supposed lack of abundance is a real condition or an apparent one resulting from its secretive behavior, the habitat it uses, and its low ranking as a preferred game species. It is noteworthy, however, that the 1968 Audubon breeding bird census resulted in only 31 common gallinules being counted in the 48 contiguous states, Alaska, and all Canadian provinces except Newfoundland (Robbins and Van Velsen 1969). The overwhelming impression resulting from a state-by-state survey requesting information on gallinule popu- lations was that this species received little attention from anyone — hunters, game biologists, or professional ornithologists — and that there was, therefore, little basis for knowledgeable responses to any questions regarding it. Where research has been conducted recently, the gallinule rises to the status of a fairly common species, at least locally (Iowa, Fredrickson 1971; Wisconsin, Krauth 1972; Ohio, Andrews, in progress, and Trautman and Trautman 1968; Louisiana, Causey et al. 1968; Arizona, R. L. Todd, personal communication).

Further indication of the breeding range is given by the following list of published surveys and studies involving nesting of the common gallinule: New Jersey, Abbott (1907), Harlow (1918), and Miller (1946); Pennsylvania, Miller (1910, 1946), and Harlow (1918); New York, Burtch (1911); Texas, Simmons (1915) and Cottam and Glazener (1959); Washington, D.C., Court (1921); Ontario, Perkins (1922); Minnesota, Roberts (1932); Delaware, Miller (1946); Arkansas, Meanley and Neff (1953); Maryland, Stewart and Robbins (1958); New Mexico, Ligon (1961); Oklahoma, Sutton (1967); Louisiana, Causey et al. (1968); Iowa, Fredrickson (1971) and Tinker (1919); and Wisconsin, Krauth (1972) and Deusing (1941).

In response to survey questions asked about habitat, the consensus of the respondents was that the common gallinule occurs in *Typha-Scirpus* marshes, but the tone of the responses from the respondents suggests that their consensus

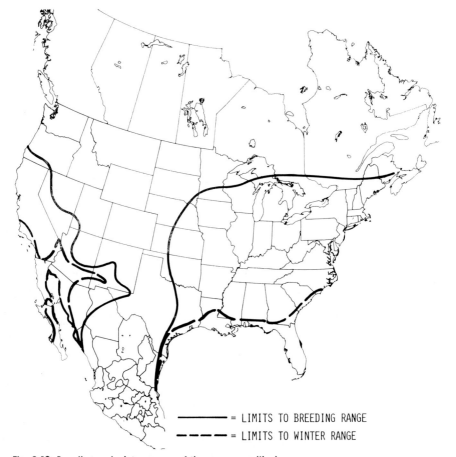

Fig. 3-12. Breeding and winter ranges of the common gallinule.

is a generalization only. The respondent in New Jersey specifically mentioned *Phragmites,* the one in Arizona included *Carex* and three-square (I assume *S. americanus*), and a study in Wisconsin indicated that *Sparganium* is important there. In Louisiana the rice (*Oryza sativa*) fields are used as habitat (including nesting habitat). Several respondents indicated that the gallinule inhabits the same situation as the coot, raising the question of whether some form of competitive exclusion might occur. Krauth (1972) found that in Wisconsin the gallinule seemed more aggressive than the coot and physically displaced it.

All parts of the country report decreases in the extent of habitat, especially on privately owned land. The primary cause of the loss is filling of marshes, but in the Southwest, where marshes are often restricted to watercourses, the habitat is often destroyed by trampling by cattle.

CENSUS PROCEDURES AND POPULATION TRENDS

No specific census techniques were reported by persons responding to the survey questions, nor do any appear to exist in the literature. The impression given by experienced respondents and from literature comparisons is that the gallinule populations are decreasing, at least in the upper Midwest and the Lake States, where the populations appear large enough for differences to be noticed.

CURRENT HARVEST AND HUNTING

For most states it is not possible to provide an estimate of the number of gallinule hunters. Louisiana provided the only specific figure, 6,106 for the 1971–72 season. California and Arizona estimated fewer than 1,000 hunters for each state. Respondents from almost all of the states replying to the questionnaire (Louisiana may be the exception) believe that gallinules are hunted only incidentally to waterfowl, that identification by hunters is poor, and that hunters' opinion of gallinules is low and the harvest is light. Hunting was allowed during 1974 in all states except Alaska, Hawaii, Illinois, Iowa, Kansas, Nebraska, North Dakota, South Dakota, and Texas. In Colorado, Montana, and Wyoming hunting was allowed only in the Pacific Flyway portions.

With poor information on population levels and little appraisal of current harvest, there is no way to determine whether the harvest is too high or too low. The impression given is that the birds are too uncommon to contribute significantly to the bag, but also that, with such an apparently low population, even minor hunter harvest might affect the species adversely.

POTENTIAL HARVEST

Again, given the relative lack of information on population levels and poor hunter awareness and appreciation of the common gallinule, it is not possible to comment on harvest potential. Based on observations of the attitudes of hunters toward coots, my personal impression is that there is little potential for a valid harvest (as opposed to random kill) until hunters are educated in species identification and their attitudes about the worth of gallinules are improved.

NEEDS OF THE SPECIES

The common gallinule's major need is for habitat. Maintenance of habitat can be accomplished coincidentally with protection and management of waterfowl habitat, but preservation of habitat for gallinules involves attention to deeper types of marshes than are usually most beneficial for ducks. The gallinule also appears to be a resident of more easterly parts of the United States than are usually considered prime duck breeding areas, so special efforts at habitat preservation are necessary in the eastern United States.

NEEDS OF THE PUBLIC

Because the common gallinule is so similar to the coot, it likely shares the coot's general characterization as a *trash* species. The primary need of the hunting public is to be educated to the worth of this species and to the proper esthetic and management-oriented philosophy of hunting.

MANAGEMENT NEEDS

Immediate management needs seem to be for a census of populations at key times of the year and for preservation of deepwater marshes. Perhaps taking precedence over these two needs is the need for most states to address themselves to the question of whether the common gallinule is a significant game bird and to include consideration of it and other rails in the job description of a game biologist. Among those states that replied to the questionnaire (17 states did not reply), the most common situation was that no one was involved with this species and no one had any answers regarding it.

RESEARCH NEEDS

Research is necessary in the areas of censusing and habitat appraisal. There are no good census techniques and almost no data available, even from poor techniques. Once the basics are known, the more specific aspects might be applied from studies already made in Louisiana and the upper midwestern states, or those designed for other key geographic areas.

The glaring need at the state level is for directing personnel toward consideration of rail species, and at higher levels for providing financial support for research into techniques and broad-scale population and habitat appraisal.

In view of the lack of state game department personnel having responsibilities for nonwaterfowl wetland game birds, one reasonable suggestion for acquiring information on gallinules is to involve the Cooperative Wildlife Research Units or other appropriately oriented and located university departments. It seems that there are several geographic areas from which information is needed, either because little exists so far or because these areas appear important to gallinules and their management. The following regions are suggested: Northeast, New York or New Jersey; upper Midwest, from Michigan to the Dakotas; Northwest (virtually no information from this region), probably Oregon; Southwest, Arizona; and South, Louisiana to Georgia. At least two of these regions (Midwest and South) appear large enough to warrant two centers of investigation each.

At each of these regional investigation centers the following goals should be achieved:

1. A broad-spectrum population appraisal.
2. Characterization of habitat.
3. Appraisal of extent and nature of habitat loss.
4. Population dynamics at selected representative sites.
5. Banding program and migrational information.
6. Consideration of the impact of hunters and their attitudes on this species.

This approach involves several obvious steps (which likely will require several workers) and also necessitates communication between regions. The demand for multiple personnel is another reason for suggesting that universities and graduate wildlife biology programs be involved. Three major avenues of consideration seem to exist in the above list of tasks: populations and habitat survey, population dynamics study, and movement and mortality study through a banding program. With research assistantship money, these investigations could be capably performed by graduate students and could provide the bases for relevant theses in the field of wildlife biology. Costs of assistantships, mileage, and supplies are estimated in Table 3-12.

LITERATURE CITED

Abbott, Clinton O. 1907. Summer bird-life of the Newark, New Jersey marshes. Auk 24(1):1-11.

Burtch, Verdi. 1911. A nest of the Florida gallinule. Auk 28(1):108-109.

Causey, M. K., F. L. Bonner, and J. B. Graves. 1968. Dieldrin residues in the gallinules *Porphyrula martinica* L. and *Gallinule chloropas* L. and its effect on clutch size and hatchability. Bulletin Environmental Contamination and Toxicology 3(5):274-283.

Cottam, Clarence, and W. C. Glazener. 1959. Late nesting of water birds in south Texas. Transactions North American Wildlife Conference 24:382-394.

Court, E. J. 1921. Some records of breeding birds for the vicinity of Washington, D.C. Auk 38(2):281-282.

Deusing, Murl. 1941. Notes on the nesting of the Florida gallinule. Passenger Pigeon 3(9):79-81.

Fredrickson, L. 1971. Common gallinule breeding biology and development. Auk 88(4):914-919.

Table 3-12. Budget requirements for a 10-year common gallinule management plan.

Major Program or Area for Funding	Specific Jobs Within Each Program	Research or Management (R or M)	Job Priority	Estimated Cost of Jobs for Each Fiscal Year (in thousands of dollars)										Total Cost by Job (thousands)	Continuing Job
				1	2	3	4	5	6	7	8	9	10		
Population and Habitat Survey	Estimate regional populations and appraise type and amount of habitat and habitat loss	M	1	28	28									$ 56[a]	No
Population Dymanics	Chronology of production and agents of natural mortality	R	3			28	28	28						84[a]	No
Movements and Mortality	Band birds to study movements and mortality	M	2			28	28	28	28	28				140[a]	No
Grand Total Cost of All Programs by Fiscal Year				28	28	56	56	56	28	28				280	

[a] Total cost for seven geographic areas centering around New York, Wisconsin, North Dakota, Oregon, Arizona, Louisiana, and Georgia.

Harlow, Richard C. 1918. Notes on the breeding birds of Pennsylvania and New Jersey. Auk 35(1):18-29.

Howard, E. 1940. A waterhen's world. Cambridge University Press, London.

Krauth, S. 1972. The breeding biology of the common gallinule. M.S. Thesis. University of Wisconsin, Oshkosh.

Ligon, J. Stokely. 1961. New Mexico birds. University of New Mexico Press, Albuquerque. 360pp.

Meanley, Brooke, and Johnson A. Neff. 1953. Bird notes from the Grand Prairie of Arkansas. Wilson Bulletin 65(3):200-201.

Miller, Richard F. 1910. Notes on the Florida gallinule (*Gallinula galeata*) in Philadelphia County, Pa. Auk 27(2):181-184.

———. 1946. The Florida gallinule; breeding birds of the Philadelphia region. Cassinia 36:1-16.

Perkins, Anne E. 1922. Breeding of the Florida gallinule in Ontario. Auk 39(4):564-565.

Robbins, Chandler S., and Willet T. Van Velsen. 1969. The breeding bird survey, 1967 and 1968. U.S. Bureau of Sport Fisheries and Wildlife, Special Scientific Report No. 124. 107pp.

Roberts, Thomas S. 1932. The birds of Minnesota. The University of Minnesota Press, Minneapolis. Vol. I. 691pp.

Simmons, George F. 1915. On the nesting of certain birds in Texas. Auk 32(3):317-331.

Stewart, Robert E., and Chandler S. Robbins. 1958. Birds of Maryland and the District of Columbia. United States Fish and Wildlife Service. North American Fauna No. 62. 401pp.

Sutton, George M. 1967. Oklahoma birds. University of Oklahoma Press, Norman. 674pp.

Tinker, A. D. 1919. Notes on the ornithology of Clay and Palo Alto counties, Iowa. Auk 31(1):70-81.

Trautman, Milton B., and Mary A. Trautman. 1968. Annotated list of the birds of Ohio. The Ohio Journal of Science 68(5):257-332.

Rails and Gallinules

Dan C. Holliman, Professor of Biology, Birmingham-Southern College, Birmingham, Alabama.

SUMMARY

The accompanying table summarizes the projected budget requirements for a 10-year management plan for rails and gallinules. An equitable amount of money is being suggested for each of the eight different species for jobs that have been specifically recommended by committee members. Monies could either be prorated over a 10-year period or be administered by priorities depending upon the most pressing species needs or the availability of funds. Since most of these wetland birds have similar habitat requirements, an attempt was made to combine certain research and management jobs. A combination is particularly appropriate where habitat acquisition involves substantial sums of money over a long period of time. In the separate species accounts, separate management and research budgets were prepared for seven of the eight species. The separate budgets total $9.922 million compared with $2.6 million in the combined budget (Table 3-13). Although separate budgets for land acquisition were prepared for only four species, when added together the individual budgets total $10.25 million compared with $5.0 million for habitat acquisition under the combined budget (Table 3-13). The committee does not presume to place priorities on the major program areas but simply offers statements of philosophy regarding their justification.

HABITAT STUDIES

Paramount for the survival of rails and gallinules is the acquisition and maintenance of marsh habitat. It is impossible to place a monetary value on wetlands because of their importance to the productivity of the biosphere. Constant monitoring of marshland parameters is necessary for the welfare of all trophic levels. Habitat acquisition should be given first priority in this major program. All federal land-use and coastal-zone management plans should include provisions for continuing habitat evaluation, inventory, and improvement studies. Subsidies to landowners could aid in the stewardship of these lands.

PUBLIC EDUCATION

Basic to the conservation of any of our natural resources is the education of the public. This problem is compounded by the present increasing developmental pressures on wetlands. Since marshes cannot be re-created once they are gone, it is exceedingly important to formulate a sound conservation ethic that will give the public the wisdom it needs to recognize the value of this nonrenewable resource. Owners of marshlands should be informed of the significance of their possessions.

HARVEST
Most of the research and management efforts for rails and gallinules are supported by the hunter's dollar. Studies on the effects of hunting regulations — for example, the rate of harvest and the amount of hunting pressure — yield limited data that in many cases justify the expenditures of monies for work on these webless migratory birds. Now with the advent of recession, it may be realistic to seek other sources of revenue to supplement ARP funds. The institution of a hunting stamp for these game birds may be a source of additional income.

POPULATION DYNAMICS
Even today there is little knowledge about these game birds. Research efforts have been scattered, leaving sizable portions of the ranges of these birds unstudied. It is understandable that the clapper rail (*Rallus longirostris*) has received the most attention because of its popularity as a game bird, even though this popularity is limited. It is significant, moreover, that only recently have studies led to the placement of the California clapper rail (*R. l. obsoletus*), the light-footed clapper rail (*R. l. levipes*), and the Yuma clapper rail (*R. l. yumanensis*) on the federal register of endangered fauna. Other populations, particularly of the black rail (*Laterallus jamaicensis*) in certain parts of its range, may become endangered before complete details of their population dynamics are known. Modern technology has provided the field biologist with a new set of tools. Telemetry and studies of heavy metal and pesticide residues require expensive equipment, although in many cases instrumentation for these studies is a one-time expenditure. The increasing expenses that accompany developing technology substantially elevate research costs. Because of the present economic situation, some hard decisions will have to be made to insure a meaningful balance among the proposed specific jobs involved in studies of population dynamics.

The committee offers two recommendations relative to the implementation of this projected budget:
1. Research and management programs should be rangewide rather than confined by state boundaries.
2. The possibility of cooperation with educational institutions should be investigated so that specific jobs in each institution's major program area can be accomplished on a cost-sharing basis and at the same time can offer training for potential field biologists.

Table 3-13. Budget requirements for a 10-year rails and gallinules management plan.

Major Program or Area for Funding	Specific Jobs Within Each Program	Research or Management (R or M)	Job Priority	Estimated Cost of Jobs for Each Fiscal Year (in thousands of dollars)										Total Cost by Job (thousands)	Continuing Job
				1	2	3	4	5	6	7	8	9	10		
Habitat Studies	Evaluate and inventory habitat (by remote sensing and ground truth studies)	M	2	20	20	20	20	20	20	20	20	20	20	$ 200	Yes
	Improve habitat (landowner subsidy)	M	3	50	50	50	50	50	50	50	50	50	50	500	Yes
	Study habitat preferences	R	4	10	10	10	10	10	10	10	10			80	No
Public Education	Expand educational efforts related to the preservation, management, and improvement of wetland habitat	M	1	10	10	10	10	10	10	10	10	10	10	100	Yes
Harvest	Conduct harvest survey	M	1	20	20	20	20	20	10	10	10	10	10	150	Yes
	Study effects of hunting	M	2	15	15	15	15	15						75	No
Population Dynamics	Conduct banding studies	M	1	25	25	25	25	25	25	25	25			200	No
	Develop census techniques	M	2	20	20	20	20	20	20	20	20			160	No
	Conduct density studies	R	3	15	15	15	15	15	15	15	15			120	No
	Conduct productivity studies	M	4	15	15	15	15	15	10	10	10			105	No
	Study distribution	R	5	15	15	15	15	15	15	15	15			120	No

Program		No.											Total	
Study life history	R	6	20	20	20	20	20	20	20	20			160	No
Develop trapping techniques	M	7	10	10	10	10	10	10	10	10			80	No
Conduct pesticide studies	R	8	80	80	10								170	No
Conduct disease studies	R	9	10	10	10	10	10	10	10	10			80	No
Conduct telementry studies	R	10	50	50	50	10	10						170	No
Study heavy metal residues	R	11	50	50	10	10	10						130	No
Grand Total Cost of All Programs by Fiscal Year			435	435	325	275	275	225	225	225	90	90	2,600	
Habitat Acquisition	M	1	500	500	500	500	500	500	500	500	500	500	5,000	Yes

4

American Coot
(Fulica americana)

Leigh H. Fredrickson, Associate Professor of Wildlife and Director, Gaylord Memorial Laboratory, School of Forestry, Fisheries, and Wildlife, University of Missouri — Columbia, Puxico, *Chairman.*

John M. Anderson, Director, Sanctuary Department, National Audubon Society, Sharon, Connecticut.

Frank M. Kozlik, Waterfowl Coordinator, California Department of Fish and Game, Sacramento.

Ronald A. Ryder, Professor of Wildlife, Department of Fishery and Wildlife Biology, Colorado State University, Fort Collins.

SUMMARY

The coot is the most aquatic member of the family Rallidae. Both sexes share in nest building, incubation, and brood rearing, but males leave broods first. They construct over-water nests that are attached to emergent vegetation. Nesting and hatching success are usually high, renesting is common, and some birds in Utah and California have second broods. Because coots are monomorphic and share brooding duties, brood counts are difficult. Coots are vegetarians most of the year, but young are fed invertebrates at hatching. Coots are less abundant now than when Europeans first arrived in North America, but the decline is not well documented. Their present distribution is widespread in temperate North America, but breeding concentrations are most common in the prairie marshes of the north central United States and south central Canada. Coots concentrate in large numbers and migrate in a broad front across the United States. Winter concentrations occur in California, Florida, Louisiana, and Texas, but not all available habitat in Louisiana and Texas is used. In California wintering coots cause depredation problems. Coots are not prized as game birds or for food except in local areas. In most states, waterfowl biologists suggest that harvest can increase without endangering the population. However, only five states have a significant number of hunters that are interested in taking coots and this interest is local. Where local interest in harvesting coots is high, 90 to 95 percent of the birds available have been harvested in one day. Waterfowl programs have provided an adequate supply of breeding, migration, and winter habitat for coots. Because recovery rates for coots are so low, few states presently band coots. Management and research needs for the species include (1) improved inventories and censuses, (2) improved harvest information, (3) better information on available habitat and utilization of this habitat, (4) ways to make coots desirable as a game species to hunters, (5) information on competition with waterfowl and other marsh species, (6) information on age-related productivity, and (7) information on migratory patterns, differential migration, and food habits.

DESCRIPTION

The coot is the largest and most aquatic member of the family Rallidae in North America. The bill is stout and chickenlike; there are three lobes on each toe; the tail is short; the plumage is soft, with a few barbules at the tips of contour feathers; and the sexes are nearly alike but the females are smaller.

Measurements in Spring

The culmen-shield of 150 males averaged 47 mm (41-52) (1.8 inches, 1.6-2.0), and in 140 females it averaged 44 mm (37-49) (1.7 inches, 1.4-1.9). The wing in 146 males averaged 203 mm (183-221) (8.0 inches, 7.2-8.7), and in 134 females it averaged 190 mm (169-205) (7.5 inches, 6.6-8.1). The metatarsus-midtoe of 151 males averaged 133 mm (117-146) (5.2 inches, 4.6-5.7); the shorter metatarsus-midtoe of 140 females averaged 123 mm (110-135) (4.8 inches, 4.3-5.3) (Fredrickson 1968).

Weight in Fall

The weights of 27 males ranged from 576 to 848 grams (average 724 grams) (1.3 to 1.9 lb, average 1.6 lb), and those of 20 females ranged from 427 to 628 grams (average 560 grams) (0.9 to 1.4 lb, average 1.2 lb) (Fredrickson, personal communication).

Plumage

The plumages are similar the year around; there is one complete prebasic molt each year after breeding (Gullion 1953a), with a simultaneous wing molt. The leg scutes are shed 45 days before the wing molt.

Adults. — The head and neck are black, the iris reddish, the back blackish gray, and the underparts dark gray; some feathers are tipped with white. The leading edge of the underwing and the tips of the secondaries and undertail coverts are white. The bill is also white, with two chestnut spots near the tip. The frontal shield is chestnut, the legs are greenish, the tarsus on older birds is yellow lime to scarlet orange, and the feet are greenish.

Juveniles. — They are similar to adults, but their plumage is grayish, especially below; the frontal shield is smaller; the iris is brownish; and the legs and feet are more gray than green.

Downy Young. — The downy young are blackish gray, with white below; the throat, head, and upper parts have numerous scarlet orange, hairlike feathers. The lores and bill are reddish and the bill is tipped with black.

Voice

The voice is guttural; the calls are described as *puhlk, poonk, kuh-kuh-kuk, cack-ka, puhk-uh, cou-ah,* and *punk-cow-ah.* There is a distinct sex difference. The female's voice has a nasal quality and a low pitch; the male's voice lacks nasal quality and has a somewhat higher pitch (Gullion 1950).

LIFE HISTORY

Habitat

American coots breed primarily on freshwater wetlands, although nesting occurs in brackish water on Clipperton Island (10° 18′ N, 109° 131′ W), the most easterly coral atoll in the Pacific Ocean, where birds appear to be in poor health and have small clutches (Stager 1964:363). Coots may be restricted to freshwater habitat because their rate of salt excretion is insufficient for all their normal water needs to be met by consumption of seawater (Carpenter and Stafford 1970). Highest nest densities occur on Type IV wetlands (Shaw and Fredine 1956:51) in the glacial marshes of the north central United States and south central Canada. Those wetlands with a good interspersion of robust emergent vegetation such as bulrush (*Scirpus* sp.) and cattail (*Typha* sp.) have the highest use. Coots are very adaptable and use ephemeral habitat when conditions are suitable.

During migration, coots may concentrate on rivers, lakes, ponds, reservoirs, and sewage lagoons. Coots winter in both brackish and freshwater. The southern coastal wetlands are most important, but in certain areas coots utilize golf courses, lawns, pastures, rice (*Orzya sativa*) fields, and vegetable and forage croplands.

Migration

Coots migrate in a broad front across North America, but concentrations occur in staging areas. Coots are nocturnal migrants and have differential migration according to age (Burton 1959). Because migrating coots are rarely seen flying during daylight, most birds apparently land on the nearest water or in unusual places at daybreak. For example, coots have been seen in the Ozark forests during migration (Fredrickson, personal communication). The lack of diurnal migration may partially explain the widespread use of wetland habitat across North America during the fall and spring movements.

Females move farther south than males. During a study of radiocesium levels in wintering coots, Brisbin et al. (1973) found more males than females wintering in North Carolina, but the ratios changed in favor of females once spring migration began.

Coots are killed by flying into buildings and TV towers during migration (Stoddard and Norris 1967:52). Vocalizations heard during migration also suggest that coots fly low. A plane struck a coot at 4,500 feet (1,372 m) near Memphis, Tennessee, so some coots fly at considerable altitudes (Erickson 1942).

Some coots move north as soon as the ice goes out, but the main movement is later and reaches the Canadian border about 1 May. By mid-July, males congregate in flocks in southern Manitoba (Ward 1953:323). Coots concentrate on the larger lakes in southern Canada (Ward 1953:323, Bergman 1973:167) before the main movement south begins in mid-September and reaches a climax in early October. Peak numbers reach Iowa, Illinois, and Missouri by mid-October. Winter concentrations reach a peak in December.

Reproduction

Pair formation is subtle and not well understood, but billing, bowing, and nibbling are obvious displays. Coots are highly territorial and have a variety of displays of varying intensities (Gullion 1952a, Fredrickson 1970:446). Intraspecific territorial displays are described as *patrolling, charging, chasing* or *splattering, paired display,* and *fighting.* Other intraspecific displays include *warning, bracing,* and *arching* by adults and *begging* by young (Gullion 1952a). The displays *swanning* and *churning* are used during interspecific encounters (Gullion 1952a). Territories are established prior to nesting and are maintained throughout brood rearing. Intraspecific interactions are most intense, but interspecific interactions are common. Coots have been recorded as interacting with a variety of birds, mammals, and reptiles within their territorial boundaries. However, no conclusive evidence currently available on competition indicates that territorial activity of coots restricts the productivity of other species.

Coots probably breed when 1 year old and build floating platforms for copulation and brood rearing (Fig. 4-1A) as well as for nesting. Fewer platforms are constructed if the nesting area has an abundance of muskrat (*Ondatra zibethicus*) feeding platforms or other structures (Fredrickson 1970:447-448). Coots nest over water and attach the nest to emergent vegetation. Both sexes take part in nest building. Normally, one member of each pair remains at the nesting site and arranges material collected by its mate. Both sexes spend time collecting materials and building the nest. Materials used in construction are those most readily available in the nesting habitat (Fredrickson 1970:448).

Coots lay one egg a day at intervals of slightly less than 24 hours (Sooter 1941:40-41, Gullion 1954:374). The normal clutch size is 9 or 10 (range 4 to 17) eggs (Fredrickson 1970:452). Clutches with more than 12 eggs are probably laid by two or more females. Late-season clutches are smaller (Gullion

Fig. 4-1. A. Coot brood platform. Dewey's Pasture, Clay County, Iowa.

Fig. 4-1. B. Newly hatched coots and eggs in nest. Incubation is initiated before the clutch is complete; hence, hatching is staggered. Dan Green Slough, Clay County, Iowa.

Fig. 4-1. C. Adult coot feeding newly hatched young at the nest. Dewey's Pasture, Clay County, Iowa.

Fig. 4-1. D. Adult coot with young. Smith's Slough, Clay County, Iowa.

Fig. 4-1. E. Adult coot removing eggshell from successful nest. Dewey's Pasture, Clay County, Iowa.

Fig. 4-1. F. Ideal interspersion of cover and water for coot nesting. Smith's Slough, Clay County, Iowa. (All photographs in Fig. 4-1 by Leigh H. Fredrickson.)

1954:375, Fredrickson 1970:452) and probably represent renesting or first nests of young birds.

Renesting is common in some areas. In Utah, coots renested when nests were intentionally destroyed (Ryder 1961:142), and most renests were within 50 feet (15.2 m) of the first nests. In South Dakota, coots renested in 9 of 10 cases where eggs were removed early in incubation (Vaa 1972:17). Six coots renested in the original nest bowls, but three renested elsewhere.

Second broods occur in California and Utah, but they have never been recorded in the Plains States. Gullion (1954:398) first recorded the occurrence of second broods in California when five females each reared two broods in one season. In Utah, 13 percent (38 of 280) of the nesting females reared second broods during two nesting seasons (Ryder 1961:140).

Coots initiate incubation before the clutch is complete. Some birds begin incubation with the first egg in second clutches, but not before the second egg in first clutches (Gullion 1954:377-378). In Iowa, some coots were increasingly attentive while laying the first three or four eggs, but incubation was insufficient for embryonic development (Fredrickson 1970:454).

Both members of the pair incubate, but males are most often on the nest at night (Gullion 1954:380). No ceremony connected with incubation relief has been recorded, but vocalization cannot be ruled out.

Because incubation commences before the clutch is complete, determination of the incubation period is difficult. Eggs hatched in 23 days in California (Gullion 1954:383) and between 21 and 27 days in Iowa (Fredrickson 1970:454).

Because not all eggs in the clutch hatch simultaneously (Fig. 4-1B), coots must continue to incubate and at the same time feed and brood the young that have hatched (Fig. 4-1C). Newly hatched coots are mobile (precocial), are covered with down (ptilopaedic), and are able to leave the nest as soon as they are dry (nidifugous). Both parents brood the young. Young coots travel equally with both parents during the day (Fig. 4-1D) but appear to favor the male for brooding at night (Fredrickson 1970:455).

Young birds are particularly prone to wetting for a few days after hatching. Feathers of the young birds are oiled directly by billing movements of the adults from their oil glands to the young. Adults also oil their young by rubbing their own oiled underwing and breast feathers on the newly hatched chicks (Fredrickson 1970:455).

In favorable habitat, nesting success is normally high if no severe storms occur during nesting. High success occurs in Manitoba (97 percent of 380 nests) (Kiel and Hawkins 1953:320), Iowa (87 percent of 161 nests) (Fredrickson 1967:74), and Utah (91 percent of 318 nests) (Ryder 1961:141).

Coot nests subjected to severe wind or wave action, or both, and the fluctuating water levels have lower rates of success. Coots normally have high hatching success. In Utah, 93 percent of 2,414 eggs hatched (Ryder 1958), and in Iowa, 90 percent of 1,998 eggs hatched (Fredrickson 1967:88).

As soon as young coots are dry, they peck at eggshells and larval insects in the nest. During the first days after hatching, the young depend on their parents to find food for them. The nonincubating member of the pair collects and presents food to the incubating bird, which in turn feeds the young. In California, the female collected most of the food (Gullion 1954:390), but in Iowa both sexes shared this duty (Fredrickson 1970:455). Larvae of aquatic insects and small crayfish are commonly fed to chicks (Gullion 1954:390, Fredrickson 1970:455).

Both sexes remove eggshells (Fig. 4-1E) and vitelline membranes from the nest soon after the chicks hatch (Fredrickson 1970:455). The adults either eat the eggshells or carry them from the nest and drop them into the water. Eggshells eaten at the nest account for many of the small chips that normally are found in successful coot nests.

In Manitoba, flightless young coots leave the home territory when they are about 7 weeks old and congregate in small flocks by walking overland (Ward 1953:323). In California, young coots begin to fly at about 75 days and leave the home territory in 80 days (Gullion 1954:395-396). Adult males leave the brood before the females do and congregate in flocks (Ward 1953:323). The females begin molting before the young leave the territory and are probably flightless before the young disperse (Ward 1953:323).

Although coots are strongly territorial during the breeding season, they become gregarious during the rest of the year. Resident birds in California have smaller territories in winter than in summer (Gullion 1953b:171).

Food

Coots are vegetarians during most of the year. Principal foods are pondweeds, sedges, algae, and grasses (Jones 1940). No reliable information indicates that coots switch to animal foods before and during the nesting season. The young are fed animal foods for the first few weeks after hatching. During the winter, coots often graze on pastures, golf courses, and lawns, and may also feed on forage crops.

Parasites, Diseases, and Other Mortality Factors

Coots are hosts for a variety of parasites and have several diseases. Diseases reported in coots are aspergillosis (Gullion 1952b), fowl cholera (Rosen and Bischoff 1949), botulism (Alcorn 1942, 1944, Parrish and Hunter 1969), and pullorum (Rausch 1947). Coots are particularly susceptible to fowl cholera.

Parasites from 17 coots collected in Iowa included four species of protozoans, four species of trematodes, two species of nematodes, and eight species of bird lice (Roudabush 1942). Generally, parasites are not an obvious cause of mortality, but the trematode *Sphaeridiotrema,* presumably *S. globulus,* appeared to be the cause of the deaths of 700 coots in Wisconsin (Trainer and Fischer 1963). Most deaths occurred in the spring and were probably caused by the cumulative effect of the stresses of parasitism, migration, and prebreeding activities.

Because coots nest over water, they are relatively free from nest predators. Coot remains were found in pellets of great horned owls (*Bubo virginianus*) (Errington et al. 1940:797-798) and bald eagles (*Haliaeetus leucocephalus*) (Broley 1947:17). Collisions with wires, fences, power lines, towers, and buildings are not uncommon. Lead poisoning is not a problem because few coots ingest lead shot (Jones 1939, Fredrickson 1969*b*). Coots often die after snow and ice storms that reduce available food sources (Fredrickson 1969*b*).

HISTORICAL REVIEW

When Europeans first reached North America, coots presumably were present in vast numbers. As the human population increased, coot numbers declined in the Northeast during the late 1800's and early 1900's (Forbush 1912:222). Coots were used as food and were common on settlers' tables (Forbush 1912: 222).

Reliable estimates of the decline in coot numbers are not available, but the continental coot population undoubtedly declined drastically when settlers reached the good breeding areas of the plains states. Between 1870 and 1930, Iowa lost nearly all of its wetlands, and extensive drainage occurred in southern Minnesota and in the Red River valley of North Dakota. Undoubtedly, all of these areas were important for coot production. After World War II, the remaining wetland habitat of the prairies was severely reduced by government support programs that encouraged drainage.

Coots are not prized as a game species or for food (Leftingwell 1888:193). Forbush (1912:222) reported that hunters shot coots just to see how many they could kill with a single shot. Some hunters use coots to *warm up* (Ward 1953: 325) or fail to retrieve coots (Baumgartner 1942:89). However, large numbers of coots are harvested in some locations. On one 1,800-acre (728.4-ha) lake in Illinois, opening-day hunters took 23,800 coots in one year or 90 percent of the birds present and in the next year took 18,225 or 85 percent of the birds present (Bellrose 1944:7-9).

Only 32,800 of 175,000 waterfowl hunters in California kill coots (Kozlik, personal communication). During a special 2-day depredation hunt for coots, 650 hunters normally take about 7,500 coots, but during the waterfowl season, 10,000 hunters take only 500 coots.

Interest in coot research has never been high. The biology of coots was first studied in detail by Sooter (1941) in Iowa. The studies in California in the early 1950's made by Gullion (1950, 1952*a*, 1953*a*, 1953*b*, 1954) provided insight into behavior, molt, and reproduction. Kiel (1955) provided additional information on breeding. Competition between coots and waterfowl was studied in Utah by Ryder (1959). More detailed information on reproductive biology was reported by Fredrickson (1969*b*, 1970). Some current projects deal with differential migration and radioactive contaminants (Brisbin et al. 1973), age-related productivity (Crawford, personal communication), food habits (Hammer, personal communication), and behavior (Fredrickson, personal communication).

Because of the close association between coots and waterfowl, regulations for coot harvest have been similar to the waterfowl regulations, and the seasons run concurrently. During the drought of the late 1950's and early 1960's, restrictive harvest regulations were in effect for both coots and waterfowl. Regulations have been liberal in the Pacific Flyway but more restrictive in the rest of the country.

DISTRIBUTION AND DENSITY

Breeding

Coots breed throughout North America where suitable habitat is available, but the greatest breeding densities occur in the prairie pothole region of the north central United States and southern Canada, particularly in the Dakotas, Manitoba, and Saskatchewan (Fig. 4-2). Coots nest in lesser numbers throughout the West wherever there are suitable wetlands, and locally there are high nest densities. Few coots nest in the East, where most habitat is along the marshy borders of creeks and rivers. In the South, a few coots nest in the coastal wetlands of Florida, Louisiana, and Texas, but millions winter in this habitat. The A.O.U. checklist (American Ornithologists' Union 1957:162) gives a detailed description of the breeding range.

Coots are adaptable, but populations fluctuate according to water and marsh conditions. In Iowa, the highest breeding populations occurred when cattail marshes had 50 percent open water and 50 percent emergent cover (Weller and Fredrickson 1973:285-287). Coots continued to nest in the late stages of the marsh cycle when only scattered clumps of vegetation remained (Crawford, personal communication). Under ideal cover and water conditions in the prairies (Fig. 4-1F), coot breeding populations reach peak densities of 432 pairs per square mile (166.8 pairs per square km) (Table 4-1) in North Dakota (Stewart and Kantrud 1972:781) and 100 pairs per square mile (38.6 pairs per square km) at Minnedosa, Manitoba (Stout, personal communication). Recently about 20 pairs nested in Delaware annually (Florio, personal communication). Coots breed in high densities locally in the West where habitat is available, for example, in Utah, Oregon, and California. Under ideal conditions, as many as 7,400 pairs breed on the 50,000-acre (20,235-ha) Malheur National Wildlife Refuge in Oregon. In recent years, biologists in California and Utah have reported 25,000 and 35,000 breeding pairs, respectively. In California, nesting occurred regularly in rice fields and once, in 1964, in cotton (*Gossypium* spp.) fields in Tulare Lake basin after flooding (Kozlik, personal communication). After severe flooding along the Mississippi River in 1973, coots nested in wheat (*Triticum aestivum*) fields in southern Illinois (Kennedy 1974).

Type IV wetlands (Shaw and Fredine 1956) are of the greatest value for breeding coots, but Types III and V wetlands are used when suitable vegetative and water conditions occur locally. In 1955, the United States had 2,346,000 acres (949,413 ha) of Type IV, 2,969,000 acres (1,201,538 ha) of Type III, and 2,596,000 acres (1,050,587 ha) of Type V wetlands, or a total of 8,911,000 acres (3,606,232 ha) of habitat that was suitable for nesting coots. Estimates of available habitat by state are shown in Table 4-2. Canada has an unknown number of additional acres of prime habitat that provide nesting cover for coots.

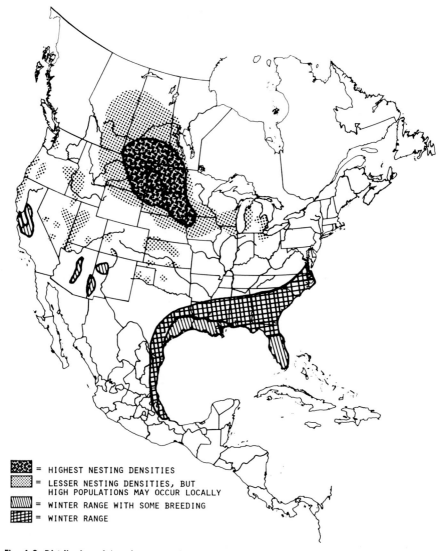

= HIGHEST NESTING DENSITIES
= LESSER NESTING DENSITIES, BUT HIGH POPULATIONS MAY OCCUR LOCALLY
= WINTER RANGE WITH SOME BREEDING
= WINTER RANGE

Fig. 4-2. Distribution of American coots during nesting and wintering.

Table 4-1. Status and estimated peak numbers (in thousands) of American coots in the United States during nesting, migration, and wintering.

State	Nesting Status[a]	Nesting No. of Pairs	Migrating Status	Migrating Number	Migrating Date[b]	Wintering Status	Wintering Number	Resident Status	Resident Number
Alabama	NR		C	50	1-1	C	60	NR	
Alaska	NR		R			R		NR	
Arizona	UC	4	C	100	15-10	UC	50	Y	
Arkansas	NR		C			UC	50	NR	
California	UC	25	C	300	15-10	A	1,000	C	50
Colorado	UC	8	C	54	15-10	R	1	NR	
Connecticut	NR		R	0.5	15-11	R	0.05	NR	
Delaware	R	0.02	UC			UC		NR	
Florida	UC	2	C	500	1-1	C	500	UC	10
Georgia	NR		C	300	1-1	C	300	NR	
Hawaii	EN	0.8				EN		EN	1.7
Idaho	UC		C	82	7-10	UC	38	NR	
Illinois	NR		C	220	27-10	R		NR	
Indiana	NR		C	40	1-11	UC		NR	
Iowa	UC		C			NR		NR	
Kansas	R	0.5	C	28	15-10	R	0.4	NR	
Kentucky	NR		Y			Y		NR	
Louisiana	UC		A	650	15-10	A	1,500	UC	36
Maine	NR		UC			R		NR	
Maryland	R		UC	42	5-11	UC	14	R	0.3
Massachusetts	R		UC			UC		NR	
Michigan	UC		C	600	15-10	UC		NR	
Minnesota	C		C			NR		NR	
Mississippi	NR		A	500	1-11	C	200	NR	
Missouri	NR		UC	27.7	16-10	UC	3	NR	
Montana	Y		Y			R		NR	
Nebraska	UC	15	C			NR		NR	
Nevada	UC	15	C	300	15-10	UC	9	NR	
New Hampshire	NR		UC			NR		NR	
New Jersey	NR		UC	1.1	7-10	R	0.3	NR	
New Mexico	NR		C	100	15-10	C	100	NR	
New York	UC		C			R		NR	
North Carolina	R		R			C	57	NR	
North Dakota	A	1,000	C			NR		NR	
Ohio	Y		Y			Y		NR	
Oklahoma	R		UC	15	11-10	UC	1	NR	
Oregon	UC	10	UC			UC	37	NR	
Pennsylvania	NR		UC	20	1-11	UC		NR	
Rhode Island	NR		UC	0.5	1-11	UC	0.5	NR	
South Carolina	R		C	100	1-11	C	100	NR	
South Dakota	C		C			NR		NR	
Tennessee	R		C			C		NR	
Texas	UC		NR			C		Y	
Utah	C	35	C	120	15-9	UC	5	NR	
Vermont	NR		UC			NR		NR	
Virginia	NR		UC	50	1-11	UC	50	NR	
Washington	Y		Y			Y		NR	
West Virginia	NR		UC	4	25-10	R	0.2	NR	
Wisconsin	C	50	C		15-10	R	1	NR	
Wyoming	Y		Y			NR		NR	

[a] NR = no records since 1950, UC = Uncommon (1,000-50,000), C = common (50,000-500,000), A = abundant (over 500,000), R = rare (less than 1,000), Y = present but status unknown, and EN = endangered.
[b] Day-month.

Table 4-2. Square miles of habitat available for coots (estimates by state water-fowl biologists).

State	Nesting	Migratory	Wintering	Unused
Alabama	None	NR[a]	NR	NR
Alaska	9,000[b]	9,000	None	Yes
Arizona	156	156	156	NR
Arkansas	None	NR	NR	NR
California	234	1,328	1,328 (172)[c]	No
Colorado	1,000	1,000	None	NR
Connecticut	Some	NR	NR	Yes
Delaware	206	206	206	NR
Florida	Some	58,559	58,559	Yes
Georgia	None	Yes	Yes	Yes
Hawaii	8.5	8.5	8.5	No
Idaho	36	36	None	NR
Illinois	None	469	None	NR
Indiana	NR	NR	NR	NR
Iowa	NR	NR	None	No
Kansas	55	489	None	No
Kentucky	None	NR	NR	NR
Louisiana	1,909	7,031	7,031	Yes
Maine	None	Yes	Yes	Yes
Maryland	NR	NR	NR	NR
Massachusetts	133	133	None	Yes
Michigan	NR	NR	None	NR
Minnesota	NR	NR	None	NR
Mississippi	NR	NR	NR	NR
Missouri	None		None	No
Montana	NR	NR	None	NR
Nebraska	234	234	None	NR
Nevada	1,105	1,105	1,105	No
New Hampshire	7,444	7,444	None	NR
New Jersey	Very little	Some	None	NR
New Mexico	234	234	234	NR
New York	Some	Some	None	NR
North Carolina	NR	1,250	1,250	None
North Dakota	NR	NR	None	NR
Ohio	NR	NR	NR	NR
Oklahoma	None	53	53	NR
Oregon	170	170	14	NR
Pennsylvania	None	Some	None	NR
Rhode Island	None	Some	24	Yes
South Carolina	None	547	547	NR
South Dakota	NR	NR	None	NR
Tennessee	NR	1,008	1,008	NR
Texas	4,375	4,375	4,375	Yes
Utah	1,016	1,563	1,563	NR
Vermont	NR	NR	NR	NR
Virginia	None	55	55	Yes
Washington	NR	NR	NR	No
West Virginia	None	Very little	None	No
Wisconsin	1,828	1,828	None	NR
Wyoming	NR	NR	None	NR

[a] NR = no response.
[b] One square mile = 2.59 square kilometers.
[c] Best habitat in parentheses.

Migration Areas

Most water areas throughout the United States are utilized by coots during migration (Fig. 4-2). Concentrations of coots occur in areas with adequate food supplies and may stay there until the food supply is exhausted or until cold weather forces them to move farther south.

Winter Areas

Most coots winter south of 35° North Latitude in North America (Fig. 4-2). The A.O.U. checklist (American Ornithologists' Union 1957:162) gives a detailed description of the wintering range.

Large concentrations of coots normally winter in the coastal marshes of Louisiana and Texas, in the Central Valley of California, and in Florida wetlands (Table 4-1). Unknown numbers of coots winter south of the United States in Central America and the Caribbean Islands. Texas and Louisiana have an abundance of good winter habitat, with nearly 3 million acres (1,214,-083 ha) in Texas and another 4.5 million acres (1,821,125 ha) in Louisiana (Table 4-2). Probably less than one-fourth of the habitat in Louisiana is used consistently by coots (Bateman, personal communication). In Florida, coots are widely distributed over 37 million acres (14,973,694 ha) in winter (Crider, personal communication). Lesser concentrations winter in Alabama, Arizona, Georgia, New Mexico, and South Carolina (Table 4-1).

Natural wetland ecosystems are most important for wintering, but in certain areas coots utilize golf courses, lawns, pastures, and vegetable and forage croplands. Concentrations of coots that use these systems maintained by humans may cause depredation problems. An average of 561,000 coots have wintered annually in California during the last 19 years, or about 78 percent of the average of 717,000 coots that winter in the Pacific Flyway. The majority of these birds winter on 110,000 acres (44,516 ha) in the San Joaquin Valley (Kozlik, personal communication). Such concentrations of wintering coots can cause economic damage to valuable crops.

CENSUS PROCEDURES AND POPULATION TRENDS

Accurate population estimates are not available for the American coot, but population trends can be derived from information gathered by the United States Fish and Wildlife Service and by a few states.

Census Procedures

Most data on populations are gathered by waterfowl biologists during routine investigations. Although coots utilize much of the same habitat used by dabbling and diving ducks, their habits are so different that the reliability of coot population estimates determined by waterfowl census techniques is unknown. An additional bias may be introduced by waterfowl biologists who are primarily interested in ducks and whose collection of information on coots is incidental to their main interest. As a result of these biases, the accuracy of much of the information on coots is unknown.

Information Available

The United States Fish and Wildlife Service maintains records on coots based on the breeding-ground survey (Table 4-3). Although the precision of this survey is unknown for coots, the trends follow the expected pattern in relation to water conditions on the breeding areas. For example, the drought years of the early to middle 1960's are evident in coot numbers. In the number of birds actually counted in the 17 years during which the breeding surveys have been conducted (Table 4-4), coots rank eighth behind mallards (*Anas platyrhynchos*), scaups (*Aythya marila* and *A. affinis*), pintails (*Anas acuta*), scoters (*Melanitta nigra, M. deglandi*, and *M. perspicillata*), blue-winged teal (*A. discors*), wigeon (*A. americana*), and shovelers (*A. clypeata*). Of the 1,185,501 birds seen, 64,075, or 5.4 percent, were coots.

Coot numbers were consistently higher in 12 of 39 strata sampled annually by the United States Fish and Wildlife Service for breeding waterfowl. All of these strata are located in southern Canada in Saskatchewan, Manitoba, and Alberta, and in the United States in North and South Dakota.

Louisiana and Illinois conduct regularly scheduled aerial inventories and maintain records on numbers of coots counted during each of these flights. Peak numbers reach Illinois between 15 October and 15 November and vary from 113,000 to 378,000. Few coots remain in Illinois after mid-November. In Louisiana, coot numbers increase during October. Peak numbers may occur during November, December, or January; from 635,000 to 1,639,000 wintered there annually between 1968 and 1973. Louisiana's peak wintering populations for these 5 years seem to follow the fluctuations found on the breeding grounds.

Banding

Few states currently have programs specifically intended for banding coots. In 23 states, coot banding is incidental to other banding or is done for the purpose of research on breeding biology. Some states that once banded coots, such as California and Iowa, have discontinued banding. The decline in interest is probably related to the low rate of recovery, lack of interest in coots, and increasing costs of banding and record keeping.

Burton (1959) analyzed data from 1,395 recoveries east of the Rocky Mountains, and Ryder (1963) analyzed data from more than 6,000 recoveries of 85,000 coots banded west of the Mississippi River and the eastern boundaries of Minnesota and Manitoba. Recoveries from 139 coots banded in the Prairie Provinces, the Dakotas, Minnesota, Iowa, and Illinois indicated an average annual adult survival of 43 percent (Burton 1959:204). Ryder (1963:448) calculated a mean annual mortality of 55 percent from 2,325 coots known to

Table 4-3. Summary of adjusted population estimates (in thousands) for American coots from the waterfowl breeding-ground survey conducted annually by the United States Fish and Wildlife Serivce.

Year	Strata						Total
	19	20	21	22	24	30	
1955	248.5	380.2	89.7	509.1	63.1		1,290.6
1956	628.3	370.2	159.7	617.0	136.7		1,911.9
1957	314.4	178.3	275.4	624.7	93.9		1,486.7
1958	74.4	109.8	87.4	228.6	212.6	246.5	959.3
1959	102.7	21.8	111.8	329.3	152.9	319.5	1,038.0
1960	68.6	41.1	94.0	148.8	163.5	324.3	840.3
1961	45.2	9.0	45.3	82.3	59.2	189.3	430.3
1962	35.5	31.8	8.2	87.5	35.7	349.8	548.5
1963	46.3	6.6	27.3	29.1	138.4	392.4	640.1
1964	25.3	71.2	32.3	15.1	183.1	45.4	372.4
1965	69.7	62.8	72.0	60.7	113.4	491.1	869.7
1966	80.7	23.9	27.5	33.3	69.5	507.8	742.7
1967	117.0	50.0	47.1	121.2	87.0	544.3	966.6
1968	67.3	27.5	96.9	156.3	89.3	585.0	1,022.3
1969	154.4	40.4	85.2	76.4	117.9	257.7	732.0
1970	259.5	257.7	86.7	110.6	311.5	436.9	1,462.9
1971	182.3	67.8	45.4	146.0	64.3	204.0	709.8

Notes: Population estimates are of numbers of breeding coots in six sampling strata used in the breeding-ground survey for waterfowl.

General locations of sampling strata used by the United States Fish and Wildlife Service are as follows: 19 = SW Saskatchewan, 20 = SE Saskatchewan, 21 = NC Saskatchewan (west half), 22 = NC Saskatchewan (east half), 24 = SW Manitoba, and 30 = coteau, North Dakota.

Population estimates are adjusted for habitat and for visibility rate differences.

have been shot or otherwise recently dead when recovered. Coots banded as *locals* had a much higher mean annual mortality rate (83 percent as compared with 61 percent for adults). In general, American coots have an average annual mortality rate higher than that of dabbling ducks and as high as that of some declining waterfowl species (Ryder 1963:450). Ryder (1963:451-452) used the available biological and banding information to construct a population model, which indicated that coot populations in North America are slowly declining.

CURRENT HARVEST AND HUNTING PRESSURE

Overall hunting interest in coots is low nationwide (Table 4-5). In none of 50 states is there a widespread interest in coots, but biologists in 5 states report high interest locally. Estimates of coot harvest from hunter surveys made by the United States Fish and Wildlife Service indicate that only 3 of 50 states harvest more than 100,000 birds each year (Table 4-5). Wisconsin is first with 206,000, California second with 180,200, and Louisiana third with 159,400.

Table 4-4. Comparison of numbers of American coots with numbers of waterfowl seen and identified on all sample transacts during the May waterfowl breeding-population survey conducted by the United States Fish and Wildlife Service from 1955 to 1971.

Species	Number of Birds	Percentage of Total	Relative Abundance
Coot	64,075	5.4	8
Mallard	274,344	23.1	1
Gadwall (*Anas strepera*)	48,566	4.1	9
Wigeon	66,222	5.6	6
American Green-winged Teal (*A. crecca carolinensis*)	17,583	1.5	12
Blue-winged Teal	76,823	6.5	5
Shoveler	65,559	5.5	7
Pintail	170,887	14.4	3
Redhead (*Aythya americana*)	23,311	2.0	11
Canvasback (*A. valisineria*)	29,472	2.5	10
Scaups	238,593	20.1	2
Ring-necked Duck (*A. collaris*)	10,021	1.0	14
Goldeneyes (*Bucephala clangula* and *B. islandica*)	10,363	1.0	13
Scoters	89,682	7.6	4
Total	1,185,501		

Four states — Florida, Michigan, Minnesota, and North Carolina — have a harvest of between 50,000 and 100,000 birds. Thirteen states have unadjusted harvest estimates of less than 5,000 coots each.

The United States Fish and Wildlife Service has maintained harvest records on coots for 20 years from post-hunting season surveys (Table 4-6). Kill has ranged from a high of 1,210,600 in 1970–71 to only 182,100 in 1961–62. The number of coots harvested follows the trends in coot populations (Table 4-3). If the unretrieved kill is added to the estimated kill, the annual harvest was nearly 1,600,000 in 1970–71 and 270,000 in 1961–62 (Table 4-6).

Precise hunting records from 1967 through 1972 are available from five intensively managed waterfowl hunting areas in Missouri. Although coots were available for harvest, only 1.7 percent as many coots (1,431) as ducks (85,575) were taken. This pattern probably reflects nationwide hunter attitudes. Kozlik (personal communication) reports that of 175,000 waterfowl hunters only 32,800 kill coots. The low interest in coots for sport probably stems from attitudes fairly common among hunters, classing coots as unsporting and coot flesh as unpalatable.

POTENTIAL HARVEST

Most waterfowl biologists from the 48 contiguous states report that harvest could be increased. Until reliable estimates of populations and present harvest are available, however, the potential harvest of American coots will be difficult to determine.

Table 4-5. Current harvest of and hunter interest in the American coot.

State	Hunter Interest[a]	Estimated Harvest (1971–72)[b]
Alabama	HL	15,700
Alaska	N	1,600
Arizona	N	5,400
Arkansas	N	4,200
California	SS	180,200
Colorado	N	6,700
Connecticut	N	1,800
Delaware	N	3,000
Florida	N	72,900
Georgia	N	6,500
Hawaii	CS	0
Idaho	N	6,400
Illinois	N	20,800
Indiana	N	16,100
Iowa	N	20,000
Kansas	N	9,200
Kentucky	N	3,300
Louisiana	HL	159,400
Maine	N	7,300
Maryland		3,100
Massachusetts	N	3,600
Michigan	N	67,200
Minnesota	N	96,300
Mississippi	N	7,600
Missouri	N	9,400
Montana	N	2,700
Nebraska	N	11,300
Nevada	N	3,600
New Hampshire	N	700
New Jersey	N	7,000
New Mexico	N	1,300
New York	HL	15,500
North Carolina	N	69,400
North Dakota	N	15,300
Ohio	N	20,300
Oklahoma	N	11,700
Oregon	N	18,200
Pennsylvania	N	19,400
Rhode Island	N	1,200
South Carolina	N	13,700
South Dakota	N	13,800
Tennessee	N	26,700
Texas	N	32,900
Utah	N	17,400
Vermont		400
Virginia	HL	39,400
Washington	N	20,000
West Virginia	N	700
Wisconsin	N	206,400
Wyoming	N	1,400

Note: Hunting of coots was allowed in all states except Hawaii in 1973, and there is additional potential for hunting in all states except Hawaii.

[a] HL = high interest locally, CS = closed season, N = none, and SS = special season.

[b] These are unadjusted estimates. Estimates of the number of hunters, the number of days each hunter hunted, and the total number of days hunted are not available.

Table 4-6. Number of American coots harvested (in thousands) from 1952 to 1972. Figures are from the United States Fish and Wildlife Service hunter surveys.

Season	Flyway				Alaska	Total	Crip-pling Loss
	Atlantic	Mississippi	Central	Pacific			
1952–53	190.0	564.1	41.7	115.9		911.7	291.8
1953–54	168.7	558.4	63.1	237.6	0.355	1,028.2	328.2
1954–55	280.0	400.4	52.6	270.5	0.590	1,004.1	253.2
1955–56	142.7	467.5	104.2	281.0	0.888	996.3	352.2
1956–57	115.1	374.2	77.4	322.9		889.6	278.3
1957–58	76.6	259.7	105.0	298.4		739.7	250.3
1958–59	59.4	291.6	100.0	275.2		726.2	259.8
1959–60	11.0	87.7	17.5	81.8		198.0	122.1
1960–61	28.8	202.4	24.9	84.8		340.9	139.0
1961–62	28.4	72.2	13.6	67.9		182.1	91.8
1962–63	36.0	102.4	10.3	71.8		220.5	81.1
1963–64	47.2	222.1	22.1	72.9		364.3	139.3
1964–65	72.2	286.1	23.2	99.3		480.8	188.9
1965–66	85.9	385.3	39.7	107.7	0.710	619.3	222.5
1966–67	110.5	629.4	42.0	167.7	0.888	950.5	328.4
1967–68	101.1	437.2	68.0	151.7	0.533	758.5	286.6
1968–69	60.4	246.3	31.1	86.8	0.414	425.0	168.9
1969–70	117.1	485.7	79.3	195.2	0.315	877.6	297.8
1970–71	144.4	727.7	89.9	248.1	0.474	1,210.6	393.2
1971–72	161.3	428.7	80.8	151.1	0.948	822.9	295.9

Because of the depredation problems in the San Joaquin Valley, California probably has the most urgent and immediate reason to increase coot harvest. Unusual harvest of coots in some areas suggests that caution should be exercised if attempts are made to increase the harvest. The fact that 90 to 95 percent of the coots using an area were harvested in one day (Bellrose 1944:7-9) indicates that coots are extremely vulnerable under certain conditions on some hunting areas. This type of wholesale slaughter would be highly undesirable as a means of increasing the annual harvest and could result in a drastic decline of the continental population.

SPECIES NEEDS

Because the needs of coots and waterfowl are so similar, coots have benefited from public and private programs that were designed for the benefit of waterfowl. The national wildlife refuge system, waterfowl production areas, wetland easements, state waterfowl areas, and areas owned by Ducks Unlimited and other private organizations have provided good habitat for nesting, migration, and wintering. Despite these efforts, wetland habitat continues to decline; hence, any program for acquisition or improvement of wetland habitat would be beneficial to coots. A special program for coots would be a duplication of present waterfowl programs. The habitat needs of coots are an additional justification for waterfowl programs rather than a justification for a separate program.

Historically, the Atlantic Flyway has not had an abundance of coot habitat, and the remaining habitat is constantly shrinking. The Mississippi Flyway still has an abundance of winter habitat in Louisiana, but the breeding habitat has been drastically reduced by drainage. Fluctuating productivity in the prairies is related to water and vegetative conditions. Coots have the greatest abundance of breeding habitat in the Central Flyway, but water cycles and drainage continue to determine overall productivity. Lack of winter habitat is not limiting in the Central Flyway, where Texas still has unused habitat. Winter habitat is in short supply in the Pacific Flyway, and breeding habitat there has never been as extensive as in the Central Flyway. Eight states, but particularly Texas and Louisiana, have habitat that appears to be ideal for coots but is not used. In general, most waterfowl biologists believe that additional habitat for coots is not a serious problem except in the Central Valley of California, where many ducks and coots winter on a relatively small area.

PUBLIC NEEDS

Because coots respond as a group to the management programs for waterfowl, these programs are meeting the public needs related to coots. Presently, the states provide adequate hunting areas and access to hunting areas primarily through land acquisition made possible by Pittman-Robertson funds. Even with low waterfowl populations and small bag limits for waterfowl, few hunters take advantage of liberal bag limits on coots. The national wildlife refuge system and state game management areas provide extensive areas for nonconsumptive enjoyment. Future waterfowl programs designed to meet public needs will probably also provide habitat, access to hunting, and observation areas for coots. In some localities where depredations occur, habitat acquisition or modified harvest regulations may be warranted. Unless hunter attitudes toward coots change, however, public needs in connection with this species are minimal.

MANAGEMENT NEEDS

State waterfowl biologists have suggested the following needs for better coot management: (1) improved inventories, (2) improved harvest information, (3) information on available habitat and habitat utilization, and (4) information on how to make coots more desirable as game birds.

Because no state biologists take accurate censuses of breeding coots, because the precision of the survey by the United States Fish and Wildlife Service is unknown, and because only 2 of the 48 contiguous states conduct adequate inventories during migration or wintering, the most pressing management need for coots is adequate inventories (Table 4-7). The United States Fish and Wildlife Service counts coots during the annual waterfowl breeding-ground

Table 4-7. Budget requirements for a 10-year American coot management plan.

Major Program or Area for Funding	Specific Jobs Within Each Program	Research or Management (R or M)	Job Priority	Estimated Cost of Jobs for Each Fiscal Year (in thousands of dollars)										Total Cost by Job (thousands)	Continuing Job
				1	2	3	4	5	6	7	8	9	10		
Population Studies	Evaluate waterfowl breeding-ground survey to estimate coot breeding populations	R	1	15	15	15	15	15						$ 75	No
	Evaluate harvest inventory	R	2	10	10	10	10	10						50	No
	Monitor harvest in key states	M	3				10	10	10	5	5	5	5	50	Yes
	Inventory wintering populations	M	4				10	10	10	5	5	5	5	50	Yes
	Conduct basic life-history studies on competition, age related productivity, behavior, and migration	R	7	20	20	20	20	20	15	15	15	15	15	175	No
	Monitor disease and pollutants	M	10	5	5	5	5	5	5	5	5	5	5	50	Yes
Total Cost of Program per Fiscal Year				50	50	50	70	70	40	30	30	30	30	450	
Habitat Studies	Determine breeding, migration, and winter-habitat preferences	R	5	20	20	20	10	10	10					90	No
	Develop and evaluate habitat-management techniques	R	8	5	5	10	10	10	10					50	No
	Evaluate effects of land-use practices on habitat quantity and quality	R	6				10	10	10	10	10	10		60	No
Total Cost of Program per Fiscal Year				25	25	30	30	30	30	10	10	10		200	
Hunter Interest	Develop ways of interesting hunters in coots for both sport and food	M	9	10	10	10	5	5	5					45	No
Grand Total				85	85	90	105	105	75	40	40	40	30	695	

surveys, but the relationship between birds counted and the actual numbers of breeding birds is unknown. Aerial and ground work need to be coordinated in different habitats and at different times to determine the reliability of the census technique. As our understanding of waterfowl census techniques and marsh systems improves, management of the American coot will undoubtedly improve too. The reliability of harvest information on coots is another unknown. The potential for effective management will increase once the accuracy of these sampling methods is determined.

Fourteen states lack information on available habitat suitable for coots, and 31 states lack information on habitat utilization. Biologists from all states indicated that an effort should be made to make coots more desirable as game birds. Five states already have high interest in harvesting coots locally, but in general coots are either wasted or are not considered suitable for harvest. The problem of educating the hunter to accept coots as a game species is two fold. First, hunters must be persuaded to harvest coots, and second, they must be convinced that coots are worth eating.

RESEARCH NEEDS

Management of coots could be improved if there were more detailed information on several aspects of the biology of the species. Many of the questions and problems discussed by Kiel and Hawkins (1953) remain unanswered and unsolved. For instance, kill statistics and breeding and winter inventories are still incomplete. Hunters still have a low opinion of the coot as a game bird. Because wetland drainage will continue in the future, more information on coots will be needed to assure that the species will continue to be harvestable and to determine what level of harvest is advisable. Some areas of the country have particular needs and the answers to these needs would provide information for better management. Specifically, additional information is needed on (1) competition between coots and waterfowl and other marsh species, (2) age-related productivity, (3) migratory patterns and differential migration, (4) food habits, and (5) accuracy of inventories and surveys.

Because waterfowl surveys that include information on coots are conducted annually, new or expanded surveys of coots seem unnecessary. However, studies should be initiated to determine the precision of the breeding-ground survey and to determine the reliability of the harvest surveys for coots.

Studies of age ratios and age-related productivity in coots are needed to help interpret the information obtained from the breeding-ground surveys. Similarly, a study of the productivity of coots in relation to marsh cycles would aid in estimating annual productivity.

Because we have no information on the habitat available or the extent of its use, surveys to determine area, quality, and use of habitat would be valuable for management purposes. Much of this information, though known to waterfowl biologists, has never been summarized for the coot.

RECOMMENDATIONS

A suggested 10-year management plan for the coot has been divided into three major areas of funding. These areas are population studies, habitat studies, and hunter interest (Table 4-7). Because coots have similarities to waterfowl — such as mobility and response to dynamic wetland ecosystems — past experiences with waterfowl suggest that a 10-year plan will not solve all management problems for coots. The management problems are particularly difficult because of the rapidly changing habitat conditions in North America. If this plan is implemented and funded as suggested, management of the species should be greatly enhanced over the 10-year period.

The population studies should receive priority. Because data on coots are now collected during the surveys and inventories conducted by the United States Fish and Wildlife Service, the precision of these surveys and inventories should be determined early in the 10-year period. Once the effectiveness of the inven-tories has been determined, winter populations should be inventoried and harvest should be monitored in states where large numbers of coots are most likely to be bagged.

Other studies that would be desirable during the first 5 years of the plan include life-history studies, particularly competition with other marsh-nesting species and age-related productivity. Studies on competition must include investigations on interspecific behavioral responses from time of arrival on the breeding grounds to fledging. Studies of habitat preferences and habitat management techniques also should be initiated early so that the effectiveness of such management can be studied late in the 10-year period. With the recent increase in environmental pollutants and the recent concern about disease in waterfowl populations, both diseases and pollutants should be monitored throughout the 10-year period.

Studies on hunter interest are more sociological than biological. The question is not so much how harvest can be increased as how hunters can be convinced that coots are palatable. Obviously, coots cannot replace waterfowl for wing shooting, but, in those instances where coots can be harvested, hunters should retrieve birds that are shot. Because some states harvest more than 100,000 coots annually, hunters from these states should provide an insight into the factors that make coots desirable for harvest.

ACKNOWLEDGMENTS

Members of the flyway technical sections have been particularly helpful in providing a mass of unpublished information that has put the status and state of knowledge of the coot in perspective. Those who assisted are listed by flyway, state, and agency.

Atlantic Flyway: Connecticut, Oliver E. Backley; Delaware, Anthony J. Florio; Florida, E. Dale Crider; Georgia, Oscar H. Dewberry; Maine, Howard E. Spencer; Massachusetts, Warren W. Blandin; New Hampshire, Harold C. Lacaillade; New Jersey, Robert E. Mangold; New York, Stephen D. Browne; North Carolina, Jack A. Donnelly; Pennsylvania, Dale E. Sheffer; Rhode Island, Charles C. Allin; South Carolina, Thomas H. Strange; Virginia, Charles P. Gilchrist; and West Virginia, Robert C. Kletzly.

Mississippi Flyway: Alabama, W. Walter Beshears, Jr.; Arkansas, David M. Donaldson; Illinois, George C. Arthur; Indiana, Harold A. Demaree; Iowa, Richard A. Bishop and Richard D. Crawford; Kentucky, Frank H. Dibble; Louisiana, Hugh A. Bateman; Michigan, Edward J. Mikula; Minnesota, Robert L. Jessen; Mississippi, Richard K. Wells; Missouri, A. Karl Slagle and Kenneth M. Babcock; Ohio, Karl E. Bednarik; Tennessee, James R. Fox; and Wisconsin, Richard A. Hunt.

Central Flyway: Colorado, Howard D. Funk; Kansas, Marvin D. Schwilling; Montana, Dale W. Witt; Nebraska, George J. Schildman; New Mexico, James L. Sands; North Dakota, Charles H. Schroeder; Oklahoma, Lemuel A. Due; South Dakota, Thomas L. Kuck; Texas, Charles D. Stutzenbaker; and Wyoming, George F. Wrakestraw.

Pacific Flyway: Arizona, Wesley B. Fleming; Idaho, Richard C. Norell; Nevada, Larry W. Barngrover; Oregon, Chester E. Kebbe; Utah, F. Clair Jensen; and Washington, Robert G. Jeffery.

United States Fish and Wildlife Service: George K. Brakhage, James C. Bartonek, Arthur S. Hawkins, Jerome H. Stoudt; Spencer R. Amend (maps); Henry M. Reeves (bibliographic materials); Richard S. Pospahala (breeding index data); Edward Martin (harvest data); and Harold F. Duebbert.

Canada: Saskatchewan, David S. Grey; and Manitoba, Merlin W. Shoesmith.

Atomic Energy Committee: I. Lehr Brisbin.

Hawaii: David H. Woodside.

Tennessee Valley Authority: Donald A. Hammer.

Special acknowledgement is made of Martha A. Johnson's assistance in tabulating data and organizing bibliographic information and Linda P. Korte's contribution in typing the manuscript.

LITERATURE CITED

Alcorn, J. R. 1942. Birds affected by botulism at Soda Lake, Nevada. Condor 44(2): 80-81.

———. 1944. Botulism in the Carson Sink, Nevada. Condor 46(6):300.

American Ornithologists' Union. 1957. Check-list of North American birds. 5th edition. Port City Press, Baltimore. 691pp.

Baumgartner, F. M. 1942. An analysis of waterfowl hunting in Lake Carl Blackwell, Payne County, Oklahoma, for 1940. Journal of Wildlife Management 6(1):83-91.

Bellrose, Frank C., Jr. 1944. Waterfowl hunting in Illinois: Its status and problems. Illinois Natural History Survey, Biological Notes 17:3-35.

Bergman, Robert D. 1973. Use of southern boreal lakes by postbreeding canvasbacks and redheads. Journal of Wildlife Management 37(2):160-170.

Brisbin, I. L., Jr., R. A. Geiger, and M. H. Smith. 1973. Accumulation and redistribution of radiocesium by migratory waterfowl inhabiting a reactor cooling reservoir. Pages 373-384. In Environmental behavior of radionuclides released in the nuclear industry. International Atomic Energy Agency, Vienna, Austria. 749pp.

Broley, Charles L. 1947. Migration and nesting of Florida bald eagles. Wilson Bulletin 59(1):3-20.

Burton, John H., II. 1959. Some population mechanics of the American coot. Journal of Wildlife Management 23(2):203-210.

Carpenter, Roger E., and Mary A. Stafford. 1970. The secretory rates and the chemical stimulus for secretion of the nasal salt glands in the Rallidae. Condor 72(3):316-324.

Erickson, Mary (editor). 1942. A coot and a plane. News from the Bird-Banders 17(1):7.

Errington, Paul L., Frances Hamerstrom, and F. N. Hamerstrom, Jr. 1940. The great horned owl and its prey in north-central United States. Iowa State Agricultural Experiment Station Research Bulletin 277:758-850.

Forbush, Edward H. 1912. A history of the game birds, wild-fowl and shore birds of Massachusetts and adjacent states. Massachusetts State Board of Agriculture, Boston. 622pp.

Fredrickson, Leigh H. 1967. Some aspects of reproductive behavior of American coots (*Fulica americana*). Ph.D. Thesis. Iowa State University, Ames. 110pp.

———. 1968. Measurements of coots related to sex and age. Journal of Wildlife Management 32(2):409-411.

———. 1969a. An experimental study of clutch size of the American coot. Auk 86(3): 541-550.

———. 1969b. Mortality of coots during severe spring weather. Wilson Bulletin 81(4):450-453.

———. 1970. Breeding biology of American coots in Iowa. Wilson Bulletin 82(4): 445-457.

Gullion, Gordon W. 1950. Voice difference between sexes in the American coot. Condor 52(6):272-273.

———. 1952a. The displays and calls of the American coot. Wilson Bulletin 64(2): 83-97.

———. 1952b. Some diseases and parasites of American coots. California Fish & Game 38(3):421-423.

———. 1953a. Observations on molting of the American coot. Condor 55(2):102-103.

———. 1953b. Territorial behavior of the American coot. Condor 55(4):169-186.

———. 1954. The reproductive cycle of American coots in California. Auk 71(4):366-412.

Jones, John C. 1939. On the occurrence of lead shot in stomachs of North American Gruiformes. Journal of Wildlife Management 3(4):353-357.

———. 1940. Food habits of the American coot with notes on distribution. United States Department of the Interior. Wildlife Research Bulletin 2. 52pp.

Kennedy, David D. 1974. Unusual nesting attempts by waterfowl in Southern Illinois. Journal of Wildlife Management 38(4):937.

Kiel, William H., Jr. 1955. Nesting studies of the coot in southwestern Manitoba. Journal of Wildlife Management 19(2):189-198.

———, and Arthur S. Hawkins. 1953. Status of the coot in the Mississippi Flyway. Transactions North American Wildlife Conference 18:311-322.

Leftingwell, W. B. 1888. Wild fowl shooting. Rand McNally Co., Chicago. 373pp.

MacArthur, Robert H. 1972. Geographical ecology: Patterns in the distribution of species. Harper and Row, New York. 269pp.

Parrish, John M., and Brian F. Hunter. 1969. Waterfowl botulism in the southern San Joaquin valley, 1967-69. California Fish & Game 55(4):265-272.

Rausch, Robert. 1947. Pullorum disease in the coot. Journal of Wildlife Management 11(2):189.

Rosen, Merton N., and Arthur I. Bischoff. 1949. The epidemiology of fowl cholera as it occurs in the wild. Transactions North American Wildlife Conference 15:147-154.

Roudabush, Robert L. 1942. Parasites of the American coot (*Fulica americana*) in central Iowa. Iowa State Journal of Science 16(4):437-441.

Ryder, Ronald A. 1958. Coot-waterfowl relationships in northern Utah. Ph.D. Thesis. Utah State University, Logan. 219pp.

———. 1959. Interspecific intolerance of the American coot in Utah. Auk 76(4):424-442.

———. 1961. Coot and duck productivity in northern Utah. Transactions North American Wildlife and Natural Resources Conference 26:134-147.

———. 1963. Migration and population dynamics of American coots in western North America. Proceedings International Ornithological Congress 13:441-453.

Shaw, Samuel P., and C. Gordon Fredine. 1956. Wetlands of the United States, their extent and their value to waterfowl and other wildlife. Circular 39, U.S. Fish and Wildlife Service. Washington, D.C. 67pp.

Sooter, Clarence A. 1941. Ecology and management of the American coot *Fulica americana americana* Gmelin. Iowa State College Library, Ames. 120pp.

Stager, Kenneth E. 1964. The birds of Clipperton Island, eastern Pacific. Condor 66(5):357-371.

Stewart, Robert E., and Harold A. Kantrud. 1972. Population estimates of breeding birds in North Dakota. Auk 89(4):766-788.

Stoddard, Herbert L., Sr., and Robert A. Norris. 1967. Bird casualties at a Leon County, Florida TV tower: An eleven-year study. Bulletin of Tall Timbers Research Station. Tallahassee, Florida. 104pp.

Trainer, Daniel O., and George W. Fischer. 1963. Fatal trematodiasis of coots. Journal of Wildlife Management 27(3):483-486.

Vaa, Spencer J. 1972. Use of waterfowl production areas by ducks and coots in eastern South Dakota. M.S. Thesis. South Dakota State University, Brookings. 31pp.

Ward, Peter. 1953. The American coot as a game bird. Transactions North American Wildlife Conference 18:322-329.

Weller, Milton W., and Leigh H. Fredrickson. 1973. Avian ecology of a managed glacial marsh. The Living Bird 12:269-291.

5

American Woodcock
(Philohela minor=
Scolopax minor of Edwards 1974)

Ray B. Owen, Jr., Associate Professor of Wildlife Resources, School of Forest Resources, University of Maine, Orono, *Chairman.*

John M. Anderson, Director, Sanctuary Department, National Audubon Society, Sharon, Connecticut.

Joseph W. Artmann, Wildlife Biologist, Office of Migratory Bird Management, United States Fish and Wildlife Service, Laurel, Maryland.

Eldon R. Clark, former Biologist, Office of Migratory Bird Management, United States Fish and Wildlife Service, Laurel, Maryland. Present address: Calais, Maine.

Timothy G. Dilworth, Associate Professor, Biology Department, University of New Brunswick, Fredericton.

Larry E. Gregg, Biologist, Wisconsin Department of Natural Resources, Park Falls.

Fant W. Martin, Director, Migratory Bird and Habitat Research Laboratory, United States Fish and Wildlife Service, Laurel, Maryland.

John D. Newsom, Leader, Louisiana Cooperative Wildlife Research Unit, Louisiana State University, Baton Rouge.

Samuel R. Pursglove, Jr., Research Associate, Southeastern Cooperative Wildlife Disease Study, College of Veterinary Medicine, University of Georgia, Athens.

SUMMARY

The Accelerated Research Program for Webless Migratory Game Birds has provided essential funds for and stimulated increased interest in woodcock management and research. Annual status reports are sent out by the United States Fish and Wildlife Service, and Regional Technical Advisory Committees have been formed. In addition, banding has revealed much about migration routes and winter areas and important information on life history has been obtained. However, as pointed out in this report, current management is inadequate. The harvest of woodcock has increased twofold since 1966, but we still cannot make an accurate census of the breeding population nor do we have a valid measure of harvest or a good indication of the effect of hunting on population levels. Population changes cannot be detected early enough to permit compensatory changes in regulations. The amount of available habitat is unknown but is apparently decreasing rapidly in some areas. Also, there is little information on the effects of accelerated land-use practices on habitat. This report contains a series of recommendations for improved management and needed research.

The costs are high, but we feel that they are justified in light of the increased popularity of the bird. The most urgent need at this time is the initiation of a Woodcock or Webless Migratory Game Bird Stamp.

DESCRIPTION

The American woodcock is a member of the order Charadriiformes, family Scolopacidae and subfamily Scolopacinae. Its nearest relatives are the Eurasian woodcock (*Scolopax rusticola*) and the common snipe (*Capella gallinago = Gallinago gallinago* of Edwards 1974).

Although classified as a shorebird, the woodcock is physically and behaviorally adapted to a forested habitat. It is a mottled brown bird whose protective coloration blends in with the dry-leaf pattern of the forest floor. Its short, rounded wings enable it to fly in dense cover. Distinguishing characteristics are the transverse bars on the head, short legs, large eyes set high and far back on the head, and a 6.4-cm (2.5-inch) bill. The bill, prehensile at the tip, is used for grasping earthworms and other soil invertebrates. The outer three primary feathers on the wing are narrow and can be used to differentiate the sexes, for the combined width of the three primaries measured 2 cm (0.8 in) from the tip is less than 12.4 mm (0.5 in) in males and greater than 12.6 mm (0.5 in) in females (Greeley 1953, Blakenship 1957). Woodcock can be aged throughout the year by differences in pattern, color, and wear of secondary feathers (Martin 1964a). The weights of females, depending on the season, range from 160 to 240 grams (0.4 to 0.5 lb) whereas the weights of males vary between 125 and 190 grams (0.3 and 0.4 lb) (Owen and Krohn 1973).

LIFE HISTORY

The migration north begins in late January or early February in the southern part of the winter range (Glasgow 1958), and most birds arrive on the northern breeding grounds during late March and April (Sheldon 1967:103). Data indicate that males migrate first, often arriving while snow still covers the ground. Both sexes are periodically subjected to severe weather during the early part of the courting and nesting periods (Fig. 5-1).

In the spring, male woodcock perform courtship displays at dawn and dusk on singing grounds. These grounds range in size from about 0.25 acre (0.1 ha) to more than 100 acres (40.5 ha) and consist of old fields, forest cuttings, bogs, and other openings (Fig. 5-2).

The display consists of an aerial flight over the singing ground lasting about 40 to 60 seconds, during which the male performs acrobatics accompanied by the twittering of wings and vocal chirps. The aerial display is followed by a ground display, during which he utters a series of *peent* calls. This repertoire is repeated 10 to 20 times during the courtship session, which lasts from 30 to 60 minutes (Pettingill 1936:297 and others). Mating apparently occurs on the

Fig. 5-1. Nesting is unaffected by a late spring snowstorm in Michigan. The typical clutch has four eggs. (Photo by R. J. Harrington, Michigan Department Natural Resources.)

Fig. 5-2. Old fields make excellent singing grounds in the spring and roosting fields during the remainder of the year. (Photo by Maine Fish & Game Department.)

singing grounds during this courtship period. Males appear to be polygamous (Sheldon 1967:47).

Most nests are located within a few yards (meters) of brushy field edges. However, nest cover varies from open fields to young or middle-aged hardwoods or mixed types of light-to-medium density (Fig. 5-3). The nest consists of a well-formed cup on the ground and generally contains four eggs. Incubation (Fig. 5-4) lasts for about 21 days, and the majority of woodcock in the northern part of the range hatch in May (Mendall and Aldous 1943:95). Renesting may occur if initial nesting fails, but there is no evidence of multiple broods (Sheldon 1967:72). Nesting success in Maine is approximately 75 percent, among the highest rates for all game birds (Mendall and Aldous 1943:103).

The chicks are precocial (Fig. 5-5), are able to fly short distances at 2 weeks of age, and are almost full grown after 4 weeks. Nesting habitat and early brood habitat appear to be similar if not identical (Mendall and Aldous 1943:114).

Alder (*Alnus* spp.) swales (Fig. 5-6) and surrounding pockets of second-growth mixed and hardwood types are the favorite daytime haunts of woodcock. One of their major requirements is fertile, moist soil, which enables the birds to probe for earthworms, which constitute 50 to 90 percent of their diet (Sperry 1940). Other animal foods, such as beetles and fly larvae, are apparently taken when readily available, but plant materials are a minor food source (Sheldon 1967:79).

In the evening, woodcock leave diurnal coverts to roost in fields and in small forest openings; these same areas often serve as courtship sites in the spring. Large numbers of birds concentrate on some of these fields (Glasgow 1958, Sheldon 1967:85). During the summer, both adults and juveniles undergo extensive molts, with peak intensity occurring during August and early September (Owen and Krohn 1973).

Fig. 5-3. Dog pointing an incubating hen. (Photo by G. A. Ammann, Michigan Department Natural Resources.)

Fall migration usually begins in Canada during late September after the molt and continues until mid-December, when most birds reach the southern wintering grounds. Most of the woodcock that nest or are hatched on the eastern side of the Appalachian Mountains appear to winter mainly in the South Atlantic states (Krohn (1973a). Woodcock that breed west of the Appalachians are believed to winter in Arkansas and in Louisiana and other Gulf States (Martin et al. 1969).

Habitat characteristics of the wintering grounds vary. In the South Atlantic and eastern Gulf Coast states, woodcock are found on both the Piedmont and the coastal plain and are usually associated with alluvial soils (Pursglove and

Fig. 5-4. The incubating female with her protective coloration blends with the forest litter. (Photo by Maine Fish & Game Department.)

Doster 1970). Few data are available on the types of openings used at night in this region, although nocturnal use of fields continues during migration and throughout the winter. Migrants at Cape May, New Jersey, occasionally feed in alfalfa (*Medicago sativa*) and weedy fields at night (Krohn 1973*b*).

In Louisiana, woodcock concentrate on the bottomlands during winter months. Extensive use is made at night of harvested croplands, pastures, and weedy old fields, where sporadic feeding occurs in early evening and before dawn (Glasgow 1958). In summary, daily patterns of behavior, life forms of the vegetation in the diurnal coverts, and requirements for open nocturnal sites are similar throughout the range of the species.

HISTORICAL REVIEW

No attempt has been made to review the hundreds of articles pertaining to woodcock. Instead, this report includes the most comprehensive studies available, the most recent articles covering specific biological aspects, articles containing material of geographic importance, and studies containing valuable management information.

Pettingill (1936) conducted the first major study of the American woodcock.

Fig. 5-5. Banded day-old chick. (Photo by R. J. Harrington, Michigan Department Natural Resources.)

Fig. 5-6. Alder swales with their abundant earthworms provide excellent diurnal habitat for woodcock. (Photo by Maine Fish & Game Department.)

Much of the early literature is reviewed in his monograph. Mendall and Aldous (1943), Sheldon (1967), and Liscinsky (1972) are also valuable comprehensive studies.

Data on singing grounds and censusing can be found in Pitelka (1943), Dangler (1947), Yerger (1947), Kozicky et al. (1954), Westfall (1954), Weeden (1955), Blankenship (1957), Marshall (1958), Goudy (1960), Duke (1966), and Modafferi (1967). Specific information about the behavior of woodcock on the singing grounds and the census method developed to provide an index of males using these grounds can be found in Sheldon (1953). Krohn (1970, 1971), Gregg (1972), and Whitcomb (1972) have described certain characteristics of summer fields, patterns of field use, and summer banding. Recently, telemetry has been used to study the behavior of females with broods (Wenstrom 1973) and the summer behavior of juveniles (Dunford and Owen 1973) and adults (Owen and Morgan 1975). Beightol and Samuel (1973) presented a sonogram analysis of woodcock calls, and Owen and Krohn (1973) studied molt and weight changes throughout the summer and fall.

Migratory pathways along the Atlantic coast, concentration points, and banding operations during migration have been discussed by Rieffenberger and Ferrigno (1970) and Krohn (1972, 1973a,b). Glasgow (1958) and Britt (1971) have provided studies of the winter grounds in Louisiana. An indication of the woodcock habitat in the South Atlantic and eastern Gulf Coast states has been given by Pursglove and Doster (1970). Detailed analyses of band recoveries have been published only for birds captured in Louisiana (Williams 1969, Martin et al. 1969, Britt 1971). Martin (1964a) outlined an effective method of sexing and aging woodcock based upon characteristics of the primary and secondary flight feathers.

The first comprehensive study of woodcock feeding habits was made by Sperry (1940). Information on earthworm distribution and densities was provided by Miller (1957) for Pennsylvania and Ensminger (1954) for Louisiana. Numerous studies have related pesticide residues to soils, earthworms, woodcock, and eggshells (Wright 1960, 1965, Davey 1963, Stickel et al. 1965*a,c*, Gish 1970, McLane et al. 1971, Dilworth et al. 1972, Kreitzer 1973). Blankenship (1957) and Pursglove (1969) studied parasites and diseases of woodcock in Michigan and West Virginia, respectively. Recently Pursglove (1973) presented detailed information on woodcock parasites throughout the range of the bird. Effects of intensive hunting on a local woodcock population were described by Goudy et al. (1970). Martin et al. (1965) analyzed wing-collection data, and Stickel et al. (1965*b*) described the care of captive woodcock.

The Woodcock Status Reports (Robbins 1958, 1959, 1960, Martin 1961, 1962, 1963, 1964*b*, Goudy and Martin 1966, Goudy 1967, 1969, and Clark 1970, 1971, 1972) have provided up-to-date information on population surveys, including productivity and harvest. Preliminary information on recent woodcock management and research was given at two American Woodcock Workshops (Fourth American Woodcock Workshop Proceedings 1971, Fifth American Woodcock Workshop Proceedings 1974). Finally, Biologist H. M. Reeves, Office of Migratory Bird Management, United States Fish and Wildlife Service, has compiled a detailed annotated bibliography on woodcock that covers most of the material published before the middle of 1972.

A questionnaire was sent to the 34 states within the range of the woodcock and to the Canadian Wildlife Service to obtain the most current information about the species. Each questionnaire was followed by a telephone call. We requested data on the number of woodcock hunters, harvest, additional hunting opportunities, typical woodcock habitat, whether any woodcock habitat inventory had been made or was anticipated, and the particular needs of the species and of the public. All states responded and the data are presented in this report.

DISTRIBUTION AND DENSITY

Present Range and Relative Densities

Woodcock are restricted to the forested regions in the eastern half of the continent (Fig. 5-7). The northern limit of the range is poorly defined but is probably in the neighborhood of James Bay and southern Labrador. The breeding range overlaps much of the winter range, and recent reports indicate that more birds may breed in the South than was previously believed. Several hundred woodcock were released in California during 1972–73, but the success of this attempt is unknown.

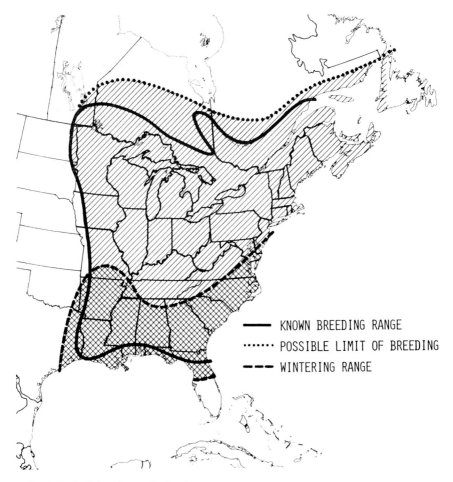

Fig. 5-7. Woodcock breeding and wintering ranges.

The relative breeding density of the bird throughout its range is shown in Figure 5-8. Highest breeding densities are in the northern portions of the range: in eastern Canada, northern New England, New York, and the northern part of the Great Lakes region.

The distribution and density of birds throughout the wintering grounds are poorly known. Few studies of the wintering range have been conducted and the bird is relatively unknown to most sportsmen in that area. Until recently is was believed that the majority of woodcock wintered in Louisiana and southwestern Mississippi. Recent banding analyses, however, indicate that birds breeding primarily west of the Appalachian Mountains concentrate in winter in Arkansas, Louisiana, Mississippi, and Alabama (Williams 1969, Martin and Britt 1971).

Breeding birds from Maine, and probably from other eastern states and provinces, winter primarily throughout the South Atlantic region (Krohn 1973*a*). The exact wintering areas of the eastern Ontario, Quebec, and western New York birds are still unknown. The data collected thus far suggest the existence of two flyways — Atlantic and Central.

Substantial populations of woodcock in the South Atlantic region are found throughout the Piedmont and the coastal plains of Georgia, North Carolina, South Carolina, and Virginia. In Florida the birds are confined primarily to the panhandle. The mountainous areas (all of West Virginia, western Virginia, western North Carolina, northwestern South Carolina, northwestern Georgia, and eastern and central Kentucky) contain isolated wintering populations only

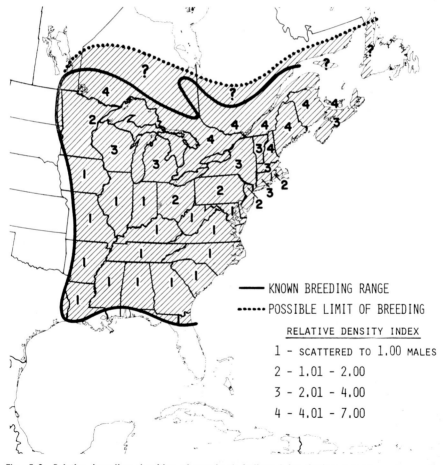

KNOWN BREEDING RANGE

POSSIBLE LIMIT OF BREEDING

RELATIVE DENSITY INDEX

1 - SCATTERED TO 1.00 MALES

2 - 1.01 - 2.00

3 - 2.01 - 4.00

4 - 4.01 - 7.00

Fig. 5-8. Relative breeding densities of woodcock indicated by singing ground surveys or by personal communications. Population indices represent the number of singing males heard per mile on comparable survey routes in 1971 and 1972.

during moderate winters. Primarily these areas support migrant populations heading for the Piedmont, the coastal plain, and the eastern Gulf Coast.

Woodcock are more concentrated in the Piedmont than in the coastal plain, possibly because of the availability of suitable habitat in the former. The birds throughout the Piedmont and coastal plains (exclusive of Florida) may be highly mobile, migrating further south with the occurrence of cold weather. It is not known whether the birds move north again with the return of warmer weather.

Wintering birds in the southwestern part of the range are primarily restricted to the Gulf States and reach very high densities along the coast, especially during cold weather.

Description of Occupied Range

Although woodcock occupy a large geographic area, their pattern of distribution is spotty within their range because of specific habitat requirements. Three major habitat requirements of woodcock are (1) forest openings used as singing grounds and nocturnal roost sites, (2) fertile, generally poorly drained soils that contain abundant concentrations of earthworms, and (3) the proper life form of vegetation to give adequate cover on both diurnal and nocturnal sites.

Woodcock habitat in the northern part of the range is generally associated with the early stages of forest succession (Mendall and Aldous 1943:125, Sheldon 1967:132, Liscinsky 1972:28). Areas that receive a high degree of utilization are dominated by shrubs or trees such as alder, aspen (*Populus* spp.), birch (*Betula* spp.), or mixtures of the three, less than 30 years old (Fig. 5-9). Old agricultural fields, burned or recently logged areas, areas too wet to support forest growth, and hardwoods adjacent to streams, ponds, and other wet areas also receive extensive use by woodcock. Two types of habitat also mentioned as important in reports from individual states were stands of larch (*Larix laricina*) and old apple (*Pyrus malus*) orchards.

Old farms reverting to forests probably provide the optimum habitat in the Northeast. These areas usually contain young to middle-aged hardwoods, mixed types, alders, and openings. As plant succession progresses on these old fields, woodcock densities appear to decline. Timber harvest then becomes a major tool for re-creating woodcock habitat. It is unknown at present whether various forestry practices can create the quantity and diversity of habitats associated with old-field succession. The use of fire may have considerable potential for rejuvenating older habitats, especially in areas where the trees have little commercial value.

In the northwestern portion of the range, the best woodcock habitat is found in the aspen-birch forests, but many of these forests have progressed beyond the stage where they are good for woodcock. However, the increase in the commercial harvest of aspen should help to counteract the trend of deteriorating woodcock habitat in aspen-birch forests.

Fig. 5-9. Typical brood habitat in northern Michigan and other Lake States. The dog is pointing a hen with chicks in an open glade adjacent to a larger opening (not shown). Photo by G. A. Ammann, Michigan Department Natural Resources.)

Specific habitat preferences of woodcock wintering in the southeastern portion of the range are largely unknown (Pursglove and Doster 1970). Birds apparently prefer alluvial floodplains that have a brush understory of the proper density. Swamp privet (*Forestiera acuminata*) seems to be highly preferred, and holly (*Ilex* spp.), switch cane (*Arundinaria tecta*), and honeysuckle (*Lonicera* spp.) are also important. Composition of the tree overstory appears to be unimportant. Isolated groups of woodcock are often encountered near small streams or seepages on pine (*Pinus* spp.) hills and ridges.

The most detailed studies of woodcock habitat in the southwestern portion of the range, conducted in Louisiana (Glasgow 1958, Britt 1971), show woodcock using two types of habitat: agricultural fields and bottomlands and upland sites covered by several species of pine interspersed with streams, seeps, and clearings. The bottomland habitat appears to be the more important and consists of a mixture of hardwood forests, croplands, pastures, and brushy borders. The birds are commonly found in croplands and pastures at night. Diurnal habitat is composed of such species as greenbrier (*Smilax* spp.), blackberry (*Rubus* spp.), switch cane, and saplings.

CENSUS PROCEDURES AND POPULATION TRENDS

Recent band-recovery data suggest little intermingling of woodcock between the Central and Atlantic regions. Because there are indications that these two regions differ in productivity, hunting pressure, weather conditions, ratio of demand to hunting opportunity, and trends in land use, they will be treated here as separate entities. The Atlantic region encompasses all Atlantic coastal states and provinces plus Quebec, Vermont, and West Virginia; the Central region includes the states and provinces within the woodcock's range west of the axis of the Appalachians. It may prove advantageous in the future to manage these two regions separately.

Woodcock hunting seasons are presently based on two annual surveys: the singing-ground survey and the wing-collection survey.

Singing-Ground Survey

Singing-ground surveys were initiated by Gustav A. Swanson in Maine in 1936 as a method of determining trends in breeding populations of woodcock. Currently the procedure consists of driving a randomly selected route approximately 20 minutes after sundown and stopping every 0.4 mile (0.6 km) to count male woodcock active in their courtship displays. Data from many such routes throughout the principal woodcock breeding range provide an index, which is the sole measure of the woodcock breeding population. As an index, singing-ground surveys should indicate major annual changes in the population, but they will not show actual numbers.

Recent unpublished data collected independently by Dilworth in New Brunswick, Krohn in Maine, Rieffenberger in West Virginia, and Whitcomb in Michigan (personal communications 1973) indicate that there may be as many as three noncourting males for each courting male. If the proportion of singing males to nonsinging males varies from year to year or from state to state, the survey is not a valid measure of the relative size of the adult male segment of the spring population. Further, since it appears that some males breed with more than one female, whereas other males do not breed, it is necessary to know the adult sex ratio in the spring to measure the comparative number of females.

There have been no significant annual changes in the breeding-population index in recent years (Fig. 5-10). Annual changes in the past 9 years based on data weighted regionally and rangewide are shown in Table 5-1.

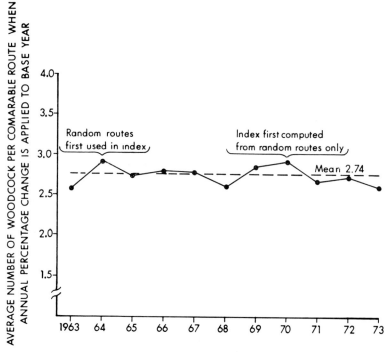

Fig. 5-10. Trends in numbers of singing male woodcock as determined from annual singing ground surveys; base year, 1970.

Table 5-1. Summary of annual population changes in the woodcock; 1965–73.

Year	Percentage Change from Previous Year		
	Atlantic Region	Central Region	Entire Range
1965	−0.4	−11.1	−6.5
1966	+2.4	−0.5	+1.7
1967	+1.5	−3.5	0.0
1968	−8.4	−4.5	−6.9
1969	+4.2	+12.1	+8.8
1970	0.0	+3.1	+2.1
1971	−9.8	−7.3	−8.4
1972	+1.6	+3.7	+2.7
1973	−6.3	−2.8	−4.3

Wing-Collection Survey

The woodcock wing-collection survey was initiated in the United States in 1959. The primary objective has been to determine woodcock reproductive success as reflected by the age and sex composition of the annual harvest. The survey also produces information on changes in geographic and chronologic distribution and size of the harvest. Wing receipts presently average about 19,000 annually (Clark 1972).

Because we lack a sampling frame that permits a random selection of co-operators, it has been necessary to conduct the wing-collection survey nonrandomly. The mailing lists have included (1) all hunters who responded the previous year, (2) a sample of those who indicated on the mail survey of waterfowl hunters that they hunted woodcock, (3) hunters who asked to participate or were recommended by fellow hunters, and (4) hunters on lists provided by states from their harvest surveys or other sources. Significant biases are introduced from each of these sources.

Obviously, precise analysis of a survey sample originating from such varied sources is impossible, but major changes in woodcock productivity probably can be detected.

Productivity Index. — The ratio of immatures to adult females in the harvest, as determined from the wing-collection survey, provides a measure of reproductive success for the preceding breeding season. Variation in the productivity index due to differences in hunters sampled has been reduced by using data only from hunters who participated in the survey both years in computing the change in weighted index.

When rangewide data were weighted and combined, as was done before the 1970–71 season, the annual change in age ratios was small (Fig. 5-11). The greatest fluctuations to date occurred in 1970–71 and 1971–72, which had a 25 percent increase and a 27 percent decline, respectively.

The causes of these unusual fluctuations in the age ratios have not been determined, but there is some indication that adverse or favorable weather during the incubation and early brood-rearing season may be a factor.

Index of Hunter Success. — Trends in the daily and seasonal woodcock harvests have been appraised by determining annual percentage changes in the number of wings submitted by hunters who participated in the survey for 2 consecutive years. Average daily harvests have changed little from year to year. The trend was downward from 1963 to 1964 and upward from 1966 to 1968 and has been slightly downward since 1968.

The seasonal harvest has shown slightly greater annual percentage changes than has the daily harvest. The apparent upward trend through 1970–71 (Fig. 5-11) is misleading because the substantial increases in 1964–65 and 1967–68 probably resulted from greater hunting opportunities. Hunting was curtailed by hazardous fire conditions in the Northeast in 1963. The return to normal conditions in 1964 resulted in a substantial increase in seasonal harvest per hunter. The increased harvest in 1967–68 may be attributed to an increase in length of season from 50 to 65 days. When the sharp increases in 1964–65 and 1967–68 are discounted, the trend is almost steadily downward. Although we do not know what is causing this trend, it is reason for concern and highlights

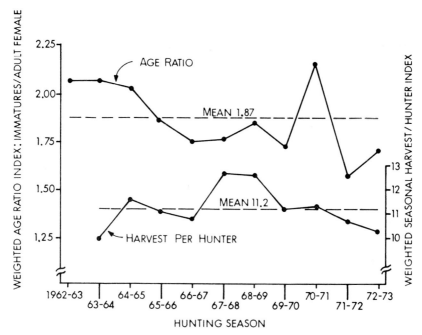

Fig. 5-11. Indices of weighted age ratio and seasonal harvest per hunter, as determined from annual woodcock wing-collection survey data from comparable hunters; base year, 1969–70.

the need for better techniques for collecting data. Hunter success, along with other factors, needs further study before hunting pressure can be equated with woodcock population trends.

HARVEST AND HUNTING PRESSURE

During the past decade, the American woodcock has become a popular game bird with an increasing number of hunters over an increasing portion of its range (Fig. 5-12). State and federal agencies give much more of their funds and time to waterfowl than to other migratory game birds. It is easy to consider waterfowl as the common denominator of interest and effort in migratory game birds. By way of comparison, the ratio of waterfowl hunters to woodcock hunters in the two northern states for which data are available has been 2:1 or less, whereas the harvest ratio has varied between 5:1 and 2.5:1 (Table 5-2).

Since there is no suitable sampling frame from which to conduct annual woodcock harvest surveys, other sources of information are utilized. Data from these sources are sketchy and provide only crude harvest estimates. But there is no alternative at present. Table 5-3 includes harvest estimates from 23 states. Reports indicate that several states do not monitor woodcock harvest and that harvest figures from other states are far from precise. Keeping these facts in

Fig. 5-12. The rewards of good management. (Photo by Maine Fish & Game Department.)

Fig. 5-13. Christmas-tree plantation on former banding field in Penobscot County, Maine. Use of field for courting and roosting decreases greatly once trees exceed 4–6 feet in height. (Photo by R. B. Owen, Jr.)

mind, we estimate that more than 0.5 million hunters are harvesting about 1.5 million woodcock annually in the United States. Thus, the species has advanced from being a specialty game bird highly regarded by only a few hunters to being a broader-based source of recreation providing between 2.5 and 3.0 million man-days of hunting annually.

In Canada, hunters of migratory game birds are required to obtain federal hunting permits. Thus, Canada has been able to monitor woodcock harvests in recent years with considerably more precision than has been possible in the United States. The 1972 Canadian survey shows a harvest of 121,829 woodcock. This number added to the estimate for the United States indicates that the continental woodcock harvest is approximately 1.6 million annually and is still increasing!

In the 1972–73 woodcock wing-collection survey, hunters were asked to provide information on number of woodcock flushed, number retrieved, and number crippled but not retrieved. Most hunters supplied the information requested. Those reporting gave totals of 56,484 woodcock flushed, 21,435 retrieved, and 1,151 crippled but not retrieved. These figures indicated a weighted crippling loss of approximately 5 percent of the retrieved bag. Pursglove (personal communication 1973) estimated that 18 percent of 200 birds hit were not retrieved. His observations were based on hunts where dogs were used and an intensive effort was made to find all birds. He believed that the crippling figures would be higher for the average hunter, especially for hunters not using dogs. Further work needs to be done to measure losses from crippling.

Table 5-2. Comparison of waterfowl hunting and woodcock hunting in two states as reported in harvest surveys of those states.

State and Year	Waterfowl		Woodcock		Ratio of Waterfowl to Woodcock	
	Hunters	Harvest	Hunters	Harvest	Hunters	Harvest
MICHIGAN						
1967	102,910	561,080	87,050	180,360	1.3:1	3.1:1
1968	96,180	373,360	88,040	162,760	1.1:1	2.3:1
1969	109,430	609,670	75,640	141,950	1.5:1	4.3:1
1970	138,260	772,230	76,650	153,380	1.8:1	5.0:1
1971	123,000	719,230	77,800	199,980	1.6:1	3.6:1
1972	163,750	591,070	82,760	188,840	2.0:1	3.1:1
NEW YORK						
1966	86,506	320,301	42,262	118,764	2.1:1	2.7:1
1967	85,666	339,305	51,835	134,566	1.7:1	2.5:1
1968	102,927	375,002	50,020	138,252	2.1:1	2.7:1
1969	99,245	437,636	59,839	158,397	1.7:1	2.8:1

POTENTIAL HARVEST

Because of inadequate information on population size, harvest level, and survival rates, the potential harvest of woodcock cannot be determined. It is apparent, however, that the harvest has doubled in the past decade.

Banding on the breeding grounds has been inadequate to measure trends in the kill or annual survival. First-year recovery rates from these bandings are low (2-8 percent) and suggest that current shooting pressure is not the major cause of mortality. Long-term bandings on the Louisiana wintering grounds also reflect low hunter harvests, but first-year indirect recovery rates from these bandings have suggested a significant increase in females harvested in recent years. The rates for females averaged 0.8 percent in years before the 1963–64 season and 1.1 percent from 1963–64 to 1969–70.

Average survival rates estimated from the bandings on the Louisiana wintering grounds suggest that adult females had higher survival rates than adult males in the earlier years but that female survival may have declined in recent years. These estimates are imprecise because of small samples and broad confidence limits.

Measurements of the size of the breeding population and of the age and sex composition in the harvest over the years have suggested that there is little change in population status as the result of increased harvest. It is possible that woodcock are much more abundant than was formerly believed. Consequently, additional harvest may be possible without affecting future numbers. Nevertheless, we do not know the reliability of woodcock population surveys. Also, the reproductive potential of woodcock is low compared with that of most other species. Thus, it is more difficult for the woodcock than for most species to recover from overharvest. For this reason, until reliable surveys become available, management should remain conservative with respect to potential harvest.

SPECIES NEEDS

Adequate habitat is the primary need of woodcock. We present here a discussion highlighting important habitat trends throughout the range of the bird.

Breeding Range

All states indicated that woodcock habitat was generally declining. Several states noted that many of their forests were already past early successional stages and were therefore of little value to woodcock. Pole-timber stands are now the dominant size class throughout the Lake States (Stone and Thorne 1961, Stone 1966, Chase et al. 1970). Burned and logged lands and reverting agricultural lands were judged insufficient to replace lands going out of woodcock productivity. Further declines in logging were anticipated in most states except the most northerly ones. Increased use of land for residential and commercial developments, highways, and impoundments will steadily reduce the amount of habitat available to woodcock.

In addition to declining habitat caused by maturing forests, woodcock cover is also being reduced in the Lake States through conversion of intolerant types such as aspen-birch to less desirable stands of northern hardwoods or spruce-fir (*Picea* spp.-*Abies balsamea*). Although Minnesota now has a greater acreage in the aspen-birch type than ever before (Stone 1966), the area occupied by this type as been declining in Michigan and Wisconsin.

Forest openings, used extensively by woodcock for breeding, nesting, and roosting, represent another critical habitat component. On loamy soils in northern Wisconsin, forest openings are disappearing (McCaffery and Creed 1969). Sizable reductions in the amount of nonstocked (grass and brush) commercial forest land in Minnesota and northern Michigan between the time of the first (mid-1930's) and third (mid-1960's) forest inventories indicate that these states, too, are losing forest openings through natural regeneration and reforestation. Throughout much of the breeding range, plantations of Christmas trees (Fig. 5-13) and residential developments are further accelerating the loss of forest openings.

Woodcock habitat in the Corn Belt States, though already scarce, may be growing even scarcer. Expanding suburbs, intensive farming, and extensive grazing of woodlots throughout the agricultural areas of the Midwest represent important threats to the existence of woodcock cover in this region. Some of the forested land in the Midwest is grazed so heavily that there is no tree reproduction and severe erosion occurs (Murphy 1968). In addition to destruction of habitat by the grazing of woodlots, millions of acres of poor-site hardwoods

Table 5-3. Estimated harvest of woodcock in states open to hunting in 1972. Data were obtained primarily from state hunter questionnaires.

State	Estimated Number of Hunters	Estimated Days Each Hunter Hunted	Estimated Total Days Hunted	Estimated Harvest	Additional Hunting Potential
Alabama	6,888	5.5	38,197	32,882	Yes
Arkansas	ND	ND	ND	ND	Yes
Connecticut	ND	ND	ND	ND	Yes
Delaware	1,164	6.5	7,533	2,090	Yes
Florida	6,900	6.4	44,300	18,800	Yes
Georgia	6,524	3.4	21,975	23,650	Yes
Illinois	12,700	2.6	32,900	27,300	Yes
Indiana	ND	ND	ND	1,500	No
Iowa	ND	ND	ND	ND	Yes
Kansas	ND	ND	ND	ND	Yes
Kentucky	3,500	3.1	11,000	15,000	Yes
Louisiana	41,000	ND	ND	ND	Yes
Maine	26,613	ND	ND	134,199	Yes
Maryland	6,597	4.2	27,739	14,865	Yes
Massachusetts[a]	26,727	ND	ND	67,886	Yes
Michigan	82,760	6.3	522,450	188,840	Yes
Minnesota	15,000	ND	ND	56,000	Yes
Mississippi[b]	3,902	6.3	24,688	26,392	Yes
Missouri	5,000	4.3	21,400	15,450	Yes
New Hampshire	9,800	6.9	67,280	ND	Yes
New Jersey	27,734	6.9	191,365	63,090	Yes
New York[c]	59,839	4.5	266,949	158,397	Yes
North Carolina	3,672	6.1	22,437	12,951	Yes
Ohio	15,923	4.6	73,247	64,018	?
Oklahoma	ND	ND	ND	ND	Yes
Pennsylvania	138,000	5.4	747,000	210,000	No
Rhode Island	ND	ND	ND	ND	Yes
South Carolina	ND	ND	ND	ND	Yes
Tennessee	ND	ND	ND	1,000	Yes
Texas	ND	ND	ND	ND	Yes
Vermont	ND	ND	ND	ND	Yes
Virginia[c]	11,400	4.1	47,000	42,000	Yes
West Virginia[a]	5,000	ND	ND	15,000	Yes
Wisconsin	ND	ND	ND	137,000	Yes

[a] 1970–71 survey.
[b] Residents only.
[c] 1969–70 survey.

in the Midwest are being converted to grasslands for production of beef cattle (Crawford 1968).

Although woodcock habitat in the Midwest is declining, large-scale habitat-improvement programs now under way in Michigan and Wisconsin may be helping to reduce the rate of loss. These programs, aimed primarily at white-tailed deer (*Odocoileus virginianus*), are designed to maintain aspen and forest openings, critical types for woodcock as well as for whitetails. In Michigan, plans have been made to treat 400,000 acres within the next 10 years (Byelich et al. 1972).

In the Lake States, where much of the forested land is publicly owned, one can be reasonably confident that wildlife production as well as wood production will be considered in forest-management planning. Much of the forested land in the Northeast and the Corn Belt States, however, is privately owned and the type of land use that yields the greatest economic return will probably dominate.

With future decreases in woodcock habitat almost certain, management of existing habitat will become even more important. Reports indicated that improved management for woodcock may present problems to several states because they lack both money for management and specific information on woodcock needs.

None of the responding states indicated that they had made, or planned to make, an adequate appraisal of how much woodcock habitat, actual or potential, was within their borders. Generally, the only information available on woodcock habitat was that which could be inferred from general data on land use, forest inventories, and wetlands surveys. Whether this information is adequate for future management plans depends upon the intensity of the planning.

With the supply of woodcock habitat decreasing in the future and hunter interest probably increasing, reports from several states predicted excessive hunting pressures.

Wintering Range

All but two states (West Virginia and Florida) reported that woodcock habitat was decreasing. All states noted large increases in various intensive land-use practices that are detrimental to woodcock, including channelization (Fig. 5-14), dam building, land clearing for urban and industrial purposes, clean farming and associated drainage, pine plantations, and clearance of pasture-land and clear-cuttings by timber companies right up to riverbanks.

As noted earlier, many woodcock in the wintering range concentrate in habitat along rivers and streams. Many of the practices mentioned above destroy this critical habitat. Prescribed burning is done in much of the Southeast, but it is unknown what effect this practice will have on woodcock populations.

Hardwood forests throughout the Mississippi Delta region and elsewhere in the Gulf States provide optimum winter habitat (Fig. 5-15). Clearing and draining of these forests, particularly for soybeans (*Glycine max*) and livestock, are important causes of habitat destruction. This trend is typified in the northern parishes of Louisiana. Yancey (1969) noted that the original 5.6 million acres (2.3 million ha) of bottomland hardwood forest in northern Louisiana had declined to 3.3 million acres (1.3 million ha) by 1961 and to 2.5 million acres (1.0 million ha) in 1969; he estimated that these forests will be essentially eliminated by 1991 if the current rate of clearing continues. Land clearing has not progressed to the point where a shortage of habitat is affecting woodcock abun-

Fig. 5-14. Channelization of Potato Creek near Barnesville, Georgia. Similar projects are resulting in significant losses of woodcock diurnal habitat. (Photo by Georgia Department of Natural Resources.)

dance. Nevertheless, the outlook is bleak, for the alluvial soils in much of the better woodcock habitat are extremely fertile and are desirable for the production of agricultural crops. In contrast, forested habitat is increasing in the upland and less fertile regions of the Gulf States. Much of this timber, however, consists of pines and provides poor habitat for woodcock and other wildlife.

It appears that woodcock habitat in the Gulf States is declining at a faster rate than elsewhere on the breeding and wintering grounds. In the long run, such reduction will have a profound effect, for this area winters a large fraction of the woodcock population, especially during cold winters.

Another area of concern to the well-being of the species throughout its range is the effect of environmental pollutants, such as pesticides and heavy metals. It has been demonstrated that woodcock accumulate these materials when they feed in contaminated environments (Stickel et al. 1965a, Pearce and Baird 1971).

PUBLIC NEEDS

Public Attitudes

There is a need to document the aesthetic and recreational values attributed

Fig. 5-15. Excellent diurnal cover for woodcock in the bottomland hardwoods of the Atchafalaya Basin, Louisiana. Note bird dog on point. (Photo by F. W. Martin, U.S. Fish and Wildlife Service.)

to woodcock. The unique courtship display of woodcock provides enjoyment for bird watchers, nature study groups, and hunters. Dog owners consider woodcock a top game bird. The attitudes of people enjoying this resource should be documented to highlight the importance of the species and the need to manage it for the benefit of all interested parties.

Public Access

Changes in patterns of land ownership, increased human population, and hunting pressures are reducing the public's access to woodcock areas. For example, in Maine, about 700,000 acres (283,286 ha) are already posted in the southern half of the state. These areas are characteristically old farmlands, which provide the best woodcock habitat. Leasing of large tracts to small hunting groups by timber companies and farmers is on the increase. More access via national forests, state forests, and cooperative agreements with farmers and timber companies is needed.

Public Awareness

There is a pressing need for state administrators and the public throughout the wintering range to understand the importance of their geographical region to the well-being of the species. The woodcock population will be unable to sustain the rapidly increasing harvest unless administrators support research and management designed to assure an adequate wintering population. This support must be given even though the species is only lightly harvested throughout much of the South.

Altered Hunting Seasons

For the sake of simplifying regulations, many southern states set opening dates for the woodcock season to correspond with the opening date for bobwhite (*Colinus virginianus*) and other small game. For some of these states, such as Kentucky and Tennessee, changes in dates may be necessary to enable sportsmen to take advantage of the woodcock resource.

MANAGEMENT NEEDS

Population Management

Information needed for monitoring woodcock numbers and regulating their harvest is similar to that required for other migratory game birds. Ideally, a management program should include the following annual measurements: (1) population size (preferably of breeding birds), (2) recruitment (immatures per adult female), (3) harvest size, (4) rate of harvest (fraction of birds in banded samples retrieved by hunters), and (5) annual survival rates. Such information can be gathered by means of breeding-population, wing-collection, and harvest surveys, together with preseason bandings. Collectively, the various parts of the program would make it possible to identify different population segments, determine their annual status, and evaluate effects of shooting and natural mortality factors upon abundance. Some type of stamp or permit is essential to provide the proper sampling base for carrying out this minimal program effectively.

The cost of implementing fully the management program described above cannot be determined precisely but would probably be about $300,000 per year. A large fraction of the expense would result from preseason bandings (Fig. 5-16) for the purpose of measuring harvest rate, determining age and sex differences in harvest and survival rates, and evaluating the contribution of hunting and natural losses to mortality. At least 3,000 woodcock must be banded annually in each of four states — Maine, New York, Michigan, and Wisconsin — to accomplish this objective.

Pesticide monitoring should be continued. The recent closure of the woodcock season in New Brunswick and the heavy use of pesticides throughout the bird's winter range highlight the importance of monitoring pesticides. Currently, both Canada and the United States are monitoring pesticides in a sample of wings every 3 to 5 years.

Habitat Management

The majority of the states within the breeding range indicated the need for habitat management. Suggestions were for land acquisition, access agreements, maintenance of existing habitat, and creation of new habitat. Costs ranged from $15,000 to $20,000 per year per state or a total of $500,000 per year if most states were to initiate programs.

The migration concentration site at Cape May, New Jersey, and winter concentration areas in the bottomland forests of the Mississippi Delta need immediate protection. Land acquisition by the U.S. Fish and Wildlife Service or by state agencies will probably be the only means of preserving these locations essential to the well-being of the species. Other critical areas will probably be found as the biology of the species is better understood.

Because of the cost, large-scale habitat management is not anticipated, but local management may be practical. Existing information on habitat management should be made available to land-management agencies and private landowners. Wildlife, forestry, and agricultural extension agents could suggest effective habitat-management techniques to interested landowners. Minor changes in land-use practices often have beneficial effects on woodcock numbers. For example, the provision of small openings in the forest canopy creates singing grounds and roosting fields. In the Northeast, advocates of tree farming have been planting seedling trees in many of the old fields, with the result that in a few years these fields are no longer used by woodcock. A slight modification of existing procedures to leave small 0.25- to 0.5-acre (0.1- to 0.2-ha) openings unplanted would maintain game habitat.

We need periodic measurements of breeding and wintering habitat to help us determine trends, ascertain the causes of changes in woodcock abundance, and assess the effects of habitat changes on future population levels. The cost of such measurements will be small if existing sources of information on land use can be utilized.

Early successional stages of vegetation support abundant wildlife, both game and nongame. In addition, these vegetation types break up the homogeneous climax forest and create a diversity of habitat. A major effort should be made to highlight the importance of these facts. Biologists should meet periodically to explore ways of managing land for the benefit of all wildlife species. Woodcock certainly benefit from management designed to help ruffed grouse (*Bonasa umbellus*) and deer.

Only two states, Florida and West Virginia, are undertaking inventories of

Fig. 5-16. Band returns provide needed information on harvest and survival rates. (Photo
by Maine Fish & Game Department.)

Fig. 5-17. Mist netting is one of the common
methods of capturing woodcock. (Photo by
Maine Fish & Game Department.)

woodcock habitat, although several states are attempting to relate wetland and
other land-use inventories to woodcock. There is a need for some type of
inventory in view of the current competition for man's uses of quality woodcock habitat, especially adjacent to rivers and streams.

RESEARCH NEEDS

The major effort in woodcock research should be to develop an effective management program that will ensure a continuing abundance of woodcock for
the enjoyment of hunter and nonhunter alike. Much additional research is
needed to reach this goal and the cost will be high.

Largely because of inadequate funding, it has been impossible to evaluate
the present woodcock management program, and there are many gaps in our
basic knowledge of the species; for example, our understanding of its population status is more limited than is generally realized. As pointed out earlier, the
size of the woodcock harvest has increased greatly in recent years and will
continue to increase as more hunters recognize the woodcock's sporting qualities.
Therefore, there is an immediate need for measurement and regulation of the
harvest of this species. We present here our recommendations for research.

Population Research

Singing-ground Survey. — The survey of singing grounds may be a direct measure of relative abundance of woodcock each year. It is conducted after the
high losses that may occur as a result of winter storms, and it provides timely
information needed for setting hunting regulations.

There is an immediate need for evaluation of survey reliability and perhaps
for its improvement. This research should be conducted concurrently in different parts of the breeding range. Considerable ingenuity will be required, particularly in appraising adult sex ratios. It seems worthwhile to judge the value

of the wing-collection survey as an index of the sex composition of breeding birds in the spring after the survey.

Indirect Measurements. — If development of a preseason banding program and improvement of the wing-collection survey prove fruitful, it may then be possible to use indirect measurements to determine numbers of immature and adult woodcock each year (as is now being done with some species of waterfowl). This approach requires information on the size and rate of harvest and on the age and sex composition of the harvest. Resulting population estimates might be useful in evaluating the reliability of the singing-ground survey.

Banding. — In recent years progress has been made in locating concentrations of woodcock and improving capture techniques (Fig. 5-17). Nevertheless, additional research is needed to develop less expensive capture methods. This research should consider methods, such as burning and mowing, to attract woodcock to banding sites, particularly at night.

New Approaches. — Because of the woodcock's unique characteristics, it has proved difficult to obtain fundamental information on its life history and vital statistics. Many techniques commonly used for other migratory birds are not easily applied to woodcock. Therefore, there is a challenge to develop new approaches. For example, parasites, feather minerals, or some other type of *biological* tag might be used to identify different populations. Clearly, creative research will be essential to understanding and managing this valuable resource in the future.

Crippling Loss and Band-Reporting Rates. — To estimate the kill rate, we must determine the percentage of birds lost by crippling and the percentage of bands found by hunters but not reported. There are conflicting data on the importance of crippling, and band-reporting rates are presently unknown.

Life-History Research. — As stressed earlier, many aspects of woodcock life history are poorly understood. For example, the annual singing-ground survey is based on counts of singing males. Yet the reliability of this important survey is not known, largely because our knowledge of woodcock breeding behavior is sketchy.

The singing-ground survey is not valid in the southern states, where breeding birds are mixed with migrants and all are singing. Some other type of index is needed to determine the number of breeding birds in the South and to determine their contribution to the total annual production of woodcock.

Little is known about the importance of mortality factors other than hunting. Information on predation, parasites and other disease-causing entities, and pollutants would be useful in assessing changes in the population.

Habitat Research

Habitat Preference. — There is an urgent need throughout the wintering grounds to determine what is preferred woodcock habitat. Most of the personnel in the states contacted remarked that they did not know what woodcock habitat was and therefore were in no position to comment on management needs.

Habitat Manipulation. — In the long run, land-use practices will determine the amount of habitat and the abundance of woodcock. Therefore, it is unlikely that habitat management by public agencies could markedly influence woodcock numbers. However, habitat management by governmental agencies and interested landowners could increase the number of woodcock in local areas. Research is needed to determine economical ways of increasing or attracting woodcock. The research should be conducted on both breeding and wintering areas and should include the study of potential management tools such as burning, grazing, thinning, clearing, and planting.

Habitat research should be conducted on demonstration areas representative of major habitat types. Moosehorn National Wildlife Refuge in Maine was established for woodcock and should be the center of research on habitat management in the Northeast. Other demonstration areas should be selected in one of the Great Lakes States and elsewhere on both breeding and wintering grounds. The research should include a study of habitat requirements for many species of wildlife.

Besides providing information essential for woodcock habitat management, such research would be valuable in assessing woodcock habitat needs, in land-use planning, and in preparing environmental impact statements appraising the potential effects of land-use changes on woodcock abundance.

Habitat Change. — Research is needed to determine ways of measuring trends in habitat quantity and quality. It may be feasible to assess changes in breeding-ground habitat simply by measuring annual changes in the proportion of stops (listening points) occupied by one or more singing males heard on existing randomly selected routes. A census on a sample of old nonrandom routes, when compared with past counts, also would provide a measure of habitat change on breeding grounds. This method, combined with the use of aerial photographs to assess actual habitat changes, is currently being investigated in New Brunswick.

Forest inventory data from both Canada and the United States are another potential source of information. This information for southern states in particular should be examined to appraise decreases in wintering habitat resulting from extensive timber-clearing operations and other land-use practices detrimental to woodcock habitat.

Finally, a study is needed to determine the practicality of measuring habitat abundance by remote sensing.

Budget Requirements

Table 5-4 outlines the cost of an effective 10-year woodcock management and research plan. Priorities are given and the total cost is about $7 million.

Table 5-4. Budget requirements for a 10-year woodcock management plan.

Major Program or Area for Funding	Specific Jobs Within Each Program	Research or Management (R or M)	Job Priority	Estimated Cost of Jobs for Each Fiscal Year (in thousands of dollars)										Total Cost by Job (thousands)	Continuing Job
				1	2	3	4	5	6	7	8	9	10		
Population Studies	Evaluate singing-ground survey	R	1	60	60	60	60	60						$ 300	No
	Develop other direct and indirect methods of population enumeration	R	2	40	40	40	40	40						200	No
	Conduct singing-ground or other population survey	M	3	15	15	15	15	15	15	15	15	15	15	150	Yes
	Develop and conduct harvest survey	M	4	25	15	10	10	10	10	10	10	10	10	120	Yes
	Improve and conduct productivity survey	M	5	25	10	10	10	10	10	10	10	10	10	115	Yes
	Improve banding technique	R	6	25	25	25	25	25	25					150	No
	Initiate preseason banding in selected areas to measure harvest rates, define harvest units, determine age and sex differences in survival, evaluate effects of regulations on harvest, and assess effects of shooting on population status	R	7			250	250	250	250	250				1,250	No
	Monitor harvest rates in key states	M	16								50	50	50	150	Yes
	Conduct basic studies of life history	R	13	30	30	30	30	20	20	20	20	20	20	240	No
	Develop new approaches to population management	R	14	10	10	10	10	10	5	5	5	5	5	75	Yes
	Monitor disease and pollutants	M	15	5	5	5	5	5	5	5	5	5	5	50	Yes

													Total Cost per Program	
Total Cost of Program per Fiscal Year			235	210	455	455	445	340	315	115	115	115	2,800	
Habitat Studies														
Determine breeding, migration, and winter-habitat preferences	R	8	50	50	50	50	50						250	No
Develop and evaluate habitat-management techniques on selected demonstration areas	R	9	50	50	100	100	100	100	100	50	50	50	750	No
Evaluate effects of land-use practices on habitat quantity and quality	R	10			25	25	25	25	15	15	15	15	160	No
Acquire habitat and provide access to it	M	11			100	300	300	300	300	300	300	300	2,200	Yes
Inventory habitat	R	12			125	125	125						375	No
Manipulate habitat	M	17						100	100	100	100	100	500	No
Total Cost of Program per Fiscal Year			100	100	400	600	600	525	515	465	465	465	4,235	
Grand Total Cost of All Programs by Fiscal Year for 10-Year Period			335	310	855	1,055	1,045	865	830	580	580	580	7,035	

RECOMMENDATIONS

The objectives listed by Liscinsky (1966) were similar to our objectives. Considerable progress has been made since 1966, and most of his general recommendations have been put into practice. In addition, banding has revealed much about migration routes and winter areas, and important life-history information has been obtained. However, it is appalling that most of the specific recommendations contained in the 1966 report must be reiterated here, now with even greater urgency. Since 1966, there has been approximately a two-fold increase in the harvest, but we still cannot take an accurate census of the breeding population. There is still no valid measure of the harvest and no good indication of the effect of hunting on population levels or on the survival of individuals. The amount of available habitat is unknown, and there is no adequate measure of habitat change. Change in land-use practices has intensified greatly since 1966, but little is known about the effects of these practices on habitat and population levels.

To summarize, woodcock management is inadequate. Population changes cannot be detected early enough to permit compensatory changes in regulations. Population levels appear to be holding up, but harvest is increasing rapidly and almost all states report that habitat is decreasing. This decline in habitat is the principal reason for concern. Both political and financial support are necessary if we are to have the needed management and research. Continuation of the status quo is impossible and will result in valid criticism if the public, especially the nonhunting public, realizes the inadequacy of the program. The sportsman must support the initial increase in effort through the purchase of a stamp for hunting migratory birds other than waterfowl or through a separate woodcock stamp. This stamp is needed, first to provide a sampling base for several of the essential surveys, and second to provide funds to help support the needed management and research program. Additional public support can be requested once this initial step is taken.

Throughout most of the South, there is little interest in the sporting qualities of the bird or in its management. Many states appear apathetic toward the whole situation. Support for the needed research and management in this region can come only through increased federal funding.

In the North, where there is hunter interest, states should be encouraged to expend additional funds to help support woodcock work. Most recent research on the species has been funded through the Accelerated Research Program. But present levels of funding are inadequate to allow us to reach the minimum goals outlined in this report.

Major Recommendations

The following major recommendations are listed in order of priority, although no priority is indicated for the other recommendations. Further rationale is given in the main text, especially in the sections on Management Needs and

Research Needs. Costs associated with each recommendation are given in Table 5-4.

1. Initiate a woodcock or webless migratory game-bird stamp immediately. *Rationale:* If funds are not available for extensive banding to determine annual survival rates, a stamp is necessary to establish a sampling base for harvest data and productivity indices. It is unlikely that the state surveys, even if they all included woodcock, would ever be uniform enough to provide statistically reliable data. Canada requires all woodcock hunters to purchase a migratory bird stamp and uses this stamp to obtain harvest and productivity data from a sample of hunters. The stamp will also help supply needed funds for management and research. Several national conservation organizations will back this proposal.

2. Evaluate the singing-ground survey. *Rationale:* Currently this survey provides the only available index of annual changes in the breeding population. An effort must be made to place this survey on a firmer base.

3. Develop alternative indices of population levels. *Rationale:* Alternative indices are needed to assess the accuracy of the singing-ground survey. They may add supporting data to this survey or, if it is invalidated, they may even replace it.

4. Continue to refine the wing-collection and harvest surveys. *Rationale:* In lieu of adequate survival data, these surveys, combined with a good sampling base, will provide keys to changes in productivity, population levels, and impact of the gun.

5. Improve banding techniques. *Rationale:* At present it costs about $22 to band one woodcock. The cost of banding large numbers would be almost prohibitive. New techniques should be developed and old ones refined to make banding operations more efficient and less costly.

6. Increase the banding effort in selected areas. *Rationale:* Again, without an enormous banding effort to determine annual changes in survival rates, moderate preseason banding is needed to furnish estimates of harvest distribution, average annual mortality, and differential vulnerability. These data, with estimates of band-reporting rates, can be used to monitor harvest rates. Banding is also needed to delineate more accurately the Atlantic and Central flyways.

7. Determine preferred woodcock habitat throughout most of the wintering grounds. *Rationale:* Personnel in southern states admitted knowing little or nothing about the bird or its requirements. Before any assessment of habitat change or management of habitat occurs, we must determine what is good woodcock habitat in this region.

8. Encourage the development and dissemination of habitat-management techniques. Moosehorn National Wildlife Refuge should be the center for this in the Northeast. *Rationale:* Current management techniques should be publicized and new techniques developed that can be used by state

agencies and landowners. Several centers throughout the range of the species should be established to test, evaluate, and demonstrate these management methods. The refuge and research branches of the United States Fish and Wildlife Service should support this effort by aiding in the evaluation and dissemination of the results.

9. Support studies designed to determine specifically what effect individual long-term land-use practices have on woodcock habitat and populations. *Rationale:* In many areas new land-use practices are becoming dominant over old established ones. For example, in the Northeast, agriculture has been diminishing for many years and reverting old farms have created ideal habitat. To what extent will timber harvest be able to re-create habitat formerly available for the bird? What is the effect on woodcock of the extensive aspen management in the Lake States? How do woodcock react to the large-scale controlled burning and clear-cutting in the South Atlantic states? How detrimental will the increased clearing of land on the bottomlands in the Gulf Coast States be to the bird? These questions and many more need to be answered.

10. Acquire critical geographical areas. *Rationale:* At certain times of the year woodcock concentrate in specific regions. Cape May, New Jersey, and the bottomland forest of the Mississippi Delta are two such areas and are in danger of being lost as good woodcock habitat because of intensified land use.

11. Develop techniques for making large-scale inventories of woodcock habitat and measuring changes in the quality and quantity of habitat. *Rationale:* To talk about habitat manipulation and habitat loss or gain, one must first determine how much habitat exists. Such aids as land-use inventories, aerial photography, and remote sensing should be investigated.

12. Continue to support life history studies. *Rationale:* Many aspects of the life-history of woodcock remain unknown. Studies are needed primarily on those factors that could have important management implications.

13. Analyze and compare data on woodcock populations, harvest, and habitat collected from the two separate flyways. If significant differences exist, then the species should be managed on a two-flyway basis. *Rationale:* Banding data indicate that two separate flyways exist and that there is only limited exchange between them. Productivity indices, habitat trends, and major land-use practices differ considerably between the two flyways.

14. Monitor regularly pesticide and other environmental contaminant levels on a 3- to 5-year basis and study the effects of different environmental contaminants, if deemed appropriate. *Rationale:* The woodcock, a carnivore feeding on soil organisms, can accumulate large amounts of pesticides rapidly. For the good of the species, and for public relations, birds should be monitored regularly.

15. Obtain more precise data on crippling loss and on band-reporting rates.

Rationale: The only data available on crippling loss are conflicting. To determine harvest rate, we must have accurate data on crippling and reporting of band recoveries.

16. Constitute an advisory committee, representative of the range of the woodcock, composed of delegates from the United States Fish and Wildlife Service, the Canadian Wildlife Service, the states, the provinces, and the universities that are actively engaged in woodcock management and research. *Rationale:* There needs to be closer scrutiny of proposals for research and management. Proposals cross regional boundaries, and this committee could advise regional technical committees as to whether a proposal should have priority.

Additional Recommendations

Increase coordination between the work in Canada and that in the United States. Present management data should be combined and published as a joint United States–Canadian effort. *Rationale:* Since the bird breeds extensively in Canada and winters exclusively in the United States, it will be of mutual benefit to cooperate as much as possible in all research and management efforts.

Determine the effects of climate on productivity and migration and on distribution and mortality on the wintering grounds. *Rationale:* It has been shown that a relationship existed between temperature and productivity during two breeding seasons (Clark 1972). This relationship may prove to be an important tool for estimating productivity before the hunting season. There is some indication that adverse weather conditions may force wintering birds into marginal habitat and possibly restrict their food supplies, as occurred in 1940 (Sheldon 1967:19). These relationships should be studied further.

Provide to the public as much free access as possible to good woodcock habitat. *Rationale:* As habitat continues to decrease and hunting pressure increases, there will be more and more leasing or purchasing of good covers. The states should encourage landowners to manage their land for the benefit of woodcock and to provide free access to the public.

Document public attitudes toward the species. *Rationale:* An understanding of the public's interest in and concern for the species is needed so that all groups enjoying this resource may be better represented in the long-range planning for this species.

Do not extend present bag limits until population trends and the effects of hunting on survival are known. If there is any indication that hunting is markedly affecting survival, bag limits or season lengths, or both, should be curtailed. *Rationale:* Until an adequate sampling base exists or more extensive banding is undertaken, regulations must be conservative. Survey data do not seem sensitive enough to detect small population changes or even trends.

Set outside dates for hunting seasons of 15 September and 31 January. *Rationale:* The molt continues through the first 2 weeks of September. Hunting before 15 September subjects birds to unduly high stresses. In addition, the birds are of low body weight and low fat content during the molt. February seasons result in the hunting of local breeding birds and migrants on the way north. The woodcock is one of the few migrant species that currently is hunted during both its southerly and its northerly migrations.

Support periodic meetings designed to bring individuals working with woodcock up to date on recent developments. Also support regional meetings designed to bring together biologists working with a variety of species that have overlapping habitat requirements. *Rationale:* The five woodcock symposia held thus far have been highly successful in generating enthusiasm and providing a forum for the exchange of ideas. These symposia should be continued at about 3-year intervals. The last was held in the Southeast to highlight the importance of this region. Habitat requirements of many game and nongame species show considerable overlap. An effort should be made to coordinate habitat-management activities so that all species benefit.

ACKNOWLEDGMENTS

The committee members express their appreciation to George A. Ammann, John C. Baird, John Dobell, Stephen A. Liscinsky, Howard L. Mendall, William G. Sheldon, Howard E. Spencer, and Douglas A. Whitcomb for their excellent suggestions concerning both the content and organization of this report. We give special recognition to William B. Krohn for his many hours of discussion and editing. We also thank the many state personnel who furnished information on harvest and specific regional needs.

LITERATURE CITED

Beightol, Donald R., and David E. Samuel. 1973. Sonagraphic analysis of the American woodcock's peent call. Journal Wildlife Management 37(4):470-475.

Blankenship, Lytle Houston. 1957. Investigations of the American woodcock in Michigan. Ph.D. Thesis. Michigan State University, East Lansing. 217pp.

Britt, T. L. 1971. Studies of woodcock on the Louisiana wintering ground. M.S. Thesis. Louisiana State University, Baton Rouge. 105pp.

Byelich, John D., Jack L. Cook, and Ralph I. Blouch. 1972. Management for deer. Pages 120-125. *In* Aspen Symposium Proceedings. General Technical Report NC-1. North Central Forest Experiment Station, St. Paul, Minnesota.

Chase, Clarence D., Ray E. Pfeifer, and John S. Spencer, Jr. 1970. The growing timber resource of Michigan, 1966. Resource Bulletin NC-9. North Central Forest Experiment Station, St. Paul, Minnesota. 62pp.

Clark, Eldon R. 1970. Woodcock status report, 1969. U.S. Bureau Sport Fisheries and Wildlife. Special Scientific Report: Wildlife No. 133. 35pp.

———. 1971. Woodcock status report, 1970. U.S. Bureau Sport Fisheries and Wildlife. Special Scientific Report: Wildlife No. 140. 38pp.

———. 1972. Woodcock status report, 1971. U.S. Bureau Sport Fisheries and Wildlife. Special Scientific Report: Wildlife No. 153. 47pp.

Crawford, Hewlette S., Jr. 1968. Midwestern deer habitat. Pages 12-22. *In* White-tailed deer in the Midwest. Research Paper NC-39, North Central Forest Experiment Station, St. Paul, Minnesota.

Dangler, E. W. 1947. The ecology of the American woodcock on the Cloquet Forest with some management suggestions. M.S. Thesis. University of Minnesota, Minneapolis. 104pp.

Davey, Stuart P. 1963. Effects of chemicals on earthworms: A review of the literature. U.S. Bureau Sport Fisheries and Wildlife. Special Scientific Report: Wildlife No. 74. 20pp.

Dilworth, T. G., J. A. Keith, P. A. Pearce, and L. M. Reynolds. 1972. DDE and eggshell thickness in New Brunswick woodcock. Journal Wildlife Management 36(4): 1186-1193.

Duke, Gary E. 1966. Reliability of censuses of singing male woodcocks. Journal Wildlife Management 30(4):697-707.

Dunford, Robert D., and Ray B. Owen, Jr. 1973. Summer behavior of immature radio-equipped woodcock in central Maine. Journal Wildlife Management 37(4): 462-469.

Ensminger, A. B. 1954. Earthworm populations on wintering areas of the American woodcock in the vicinity of Baton Rouge, Louisiana. M.S. Thesis. Louisiana State University, Baton Rouge. 97pp.

Fifth American Woodcock Workshop Proceedings. 1974. University of Georgia, Athens. n.p.

Fourth American Woodcock Workshop Proceedings. 1971. Higgins Lake Michigan.

Gish, C. D. 1970. Organochlorine insecticide residues in soils and soil invertebrates from agricultural lands. Pesticides Monitoring Journal 3(4):241-252.

Glasgow, Leslie L. 1958. Contributions to the knowledge of the ecology of the American woodcock, *Philohela minor* (Gmelin), on the wintering range in Louisiana. Ph.D. Thesis. Texas A&M University, College Station. 158pp.

Goudy, William H. 1960. Factors affecting woodcock spring population indexes in southern Michigan. M.S. Thesis. Michigan State University, East Lansing. 44pp.

————, Compiler. 1967. Woodcock research and management, 1966. U.S. Bureau Sport Fisheries and Wildlife. Special Scientific Report: Wildlife No. 101. 40pp.

————, Compiler. 1969. Woodcock research and management programs, 1967 and 1968. U.S. Bureau Sport Fisheries and Wildlife. Special Scientific Report: Wildlife No. 123. 32pp.

————, and Fant W. Martin. 1966. Woodcock status report, 1965. U.S. Bureau Sport Fisheries and Wildlife. Special Report: Wildlife No. 92. 43pp.

————, Robert C. Kletzly, and Joseph C. Rieffenberger. 1970. Characteristics of a heavily hunted woodcock population in West Virginia. Transactions North American Wildlife and Natural Resources Conference 35:183-195.

Greeley, Frederick. 1953. Sex and age studies in fall-shot woodcock (*Philohela minor*) from southern Wisconsin. Journal Wildlife Management 17(1):29-32.

Gregg, L. E. 1972. Summer banding of woodcock in Michigan. M.S. Thesis. Michigan State University, East Lansing. 37pp.

Hawn, L. J. 1973. Michigan small game kill estimates, 1971. Michigan Department Natural Resources, Surveys and Statistical Services Report No. 119. 8pp.

Kozicky, E. L., T. A. Bancroft, and P. G. Homeyer. 1954. An analysis of woodcock singing ground counts, 1948-1952. Journal Wildlife Management 18(2):259-266.

Kreitzer, J. F. 1973. Thickness of the American woodcock eggshell, 1971. Bulletin Environmental Contamination and Toxicology 9(5):281-286.

Krohn, William B. 1970. Woodcock feeding habits as related to summer field usage in central Maine. Journal Wildlife Management 34(1):769-775.

———. 1971. Some patterns of woodcock activities on Maine summer fields. Wilson Bulletin 83(4):396-407.

———. 1972. American woodcock banding and recovery data, 1950–1970. Migratory Bird Populations Station Administrative Report No. 213. 11pp.

———. 1973a. Banded Maine woodcock. Maine Fish and Game 15(2):4-7.

———. 1973b. Cape May woodcock: Their migration and behavior. New Jersey Outdoors 24(3):2-7.

Liscinsky, S. A., Chairman. 1966. American woodcock research and management program. Paper prepared for the International Association of Game and Fish Commissioners. 42pp. (Mimeo.)

———. 1972. The Pennsylvania woodcock management study. Research Bulletin No. 171. Pennsylvania Game Commission, Harrisburg. 95pp.

Marshall, William H. 1958. Woodcock singing grounds at the Cloquet Experimental Forest, 1947–1956. Transactions North American Wildlife and Natural Resources Conference 23:296-305.

Martin, Fant W., Compiler. 1961. Woodcock status report, 1961. U.S. Bureau Sport Fisheries and Wildlife. Special Scientific Report: Wildlife No. 58. 29pp.

———, Compiler. 1962. Woodcock status report, 1962. U.S. Bureau Sport Fisheries and Wildlife. Special Scientific Report: Wildlife No. 69. 36pp.

———, Compiler. 1963. Woodcock status report, 1963. U.S. Bureau Sport Fisheries and Wildlife. Special Scientific Report: Wildlife No. 76. 43pp.

———. 1964a. Woodcock age and sex determination from wings. Journal Wildlife Management 28(2):287-293.

———, Compiler. 1964b. Woodcock status report, 1964. U.S. Bureau Sport Fisheries and Wildlife. Special Scientific Report: Wildlife No. 88. 43pp.

———, and T. L. Britt. 1971. Woodcock studies in Louisiana. A progress report. In Proceedings Fourth American Woodcock Workshop. Higgins Lake, Michigan. n.p.

———, Aelred D. Geis, and William H. Stickel. 1965. Results of woodcock wing collections, 1959 to 1962. Journal Wildlife Management 29(1):121-131.

———, S. O. Williams, III, J. D. Newsom, and L. L. Glasgow. 1969. Analysis of records of Louisiana-banded woodcock. Proceedings Southeastern Game and Fish Commissioners Conference 23:85-96.

McCaffery, Keith R., and William H. Creed. 1969. Significance of forest openings to deer in northern Wisconsin. Wisconsin Department Natural Resources. Technical Bulletin 44. 104pp.

McLane, M. Anne R., Lucille F. Stickel, and John D. Newsom. 1971. Organochlorine pesticide residues in woodcock, soils, and earthworms in Louisiana, 1965. Pesticides Monitoring Journal 5(3):248-250.

Mendall, Howard L., and Clarence M. Aldous. 1943. The ecology and management of the American woodcock. Maine Cooperative Wildlife Research Unit, Orono. 201pp.

Miller, D. R. 1957. Soil types and earthworm abundance in woodcock habitat in central Pennsylvania. M.S. Thesis. Pennsylvania State University, University Park. 69pp.

Modafferi, R. D. 1967. A population behavior study of male American woodcock on central Massachusetts singing grounds. M.S. Thesis. University of Massachusetts, Amherst. 57pp.

Murphy, D. A. 1968. Deer range appraisal in the Midwest. *In* Proceedings Third American Woodcock Workshop. University of Maine, Orono. n.p.

Owen, Ray B., Jr., and William B. Krohn. 1973. Molt patterns and weight changes of the American woodcock. Wilson Bulletin 85(1):31-41.

————, and J. W. Morgan. 1975. Summer behavior of adult radio-equipped woodcock in central Maine. Journal Wildlife Management 39(1):179-182.

Pearce, Peter A., and John C. Baird. 1971. DDT closes New Brunswick woodcock season. Canadian Field-Naturalist 85(1):82.

Pettingill, Olin Sewall. 1936. The American woodcock *Philohela minor* (Gmelin). Memoirs Boston Society Natural History 9(2):169-391.

Pitelka, Frank A. 1943. Territoriality, display, and certain ecological relations of the American woodcock. Wilson Bulletin 55(2):88-114.

Pursglove, Samuel R., Jr. 1969. A survey of the internal parasite fauna of American woodcock in the Canaan Valley of West Virginia. M.S. Thesis. West Virginia University, Morgantown. 97pp.

————. 1973. Some parasites and diseases of American woodcock, *Philohela minor* (Gmelin). Ph.D. Thesis. University of Georgia, Athens. 221pp.

————, and Gary L. Doster. 1970. Potentialities of the woodcock as a game bird resource in the southeastern United States. Proceedings Southeastern Game and Fish Commissioners Conference 24:223-231.

Rieffenberger, J. C., and F. Ferrigno. 1970. Woodcock banding on the Cape May Peninsula, New Jersey. Bird-Banding 41(1):1-10.

Robbins, Chandler S. 1958. Woodcock newsletter No. 1. U.S. Bureau Sport Fisheries and Wildlife, Washington, D.C. 28pp.

————, Compiler. 1959. Woodcock newsletter No. 2. U.S. Bureau Sport Fisheries and Wildlife, Washington, D.C. 24pp.

————, Compiler. 1960. Woodcock status report — 1960. U.S. Bureau Sport Fisheries and Wildlife. Special Scientific Report. Wildlife No. 50. 26pp.

Sheldon, William G. 1953. Woodcock studies in Massachusetts. Transactions North American Wildlife and Natural Resources Conference 18:369-377.

————. 1967. The book of the American woodcock. University of Massachusetts Press, Amherst. 227pp.

Sperry, Charles C. 1940. Food habits of a group of shore birds: Woodcock, snipe, knot, and dowitcher. U.S. Biological Survey. Wildlife Research Bulletin 1. 37pp.

Stickel, William H., Don W. Hayne, and Lucille F. Stickel. 1965a. Effects of heptachlor-contaminated earthworms on woodcocks. Journal Wildlife Management 29(1):132-146.

————, William G. Sheldon, and Lucille F. Stickel. 1965b. Care of captive woodcocks. Journal Wildlife Management 29(1):161-172.

————, Wendell E. Dodge, William G. Sheldon, James B. DeWitt, and Lucille F. Stickel. 1965c. Body condition and response to pesticides in woodcocks. Journal Wildlife Management 29(1):147-155.

Stone, Robert N. 1966. A third look at Minnesota's timber. Resource Bulletin NC-1. North Central Forest Experiment Station, St. Paul, Minnesota. 64pp.

————, and Harry W. Thorne. 1961. Wisconsin's forest resources. Station Paper No. 90. Lake States Forest Experiment Station, St. Paul, Minnesota. 52pp.

Weeden, R. B. 1955. Cover requirements of breeding woodcock in central Maine. M.S. Thesis. University of Maine, Orono. 107pp.

Wenstrom, William Peter. 1973. Habitat utilization and activities of female American woodcock *Philohela minor* (Gmelin) in northeastern Minnesota during spring and summer. Ph.D. Thesis. University of Minnesota, Minneapolis. 203pp.

Westfall, C. Z. 1954. A study of woodcock behavior on their breeding grounds in central Maine. M.S. Thesis. University of Maine, Orono. 117pp.

Whitcomb, D. A. 1972. Nocturnal use of forest clearings during summer by an insular woodcock population. M.S. Thesis. Michigan State University, East Lansing. 33pp.

Williams, S. O., III. 1969. Population dynamics of woodcock wintering in Louisiana. M.S. Thesis. Louisiana State University, Baton Rouge. 65pp.

Wright, Bruce S. 1960. Woodcock reproduction in DDT-sprayed areas of New Brunswick. Journal Wildlife Management 24(4):419-420.

————. 1965. Some effects of heptachlor and DDT on New Brunswick woodcocks. Journal Wildlife Management 29(1):172-185.

Yancey, R. K. 1969. The vanishing delta hardwoods and their wildlife resource. Paper presented at the Governor's Seminar. Little Rock, Arkansas. 18pp. (Mimeo.)

Yerger, R. W. 1947. Breeding populations of woodcock (*Philohela minor*) in central Pennsylvania. M.S. Thesis. Pennsylvania State College, University Park. 65pp.

6

Common Snipe
(Capella gallinago delicata= Gallinago gallinago of Edwards 1974)

Michael J. Fogarty, Former Biologist, Wildlife Research Projects, Florida Game and Fish Commission, Gainesville, *Cochairman*. Present address: 1101 5th, Palm City, Stuart, Florida.

Keith A. Arnold, Associate Professor, Department of Wildlife and Fisheries Sciences, Texas A&M University, College Station, *Cochairman*.

Larry McKibben, Associate Wildlife Manager–Biologist, California Department of Fish and Game, Gridley.

Leo B. Pospichal, Biologist, Michigan Department of Natural Resources, Harsens Island.

Robert J. Tully, Chief of Wildlife Management, Colorado Division of Wildlife, Department of Natural Resources, Denver.

SUMMARY

Around the turn of the century, interest in snipe hunting was high. The tradition of snipe hunting, however, waned significantly and was practically eliminated by the 13-year closed season beginning in 1941. Apparently, a spark of interest in this game bird resource has rekindled and a new jacksnipe following seems to be gathering momentum. This renewed interest was pointed out to some degree by the responses the committee received to the questionnaire regarding this species in the various states. Recent publications have mentioned this same trend, particularly among the western states and Alaska. Little accurate knowledge is available regarding present snipe populations and current harvest. Since this resource is considered minor, few states have utilized the fairly standard techniques for estimating populations or even included the species on their statewide surveys. However, an attempt was made for this report to compile a continentwide annual harvest figure from the data supplied by the states. Although the estimated harvest for any species of low hunter interest is generally overestimated, the annual harvest may approach 900,000 birds. The potential harvest of common snipe appears to be great. At least one author has recently speculated that the North American population of common snipe may be greater than the total number of all the other shorebirds combined. Be that as it may, many agencies expressed the belief that hunters in their states were satisfied with the present daily bag and season limits. Respondents from most states believed that the needs of the public and the species were being met. However, there was a general fear that all wetlands species would be jeopardized if attempts to secure additional wetland habitat within their respective borders were not accelerated. Research needs for the species are basic. Respondents from nearly every state expressed a need for an inventory to determine the size of the resource and an inventory of the available wetlands and their utilization by the common snipe. Many states also wished to proceed with modest life-history studies and banding programs. Estimated expenditures for these programs, based on a 5- to 10-year completion schedule, amount to approximately $1.35 millions. Although the snipe resource in most states is generally considered a minor one, the species possesses the qualities of a fine game bird. The snipe is a swift, erratic flyer, can be successfully hunted without a dog, has a widespread range that makes it available to many sportsmen, and is a succulent table bird. The snipe also shares its wetland habitat with many other interesting and visible species, enhancing its attractiveness to the nonhunting outdoorsman.

DESCRIPTION

The common snipe ranges from 265 to 295 mm (10.4 to 11.6 in) including the bill, which averages about 64 mm (2.5 in); the wingspread reaches as much as 450 mm (17.7 in); and the weight is about 100 (range, 70 to 155) grams (3.5 oz; range 2.5 to 5.5 oz). It has a long, straight bill, a longitudinally striped crown, variegated upperparts, and a white belly and undertail coverts (Fig. 6-1). The narrow tail feathers have rounded ends and little white except in the outer pair. The sexes are similar in plumage, but the female is heavier and has a longer bill.

The bill is flesh-colored, darkening distally to muted deep brown. The iris is medium brown. The legs and feet are greenish gray to yellow green. There are broad blackish, sometimes flecked, crown stripes and also a dark stripe through the eye and a patch on the lower cheek; the in-between areas are various buffs with dark markings. The underparts are various dark browns; some of the light feather edgings are so broad as to form light (buffy) lines or stripes along the sides of the back. The rump is tawny rufous. The breast is buffy with dark streaking; the belly is white from the lower breast to the vent (but there is blackish barring on the upper sides); and the undertail coverts are brownish. The tail has middle feathers that are largely blackish, with progressively less black and more brown (near chestnut) laterally and an increasing amount of white on the ends. There is much white in the outer pair. The wings are dark, and the coverts and secondaries have a broken pattern, as does the back. The downy young have transverse dark areas on the crown. Their underparts are variegated deep browns with darker markings and some silvery feather tips that pale to unmarked tan on parts of the face, neck, and ventral surface (Stout 1967).

Fig. 6-1. Common snipe, Allerton Park, Piatt County, Illinois, 17 October 1974. (Photo by Jean W. Graber, Illinois Natural History Survey.)

In the field, the species is identified by its rapid and irregular wing beat, fast flight, and the *scaipe* note emitted when the bird is flushed. In flight, the snipe shows a white breast and longitudinal stripes on its dark back.

There is no reliable way to age this species after the postjuvenile molt. Furthermore, although Sloan (1967) presented a technique for sexing the common snipe based on the number of bars on the outermost rectrix, this method has been shown by Fogarty and Arnold (personal communications) to be unreliable. Other characteristics of the outmost rectrix may, however, prove to be reliable for sexing this bird (Arnold, unpublished data).

LIFE HISTORY

There was a dearth of information on the common snipe until the appearance of Tuck's (1972) acclaimed monograph on the species. Much of the material in this section of our report has been condensed from his monograph.

During mid-March in the South, snipe begin to show signs of impending migration. The birds flush from the marsh for no apparent reason and wheel about in tight flocks before dropping abruptly back to the ground (Fogarty 1970). On the first moonlit night during this period, northward migration begins. Although fair numbers of birds are still in Florida during early April, by then large flights are already arriving in lower Canada. The males arrive about 10 days to 2 weeks before the females and immediately establish territories, even though the summer population may not peak until the end of May.

Upon arrival, the males begin the spectacular *bleating* or *winnowing* displays over large sections of the breeding areas. These displays are intensified and the areas that they cover are reduced upon arrival of the females. The winnowing display may occur at any time but is most frequently observed at dusk and on moonlit nights. The bird rises on rapid wing-beats to some 300 feet (91.5 m) and then plummets toward the ground at about a 45-degree angle. The tail is spread horizontally and the wings are held at about a 45-degree angle. As the speed increases during the dive, the air passing over the outer tail feathers causes them to vibrate, producing a loud humming sound. The vibration could reach a frequency that would damage the feathers were not it for the wings, which regulate the airflow passing around the tail feathers. This wing-regulated damping effect produces the tremolo quality of the vibration. The male rises again to repeat his winnow as many as eight times per minute. The displaying male will usually follow an elliptical flight path when winnowing over a female.

As pair formation begins, the male will often hold his wings over his back when in the presence of the female and drop to the ground in a graceful downward-curving trajectory with the feet dangling or trailing (Sutton 1923). This performance is usually accompanied by a *yakking* call. Strutting climaxes the precopulatory displays of the male; he drops his wings and struts before his mate with his tail fanned and sometimes turned at an angle of 90 degrees to his body with the upper surface towards the female. Often the female joins in this display.

The clutch consists of four heavily blotched, buffy eggs deposited in a location selected by the female, in a nest that usually begins as a mere scrape. The nest is added to as laying progresses, sometimes acquiring a canopy, until it is often a structure that can be lifted out intact (Rockwell 1912). Eggs are deposited from mid-April to early June, but fresh clutches are sometimes noted in August. These are presumed to be from late-hatched females of the previous year.

The female incubates the eggs for about 19 days. At hatching, the male, who has been spending more time near the nest and less time winnowing, appears on the scene to lead away and rear two chicks, usually the oldest.

The young, which weigh about 10 grams (0.35 oz) at hatching, grow rapidly and are making short, fluttering flights when about 14 days old. Sustained flight is acquired at about 20 days, when the snipe weigh about 90 grams (3.2 oz). Up until about 10 days of age, the chicks are fed by the parents — the adult probes the muck and the young peck at the bill when it is withdrawn. Since the chicks are fed and since the precocial young are brooded on cold, damp nights, there are advantages in dividing the brood between the two parents (Palmer 1967). Food of the common snipe, on both the breeding and the wintering ranges, is over four-fifths animal matter — largely insects (and their larvae), earthworms, crustacea, arachnids, and mollusks. Other items appearing incidentally in the stomach contents (plant matter, seeds, fibers, and grit) are not considered food (Sperry 1940, Whitehead 1965, White and Harris 1966, Owens 1967, Booth 1968).

Fall migration begins in August and heavy flights have reached the mid-section of the United States by the end of this month. Heavy flights continue for the next 2 months. By November, only stragglers are left in eastern Canada. There is no definitive evidence that immature birds precede adults in migration, but there is some hint that adult females migrate ahead of adult males.

HISTORICAL REVIEW

On 16 March 1821, Audubon was invited by some French gunners to accompany them on an American golden plover (*Pluvialis dominica*) shoot. The plovers were on their spring migratory flight and frequently stopped over on a section of Bayou St. Johns near New Orleans. The gunners formed teams of from 20 to 50 each and assembled in different places along the bayou. The plovers were shot as they proceeded down the bayou running the proverbial gauntlet. Audubon estimated that the party of about 200 men killed some 48,000 birds that day (Matthiessen 1959:162).

Forbush (1912) described similar instances of intense gunning pressure during spring and fall migration. He noted that a gunner of the period said that he and a friend killed 340 snipe in one day in Illinois and rarely bagged less than 150 a day during the peak of migration.

Accounts of this type are numerous with regard to almost all of the shorebirds. The birds were considered, like the passenger pigeon (*Ectopistes migratorius*), inexhaustible. When the great flocks began to disappear, gunners assumed that the birds had merely altered their migration routes. The gunners were unwilling to accept the possibility that unlimited spring and fall shooting were taking a serious toll (Stout 1967).

Since snipe do not demonstrate the "flock behavior" of most shorebirds, and since they have an affinity for inaccessible haunts, the species [and the American woodcock (*Philohela minor* = *Scolopax minor* of Edwards 1974), because of its behavioral similarities] did not suffer the extreme depredations suffered by most shorebirds and did not show the precipitous population declines. However, drought on the breeding range and extended cold periods on the traditional wintering ranges can severely reduce the populations. These stresses occurred and caused the United States to impose a closed season on snipe hunting from 1941 to 1953, as provided for by the Migratory Bird Treaty Act. Canada gave partial protection to the species by reducing the daily bag limit.

Snipe hunting resumed in 1954; but after a 13-year break, a generation gap existed — the hunting of this sporty little speedster was not passed from father to son, and snipe hunting declined to the point where the snipe is now rarely hunted. It is usually killed incidentally to the shooting of other species, and this is a pity. The snipe is an outstanding game bird. Its rapid and irregular zigzag flight over habitat sometimes difficult to hunt taxes the skill of even the best wing shooters. It is also an excellent table bird.

With the advent of the Accelerated Research Program, initial research on the snipe was based on the principle that, should hunting pressure increase because of renewed interest or decreasing waterfowl populations, it would be extremely beneficial to have knowledge about the species now — baseline data, in effect.

DISTRIBUTION AND DENSITY

The common snipe is distributed throughout almost the whole North American continent, from Point Hope, Alaska, on the Arctic Ocean, south to Brownsville, Texas, on the Gulf of Mexico, and through most of central and eastern Mexico, all of Central America, and the northern part of South America in Colombia and Venezuela. Snipe occur from the Aleutian Islands and the California coast on the Pacific Ocean to Newfoundland and the Florida coast on the Atlantic Ocean. They are found in the brackish marshes at sea level as well as in the mountain meadows of the Rocky Mountains, near 10,000 feet (3,050 m) elevation.

The northern limit of the breeding range extends from the Chukchi Sea coast of northwestern Alaska through the northern Yukon and Northwest Territories to about Churchill, Manitoba, on Hudson Bay; and eastward from Fort Chimo, Quebec, north of James Bay, through central Labrador and all of Newfoundland. The general southern boundary of the breeding range extends from Los Angeles, California, northward through northwest Nevada and north central Utah to south central Colorado; eastward through central Iowa, northern Illinois, and Ohio to northeastern West Virginia; through northwestern Pennsylvania and southern New York; and along the eastern coast of Connecticut, Massachusetts, Maine, and Nova Scotia through Newfoundland. Isolated breeding areas not shown on the distribution map have been reported from near Springerville in east central Arizona and from central Mexico.

Snipe generally winter south of a line along the panhandle of Alaska, through southern British Columbia, western Washington, southern Idaho, north central Utah, southern and east central Colorado, central Missouri, Illinois, Indiana, western Kentucky, and northern Virginia. They also are commonly seen in Mexico, Central America, the West Indies, Bermuda, and the northern coastal regions of Colombia and Venezuela. Occasionally, during mild winters or in local areas with special climatic and habitat conditions, small populations have wintered in the states bordering Canada from Montana to New York and in the northern New England states, southern Ontario, Nova Scotia, and Newfoundland.

The overall breeding and wintering areas of the common snipe are shown in
Figure 6-2. Only the general outline of the range is included because detailed

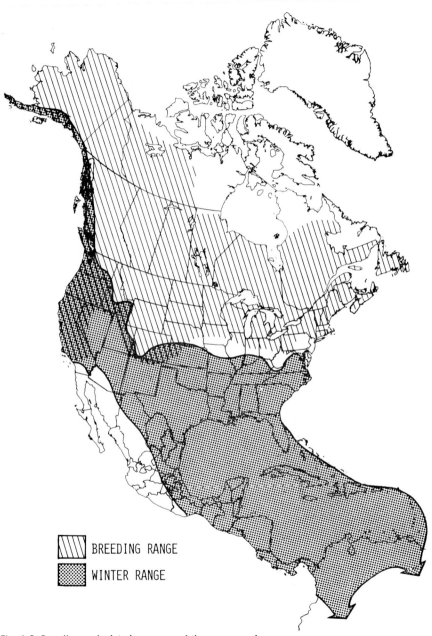

BREEDING RANGE

WINTER RANGE

Fig. 6-2. Breeding and wintering ranges of the common snipe.

information from the responding states and the literature is severely lacking. In some cases, as in Mexico, British Columbia, and several states, it was necessary to extrapolate from one area or state to another — for example, through Kansas. From the information available, it is evident that one of the major objectives of immediate concern throughout the United States is to identify more accurately the major snipe breeding and nesting grounds, the primary migration routes, and the winter concentration areas.

Present, but limited, data indicate that all of the potential range apparently is occupied during some portion of the year or, if the climatic conditions are right, during the entire year.

As with many species of both migratory and resident wildlife, the primary need is related to the status of the population. Because of the snipe's status as a minor game species in all states where it occurs, annual statewide census procedures have not been utilized, even in states with significant harvests, such as Louisiana, California, Florida, Georgia, and Washington. Inventories have been taken in Newfoundland, Ontario, California, Florida, Louisiana, Oregon, and several other states. However, they usually have been conducted in localized areas and on too small a scale to be useful in establishing trends or estimating total populations even for the area, let alone for a province, state, or larger unit. Estimates of population densities for individual states and for the entire range are thus not available.

Estimates from a few research projects vary from spring densities averaging 11.6 birds per 100 acres (28.7 birds per ha) (1968–72) in northwest Oregon to winter densities of over 275 birds per 100 acres (680 birds per ha) (1967–68) in Paynes Prairie, Florida. Similar data for either major breeding grounds in the United States or major wintering areas are insufficient even to make possible good subjective population estimates for any given time period, state, or management unit.

There is no question but that the snipe is common to abundant throughout its major ranges; however, this conclusion is based on considerable well-qualified opinion but little hard population data.

Although many hundreds of thousands of snipe probably breed in the contiguous states, fall and winter populations, especially in the southern United States, are for the most part dependent on Canadian habitats, where a majority of North American snipe are produced. This fact must be considered annually when estimating fall populations for any area of the United States. Although it is presently impossible to estimate the total snipe population in North America, it is possible that it exceeds five million birds.

Whether within their breeding or their wintering range, common snipe occupy only habitats that fall in the general category of wetlands. The nesting area in North America is primarily Canadian peat lands. Peat lands are scattered within the boreal forest biome of spruce (*Picea* spp.), fir (*Abies* spp.), and larch or tamarack (*Larix laricina*) and are composed of an ecosystem of fens, bogs, and swamps (Tuck 1972:119). The differences among these breeding habitats were described by Sjörs (1959), Ritchie (1960), Heinselman (1963), Damman (1964), and Pollett (1967). Various mosses, sedges, grasses, and low shrubs provide snipe with the desired low cover characteristic of summer breeding and feeding habitats.

Snipe principally overwinter in the extensive fresh and brackish marshlands of the Atlantic and Gulf coasts, Mexico, and northern Venezuela (Tuck 1972). They are also found in fewer numbers in almost any wetlands within the winter range. These include the edges of lakes and rivers, ditches, periodically inundated fallow or harrowed agricultural fields, wet cattle pastures, and rice (*Oryza sativa*) fields. High, thick cover apparently is the main factor that precludes snipe utilization of otherwise attractive summer and winter habitats.

CENSUS PROCEDURES AND POPULATION TRENDS

The secretive habits of migratory shorebirds, including snipe, make them difficult to study in many respects. Population estimation is an important management parameter but is also difficult to measure. There are six survey methods recommended by the committee as having application in the study of snipe.

1. *Bleating or winnowing counts* on the breeding grounds.
2. *Territorial response* involving playback of recorded calls on the breeding grounds.
3. *Strip census or King method* on both breeding and wintering areas.
4. *Direct counts* of birds during migration and on wintering areas. This type of count can be aided by the use of delayed-detonating shotgun shells causing birds to flush for accurate counts.
5. *The Lincoln-Peterson Index* method by capturing and banding or marking, or both, and recapturing snipe in concentration areas.
6. *Snipe wing survey* to examine and monitor annual productivity and hunter harvest based on the federal waterfowl harvest survey.

These techniques will be discussed in greater detail below. The United States Fish and Wildlife Service made attempts in the early 1950's to obtain information on the population status of snipe. These attempts centered on annual surveys of the breeding and wintering grounds. Later the surveys were terminated for reasons to be explained, but the information gained should be of value in planning future population surveys.

Bleating or Winnowing Counts

Breeding ground estimates for snipe were attempted by the United States Fish and Wildlife Service in a few northern states and parts of Canada by making winnowing counts. This attempt to eventually census large areas of snipe breeding range was discontinued largely because of lack of access to a large portion of the breeding habitat over the vast land area involved. Some additional drawbacks to indexing on breeding grounds are (1) all birds heard winnowing are not paired, (2) both sexes are known to winnow, and (3) factors such as weather conditions, moon phase, time of day, and phase of breeding cycle affect winnowing activity.

Tuck (1972) recommends the use of straight-line census routes to count winnowing birds. Stops should be about every 0.8 km (0.5 mi). The number of birds heard may be extrapolated to include the total area. The peak period for winnowing is during the 10-day interval after the females arrive, and this period is considered to be the most reliable time to census. The timing of this peak of course varies in different parts of the breeding range. The calling period at dusk should be used; this period appears to be more reliable than the dawn period. A rangewide survey might be hampered somewhat by lack of roads through much of the snipe breeding habitat. If one is aware of and takes into consideration the drawbacks, a comparative index can be obtained over rather broad expanses of breeding territory.

Territorial Response

This method involves playback of recorded territorial calls from predetermined locations and enumerating individual responses (Tuck 1972:137, 393). This technique is the most accurate available and allows the pinpointing of males and nest sites for other studies. It can be effectively used over the entire day during the early part of the breeding season. It is more time-consuming than the other techniques but can be used in combination with other indices to census relatively large areas.

Strip Census or King Method

This method is carried out by walking a predetermined route through snipe cover and counting the number of birds and noting the distances at which they flush. The average flushing distance is determined and used to calculate the effective width of the census strip. The population is the number of birds flushed divided by the area of the strip and multiplied by the total area (Tuck 1972:394).

$$P = \frac{AZ}{ZYX}$$

where

P = population,
A = total area of study,
Z = number flushed,
Y = average flushing distance, and
X = length of line.

This technique has application on both the breeding and the wintering grounds and is stressed for that reason. It probably would be most practicable in localized studies.

Direct Counts

Direct counts of snipe on the wintering ground were also made by the United States Fish and Wildlife Service in the early 1950's, and continued through 1963. Counts were made in snipe concentration areas by local cooperators in 10 to 15 southern states. Supplementary information on snipe numbers was obtained from the National Audubon Society Christmas Bird Count.

This estimate attempt was discontinued because of large variability among years in the number of snipe observed at census areas. Both tidal and upland water levels affected location and size of snipe concentrations as did prevalence of winds and storms. Human disturbance by both legal and illegal hunters was a factor. An unknown number of snipe winter in Mexico and farther south, and the number of snipe wintering in southern United States may fluctuate depending on the severity of winter weather to the north. These locally high changes in bird abundance probably affected the reliability of the overall estimate and masked any actual population changes. A much larger sample size was needed to increase the accuracy and repeatability of the estimates, and perhaps randomization of census areas would have been helpful. The use of delayed-detonating shotgun shells may aid in increasing accuracy of individual counts. These can be fired into fields in order to flush birds for counting.

The Lincoln-Peterson Index

This method involves trapping and banding or marking a portion of the resident population and using the recapture rate to compute the total population. This technique is beneficial on the wintering grounds if high and stable concentrations of snipe are available to work with so as to justify the time expended. In many situations where a continuous banding operation is in effect, the original Lincoln Index will not suffice; however, modifications are available that may be pertinent to these situations (Jolly 1965).

Wing Survey

An annual wing survey, similar to the waterfowl wing survey conducted by the United States Fish and Wildlife Service, would provide a ratio of adults to juveniles and an index to the annual production. It is impossible to use this method, of course, until some system of obtaining names of migratory shore and upland game bird hunters is agreed on and made operational, and until reliable techniques are available to determine age and sex of snipe during the hunting season.

The population trend of common snipe appears stable. Kill figures from responding states exhibit a sustained yield, with generally minor yearly variations. However, snipe populations can be subjected to extreme fluctuations if conditions on the wintering grounds become severe. Extreme fluctuations were demonstrated in the early 1940's. Drought on the breeding range can also restrict production.

The vicissitudes of weather certainly affect snipe populations. These conditions are built into the evolution of the species and do not cause permanent changes in the overall population. The elimination of breeding and wintering ranges by agricultural practices involving drainage and the urbanization of wintering grounds, however, will cause permanent change, obviously a downward one.

CURRENT HARVEST AND HUNTING PRESSURE

Accurate data on harvest and hunting pressure on the common snipe are presently unavailable. The species is considered minor by all states and many do not include it in their statewide kill estimates. Nonetheless, all but 4 of the 49 states polled supplied some information in response to the committee's request. These figures, as received from the various state agencies, are presented in Tables 6-1, 6-2, and 6-3.

A harvest estimate of 159,000 snipe for the 22 states in Table 6-3 (states with no harvest data available but considered to have light hunting pressure) was arrived at after consideration of each state's geographic location, availability of habitat, reported hunting interest, and when feasible, comparison with adjacent states. This figure, when combined with those supplied by the states listed in Tables 6-1 and 6-2, resulted in a nationwide estimate of 831,000 snipe harvested per year.

According to Tuck (1972:369), an additional 80,000 snipe are taken in Canada (primarily in Quebec, Ontario, and Newfoundland) and an unknown number in Mexico and Central and South America. The total annual harvest of common snipe based on these figures apparently approaches 911,000 and this estimate probably has a range of ± 20 percent. Hunting pressure generally appears to be very light throughout North America. Relatively few individuals are snipe hunters in the sense that they concentrate on this species.

A large part of the bag apparently is shot incidentally to the hunting of waterfowl, American woodcock, and the other species that share snipe habitat. It seems that the snipe-hunting tradition, which flourished in the early 1900's, dwindled and was lost following the extended closure from 1941 to 1953. Interest now appears to be increasing in some areas, however.

POTENTIAL HARVEST

The potential harvest for common snipe is unknown. Few states include snipe on their hunter harvest questionnaire. Consequently, even present levels of

Table 6-1. Snipe harvest data from states with hunter surveys.

State	Number of Hunters	Number of Snipe Harvested	Year	Average Harvest
Alaska	10,400	3,100	1971	3,100
California	12,200	92,000	1971	82,200[a]
Colorado	500	1,400	1971	1,100[b]
Delaware	200	500	1972	500
Florida	16,600	204,000	1972	197,300[a]
Idaho	ND	1,900	1971	1,900[b]
Iowa	3,600	7,700	1972	7,600[a]
Maryland	600	800	1972	1,300[a]
Nebraska	ND	1,200	1971	2,100[a]
New Mexico	100	100	1969	100[a]
Oregon	4,100	14,300	1971	13,500[b]
Utah	1,700	4,000	1971	4,900[a]
Virginia	1,800	7,900	1969	7,900
Washington	7,000	34,700	1972	36,000[a]
Total				359,500

[a] Based on latest 3 years of available data.
[b] Based on latest 2 years of available data.

Table 6-2. Snipe harvest estimates from states without hunter surveys.

State	Number of Hunters	Number of Snipe Harvested[a]	Average Harvest
Georgia	15,000	20,000	20,000
Indiana	600	500-1,200	800
Louisiana	23,000	262,000	262,000
Michigan	5,000	10,000	10,000
Minnesota	ND	ND	14,400
Missouri	1,000	ND	ND
New Hampshire	200	600	600
Texas	100	ND	ND
West Virginia	ND	5,000	5,000
Total			312,800

[a] Based on latest 3 years of available data.

Table 6-3. Snipe-hunting states with no harvest data; all have light hunting pressure.

Alabama	Mississippi	Rhode Island
Arizona	New Jersey	South Carolina
Arkansas	North Carolina	South Dakota
Connecticut	North Dakota	Tennessee
Illinois	Ohio	Vermont
Kentucky	Oklahoma	Wisconsin
Maine	Pennsylvania	Wyoming
Massachusetts		

hunting pressure and concurrent harvest are not accurately known. Limited band-retrieval data indicate a low hunter harvest in the United States. Tuck (1972:356) calculated the hunter harvest rate for North America at about 1.1 percent.

The consensus from responding states is that snipe are underexploited, but the committee believes that without further positive field information it would be unwise to alter hunting regulations significantly. At the present time, respondents from all states reporting believe that the present hunting demand for snipe is being met.

SPECIES NEEDS

The needs of the species are presented here, first with a general discussion of the habitat requirements of the species, on both summer and winter ranges, and second with a discussion of need for increased research. The snipe has certain basic requirements for food and cover. Because the species is migratory, meeting these requirements becomes complicated for managers. Good breeding grounds must be available in the North to insure sufficient reproduction. Rest areas must be available to the flocks during migration, and winter habitat and food sources must be available in the South to hold them through the winter.

In North America, the optimum breeding range of the common snipe is restricted to organic soils, primarily peat lands within the northern coniferous forest region of the United States and Canada. The snipe breeding biotype does not include all this vast area of peat, but only parts of the pioneer and consolidation stages of the bogs. Further, the shallow fringe areas are considered the best-quality breeding habitat. Efforts should be made to preserve these areas.

Little research has been done on breeding populations in the southern portion of the range, where snipe inhabit areas of decomposed wet plant litter along ponds, meandering rivers, and brooks, and in similar marshy localities. Although breeding birds may be widely scattered, they probably contribute substantially to the overall breeding population and in turn to the total population.

As summer progresses, the breeding habitat begins to dry up forcing snipe to move and begin to concentrate in areas of more suitable habitat. It is important that resting and feeding areas be available as flocks move southward on their fall migration. Respondents from most states believe that this need is met primarily by waterfowl areas or natural marsh and riparian habitats. In a few states, respondents feel that there is a need for additional lands preferred by snipe. Habitat throughout the wintering range is composed, in various quantities and quality, of marsh (coastal and freshwater), wet rice fields, fallowed agricultural fields, borders of marshy lakes, riparian habitat, and wet pasture.

Most states report that sportsmen show a lack of interest in the snipe as a game bird. For this reason, little emphasis has been placed on the status of the species or its habitat. Beyond the known basic habitat requirements of the common snipe, the greatest need of the species is accelerated research.

Wetlands of good quality, primarily in the winter range, need to be maintained. Land acquisition for snipe alone is usually not feasible. However, the need to provide habitat for snipe may help to justify purchase of wetlands for several species of shorebirds.

There is a need to detail the winter and summer range throughout the United States as well as to learn more about the total range outside the United States. We know generally in which states snipe are found at various times of the year but not in what numbers and over how much area.

Staging areas within the breeding range also need to be located. This information would be invaluable for estimating breeding success and fall populations.

Although several studies of the food habits of snipe have been made, there is a need to document their food habits in greater detail for many areas of the United States. Studies have shown that food items, although usually over 60 percent animal matter, tend to vary according to habitat type. Our knowledge of the snipe's range and adaptability to various food situations should be refined as an aid to management.

A pressing need for wetlands inventory and evaluation for snipe and other riparian species was mentioned in reports from all states polled. Some states submitted actual proposals for land purchase. Respondents from other states not submitting proposals expressed some desire for a population inventory of snipe in their states. If population data indicated a need, they might be prepared to consider habitat purchases.

From Maryland came the unique opinion that acquisition of tidal wetlands by state and federal agencies may lead in some instances to the destruction of snipe habitat because such management practices as drainage would be instituted to provide more habitat for upland game. Also, private interests in many areas are rapidly adapting shorelines to human needs by constructing bulkheads, dredging, and similar activities. Respondents from Maryland, therefore, made the suggestion that governmental agencies and private interest groups give increased recognition to the importance of such game species as the snipe and their associated habitats.

At the other end of the spectrum, respondents from Alaska did not see any immediate need for purchase of wetlands because that state presently has 100,000 square miles (259,000 km²) of breeding habitat for snipe.

PUBLIC NEEDS

There is a definite need to increase the public's ability to identify snipe correctly. Dowitchers (*Limnodromus* spp.), several kinds of sandpipers, phalaropes

(*Steganopus tricolor, Phalaropus fulicarius,* and *Lobipes lobatus*), and other species are sometimes mistaken for and occasionally shot in place of the common snipe. A planned educational program primarily aimed at identification should also include information on the snipe's habits and habitat. With increased hunter and nonhunter interest, such as would result from a proper educational campaign, conservation agencies would exhibit more enthusiasm toward improved management of this renewable wildlife resource.

It is suggested that the United States Fish and Wildlife Service, in cooperation with the states in the several management units, develop species identification brochures similar to those for ducks. The technical committees of the respective management units should further develop educational materials for use in the individual states. It is the responsibility of each state that authorizes a season to provide to its users material on identification, concentration areas, snipe hunting, populations, and habitat conditions.

Respondents in a majority of states concur that there is insufficient knowledge to recommend significant changes in either the federal framework for hunting or the seasons selected by the states. The Alaska hunters would, however, benefit if the possession limit were expanded to equal a 3-day bag.

Throughout the United States there are federal and state lands as well as many private acres to which public access for either nonconsumptive viewing or sport hunting is prohibited. State parks and other state public lands are often administered with little regard for the hunter or the wildlife observer. In some areas of the West, access to federal lands is blocked by private landowners. The present general lack of public interest in snipe and snipe hunting precludes providing access to these lands solely for hunting snipe; however, when snipe are considered in combination with woodcock, dove, waterfowl, any many resident wildlife species, we can clearly see that the individual states must identify key areas and provide access to these lands through purchase, lease, and cooperative agreements to meet future demands.

MANAGEMENT NEEDS

The drainage and destruction of wetlands throughout the United States and portions of the production areas in Canada are well documented. Considering nonconsumptive as well as hunting areas, we can see that there is a continuing need to preserve and improve all classes of marshes, bogs, and other permanent and temporary wetlands, both inland and coastal. To serve the future needs of the public in snipe management, there should be an expanded educational effort toward the preservation, maintenance, and improvement of all necessary wetland habitats, especially those in private ownership. The coastal marshes and shoreline mud flats of the Atlantic coast and the Gulf of Mexico, which are rapidly being lost to urbanization, are of special importance to wintering snipe.

State and federal refuges, public hunting lands, and wildlife management areas should seldom be managed to benefit one species or group, such as waterfowl, with little consideration for other wildlife, including snipe. Respondents from several states said that migrating and wintering snipe populations can be benefited and snipe-hunting opportunities can be improved through proper water manipulation, livestock grazing, burning, disk plowing, and rotary cutting of vegetation.

RESEARCH NEEDS

The agencies responding to the request for information on snipe in their states unanimously agreed that information was unavailable because of the lack of research resulting from limited hunter interest in the species. In most cases, it was also implied that hunter interest appears to be on the upswing, an opinion documented by MacDonald and Martin (1971). Consequently, the respondents thought that there was an immediate need for information on population density and distribution and to obtain the needed information there must be an improvement in survey methods. Some techniques have more applicability than others and can be modified to fit the local situation. There is a need for research on the amount of habitat and its utilization, as well as a need for current figures on hunter harvest. A representative sample of snipe hunters should be obtained from which accurate harvest figures may be calculated. A banding program is needed to show the derivation and distribution of the harvest, and especially to monitor shooting pressure by means of band-recovery rates. Such a banding program in addition to annual harvest surveys would make it possible to monitor the population status of snipe, and aid in delineating their winter range south of the United States. Although shooting pressure is low, continued periodic banding is needed to monitor any abrupt increases in harvest pressure that might occur.

Some states are already engaged in snipe programs. Ten states (Alaska, California, Colorado, Idaho, Iowa, Maryland, Minnesota, Florida, Oregon, and Washington) are collecting data on harvest as part of their hunter surveys. In recent years there have been a few modestly funded ARP projects on snipe. These programs also generate some life-history data. In addition, West Virginia bands a few snipe every year incidentally to its woodcock night-lighting project in the Canaan Valley.

Several states conduct annual censuses of snipe on selected areas. Emphasis is given to arrival times and peak numbers. Other states utilize the Christmas and summer bird counts sponsored by the National Audubon Society.

The major research needs, their estimated costs, and approximate time frames listed by respondents from the states replying to the committee's questionnaire are summarized in Table 6-4. Many agencies listed other research programs that they believed deserving of attention. Management practices requiring ob-

Table 6-4. Budget requirements for a 10-year management plan for the common snipe.

Major Program or Area for Funding	Specific Jobs Within Each Program	Research or Management (R or M)	Job Priority	Estimated Cost of Jobs for Each Fiscal Year (in thousands of dollars)										Total Cost by Job (thousands)	Continuing Job
				1	2	3	4	5	6	7	8	9	10		
Population Studies	Determine breeding and wintering population densities by recommended census methods	R	1	100	100	100	100	100	100					$ 600	No
	Determine population characteristics by banding	R	2	100	100	100	100	100	100					600	No
	Inventory harvest	M	3	50	50	50	50	50	50	50	50	50	50	500	No
	Study life history	R	6	50	50	50	50	50						250	No
	Investigate management practices on populations	M	7	50	50	50	50	50						250	No
Total Cost of Program per Fiscal Year				350	350	350	350	350	250	50	50	50	50	2,200	
Habitat Studies	Inventory habitat	M	4	50	50	50	50	50						250	No
Total Cost of Program per Fiscal Year				50	50	50	50	50						250	
Grand Total Cost of All Research and Management Programs by Fiscal Year for 10-Year Period				400	400	400	400	400	250	50	50	50	50	2,450	
Habitat Acquisition[a]		M	5	300	300	300	300	300	300	300	300	300	300	3,000	Yes

[a] Several states have programs that would decrease costs.

jective assessment — such as discing, burning, and flooding — were suggested by respondents from Maryland, North Carolina, and Missouri. In Minnesota, Florida, and Mississippi, the gathering of baseline data on pesticide burdens in the snipe was suggested.

In the opinion of the Snipe Technical Committee, based partially on the responses from the states, there are five major research needs. They are listed here in order of priority, except for items 2 and 3, which are of equal importance (see also Table 6-4).

1. Population analysis (banding programs).
2. Harvest information.
3. Habitat inventory — breeding and wintering range.
4. Life-history studies.
5. Investigation of management practices.

The major objectives of research in these areas are as follows:

1. To determine breeding and wintering population densities by recommended census techniques (winnowing counts on the breeding range and strip flush counts on the wintering areas) and banding programs.
2. To determine the harvest through a hunter survey, to evaluate habitat types, and to measure hunter distribution and crippling loss.
3. To determine the number of square miles of habitat utilized by snipe and the seasonal availability of potential habitat.
4. To initiate studies on the biology of the species, including age and sex determination, identification of breeding populations on the wintering grounds, and daily and seasonal movements.
5. To test objectively the value of certain management practices, including such habitat manipulation as causing water fluctuation, discing, burning, using livestock, and using chemical controls (herbicides).

RECOMMENDATIONS

On the basis of responses from the agencies polled, the Snipe Technical Committee makes the following recommendations:

1. Obtain an annual nationwide population estimate through the consistent application of the census procedures discussed in this report.
2. Assess the snipe habitat in each state. Eventually funds should be made available for the purchase of these wetlands when practical.
3. Include the species on the statewide surveys in order to obtain the approximate annual harvest.
4. Initiate a wing-collection program to gather information on the age ratio of the harvest and annual productivity.
5. Issue a stamp for migratory shore and upland game birds. Although the committee realizes that there is considerable opposition to such a stamp, it

also recognizes that the potential recreational resource provided by common snipe and the other webless migratory game species far outweighs that provided by waterfowl. Consequently, the committee strongly recommends the initiation of a program or system that will provide a sampling framework for this resource in general and snipe in particular.

6. Provide for the continuation of the Snipe Technical Committee, which should include a member from each management unit and Canada. The expertise of this committee should be used in evaluating research and management proposals before they are submitted to the various management unit committees.

7. Establish a technical position in the United States Fish and Wildlife Service for an individual who coordinates research on and management of the common snipe. The responsibilities of this position should be equivalent to those held for the mourning dove (*Zenaida macroura*) and the woodcock. Whoever acts in this capacity should also serve on the Snipe Technical Committee.

ACKNOWLEDGMENTS

We thank Ronald Ryder, Department of Fishery and Wildlife Biology, Colorado State University, Fort Collins, for his review of the first draft of this report.

LITERATURE CITED

Booth, T. W., Jr. 1968. The availability and utilization of the foods of the common snipe (*Capella gallinago delicata*) in the rice growing region of southwestern Louisiana. M.S. Thesis. Louisiana State University, Baton Rouge. 168pp.

Damman, A. W. H. 1964. The distribution patterns of northern and southern elements in the flora of Newfoundland. Canada Department Forestry, Forest Research Branch. Report 64-N-15.

Edwards, Ernest P. 1974. A coded list of birds of the world. Ernest P. Edwards, Sweet Briar, Va. 174pp.

Fogarty, Michael J. 1970 (1969). Capturing snipe with mist nets. Proceedings Annual Conference Southeastern Association Game and Fish Commissioners 23:78-84.

Forbush, Edward H. 1912. Game birds, wild fowl and shore birds. Massachusetts State Board of Agriculture, Boston. 622pp.

Heinselman, Miron L. 1963. Forest sites, bog processes, and peatland types in the glacial Lake Agassiz region, Minnesota. Ecological Monographs 33(4):327-372.

Jolly, G. M. 1965. Explicit estimates from capture-recapture data with both death and immigration — stochastic model. Biometrika 52(182):225-247.

MacDonald, Duncan, and Elwood Martin. 1971. Trends in harvest of migratory game birds other than waterfowl 1964–65 to 1968–69. United States Fish and Wildlife Service, Special Scientific Report. Wildlife No. 142. 29pp.

Matthiessen, Peter. 1959. Wildlife in America. The Viking Press, Inc. New York. 304pp.

Owens, J. 1967. Food habits of the common snipe (*Capella gallinago delicata*) in the pastures of south central Louisiana. M.S. Thesis. Louisiana State University, Baton Rouge. 107pp.

Palmer, Ralph S. 1967. Species accounts. Pages 249-254. *In* Gardner D. Stout [Editor], The shorebirds of North America. The Viking Press, Inc., New York. 270pp.

Pollett, F. C. 1967. Certain ecological aspects of selected bogs in Newfoundland. M.S. Thesis. Memorial University of Newfoundland, St. John's.

Ritchie, J. C. 1960. The vegetation of northern Manitoba. V. Establishing the major zonation. Arctic 13(4):211-229.

Rockwell, Robert B. 1912. Notes on the wading birds of the Barr Lake region, Colorado. Condor 14(4):117-131.

Sjörs, Hugo. 1959. Bogs and fens in the Hudson Bay lowlands. Arctic 12(1):3-19.

Sloan, N. L. 1967. An external sexual character of the common snipe. Michigan Technical University, Houghton. Wharve-Graduate School Publication:11-12.

Sperry, Charles C. 1940. Food habits of a group of shore birds: Woodcock, snipe, knot and dowitcher. U.S. Fish and Wildlife Service, Wildlife Research Bulletin No. 1. 37pp.

Stout, Gardner D., Editor. 1967. The shorebirds of North America. The Viking Press, Inc., New York. 270pp.

Sutton, George M. 1923. Notes on the nesting of the Wilson's snipe in Crawford County, Pennsylvania. Wilson Bulletin 35(4):191-202.

Tuck, Leslie M. 1972. The snipes: A study of the Genus *Capella*. Canadian Wildlife Service. Monograph Series No. 5. 429pp.

White, Marshall, and Stanley W. Harris. 1966. Winter occurrence, foods, and habitat use of snipe in northwest California. Journal Wildlife Management 30(1):23-34.

Whitehead, C. J., Jr. 1965. Foods and feeding habits of the common snipe (*Capella gallinago delicata*) in Cameron Parish, Louisiana, with ecological notes and a discussion of methods of sexing and aging. M.S. Thesis. Louisiana State University, Baton Rouge. 199pp.

7

Band-Tailed Pigeon
(Columba fasciata)

Robert G. Jeffrey, Game Project Leader, Washington Department of Game, Stanwood, *Chairman.*

Clait E. Braun, Wildlife Researcher, Colorado Division of Wildlife, Fort Collins.

David E. Brown, Small Game Supervisor, Arizona Game and Fish Department, Phoenix.

D. Ray Halladay (Consulting Member), Senior Wildlife Biologist, British Columbia Fish and Wildlife Branch, Victoria.

Paul M. Howard, Western Representative, National Audubon Society, Sacramento, California.

Chester E. Kebbe, Staff Biologist, Small Game Management, Oregon State Game Commission, Portland.

Darrell H. Nish, Upland Game Supervisor, Utah Division of Wildlife Resources, Salt Lake City.

Walton A. Smith, Wildlife Manager–Biologist, California Department of Fish and Game, Gridley.

Thomas P. Zapatka, Wildlife Biologist, New Mexico Department of Game and Fish, Albuquerque.

SUMMARY

Summer and winter ranges of the band-tailed pigeon were mapped, but only rough estimates or none exist for either total numbers or densities. Breeding-ground densities in the Interior race (*C. f. fasciata*) vary from 1 to 10 pigeons per square mile (0.4 to 3.9 per km²), with highest densities associated with pine-oak (*Pinus-Quercus*) communities. With few exceptions, bandtails are closely linked to forests in their distribution, and abundance of these pigeons varies directly with the supply of mast, berries, and other small fruits. Accessible grainfields and orchard crops furnish both additional food resources and occasional management problems. There have been six approaches explored for censusing bandtails or estimating their numbers. Included are preseason ground and aerial counts, postseason counts, estimates based on kill, estimates based on band-recovery data, and audio censuses. Efforts to refine the last two methods are continuing, and a new postseason census method is being considered. During the 6 years for which data from British Columbia are available (1967–72), the average total kill of the Coast subspecies (*C. f. monilis*) by hunters north of

Baja California was 517,000 pigeons. Harvest distribution percentages were 58 in California, 23 in Washington, 17 in Oregon, and 2 in British Columbia. During the same period, the total number of pigeon hunters averaged 74,600. In the recent brief period (1970–72) during which Arizona, Colorado, New Mexico, and Utah all had open seasons, up to 2,500 hunters per year participated. The total annual kill by hunters averaged 5,000 to 10,000 pigeons, and the Mexican harvest of this subspecies was probably of similar size. The potential for increasing the safe harvest of Coast pigeons is not known. In the Interior race, the harvest might be doubled if hunters could be distributed properly. Identified needs of the species are food, nest cover, water, minerals, and, in general, conditions that permit the recruitment of young to equal adult mortality. Not enough is known of the habitat and the habitat requirements of the bandtail to rank species needs as to their limiting effects. Needs of the public are access to the resource, sound management of the resource, and information on the status, management, and hunting of bandtails. Management and research needs and costs are summarized and priorities are assigned. Annual costs for bandtail management, exclusive of the land acquisition program, would not exceed $125,000, with a 10-year total of $1,012,000. Acquisition, development, and maintenance of pigeon concentration areas would cost $1 million over the same period. Thus, the total cost for management would be slightly over $2 million for the 10-year period. All of the land acquisition projects and 74 percent of the remainder of the program are allotted to the management of the Coast subspecies. The university is considered to be the logical place for performing about one-third of the needed research. Research expenditures would reach a peak of $117,000 in fiscal year 1981–82 and would total $792,000 after 10 years. This amount is divided between the Coast and the Interior races, 69 percent and 31 percent, respectively.

DESCRIPTION

Band-tailed pigeons are large, stout-bodied birds (Fig. 7-1) similar in size and general appearance to blue-phase domestic pigeons (*Columba livia*). The name *bandtail* is derived from the wide, pale gray band bordered with black across the tail. Bandtails are somewhat longer (350-380 mm — 13.8-15.0 in) than domestic pigeons, although bandtails have slightly shorter wings (200-230 mm — 7.9-9.0 in) and are lighter in weight (300-500 g — 10.6-17.6 oz). Adult bandtails appear blue gray, with both sexes having a conspicuous white neck crescent above an iridescent nape. Plumage of the head and upper breast ranges from brown through pink to purple; males have the brighter colors. Differences in plumage allow sexes of adults to be separated with a high degree of accuracy. Of the two subspecies occurring north of Mexico, the Interior race is somewhat paler and smaller than the Pacific Coast race, but individual variation produces overlaps in color and size.

Fig. 7-1. Close-up of band-tailed pigeon. (Photo by C. Fred Martinsen, Washington Department of Game.)

Immatures upon fledging are slate gray in appearance, with conspicuous buffy tipping on the wing and tail coverts and on the upper breast. They lack the white crescent and iridescent nape of the adult, characters that do not start to appear until the young are 80 to 90 days of age. By the appearance of wing coverts, primaries, and secondaries, young-of-the-year can be separated accurately from adults until they are about 300 to 340 days of age (White 1973).

Bandtails are powerful, swift fliers and have been observed to reach sustained speeds of over 60 mph (96.5 km per hr). When startled, they spring into the air with a distinctive clapping of wings both above and below the body. Courtship displays are similar to those of other Columbids and consist primarily of circular gliding-flapping aerial flights and a bowing-cooing pursuit of females. Females remain somewhat passive during displays by males, although there is mutual preening during courtship. Several types of calls are emitted by bandtails, ranging from a *chirping* or *chirring* call given during display flights and during times of aggression to the typical low-pitched cooing associated with mate-seeking and territoriality.

LIFE HISTORY

In late winter, flocks of band-tailed pigeons start working their way northward from the wintering range in Mexico and California. By early April, the vanguard has reached the northern limits of nesting in British Columbia and Colorado. Spring migration is essentially complete by the middle of May.

Some bandtails are ready to enter a breeding cycle immediately; this readiness is announced by perch calls and display flights of males. Bandtails evidence some territoriality, but it does not express itself in vigorous or continuous defense of an area with definite boundaries. Males exhibit aggressive behavior on some occasions of trespass by other males, but both members of a pair spend much time away from the nest, gregariously feeding in flocks. Nests may be loosely colonial in distribution (one nest to 3 or 4 acres — about one nest per 1 or 2 ha) or well dispersed (Neff 1947:11). Bandtails are believed to be monogamous, and males share in the activities of incubation, brooding, and feeding of the young.

Nests may be located either in conifers or in broad-leaved trees and vary in height from 8 to 180 feet (2.4 to 54.9 m) above the ground. A typical site is 15 to 40 feet (4.6 to 12.2 m) high on a horizontal limb or fork close to the trunk of the tree. Nest construction is similar to that of the mourning dove (*Zenaida macroura*); the nest usually consists of a loose collection of twigs in which little or no shaping has been done. The date of inception of nesting varies with latitude and altitude. In a nesting study at Carmel, California, the first egg-laying noted was 1 February (MacGregor and Smith 1955). It is probable that some bandtails are involved in nesting activities every month of the year, depending upon location. However, throughout the range most bandtails are in a breeding cycle from mid-May to late August.

Although one egg per nesting attempt appears to be most usual for the Coastal population, up to 8 percent of the nesting attempts by the Interior population may involve two eggs (Gutierrez 1973). Eggs, which are pure white, are incubated for about 18 to 20 days. Incubation is shared, males relieve the females usually before 1000 hours, and females return to relieve the males by late afternoon. Upon hatching, the altricial young are about 25 to 30 mm (1.0 to 1.2 in) long and are covered with fine yellow down. For the first few days of life, the young are fed almost exclusively on *pigeon milk*. This substance is produced as a mass of fatty, yellowish curds by the glandular walls of the crops of both parents. Beginning with three or more a day, feedings are reduced to one daily by each parent after the parents have ceased brooding the squab (Neff 1947:15, Peeters 1962:464). As the squab grows, the crop contents regurgitated by the parents are composed of an increasing proportion of berries and seeds until finally the food of the young is nearly identical to that of the adults.

Most adult pigeons are capable of initiating a second breeding cycle with little or no rest period. The squab is fledged in about 25 days after hatching;

the nesting cycle is 45 to 50 days. Rearing of multiple broods by marked, free-living bandtails has been documented in California, and there is ample indirect evidence that some of the adult population regularly raise two or three broods even in the northernmost nesting areas (MacGregor and Smith 1955, March and Sadleir 1970, Gutierrez 1973).

By late August, some bandtails probably have migrated south. In the northern half of the range, the major part of the exodus is over by late September. The pace of migration appears to be influenced, to some extent, by availability of food and by weather; small flocks in some years remain far north of the normal winter areas. Migration in the southern half of the range, through California, Arizona, and New Mexico, tends to be slower and less predictable.

Pigeons have learned to use several agricultural crops as food, and the appearance of large numbers of spring migrants coincides, in many areas, with the planting of grain or peas. Bandtails are efficient gleaners of any seed left uncovered in the planting process. Other major spring foods include acorns, terminal buds, blossoms, tender young leaves and needles, persisting berries, and a host of small green fruits, both wild and cultivated.

Summer foods reflect the increasing availability of berries and other fruits. Pigeons will visit stubble fields where early grain has been harvested. On occasion, they will take ripening cherries and green prunes. In some portions of the Interior range, throughout the spring, summer, and fall, bandtails are heavily dependent upon waste grain found in corrals and old grainfields.

In fall, bandtails return to a diet of acorns, pine nuts, and grains, supplemented by fruits that are still available. For most of the band-tailed pigeon population, the staple winter foods are acorns, pine nuts, and other seeds.

Bandtails prefer to feed exclusively on one species or source of food as long as the supply lasts. They are very adaptable to changing food conditions, a trait that contributes to their being characterized as erratic. One season may see excellent shooting over grainfields; the following fall, the birds may feed on berries or acorns in the foothills, and no pigeons may be bagged over fields that yielded hundreds the previous year.

Beginning with the arrival of warm days in spring or early summer, Coastal pigeons and, to a lesser extent, the Interior population seek sources of mineral salts. This craving appears to be related to increased physiological needs for certain minerals, including calcium and sodium salts, and one particular bit of evidence points to calcium as the main mineral involved (March and Sadleir 1972:282-283). On numerous occasions, pigeons have been known to visit areas where salt is placed for livestock. Natural sources include certain seashore areas and mineral springs. Use of these sites by bandtails continues into the fall, and the sites often become well-known pigeon concentration areas.

Natural mortality of band-tailed pigeons appears rarely to involve large numbers in any particular event. Most feeding flocks of pigeons are regularly harrassed by avian predators, and kills are frequently observed (Braun, unpublished data). However, except in one limited nesting-success study (MacGregor and Smith 1955), the effect of predation has not been evaluated for either adults or young. No major outbreaks of disease have been documented in band-tailed pigeons, although up to 20 percent in samples of pigeons examined have been infected with *Trichomonas* (Stabler and Matteson 1950). Studies of the Interior population have revealed that about 15 percent of the adults harbor helminths, although few birds are heavily infected. Hematozoa have been found in over 80 percent of the pigeons examined from the Interior population but in only 50 to 55 percent of those sampled from the Coastal population (Braun, unpublished data). No deleterious effects from either helminths or blood protozoa have been documented, and the impact of these parasites on pigeon populations is unknown. A study in Arizona on the occurrence of pesticides in bandtails did not indicate serious residue levels in monitored populations, although chlorinated hydrocarbons were present in the tissues of all pigeons examined (David E. Brown. 1969. Band-tailed pigeon management information. Arizona Department Game and Fish. Federal Aid Report. W-53-R-19-WP3. 11pp.).

HISTORICAL REVIEW

An excellent starting point for a survey of the literature on the band-tailed pigeon is the comprehensive natural history and status report by Neff (1947). Headings include history of knowledge of the species, natural history, distribution, value as a game bird, agricultural relationships, and food habits. Neff's publication has served as a guide in the preparation of the pre-1947 part of the present review.

The type specimen of the band-tailed pigeon was collected by the Long expedition in central Colorado and was described by Say in 1823. The Pacific Coast race of the bandtail was described by Vigors in 1839 as a separate species (American Ornithologists' Union 1957:259). In the early literature there are few specific references to numbers of this pigeon, but its abundance apparently did not approach that of the passenger pigeon (*Ectopistes migratorius*). Bendire (1892:122) quotes Captain William L. Carpenter as drawing such a comparison in reference to large numbers of bandtails near the mouth of the Columbia River in 1865. More specifically, Dr. George Suckley, writing of pigeons attracted to grainfields in the Puget Sound country in 1856, estimated that some flocks contained at least a thousand birds (Coues 1874: 386).

As a game bird, the bandtail was desirable enough to attract both sport and market hunters, but travel was slow, and access to areas where the bandtail could be hunted was limited. Most pigeon shooting in the Northwest occurred in spring over freshly planted grainfields. In California, market hunting was not important until early in this century. During the winter of 1911–12, at the time of a very large incursion of pigeons into Santa Barbara County, with a resulting hunting bonanza, one market hunter shipped 2,000 birds to San Francisco and Los Angeles (Chambers 1912, Smith 1968:13). Even before the concentrated kill of 1911–12, most ornithological writers believed that hunting had reduced pigeon numbers, and this incident provided the final impetus for restrictive legislation (Grinnell 1913).

In 1913, the band-tailed pigeon was one of the species designated for complete protection under the Weeks-McLean Law. Five years later, with the passage of the Migratory Bird Treaty Act, the ban on pigeon hunting was extended, and no open seasons were permitted until 1932. During the interim, pigeon populations responded vigorously, and complaints of crop damage multiplied. Special permits to kill pigeons in the spring were the most effective control measure, and soon these permits became so numerous that a fall hunting season seemed a more desirable management approach (Neff 1947:49-50, Smith 1968: 13). Hunting was resumed in 1932 in California, Oregon, Washington, Arizona, and New Mexico, with a 15-day season and a daily bag of 10. In 1944, Colorado joined the ranks of states allowing pigeon hunting, but hunting was again closed in that state in 1945 and in Arizona and New Mexico after the 1950 season. In 1968, seasons were again authorized in Arizona and New Mexico. Participation was limited through the issuance of permits, and the pigeon harvest was closely studied. Two years later, the same type of hunt was offered to hunters in Colorado and Utah. On the Pacific Coast, hunting regulations evolved into a 30-day season and a daily limit of 8, with California being split into northern and southern regions for an early and a late season, respectively.

From 1947 to 1965, interest in pigeon research built slowly. We found only five publications for this period that contained significant amounts of original information on the bandtail. In the mid-1960's, the tempo of studies increased as Oregon State University and, to a lesser extent, Humboldt State University undertook studies of band-tailed pigeons that were of vital interest to management. In 1967, the first Accelerated Research Program (ARP) funds provided incentive for research on pigeons by several states. A cooperative study of the Interior race of the bandtail was launched in Arizona, Colorado, New Mexico, and Utah; and coastal states either published results of previous research or made increased commitments to pigeon studies.

After Neff's monograph (1947), the next bandtail publication of importance was a nest study in northwestern California by Glover (1953). He investigated nesting ecology, made estimates of breeding density and production for a limited area, and found that cooing activity was synchronized with the breeding season. MacGregor and Smith (1955) conducted a nesting study in the Carmel area of California. They documented the fledging of three young (three broods) by one pair of pigeons in a single season. Of 26 nests studied, 17 (65 percent) were successful, 5 were unsuccessful, and the fate of 4 others was undetermined.

Peeters (1962) described breeding behavior, nesting, and feeding of pigeons at Berkeley, California. Houston (1963) studied breeding behavior and physiology in the Arcata, California, area. He evaluated age and sex criteria and found plumage coloration to be 87 percent accurate in determining sex of adult birds. Drewien et al. (1966), working in the same area, weighed 386 live adult bandtails and compared the utility of weight, plumage, and cloacal characters as sex criteria.

An analysis of recovery data from pigeon banding at Nehalem, Oregon, was published by Mace and Batterson (1961), and, subsequently, mortality estimates were prepared for this same population (Wight et al. 1967). Their report marked the first investigation of a possibly untenable management situation on the Pacific Coast. For years the Coastal race had been subjected to a continuing, substantial harvest, yet its productivity apparently was quite low. Wight et al. (1967) calculated a first-year adult mortality from all causes of 31.4 percent and tentatively ascribed a mortality of 14 percent to hunting. Thus, 45 percent of the total mortality was caused by hunting. On the basis of reasonable assumptions about productivity and immature mortality, they thought that annual replacement was adequate in this population.

Silovsky (1969), however, recalculated mortalities on the basis of the band-recovery data at Nehalem but for a shorter span of years characterized by higher and more uniform recovery rates. His first-year adult mortality estimate was 33.8 percent, with about 74 percent of the first-year mortality caused by hunting, and he showed even higher mortalities for populations banded in California and Washington. The net result was that the status of the Coast bandtail remained in some doubt.

Smith (1968) discussed aspects of bandtail ecology (other than nesting) in California. He analyzed recovery data from 3,084 pigeons banded in California and described their food habits and the damage they caused to agricultural crops. Weights and age and sex ratios in the hunting bag were sampled. The use of plumage characters provided 90 percent accuracy in sexing adults and 96 percent accuracy in identifying immatures in the bag.

Braun (1972), relying on plumage differences, correctly sexed 94 to 96 percent of two samples of Colorado bandtails. Silovsky et al. (1968) published a detailed description of age criteria for the bandtail and found that the use of wing plumage characteristics permitted workers to age correctly 97 percent of the pigeons bagged in September and October. Further, it was learned that the presence of a glandular bursa was proof of immaturity through December.

Sisson (1968) was the first to investigate the use of the coo call, or perch call, of the band-tailed pigeon as a basis for an audio census. A procedure similar to that of the mourning dove call route was tested in Oregon. Sisson concluded that, if the cooing proportion of the population did not change, the technique was capable of detecting population changes. Results of further testing and refinement of the technique were reported by Keppie et al. (1970). Effects of environmental factors were measured, and the precision of the index as related to sample size was calculated.

The most recent bandtail research report from Oregon State University was that of Zeigler (1971) on crop-milk cycles. In particular, he identified a daily crop-milk cycle and described its stages, which previously may have been confused with nesting-cycle phases of the crop gland found in adults killed in September. Zeigler estimated that between 3.5 and 7.2 percent of the annual production of nestlings would be lost if one or both parents were shot in September.

The reproductive physiology of bandtails in British Columbia was the subject of research by March and Sadleir (1970). They described the stages of the seasonal crop-gland cycle for the bandtail and monitored both crop development and gonadal cycles through the production season. Their evidence suggested that at least a part of the breeding population of the Fraser Valley produced two clutches containing one egg each in a single season. They noted that the shooting of adults in September probably resulted in some loss of squabs in the nest.

New information produced by the Four Corners States Cooperative Pigeon Study is contained in Braun (1972) and in unpublished reports (David E. Brown. 1972. Band-tailed pigeon management information. Arizona Department Game and Fish. Federal Aid Report. W-53-R-22-WP3. 15pp.; Thomas P. Zapatka. 1972. Band-tailed pigeon populations. New Mexico Game and Fish Department Federal Aid Report. W-104-R-12, WP12. 22pp.). These workers analyzed band-recovery information on pigeon mortality and distribution. In addition, Brown described the wintering range of the Interior race and Braun (1973) compared present and historical distribution of pigeons in Colorado and related distribution and relative abundance to vegetation and physical features of the environment.

In the above review of the more recent bandtail research, only those titles that represent substantial, original work exclusively with this species have been included. These publications have supplied the supporting structure and the tools of present planning and investigation. Articles of a general or popular nature on bandtails have not been included, nor have numerous papers dealing with the taxonomy and parasitology of Columbids. For a recent, readable, and thorough review of bandtail literature, the reader is referred to Fitzhugh (1970).

DISTRIBUTION AND DENSITY

The physiographic unit called the Pacific Mountain System (Hunt 1967:375) encompasses the range of the Coastal race of the band-tailed pigeon (Fig. 7-2). Except for small, local, or transient flocks, however, pigeons do not range down the eastern slopes of the thousand-mile-long Cascade-Sierra Mountains. The principal exceptions are the Wenatchee Mountains in Washington, the forested regions of Hood River and Wasco counties in Oregon, and the Susanville-Bishop area of northeastern California. North of the Fraser River in British

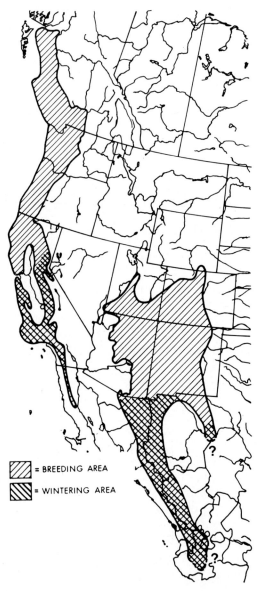

Fig. 7-2. Principal breeding and wintering distribution of the band-tailed pigeon, showing the ranges of the Interior and Pacific Coast races.

Columbia, the approximate eastern limit of pigeon observations is the Canadian Coast Range divide; the northern limit is the Skeena River. South into Baja California and west to the Pacific Ocean, summer populations of the band-tailed pigeon occupy most of the forest, woodland, and chaparral areas. Included is the whole of Vancouver Island and most other islands south along the coast.

The Interior race of the band-tailed pigeon occupies suitable habitat from north central Colorado and southern Wyoming west into southern and central Utah and throughout the forested and wooded mountains of Arizona, New Mexico, and west Texas. Although the exact distribution in Mexico is unknown, scattered breeding records are available for the pine-oak forests along the crest of the Sierra Madre Occidental Mountains from western Chihuahua to eastern Sonora and south to Guatemala (Fig. 7-2).

It is estimated that fewer than 5,000 pigeons winter north of California in the coastal habitat. According to the California Department of Fish and Game (1966), about one million bandtails winter in that state, and these mostly south of the latitude of San Francisco Bay. The coastal wintering range extends south in Baja California along the crests of the mountains to about 30 degrees north latitude. Wintering in the interior north of Mexico is irregular, with small numbers remaining in New Mexico and Arizona in some years. This occurrence apparently is related to the availability of food. To the extent that band recoveries indicate the distribution of pigeons, it appears that the bulk of the Interior population winters in the Sierra Madres of Sinaloa and Durango. The relative importance of the several states in the maximal bandtail range is summarized in Table 7-1.

Little reliable information on densities, either comparative or quantitative, exists for Coastal populations of the band-tailed pigeon. In Washington, an audio census indicates that summer-resident pigeons may be concentrated mostly below 1,000 feet (305 m) in altitude during the peak of the nest season. Also, few data are available concerning pigeon densities anywhere in the interior. At times, as many as 1,500 birds have been observed feeding in 200 acres (80.9 ha) or less. However, densities such as this are not representative of the entire range, and banding studies in Colorado have documented daily movements of up to 20 air miles (32.2 km) in 1 day during the breeding period. Present data indicate that densities may range from 1 pair of pigeons per square mile (0.4 per km²) of suitable breeding habitat to as high as 10 pairs per square mile (3.8 pairs per km²) locally. Highest population densities are closely correlated with the presence of mast-producing trees and shrubs.

DESCRIPTION OF RANGE

The Coastal pigeon range embraces a wide spectrum of climatic variation. Such a variation is predictable, for the range spans 23 degrees of latitude and

Table 7-1. Seasonal occurrences of the band-tailed pigeon and comparative amounts of habitat, by state.

State	Occurrence by Period[a]			Trend	Square Miles of Habitat		
	Breeding	Hunting	Winter		Breeding	Hunting	Winter
Arizona	C	C	U	Stable	18,300	18,300	Trace
California	C	C	C	Stable	43,000	10,300	6,500
Colorado	C	C	U	Stable	20,000	20,000	0
Idaho	P	P	A	ND	ND	ND	0
Montana	P	P	A	ND	ND	ND	0
Nevada	P	P	U	ND	ND	ND	Trace
New Mexico	C	C	U	Stable	21,000	21,000	Trace
Oregon	C	C	P	Stable	12,500	12,500	Trace
Texas	P	P	P	ND	ND	ND	Trace
Utah	C	C	A	Stable	2,500	2,500	0
Washington	C	C	P	Stable	21,000	21,000	Trace
Wyoming	P	P	A	ND	ND	ND	0

[a] C = common: established population consistent with the amount of habitat available; P = peripheral: present in most years but distribution is limited and local; U = uncommon: sporadic, not present in most years; and A = absent: does not exclude occasional sighting.

14,000 feet (4,268 m) of elevation, and the axes of the principal mountain ranges tend to be perpendicular to the prevailing westerly winds (Hunt 1967: 394-395). Throughout the length of the range, however, temperatures are moderated to a surprising degree by the oceanic influence, and precipitation tends strongly toward a seasonal pattern of winter-wet and summer-dry.

The northern half of the range of this subspecies lies within the coast forest formation (Weaver and Clements 1938:500-504). In Washington, the formation is typified by the dominants, western hemlock (*Tsuga heterophylla*), red cedar (*Thuja plicata*), and Douglas fir (*Pseudotsuga menziesii*). These species persist throughout, but in British Columbia, Sitka spruce (*Picea sitchensis*) becomes more important, whereas Port Orford cedar (*Chamaecyparis lawsoniana*) is more prevalent in southwestern Oregon. Redwood (*Sequoia sempervirens*) predominates in the fog belt of north coastal California. Red alder (*Alnus rubra*) and broadleaf maple (*Acer macrophyllum*) are conspicuous deciduous species throughout the coast forest. Most of the trees and shrubs that produce the pigeon foods of this community occur as understory but reach their best growth and fruit production as members of a subsere after logging or fire. Some of the more important food species are cascara (*Rhamnus purshiana*), elderberries (*Sambucus* spp.), wild cherries (*Prunus* spp.), huckleberries (*Vaccinium* spp.), western flowering dogwood (*Cornus nuttallii*), and Pacific madrone (*Arbutus menziesii*). The coast forest hosts only a few scattered flocks of wintering pigeons.

South of Oregon's Willamette Valley, the bandtail habitat becomes more diverse. The Sierran montane forest makes its appearance to the east of the coast forest, with major dominants consisting of ponderosa pine (*Pinus ponderosa*), white fir (*Abies concolor*), incense cedar (*Libocedrus decurrens*), and Douglas fir. Of particular value to the bandtails within this association are California black oak (*Quercus kelloggii*), Oregon oak (*Q. garryana*), and madrone. The Sierran montane forest extends the length of the Sierras, throughout the transverse ranges, and into Baja California. Its lower limits range from 2,000 feet (610 m) in the Cascades to 5,000 feet (1,524 m) in southern California. Recovery from fire or logging is slower than in the coast forest and may involve a long-persisting chaparral subclimax. From Nevada County, California, south, the montane forest serves as both breeding and winter range for pigeons.

Two other extensive plant communities originate in the pigeon range of southern Oregon. The pine-oak woodland association and the coastal chaparral often occupy the drier slopes below the conifer forests, with the chaparral being the more xeric. Both extend south through the Sierra foothills, the Coast Range, and the transverse ranges, and into Baja California. There is considerable mixing of the two associations, particularly in the Coast Range. Woodland dominants include digger pine (*Pinus sabiniana*), blue oak (*Quercus douglasii*), interior live oak (*Q. wislizenii*), piñon pine (*P. edulis*), huckleberry oak (*Q. vaccinifolia*), coffeeberry (*Rhamnus californica*), and California juniper (*Juniperus californica*). The coastal chaparral is composed mainly of evergreen shrubs, of which chamise (*Adenostoma fasciculatum*) is one of the most prevalent. There are numerous species of both manzanita (*Arctostaphylos* spp.) and buckbrush (*Ceanothus* spp.). Scrub oak (*Q. dumosa*) is the one important deciduous component of the coastal chaparral. The oak species mentioned for both associations, as well as piñon, manzanita, and juniper, have been listed as pigeon-food plants (Neff 1947:51-52, Smith 1968:7-9). South from San Francisco Bay, bandtails may be found in these habitats every month of the year.

Bandtails seasonally occupy a wide variety of habitats in the interior, ranging from agricultural areas near forests to berry-producing areas at about 11,000 feet (3,354 m). In the northern areas (Utah, Colorado, and portions of New Mexico), pigeons occur sparsely in the spruce-fir association (petran subalpine forest), which is characterized by Engelmann spruce (*Picea engelmanni*) and alpine fir (*Abies lasiocarpa*), and the subclimax species — lodgepole pine (*Pinus contorta*), limber pine (*P. flexilis*), and aspen (*Populus tremuloides*). Numbers apparently are highest at lower altitudes in areas dominated by ponderosa pine and Gambel oak (*Quercus gambelii*) (petran montane forest). Some pigeons, especially during feeding, are found in areas characterized by commercial orchards and piñon-juniper woodland. Stream courses dominated by cottonwoods (*Populus* spp.) and adjacent grainfields are often of major importance during the breeding and premigration periods. The breeding habitats used by bandtails in Arizona have been described as Rocky Mountain [petran] montane forest, Mexican pine-oak, and encinal (*Quercus*) woodlands (David E. Brown and Charles H. Lowe. 1973. A proposed classification for natural and potential vegetation in the Southwest with particular reference to Arizona. Arizona Department Game and Fish. Federal Aid Report. Appendix I of W-53-R-22-WP4. *xvii* pp.). Feeding pigeons in Arizona also are frequently observed in interior chaparral, less frequently in piñon-juniper, and occasionally in grassland or desert scrub.

Preliminary, limited data indicate that bandtails wintering in Mexico make extensive use of the pine-oak woodland and the montane conifer forest along the crest of the Sierra Madres in late fall and up to midwinter. At that time food supplies possibly become limited, and pigeons can then be found feeding throughout the subtropical deciduous and thorn scrub at elevations as low as 800 feet (244 m). Apparently pigeons can even be found in Sonoran desert scrub prior to northward migration. It thus appears that, in the interior, band-tailed pigeons breed and nest in a variety of coniferous-dominated forests ranging from 4,000 to 11,000 feet (1,220 to 3,354 m) in height and running from central Mexico at least as far north as northern Colorado and south central Utah. They winter primarily in mixed coniferous-deciduous forests from southern New Mexico and Arizona into central Mexico at elevations from 8,000 to as low as 800 feet (2,439 to 244 m).

CENSUS PROCEDURES AND POPULATION TRENDS

Preseason counts of pigeons at concentration areas have been made in Oregon for more than 20 years. The same technique was used in Washington from 1961 through 1964. In both states, the count was made in late August, and sites were either mineral springs or tidewater areas used heavily by pigeons in warm weather. In 1972, 21 concentration areas were censused in Oregon, whereas 10 was the maximum number of sites used in the Washington survey. Biologists in both states have concluded that weather conditions at the time of the census have a strong influence on the number of bandtails counted. Cool, rainy weather drastically lowers the use of salting areas by pigeons, and the effect may involve a large area for a period of a week or more.

In California, from 1960 through 1963, efforts were made to conduct surveys of population trends by counts at permanent observation stations and by roving counts after the breeding season and before the hunting season. These surveys failed to show trends in the population. Before the 1963 season, field reports were submitted listing the locations of winter concentrations of pigeons, and an aerial survey was attempted for some areas. Few pigeons were seen, and efforts to flush birds by low-level flying failed. In 1964, a post-hunting season survey was initiated. Permanent stations were not established, because pigeon concentration areas changed from year to year. An attempt was made to locate such areas each year before the census period. After conducting this survey for

5 years, workers concluded that they were counting a small and highly variable percentage of the total population. The nomadic habits of pigeons, weather conditions, and lack of access roads in certain parts of the wintering range were responsible for the unreliable data.

Experience with a system of randomized audio-census routes in Washington over a 3-year period (1971–73) has demonstrated the operational practicability of the technique in that state. However, the number of pigeons heard per route is not an estimate of the number of breeding males within a specified area and cannot be used to calculate breeding density.

The three Pacific Coast states conduct annual harvest surveys, the results of which should have high year-to-year comparability. These surveys showed no discernible trend in bandtail harvest from 1957 to 1972 (Table 7-2, Fig. 7-3), and it is likely that this stability reflected the status of the population over the same period. Since

$$harvest = population \times harvest \ rate,$$

the harvest indicates the population only when the harvest rate is constant. We have no evidence pertaining to Coastal bandtails that there has been any sustained trend in harvest-rate fluctuations since 1957. However, even from the long-range view, pigeon harvest by itself is an unsatisfactory indicator of the

Table 7-2. Estimates of harvest and hunters for the Pacific Coast race of the band-tailed pigeon north of Mexico, based on questionnaires. The data were not adjusted for reporting bias.

Year	California		Oregon		Washington		Totals[a]		British Columbia	
	Harvest	Hunters	Harvest	Hunters	Harvest	Hunters	Harvest	Hunters	Harvest	Hunters
1957	255,000	32,900	93,900	14,600	74,000		422,900			
1958	195,200	28,000	122,200	20,300	72,800		390,200			
1959	156,700	26,800	86,000	13,100	90,500		333,200			
1960	310,300	36,900	87,000	13,100	86,900		484,200			
1961	233,100	27,600	121,000	15,000	94,200		448,300			
1962	337,800	45,800	121,400	14,100	104,000		563,200			
1963	248,500	33,700	90,500	12,000	92,600		431,600			
1964	242,500	36,700	103,900	12,500	126,700	17,300	473,100	66,500		
1965	206,600	28,800	105,200	12,600	158,100	20,300	469,900	61,700		
1966	321,600	36,400	121,100	12,400	158,000	22,300	600,700	71,100		
1967	260,100	44,000	82,200	9,900	109,100	16,400	451,400	70,300	14,600	1,700
1968	307,000	44,300	94,500	12,300	152,400	22,600	553,900	79,200	16,300	1,900
1969	215,900	42,200	84,600	11,300	95,500	18,600	396,000	72,100	11,400	1,700
1970	181,100	33,000	99,400	12,900	120,300	20,700	400,800	66,600	11,600	1,700
1971	285,800	38,000	84,300	10,800	129,800	19,900	499,900	68,700	9,100	1,300
1972	536,800	50,900	87,100	11,500	100,500	18,500	724,400	80,900	11,300	1,700

[a] The totals do not include British Columbia.

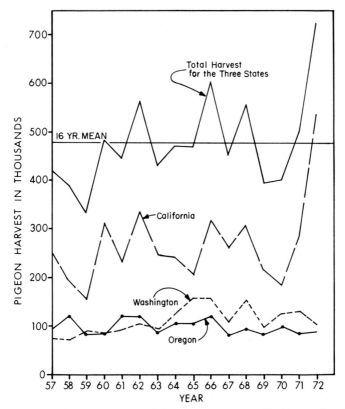

Fig. 7-3. Band-tailed pigeon harvest for California, Oregon, and Washington, based on game questionnaires. The horizontal line represents the 16-year mean for the three-state harvest.

population. Weather, food availability, and other factors may cause large annual fluctuations in the kill, and the time lag in identifying a trend is likely to be excessive.

No valid census techniques have been developed for use in the interior. Attempts have been made in Arizona, Colorado, and Utah to utilize both a call count and a fall census. No calling pigeons were heard on arbitrarily selected routes in Colorado and Utah. Presently, Arizona and Colorado are estimating pigeon numbers on the basis of bandings, recaptures, and recoveries; their methods are modifications of such established techniques as those commonly referred to as the Jolly (recaptures) and Seber (recoveries) methods. Fluctuations in populations of pigeons in Arizona appear to depend on food supply. Populations in Colorado and Utah, although exhibiting some fluctuations in localized areas, appear stable. Respondents from New Mexico are not prepared at this time to comment on trends in numbers, but it is probable that some parts of the state are similar to Colorado and other parts are more like Arizona. No meaningful long-term trends in numbers are available from any of the interior states. It is probable that banding and harvest trends will continue to give the best data for estimating pigeon numbers in this region.

CURRENT HARVEST AND HUNTING PRESSURE

Harvest statistics for bandtails are listed in Table 7-3 for states open to hunting. Harvest estimates for Arizona, Colorado, New Mexico, and Utah are based upon hunting permits and have high reliability. Harvest estimates for the Coastal race of the bandtail depend upon postseason hunter questionnaires. These vary as to format and sample size, but probably all share the inflationary biases described by Atwood (1956). However, the method employed in each state has remained relatively constant; trends in estimates based on questionnaires should represent actual changes in harvest and hunting pressure.

Hunting statistics are available for California, Oregon, and Washington for the past 16 years (1957–72) (Table 7-2). Data for British Columbia are shown for 1967–72 (Benson 1968, 1969, 1970, 1971, Cooch et al. 1973). From 1967 through 1972, the total harvest averaged 517,000 pigeons, the mean number of pigeon hunters was 74,600, and the average season bag was 6.9 pigeons. California hunters took 58 percent of the total harvest, Washington 23 percent, Oregon 17 percent, and British Columbia about 2 percent.

No comprehensive study of crippling loss from bandtail hunting has been made, but this kind of loss is known to be high in the dense cover and rough terrain of many Pacific Coast shooting areas (Fig. 7-4). Hunters interviewed as they left mineral-spring areas in Washington reported a crippling loss of 34 percent of the bag (Carl V. Swanson. 1965. Band-tailed pigeon research studies, 1964. Washington Department of Game Administrative Report. 7pp.).

Table 7-3. Current and potential harvest of band-tailed pigeons in states open to hunting in 1972.

State	Estimated Number of Hunters	Estimated Days Each Hunter Hunted	Estimated Total Days Hunted	Estimated Harvest	Additional Hunting Potential
Arizona	1,427[a]	1.8	2,569	453	Yes
California	50,900[a]	3.2	164,200	536,800	Yes[b]
Colorado	562[a]	2.6	1,461	822[c]	Yes
New Mexico	1,080[a]	2.4	2,592	3,313[c]	Yes
Oregon	11,500	4.5	51 400	87,100	No
Utah	121	1.9	230	211	Yes
Washington	18,500	3.6	66,600	100,500	Unknown
Total	84,090	3.4	289,052	729,199	

[a] Number of permits issued.
[b] Dependent upon opening private lands to hunting.
[c] Includes crippling loss.

Fig. 7-4. Heavily hunted slope overlooking a mineral spring near Clear Lake in western Washington. Dense ground cover is largely responsible for an estimated crippling loss of 34 percent of the bag in this type of habitat in Washington. (Photo by Robert Jeffrey.)

Fig. 7-5. Pigeon hunting is enjoyed by relatively few hunters in New Mexico. Here, as in other states of the Interior range, some potential exists for increased harvest, but localized overhunting might occur under fuller exploitation. (Photo by James L. Sands, New Mexico Department of Game & Fish.)

Because in modern times hunting of bandtails in the interior is of fairly recent origin, no long-term data are available on the numbers of hunters and the kill. The average number of hunters per state per year since the pigeon seasons were reopened has been about 50 in Utah, 450 in Colorado, and from 800 to 1,000 each in Arizona and New Mexico. Overall, hunting pressure is low, but hunters tend to concentrate in localized areas, thus posing a possible threat of overharvest of local flocks. To date, the harvest has not been excessive; the known harvest varies from about 150 birds per year in Utah to 1,000 in Colorado and up to slightly over 3,000 each in good years in Arizona and New Mexico (Fig. 7-5). Total harvest of the Interior population north of Mexico is between 5,000 and 10,000 birds per year, with the Mexican harvest probably of similar size.

POTENTIAL HARVEST

There is no obvious situation of either over- or underharvest in Coastal populations of the band-tailed pigeon. That is not to say that either condition, or both, may not exist, and we do not imply that the apparent stability of the resource can easily be maintained under increasing demand. According to the California Department of Fish and Game (1966), there will be in that state by 1980 from 41,000 to 55,000 pigeon hunters with a maximum bag of 400,000 birds. The unprecedented 1972 harvest exceeded the 1980 projection by a third, and the number of hunters approached the upper limit. The conditions that resulted in the 1972 harvest may not obtain again for many years, but that harvest underlines the need for better knowledge of pigeon productivity and mortality.

Smith (1968) gave a first-year mortality estimate of 38.2 percent for young and adults banded in California. Wight et al. (1967) calculated the first-year mortality for adult pigeons banded at Nehalem, Oregon, at 31.4 percent. In addition, they calculated hunting mortality to be 14 percent. Using a direct-recovery rate of 0.03 and a crippling-loss rate of 0.34 (Swanson 1965, unpublished report), and assuming a band-reporting rate of 0.30, we can calculate a kill-rate of 0.134. This estimate is in fair agreement with the above estimate of hunting mortality. However, Silovsky (1969) found a higher total mortality and also found that a higher share of the total mortality was attributable to hunting. For comparison with the hunting-mortality estimate of 14 percent made by Wight et al. (1967), we have expressed the hunting-mortality calculations of Silovsky (1969) in the same terms, as follows: Nehalem, Oregon, banding, 24.9 percent; Reedsport, Oregon, 21.2 percent; and Washington, 20.5 percent. If real hunting mortalities fall within the range set by Silovsky's estimates, a substantially larger crippling loss, a lower reporting rate, or some combination of the two is operating. Such conditions would increase the uncertainty regarding present and potential harvests and would give a high priority to more extensive work on pigeon mortality and productivity.

The present total harvest of the Interior population could probably be doubled with no harm to the overall population. It is possible, however, that local flocks or subpopulations could be adversely affected by concentrated hunting.

SPECIES NEEDS

Habitat

General. — In Oregon and Washington, forest land with a good interspersion of seral stages and openings probably provides the best bandtail habitat. In California, good habitat includes forest, woodland, or chaparral in which there is an abundance of oak. The occurrence of pine and oak betokens good pigeon habitat throughout the Interior range.

Food. — Food controls the distribution and abundance of bandtails much more frequently than any other factor. Berries, mast, other fruits, buds, flowers, grain, and other cultivated crops are sought out in season.

Nesting. — Trees, either conifer or broad-leaved, are needed; apparent preference is given to sites with moderate to steep slopes.

Water. — Smith (1968) states that water is required daily. Glover (1953) lists permanent water as one of the factors that appears to control the size and spacing of nesting territories. It is doubtful if water is limiting over an appreciable unit of habitat.

Minerals. — Mineral springs and seashores are heavily used by pigeons in spring and fall in California, and in summer in Oregon and Washington. Some populations thrive where mineral water apparently is not available, and, except in Arizona, Interior pigeons do not seem to be as strongly attracted to mineral sources. However, the Coastal bandtail's desire for certain minerals has important management implications.

Population
The primary need of the bandtail population is for conditions under which recruitment of young to adult ranks is at least equal, on the average, to adult mortality.

PUBLIC NEEDS

Access to Resource
The public should be guaranteed the opportunity for maximum safe use of the band-tailed pigeon resource, including access to traditional pigeon concentration areas, whether the desired use is hunting, viewing, or photography.

Management
The public has a right to expect enlightened and sound management of the band-tailed pigeon, with the objective of maintaining optimum numbers throughout the range of the species.

Information
The public should be kept informed on the status of the bandtail and on both the needs and the progress of management. It should be instructed in hunting methods and be kept apprised of hunting or viewing opportunities.

MANAGEMENT NEEDS
Both management and research objectives originate in the needs of the bandtail resource and its users. These objectives may be grouped into three categories: (1) information on pigeon numbers, trends, survival rates, and hunting mortalities — that is, on the status of the resource; (2) optimum use of the resource; and (3) information on the status of the habitat. Secondary objectives under these major funding areas are briefly justified and cost estimates

developed in the following pages. An abridgment of this information is presented in Table 7-4.

Expenditures recommended for management procedures and projects for the fiscal decade 1977–86 amount to $2,012,000 and are distributed between the Interior pigeon range and the Coastal range, 13 and 87 percent, respectively. Exclusive of the acquisition of mineral areas, the need for which is confined to the coast, costs would total $1,012,000, with 26 percent for the management of the Interior race and 74 percent for the Pacific Coast bandtail.

Status of the Resource

Population Indices. — These should provide annual estimates of population size or density by area. The randomized call count is an index to the status of the adult population of the bandtail in summer. It is operationally feasible in Washington and has been intensively tested in Oregon. There is concern that the road network in California pigeon habitat is not adequate for the sampling design used in Washington. Lack of roads would undoubtedly be even more of a problem in British Columbia. Route counts conducted in the interior have detected no calling pigeons except on a limited area in Arizona. Until the results of research studies are available, however, the call count should be conducted as part of the management surveys over as much of the range of the Coast pigeon as possible.

The cost has been about $28 per one-run route in Washington, although $40 might be a more realistic estimate for the next 2 or 3 years. To have a 90 percent probability of detecting a 20 percent change in numbers of calling pigeons between 2 years, at least 131 one-run routes would be needed (Keppie et al. 1970). About 100 more routes would have to be added to yield 131 operational routes. The cost of installing a random-route system would about equal the cost of one coverage. The initial cost for the Pacific Coast would be about $4,000, and the annual cost would run about $6,000.

A winter-survey procedure is to be developed (see RESEARCH NEEDS). The plans to make population surveys of the Interior race are discussed under *Banding.*

Banding. — A banding program should provide annual information on harvest rates and contribute data for periodic revisions of estimates of mortality rates, patterns and rates of migration, relative vulnerability (by age and sex) to hunting, and evaluation of production and harvest areas. The reporting rate should be evaluated periodically through reward-banding projects (see RESEARCH NEEDS). For the Interior subspecies, banding (Fig. 7-6) is presently the only feasible method of determining population size. Pending results of the census study, banding should be a part of the annual management surveys of the interior. Yearly costs would be about $5,000 per state, or $20,000. There are presently no prospects of extending the study to Mexico. The design

Table 7-4. Budget requirements for a 10-year band-tailed pigeon management plan.

Major Program or Area for Funding	Specific Jobs Within Each Program	Research or Management (R or M)	Job Priority	Estimated Cost of Jobs for Each Fiscal Year (in thousands of dollars)										Total Cost by Job (thousands)	Continuing Job
				1	2	3	4	5	6	7	8	9	10		
Status of the Resource	Develop breeding-population index	R	1	22	22	19	16	8						$ 87	No
	Develop banding capability, band for research needs, and evaluate banding data	R	2	66	50	48	44	42	30	30				310	No
	Conduct annual breeding-population survey	M	3	10	6	6	6	6	6	6	6	6	6	64	Yes
	Perform annual maintenance banding	M	4	20	20	20	20	20	20	20	50	50	50	290	Yes
	Develop and evaluate harvest surveys	R	5	8	8	8	8	28	20					80	No
	Conduct harvest surveys	M	6	8	8	8	8	8	8	8	8	8	8	80	Yes
	Define, describe, and interrelate production and harvest areas	R	8			8	8	8	43	43	8	8	8	134	No
	Develop production index	R	9						8	8	8			24	No
Total Cost of Program per Fiscal Year				134	114	117	110	120	135	115	80	72	72	1,069	
Use of the Resource	Insure access to and regulate human use of concentration areas:														
	Develop areas	M	7		32	64	128	64	32					320	No
	Maintain areas	M	7			1	2	5	6	7	7	7	7	42	Yes
	Regulate hunting and enforce regulations	M	13	36	36	36	36	36	36	36	36	36	36	360	Yes

Program	Type	No.	1	2	3	4	5	6	7	8	9	10	Total	Meets objective
Inform public on status of resource and progress of management	M	14	10	10	10	10	10	10	10	10	10	10	100	Yes
Develop habitat and enhance viewing areas	M	15	13	5	5	5	5	5	5	5	5	5	58	Yes
Control crop damage with minimal effect on populations	M	16	6	6	6	6	6	6	6	6	6	6	60	Yes
Total Cost of Program per Fiscal Year			65	89	122	187	126	95	64	64	64	64	940	
Status of the Habitat: Determine habitat requirements	R	10					16	16	16				48	No
Complete a habitat inventory	R	11							47	46			93	No
Determine habitat threats and develop management guidelines	R	12								8	8		16	No
Total Cost of Program per Fiscal Year							16	16	63	54	8		157	
Grand Total Cost of all Programs by Fiscal Year for 10-Year Period			199	203	239	297	246	246	195	207	190	144	2,166	
Habitat Acquisition[a]	M	7	64	128	255	128	63						638	No

[a] See Table 7-5 for details.

of the maintenance banding program for the Pacific Coast should await re-search findings on the comparative effectiveness of different banding periods, the distribution of bandtails, and the optimum number of birds to be banded. Starting in the year after the termination of the research project in 1983–84, annual costs for summer maintenance banding would be about $30,000 for California, Oregon, and Washington combined, and $50,000 range wide. The 10-year program total would be $290,000.

Harvest Surveys. — The wing survey should furnish an annual measure of productivity in addition to showing the geographic distribution of the kill. It should provide early data on the success of the season. In Washington, the mail survey has cost no more than $1.25 per wing, and the total cost has been about $1,400 per year. Cost of a mail survey in Oregon would be approximately $1,000. California's field-collection effort would cost about the same, for a three-state total of $3,400. Wing collection for all interior states would cost about $2,000.

The harvest questionnaire should provide an annual estimate of the number of hunters, an annual list of pigeon hunters' names for use in the wing survey, and an annual estimate of the harvest by county or other subdivision of the state. On the basis of man-days of hunting furnished by bandtails, it is thought that pigeon management should bear about 2 percent of the cost of the annual harvest questionnaire. This cost would amount to $800 for California, $280 for Oregon, and $240 for Washington. The total annual cost would come to $1,320. Costs for this survey in the interior would be $1,000.

Because the field interview is relatively costly, and because it is difficult to insure that a representative sample of hunters is being interviewed, field inter-viewing may not be justified by the amount of management information that it yields. If, however, field checking is done as a regular part of hunting-season patrol, and if proper safeguards are used, it may serve as an alternative to the wing-mail survey and provide, as well, useful data on hunting success, crippling loss, sex composition of the bag, and development of the crop gland.

Use of the Resource

Concentration Areas. — Management and public-use rights should be acquired by purchase, lease, or easement for those traditional pigeon concentration areas where present ownership does not guarantee their continuing value to birds or to the public. Problems of public access occur mostly with privately owned mineral springs and seashore areas in Oregon and Washington, but access to some sites on public land in California is denied by owners of peripheral private lands. Acquisition costs are estimated at $35,000 for California, $310,000 for Oregon, and $293,000 for Washington (Table 7-5). In addition, development and maintenance costs for these states through 1984–85 would be $320,000 and $42,000, respectively. Thus, the total expenditure for the 10-year period would be $1 million. No acquisition program is proposed for states in the Interior

Fig. 7-6. Bandtails feeding in a small grain-field in New Mexico have been detained by a rocket net until they can be banded. Band-recovery and recapture data are the best sources of pigeon-population estimates in the Interior range. (Photo by Jerry Maracchini, New Mexico Department of Game & Fish.)

Fig. 7-7. Cannon-net trapping at a mineral spring near woodland in western Washington. In warm weather, coastal pigeons typically touch the ground only at mineral springs and are on the ground for only a few seconds each day. Banding adequate samples of young and adults will be extremely difficult and expensive. (Photo by Robert Jeffrey.)

range of the bandtail; nearly all concentration areas in that range are on public (national forest) lands.

Hunting. — Hunting seasons and bag limits should be set to achieve the proper bandtail harvest, with results of the management surveys serving as a guide. Also, shooting at mineral sites should be managed for the best distribution of hunting pressure and minimizing of crippling losses (Wight 1966). In certain regions, hunting mortality probably could be effectively controlled through regulation of hunting on mineral areas. That part of the enforcement budget chargeable to pigeons was estimated as follows: California, $10,900; Oregon, $10,000; Washington, $8,600; and the United States Fish and Wildlife Service, $6,000, for an annual total of approximately $36,000. In the interior, the pigeon resource makes little demand upon law-enforcement services.

Public Information. — Agencies charged with responsibilities for pigeon man-agement should use their regular facilities and those of the news media to keep the public informed on hunting and viewing opportunities, methods and ethics of pigeon hunting, status of the pigeon resource, and progress of the research and management programs.

Annual costs of disseminating such information were estimated as follows: Arizona, $100; California, $1,200; Oregon, $300; and Washington, $600, for a total annual cost of $2,200. This amount reflects the portion of Information and Education budgets chargeable to pigeons on the basis of hunting recreation provided. Even so, it was thought that a more appropriate level of support for this program would be at least $10,000 annually for the seven-state total.

Habitat Development. — Our present knowledge of bandtails does not suggest any important practical opportunities for habitat alteration specifically to bene-

Table 7-5. Summary of needs for acquisition of band-tailed pigeon concentration areas on the Pacific Coast.

State	Area	County	Type of Area	Action	Size of Area (acres)	Cost
Washington	Cavanaugh Road	Skagit	Mineral Spring	Purchase	40	$ 21,000
	St. Martin	Skamania	Mineral Spring	Purchase	100	75,000
	Newaukum	Lewis	Mineral Spring	Purchase	120	60,000
	Green River	Cowlitz	Mineral Spring	Purchase	80	40,000
	Cedar Creek	Clark	Mineral Spring	Purchase	50	35,000
	Pigeon Bluff	Wahkiakum	Mineral Spring	Purchase	200	40,000
	Outlet Creek	Klickitat	Mineral Spring	Purchase	5	1,250
	Warm Beach	Snohomish	Seashore	Permanent Hunting Easement	3	7,500
	Sumas	Whatcom	Mineral Spring	Purchase	15	13,000
Subtotal						292,750
Oregon	Long Tom	Benton	Mineral Spring	Purchase	50	20,000
	Dutch Canyon	Columbia	Mineral Spring	Purchase	20	10,000
	Clatskanie	Columbia	Mineral Spring	Purchase	80	24,000
	Blueslide	Coos	Tidal Area	Purchase	100	30,000
	Parkersburg	Coos	Tidal Area	Purchase	80	24,000
	Hudson Slough	Douglas	Tidal Area	Purchase	50	20,000
	Cushman	Lane	Tidal Area	Purchase	40	16,000
	Cheshire	Lane	Mineral Spring	Purchase	20	10,000
	Drift Creek	Lincoln	Tidal Area	Purchase	60	30,000
	Crawfordsville	Linn	Mineral Spring	Purchase	80	32,000
	Aurora	Marion	Mineral Spring	Purchase	40	32,000
	Nehalem	Tillamook	Tidal Area	Purchase	80	56,000
	Fairdale	Yamhill	Mineral Spring	Purchase	20	6,000
Subtotal						310,000
California	Big Bend	Shasta	Mineral Spring	Purchase	200	8,200
	Brian Beaver	Butte	Mineral Spring	Purchase	190	20,000
	Bangor	Butte	Mineral Spring	Purchase	20.74	7,000
Subtotal						35,200
Grand Total						637,950

fit this bird. There are possibilities of minor projects on state game lands and federal refuges. If it is assumed that there is a shortage of pigeon foods in spring, those installations that plant grain for other wildlife species could broadcast or drill extra grain on the surface of the ground at little expense. Pigeons are not known to use standing grain; thus, there would seem to be little reason for planting food patches.

Pigeons should be available on public wildlife areas for the public to view and photograph. Use by bandtails could be encouraged by providing grain and salt during the closed season. The Oregon Game Commission has developed an artificial mineral spring that has attracted pigeons. State wildlife-recreation areas and federal refuges in western Washington offer six or eight sites where salt and food could be provided. A by-product benefit of making such provisions would be the availability of pigeons for study and banding. Costs are estimated at $500 per installation for the first year, with $200 needed for annual maintenance. Costs for all three Pacific Coast states are estimated at $13,000 for the first year and $5,000 per year thereafter.

Crop Depredation Control. — In recent years, crop depredations by pigeons have become less important; the last serious damage in California was in 1958. Coastal states receive no more than 60 complaints a year for a combined cost of $3,000. Crop damage in the interior involves scattered instances of pigeons feeding on ripening cherries; costs are estimated at about the same level as on the Pacific Coast, for a combined annual cost of $6,000. Wildlife agencies should remain alert to prevent or minimize serious crop damage in the future.

RESEARCH NEEDS
Research projects totaling $792,000 are proposed in this section. Approximately 31 percent is allocated to the Interior and 69 percent to the Coastal subspecies. Project and annual costs are summarized in Table 7-4.

Status of the Resource
The primary research need is for continued development and refinement of methods and techniques for obtaining reliable annual information on breeding populations, production, harvest, number of hunters, crippling loss, direct-recovery rates, and mortality rates.

Breeding-Population Index. — The call-count technique is the most promising method of determining the status of the breeding population of the Pacific Coast. It should be investigated further to determine whether procedures could be developed for increasing its efficiency, producing compatible data from areas with poor road access, and estimating the breeding-pair density. Such studies should involve cooperation between management agencies and a university but probably should be conducted by the latter. Costs would include support of a graduate study for 5 man-years at $8,000 per year (stipend and expenses) for a total of $40,000. It is estimated that state supportive costs would total $3,000 annually for a period of 3 years.

Because the present call-count technique may not prove to be adapted for use in the interior, it is most important to develop a simple, reliable census procedure that could be used in all states and Mexico. If done by graduate students, this research probably would require 4 man-years at a cost of $32,000.

The possibility of devising a successful method of counting pigeons on wintering grounds should be explored further. The field-cost estimate for California is $2,000 per year for 2 years. An additional $2,000 would be required for design and analysis, and the total cost would be $6,000. The winter survey would be less costly than the call count but would provide population estimates 6 months prior to the breeding season. Previous attempts at winter counting have failed. The design should include precision standards. The project total for all investigations of breeding potential would be $87,000.

The call count, the census study of the Interior subspecies, and the winter survey are alternative approaches to assessment of the brood stock. These studies should be conducted simultaneously, with a high degree of mutual awareness, if not coordination, among the workers. Ideally, a single method would be developed to serve management needs for the entire bandtail population.

Banding. — Banding is needed on the Pacific Coast to provide an index of the harvest rate and to provide estimates of hunting mortality and total mortality. Banding during July and August would be the most productive because both adults and immatures could be captured at the same place and time, and, in addition, banded samples would represent summer-resident populations. If a direct-recovery rate of between 4 and 5 percent for immatures were assumed (Silovsky 1969), a relatively large banded sample would be needed. A minimum objective of 300 banded immatures per state per year would tax banders' capabilities and might not be attainable (Fig. 7-7). Costs, at $7 per band for the first year and $5 per band thereafter, are based upon the banding of 2,000 pigeons annually in each state. The cost for each state is estimated at $14,000 for the first year and $10,000 for each of 6 succeeding years, totaling $74,000. For California, Oregon, and Washington, total costs for 7 years would be $222,000. In the interior states, some research banding is needed for the first 5 years at a cost of $10,000 per year or a total of $50,000.

Postseason and May banding should be evaluated as alternatives to preseason banding for the purpose of satisfying both research and management objectives. Relative recovery rates (adult-juvenile) for a September season could not be obtained from other than summer banding; in addition, winter or spring banding samples might be difficult to link with useful population entities. It may be necessary, however, to rely upon banding during these periods to satisfy needs for information. Winter banding would be conducted in California after the hunting season and before northward migration. A minimum of 2,000 pigeons should be banded, at a preliminary cost of $7 per band and a total cost of $14,000 for 1 year. May banding should take place after migration is essentially complete and before large, grain-feeding flocks have dispersed. It is likely that enough birds already have been banded during this period to permit the comparison of results with those of other banding periods.

The band-reporting rate, or the proportion of all the bands recovered by hunters that are reported to the banding office, must be determined periodically if calculations of mortality, harvest, and population levels are to be made with confidence from recovery data. It is proposed that enough reward bands be placed upon juvenile pigeons to guarantee 100 band recoveries in the range of the Coast subspecies during the first hunting season. Using a direct-recovery rate of 0.0421 (Silovsky 1969) and assuming a reporting rate of 0.30, we can estimate that the harvest rate for juveniles would be 0.14. The use of 1,000 reward bands ideally would result in 140 reported band recoveries. The banded sample would be distributed in rough proportion to the summer population of the three Pacific Coast states. The experiment would be conducted in the second and fifth years of the research banding program. The cost, including $10 per reported band, is estimated at $2,000 for each year, or $4,000 total.

A fluoroscopic study of the incidence of body shot in mature bandtails is proposed for the Pacific Coast band-tailed pigeon population. The objective would be to develop an alternative to the direct-recovery rate as an index to gun pressure. The relationship of body shot to harvest rate and to kill rate also should be determined. The cost of a graduate research study is estimated at $20,000 for 2.5 man-years.

Harvest Surveys. — The accuracy and precision of pigeon-harvest statistics as derived from the game-harvest questionnaire should be determined in each of the three coastal states. Costs would include design and analysis, field checks, interviews, and mail surveys and are estimated at $20,000 per year for a total of $40,000. The study could be extended to cover certain other game-bird categories at a saving to pigeon management.

Wight (1966) suggested a rangewide system for sampling hunters. Such a system would be superior to the present lack of uniformity but probably would best be postponed until a truly adequate sampling frame is available. The issuance of federal pigeon-hunting permits would provide such a frame as an important by-product contribution to management.

It is anticipated that research surveys involving field contacts with hunters would be planned and carried out by technicians for the number of seasons necessary to satisfy research objectives. Hunter contacts made at or near the hunting area should provide information on crippling loss, age and sex composition of the bag, development of the crop gland, and food habits (if desired). Hunter contacts should be distributed in proportion to numbers of hunters afield, with regard to both time and place. Cost is estimated at $6,500 per state for 5 man-months, with this effort being spread over five hunting seasons. Total cost for the three states would be $20,000, and an additional $4,000 per year would be necessary for the continuation of the field-check projects in the interior, for a total of $20,000. The project total would be $40,000.

Production and Harvest Areas. — Major production and harvest areas should be defined. The contribution of each production area to harvest areas should be compared with the derivation of the pigeon harvest in each area. The satisfaction of this need would depend upon the development of production and harvest estimates for the individual areas and a banding project on the scale of that described for preseason banding (see *Banding*). In addition, banded samples should be well distributed throughout the breeding range. Obviously, production and harvest areas could not be described completely unless surveys and banding were conducted also in Canada and Mexico. Planning should include an offer of assistance to the Province of British Columbia in the areas of banding and summer-population surveys. Planning, coordination, and analysis should be handled by the United States Fish and Wildlife Service, with actual banding done by the states. In addition to costs detailed above, $50,000 would be required for 2 years' work in Canada and $20,000 would be needed for coordination. A complete study of the biology, population dynamics, and ecology of bandtails in Mexico is a major research need for the Interior race. The cost for 8 years of graduate study would be $64,000. The total outlay for production and harvest-area studies would be $134,000.

Production Index. — A preseason assessment of production would be useful, but age-ratio counts of free-living pigeons made only in limited areas show that age ratios of trapped samples of birds cannot be translated into population ratios at present. A reliable preseason estimate of production would provide timely data that could be directly associated with production areas. The study would require 3 years of graduate work and cost $24,000.

Use of the Resource

No research projects are recommended for funding under this program; fact finding would be an integral part of the management projects.

Status of the Habitat

Habitat Requirements. — The seasonal habitat requirements of the band-tailed pigeon should be determined; making this determination would involve two 3-year graduate projects, one for the coast and one for the interior. The cost would be $24,000 for each region.

Habitat Inventory. — Breeding and wintering habitat should be inventoried by pigeon-density or pigeon-use classes. State wildlife agencies would conduct the inventory, which, it is estimated, would require 6 man-years. Interior costs would total $36,000; those for the Pacific Coast were put at $57,000, for a grand total of $93,000.

Threats to the Habitat. — Man-caused changes in vegetation, soil, and water of the coastal pigeon range should be evaluated for effects on bandtail populations. Major influences to be investigated would be land and forest management practices, fire, and development. Guidelines for habitat alteration should be established. In the light of present knowledge, the following guidelines for timber management are indicated: Within the coast forest, the primary need is to continue the practice of clear-cutting timber in small blocks (Fig. 7-8)

This system results in a good interspersion of seral stages and a juxtaposition of nesting and feeding areas. Scattered overmature trees of low value should be left standing. Tree fringes should be left along watercourses. In the coast forest of California, it is estimated that 0.25 mile (0.40 km) of timber should be left on either side of each stream.

Control of weed trees should be discontinued in areas where species being eliminated are important components of pigeon habitat. In the coast forest, this change would apply primarily to the use of herbicides on broad-leaved species. In areas where vegetation includes berry-producing shrubs and trees, spraying reduces the value of the habitat for pigeons and other wildlife (Fig. 7-9). Control of oaks is practiced on some pigeon habitat in California. As a result of an agreement between the California Department of Fish and Game and the United States Forest Service, wildlife values now are being considered in the cutting of black oak (*Quercus velutina*) for firewood.

We recommend that the above measures be regarded as interim procedures and that an evaluation of habitat management be initiated, to be completed by 1985–86. This project would require 2 years of graduate study and would encompass all bandtail range in the United States. The total cost would be $16,000.

Other Areas of Investigation

There is need for much additional research on ecology, physiology, and ethology of bandtails. It is not within the scope or capacity of the present plan to set limits or estimate costs for all of the major areas of study within these fields.

Fig. 7-8. A large clear-cut area in bandtail range near Arlington in western Washington. Clear-cutting stimulates the growth and fruiting of red elderberry (*Sambucus callicarpa*) and other berry-producing shrubs. However, the value of the practice to pigeon management is diminished or lost when the cutting area is too large and tree fringes are not left along watercourses. (Photo by Robert Jeffrey.)

Fig. 7-9. Red elderberry killed by aerial herbicide application on a conifer plantation near Conway in western Washington. The control was directed mainly at red alder, but it eliminated most of the noncompetitive, pigeon-food species as well. (Photo by Robert Jeffrey.)

We do not thereby imply that projects not included here as needs are less important. Research findings may or may not be directly applicable in management, but it would be shortsighted to view the solving of today's management problems as a guarantee of the permanent well-being of the bandtail. In this context, we offer the following partial list of areas for continued study: nutrition, pesticides and other pollutants, natural mortality, nesting, migration, reproductive physiology, parasites, and diseases.

RECOMMENDATIONS

The basic alternatives available to the agencies involved in bandtail management are three: stop all hunting and permit the species to seek an unmolested, unmanaged equilibrium within its environment; continue harvest, population monitoring, and research at about the present level; or adopt management and research programs planned to satisfy the needs of both the species and the public. We reject the first alternative because it would result in waste of a renewable resource — a recreational resource for which there is an increasing demand. Also, the future of the bandtail will not be insured by ignoring the future; the species cannot be isolated from the effects of habitat losses and conflicts with agriculture. Neither can we recommend the continuance of management at its present low intensity. The future security of pigeon populations requires immediate action to increase our knowledge of habitat, mortality, and productivity; and as the best way of insuring this, we recommend the acceptance of the third alternative.

Research begun in 1976 could not be integrated into a management program before 1979 at the earliest. Therefore, the committee recommends that the research program be initiated as soon as funded and that the following proposals be activated in the order listed:

1. Develop a breeding-population index.
2. Develop banding capability and band for research needs.
3. Develop and evaluate harvest surveys.
4. Define, describe, and interrelate production and harvest areas.
5. Develop a production index.
6. Determine habitat requirements.
7. Complete a habitat inventory.
8. Determine threats to habitat and develop guidelines for habitat management.

It is recommended that the following management program be implemented in 1976–77 in its entirety if funds are available. Otherwise, segments are listed in order of priority.

1. Conduct an annual breeding-population survey.
2. Perform annual maintenance banding.
3. Conduct harvest surveys.
4. Acquire, develop, and maintain the concentration areas listed in Table 7-5.
5. Regulate hunting and enforce regulations.

6. Inform the public on the status of the resource and on the progress of management.
7. Enhance viewing areas.
8. Control crop damage with minimal effect on populations.

A detailed revision of the management plan should be prepared upon completion of the principal research studies.

The committee recommends that a rigid schedule be adopted for the circulation of research progress reports. Final reports should be prepared to meet publication standards, and significant findings should be published. Annual status reports also should be scheduled and made available to administration well in advance of the adoption of hunting regulations. We suggest that the annual report of the Western Migratory Upland Game Bird Committee would be an appropriate vehicle for the circulation of both research progress reports and management status reports.

ACKNOWLEDGMENTS
The committee thanks the administrators of the wildlife conservation organizations represented in its membership for their patience and assistance, without which the band-tailed pigeon plan could not have been completed. Particularly, we thank Harold T. Harper, California Department of Fish and Game, for his interest and his help with committee meetings. The committee also thanks John E. Chattin, United States Fish and Wildlife Service, and Howard M. Wight, Oregon Cooperative Wildlife Research Unit, for reviewing the pigeon plan.

Permission to use preliminary data on the harvest of bandtails in Canada was granted by Denis A. Benson, Canadian Wildlife Service, and estimates of crippling loss in Washington were made available by Carl V. Swanson. Gene D. Silovsky permitted us to use material from his Master's thesis and helpfully reviewed a portion of the plan. We are indebted also to Ralph J. Gutierrez, Douglas B. Houston, Leonard H. Sisson, J. Allen White, and Don L. Zeigler for permission to cite their unpublished theses.

Classification and descriptions of plant communities follow Weaver and Clements (1938).

LITERATURE CITED
American Ornithologists' Union. 1957. Check list of North American birds. 5th ed. The Lord Baltimore Press, Inc., Baltimore. 691pp.

Atwood, Earl L. 1956. Validity of mail survey data on bagged waterfowl. Journal Wildlife Management 20(1):1-16.

Bendire, Charles. 1892. Life histories of North American birds with special reference to their breeding habits and eggs. Smithsonian Contributions to Knowledge 28. U.S. National Museum. Special Bulletin No. 1. 446pp.

Benson, Denis A. 1968. Waterfowl harvest and hunter activity in Canada during the 1967–68 hunting season. Progress Notes. Canadian Wildlife Service No. 5. 6pp.

————. 1969. Waterfowl harvest and hunter activity in Canada during the 1968–69 hunting season. Progress Notes. Canadian Wildlife Service No. 10. 6pp.

————. 1970. Report on sales of the Canada migratory game bird hunting permit and waterfowl harvest and hunter activity, 1969–70. Progress Notes. Canadian Wildlife Service No. 16. 34pp.

―――. 1971. Report on sales of the Canada migratory game bird hunting permit and waterfowl harvest and hunter activity, 1970. Progress Notes. Canadian Wildlife Service No. 22. 29pp.

Braun, Clait E. 1972. Movements and hunting mortality of Colorado band-tailed pigeons. Transactions North American Wildlife and Natural Resources Conference 37:326-334.

―――. 1973. Distribution and habitats of band-tailed pigeons in Colorado. Proceedings Western Association State Game and Fish Commissioners 53:336-344.

California Department of Fish and Game. 1966. California Fish and Wildlife Plan. Volume II. California Department of Fish and Game. 68pp.

Chambers, Willie L. 1912. Who will save the band-tailed pigeon? Condor 14(3):108.

Cooch, F. G., G. W. Kaiser, and L. Wight. 1973. Report on 1972 sales of the Canada migratory game bird hunting permit, migratory game bird harvest and hunter activity. Progress Notes. Canadian Wildlife Service No. 34. 10pp.

Coues, Elliott. 1874. Birds of the northwest: A Hand-book of the ornithology of the region drained by the Missouri River and its tributaries. U.S. Geological Survey of the Territories. Miscellaneous Publication No. 3. Washington, D.C. 791pp.

Drewien, Roderick C., Richard J. Vernimen, Stanley W. Harris, and Charles F. Yocom. 1966. Spring weights of band-tailed pigeons. Journal Wildlife Management 30(1):190-192.

Fitzhugh, Lee. 1970. Literature review and bibliography of the band-tailed pigeon of Arizona, Colorado, New Mexico and Utah. Arizona Department Game and Fish. Special Report. 33pp.

Glover, Fred A. 1953. A nesting study of the band-tailed pigeon (*Columba f. fasciata*) in northwestern California. California Fish and Game 39(3):397-407.

Grinnell, Joseph. 1913. The outlook for conserving the band-tailed pigeon as a game bird of California. Condor 15(1):25-40.

Gutierrez, Ralph J. 1973. Reproductive biology of the band-tailed pigeon (*Columba fasciata*). M.S. Thesis. University of New Mexico, Albuquerque. 28pp.

Houston, Douglas B. 1963. A contribution to the ecology of the band-tailed pigeon, *Columba fasciata* Say. M.A. Thesis. University of Wyoming, Laramie. 74pp.

Hunt, Charles B. 1967. Physiography of the United States. W. H. Freeman & Co., San Francisco. 480pp.

Keppie, Daniel M., Howard M. Wight, and W. Scott Overton. 1970. A proposed band-tailed pigeon census — a management need. Transactions North American Wildlife and Natural Resources Conference 35:157-171.

Mace, Robert U., and Wesley M. Batterson. 1961. Results of a band-tailed pigeon banding study at Nehalem, Oregon. Proceedings Western Association State Game and Fish Commissioners 41:151-153.

MacGregor, Wallace G., and Walton M. Smith. 1955. Nesting and reproduction of the band-tailed pigeon in California. California Fish and Game 41(4):315-326.

March, G. L., and R. M. F. S. Sadleir. 1970. Studies on the band-tailed pigeon (*Columba fasciata*) in British Columbia. I. Seasonal changes in gonadal development and crop gland activity. Canadian Journal Zoology 48(6):1353-1357.

―――, and ―――. 1972. Studies on the band-tailed pigeon (*Columba fasciata*) in

British Columbia. II. Food resource and mineral-gravelling activity. Syesis 5:279-284.

Morse, William B. 1950. Observations on the band-tailed pigeon in Oregon. Proceedings Western Association State Game and Fish Commissioners 30:102-104.

Neff, Johnson A. 1947. Habits, food and economic status of the band-tailed pigeon. United States Fish and Wildlife Service. North American Fauna No. 58. 76pp.

Peeters, Hans J. 1962. Nuptial behavior of the band-tailed pigeon in the San Francisco Bay area. Condor 64(6):445-470.

Silovsky, Gene D. 1969. Distribution and mortality of the Pacific Coast band-tailed pigeon. M.S. Thesis. Oregon State University, Corvallis. 70pp.

———, Howard M. Wight, Leonard H. Sisson, Timothy L. Fox, and Stanley W. Harris. 1968. Methods for determining age of band-tailed pigeons. Journal Wildlife Management 32(2):421-424.

Sisson, Leonard H. 1968. Calling behavior of band-tailed pigeons in reference to a census technique. M.S. Thesis. Oregon State University, Corvallis. 57pp.

Smith, Walton A. 1968. The band-tailed pigeon in California. California Fish and Game 54(1):4-16.

Stabler, Robert M., and Clyde P. Matteson. 1950. Incidence of *Trichomonas gallinae* in Colorado mourning doves and band-tailed pigeons. Journal Parasitology 36(6): 25-26.

Weaver, John E., and Frederic C. Clements. 1938. Plant ecology. 2nd ed. McGraw-Hill Book Co., New York. 601pp.

White, J. Allen. 1973. A study of molt of band-tailed pigeons. M.S. Thesis. Colorado State University, Fort Collins. 27pp.

Wight, Howard M. 1966. A band-tailed pigeon research and management program. In files of United States Fish and Wildlife Service, Laurel, Maryland. 9pp. Abstracted in Proceedings International Association Game, Fish and Conservation Commissioners 56:40.

———, Robert U. Mace, and Wesley M. Batterson. 1967. Mortality estimates of an adult band-tailed pigeon population in Oregon. Journal Wildlife Management 31(3):519-525.

Zeigler, Don L. 1971. Crop-milk cycles in band-tailed pigeons and losses of squabs due to hunting pigeons in September. M.S. Thesis. Oregon State University, Corvallis. 48pp.

8

White-Winged Dove
(Zenaida asiatica)

David E. Brown, Small Game Supervisor, Arizona Game & Fish Department, Phoenix, *Chairman.*

David R. Blankinship, Research Biologist, National Audubon Society, Rockport, Texas.

Philip K. Evans, Wildlife Biologist, Edinburg, Texas.

William H. Kiel, Jr., Wildlife Biologist, King Ranch, Inc., Kingsville, Texas.

Gary L. Waggerman, Wildlife Biologist, Texas Parks & Wildlife Department, Edinburg.

Charles K. Winkler, Regional Director for Wildlife, Texas Parks & Wildlife Department, Rockport.

SUMMARY

The white-winged dove is a subtropical species, peripheral in the United States, but an important migratory game bird in southern Texas and Arizona. The two major breeding areas in the United States are the Rio Grande valley of Texas and riparian habitats within the Sonoran Desert in Arizona. The populations that breed in these two areas are discrete. The winter range of the Rio Grande valley birds is in extreme southwestern Mexico and Central America, whereas the whitewings of Arizona winter near the western coast of south central Mexico. During the last 50 years, most of the woodland and forested nesting habitats in the United States have been altered or destroyed. Numerous federally funded projects continue to threaten the remaining colonial nesting sites. Although there is no threat to the survival of the species, it has been only through the intensive efforts of public and private conservation agencies that the status of the white-winged dove as a game bird has continued. The maintenance of its status as a game species has been made possible by the acquisition or protection of remnant nesting habitats and by careful regulation of the harvest. The adaptation of at least some populations to nest in citrus orchards has also been of importance. The acquisition, management, and reestablishment of nesting habitats is now the principal management objective of white-winged doves. Investigations of winter habitats, peripheral nesting areas, census techniques, and mortality factors are recommended.

DESCRIPTION

The white-winged dove can be described as having the form and size of a typical Columbid, with a band of white across the shoulder of each wing (Fig. 8-1). A detailed description is given by Cottam and Trefethen (1968:28-29).

A band of white across the middle of each wing is the certain field mark of the white-winged dove in flight. At rest or on the ground, the whitewing displays this insigne as a white border along the margin of the folded wing. No other dove in this country has similar markings.

The wing action and general appearance of the whitewing in flight are more pigeon-like than those of the mourning dove; its flight is more direct and even, with less zigzagging except when frightened. It is chunky of build and large of head in comparison to its slender, more streamlined, and more widely-distributed cousin. The tail is shorter, rounded, and carries a distinctive pattern — dark feathers tipped by a broad band of white. The mourning dove also has a white border on its tail, but the longer feathers are graduated and pointed. Those of the whitewing are more nearly of equal length, giving the tail a somewhat stubby shape, rounded across the end. The wing is noticeably longer than the tail; the wing of the mature mourning dove is about equal in length to its tail.

The adult whitewing's eye has a bright red iris surrounded by a bare patch of blue skin. The eye of the mourning dove is dark brown, and it lacks the bare eye patch. The bill of the whitewing is longer and stouter and the feet and legs are heavier than those of the mourning dove.

The average whitewing outweighs the average mourning dove by nearly 2 ounces, with a mean weight of about 6 ounces. Smaller specimens may weigh 4.5 ounces, which is the average weight of the mourning dove, but specimens up to 7 ounces have been recorded. With a full crop, a large whitewing may weigh more than a half-pound, but up to 2 ounces of this maximum may be accounted for by undigested seeds and fruits in the crop.

Although the female usually has less purple on the crown and more brown ventrally than the male, cloacal examination is necessary for accurate determination of sex. Juveniles are much grayer than adults. Their plumage is neither as heavy nor as well rounded as that of mature birds, and their necks are brownish without iridescent gloss on the sides. Ear spots are small and dull in color. Flight feathers are browner than in the adult, and the primary coverts have pale tips. Bills are brownish, a softer color than the black of adults, and the iris is brown to yellowish brown. The legs and feet of juveniles are brownish to reddish brown — never bright red as are those of adults.

Four subspecies of this slightly polymorphic species breed in the United States: the Western or Arizona white-winged dove (Z. a. mearnsi), the Eastern or Texas white-winged dove (Z. a. asiatica), the upper Big Bend white-winged dove (Z. a. grandis), and the Mexican highland white-winged dove (Z. a.

Fig. 8-1. White-winged doves drinking from a watering trough in the Sand Tank Mountains in the Sonoran Desert of Arizona. Large numbers of white-winged doves utilize desert watering holes from May through June before the advent of the summer rain. (Photo by Steve Gallizioli, Arizona Game & Fish Department.)

monticola) (Cottam and Trefethen 1968:32-41, Saunders 1968). For the purposes of this report, the first two subspecies are considered as western and eastern whitewings, respectively. All subspecies are commonly known in Mexico and the southwestern United States as white-winged doves or *palomas de alas blancas*.

Detailed descriptions of the various subspecies are given by Saunders (1968) and by Cottam and Trefethen (1968). Individuals of the Eastern race (*asiatica*) are generally heavier and darker than those of the Western race (*mearnsi*). Except at the southern terminus of their wintering range, both the breeding and the wintering ranges of the Western subspecies are discrete from those of *asiatica*. Saunders (1968) has shown that populations of *mearnsi* and *asiatica,* the subspecies of major management importance, are strongly migratory, whereas those of *grandis* and *monticola* are not.

LIFE HISTORY
White-winged doves begin arriving in numbers in the major nesting areas, both Eastern and Western, in April and continue to arrive through the middle of

May. These arrivals coincide roughly with the leafing of several subtropical deciduous trees. The two sexes arrive simultaneously and the males begin courtship activities immediately. Nesting activity also commences at this time and reaches a peak in late May or early June.

Both sexes construct the nests, which are placed on horizontal branches, usually in short trees that often occur in the interior of a dense thicket or "bosque." Numerous pairs nesting in the woodlands or other favored sites provide a colonial aspect. Nests are rather flimsy affairs, usually consisting of dead twigs, and are rarely lined. Two eggs are laid in the normal clutch, the first during the afternoon on completion of the nest and the second about 36 hours later. Incubation is shared by the two sexes; the female occupies the nest from late afternoon through the next morning and then the male takes over. During the early morning when the males are off the nest and separated from the females, calling activity is vigorous.

The normal incubation period, around 14 days, places the peak of the first hatch sometime in June. Squabs are still largely dependent on *pigeon milk* for several days after leaving the nest, which they do about 2 weeks after hatching. At this time certain native food items are normally available, such as the fruit of the giant cactus or saguaro (*Cereus giganteus*) in Arizona.

Two broods are the rule among whitewings that nest in colonies in bosques or other favored types of habitats. There is some evidence that birds in desert scrub habitats that lack proximate cultivated grains may nest only once.

Major nesting activity terminates shortly after 15 August in both the eastern and the western ranges. Immatures usually remain in the vicinity of the nest site for at least 2 weeks after fledging, often remaining in the area even after the adults have migrated. It is during this premigration period that the so-called *feeding* flights (Fig. 8-2) occur, when large numbers of both immatures and adults flock into cultivated fields to feed on safflower (*Carthamus tinctoris*), maize (*Zea mays*), and cereal crops. When the birds are in satisfactory physiological condition, migration commences. Adults usually precede the immatures.

The Eastern population in south Texas differs from the Western population in that migrations often do not begin until September, with the first abrupt drop in temperature. Such a drop in temperature usually precipitates a more leisurely southward movement from breeding ranges in the Rio Grande valley and Tamaulipas than is observed for their western counterparts. In both migrating populations, juvenile birds usually leave later than adults. The destination of the Eastern migrants is the tropic woodlands and forests of western Oaxaca, Chiapas, Guatemala, Costa Rica, El Salvador, and Honduras.

Migration of Western populations usually begins in August and is almost always under way by the first week of September. Band recoveries indicate that these whitewings travel well-established routes directly to their wintering range. Western populations travel along the western escarpment of the Sierra Madre

Fig. 8-2. Fall feeding flights of whitewings in Texas. (Photos by Texas Parks and Wildlife Department.)

Occidental in Mexico as they pass through Sonora, Sinaloa, and Nayarit to the tropic woodlands and forests inland from the coasts of Jalisco, Colima, Michoacan, and Guerrero. Here they remain until the spring cycle begins anew.

HISTORICAL REVIEW

Cottam and Trefethen (1968) gave a comprehensive review of the history and status of the white-winged dove when their book was published. This excellent book details all information available on the various white-winged dove populations known prior to its publication and also provides the most comprehensive literature review available for material published through 1968. It is not our purpose to reiterate this information and duplicate their bibliography. We will, however, outline the publications available since 1968 and mention a few that Cottam and Trefethen omitted.

Further studies of the nesting activities of Eastern populations in southern Texas and the state of Tamaulipas in Mexico were presented by Alamia (1970), Blankinship (1970), Williams (1971), and Cuevas (1974). Movement and mortality of certain Eastern populations were also discussed by Blankinship et al. (1972). Blankinship (1966), Dunks (1969), and Evans (1972) discussed the particular effects and control of predation by great-tailed grackles (*Cassidix mexicanus*) on white-winged dove eggs and young. Evans (1970) and Waggerman (1972) presented current habitat and management relationships in

Texas. Hunter participation in whitewing management in Texas was discussed by Evans (1969).

Published reports relating to particular investigations of nesting habitat of Arizona populations that are not referred to by Cottam and Trefethen (1968) are those by Shaw and Jett (1959), Carr (1960), Shaw (1961), and Wigal (1973), and unpublished reports by Carr and Shaw and Jett (J. N. Carr. 1960. Mourning dove and white-winged dove nest surveys during the summer of 1960. Project W-53-R-11, WP3, J2, Supplemental Report. Arizona Game and Fish Department, Phoenix. 6pp.; H. Shaw and J. Jett. 1959. Mourning dove and white-winged dove nesting in the Gila riverbottom between Gillespie Dam and the junction of the Salt and Gila rivers, Maricopa County. Project W-53-R-10, WP3, J2, Special Report. Arizona Game and Fish Department, Phoenix. 6pp.). Kufeld (1963) and Brown (1970) presented data on banding and mortality and discussed characteristics of Arizona populations. Texas and Arizona are the only states that include white-winged doves in a federal aid project.

Research and management of white-winged doves in Texas and Arizona has been through several Federal Aid Projects, and annual reports concerning these studies have been published each year since 1949. Saunders (1968) provided the latest information on subspeciation and racial characteristics. Physiological adaptions were investigated by MacMillen and Trost (1966). Findings relating to ornithosis in whitewings are presented by Grimes et al. (1966). A summary of the status of white-winged doves in Mexico is provided by the Mexico General Office of Wildlife (1968).

DISTRIBUTION AND DENSITY

The white-winged dove is a peripheral species in the United States, breeding only in the southwestern states. A map depicting the breeding range of the subspecies of whitewings in the United States is shown in Figure 8-3. It shows also the wintering areas and migration routes for both Eastern and Western populations of management importance in the United States, as determined through band recoveries. The ranges of these and other subspecies in Mexico and Central America are imperfectly known.

The natural and apparently preferred whitewing nesting habitat in the lower Rio Grande valley is dense, thicketlike forests of native subtropical trees 15 to 25 feet (4.6 to 7.6 m) in height with an understory of thorny shrubs. Most-favored trees and shrubs for nest sites are ebony (*Pithecellobium flexicaule*), anaqua (*Ehretia anacua*), huisache (*Acacia farnesiana*), colima (*Zanthoxylum fagara*), granjeno (*Celtis pallida*), and brazil (*Condalia obovata*). Texas honey mesquite (*Prosopis glandulosa*) is often a major component of these communities but is usually not important for nest sites except in isolated cases. White-wings also use taller and more open stands composed of many of the above species mixed with ash (*Fraxinus* sp.), hackberry (*Celtis reticulata*), and winged elm (*Ulmus crassifolia*), which are found in the first bottomlands of the Rio Grande and along its old channels. In towns of the area, shade trees of the above species provide nest sites for several thousand whitewings.

In upper south Texas, whitewings nest in single trees and groves of huisache,

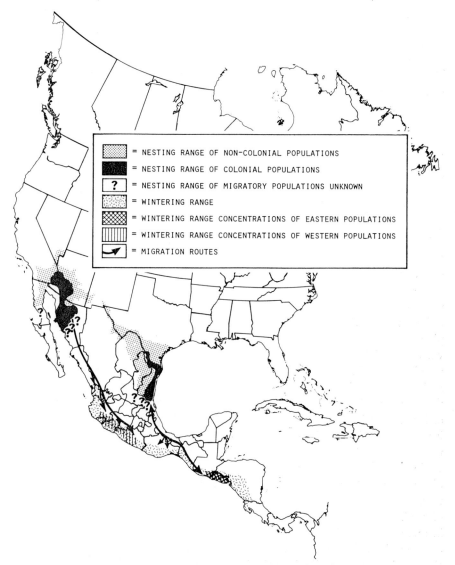

Fig. 8-3. The principal nesting and wintering areas of migratory white-winged dove populations in North America.

mesquite, granjeno, pecan (*Carya illinoensis*), hackberry, guajillo (*Acacia berlandieri*), and tamarisk (*Tamarix* sp.). Generally the largest concentrations are in towns, in lake areas, and along streams. The largest concentration of nesting whitewings in upper south Texas is in a mixture of native brush species adjacent to Lake Corpus Christi.

The whitewing colonies of northeastern Mexico are in fasciations of much the same physiognomy as those communities described for the lower Rio Grande valley but with a different species composition. Particularly notable in some areas is the heavy use by doves of large arboreal cacti; for example, prickly-pear cactus (*Opuntia* spp.).

Since 1940, with the rapid clearing of native habitat, whitewings in the lower Rio Grande valley have made increased use of the expanding citrus groves as nesting habitat. With the conversion of the native thickets to agriculture, a majority of the whitewings in Texas now nest in citrus trees. Whitewings show a marked preference for mature citrus trees — those exceeding 7 inches (17.8 cm) in trunk diameter and 12 feet (3.6 m) in height. Such trees are usually at least 7 years of age. These citrus groves are subject to damage or destruction by periodic freezes. After freezes, nesting whitewings are dependent on the limited native habitat until the citrus can recover or new trees reach maturity.

The breeding range of the white-winged dove in Arizona, Sonora, and California closely overlaps the mapped boundaries of the Arizona Upland subdivision of the Sonoran Desert of Shreve (1942, 1951) and Brown (1973). As in Texas and Tamaulipas, the largest nesting populations are found in subtropical winter- or drought-deciduous woodlands or bosques. These are found in or adjacent to the Sonoran Desert and near columnar cacti such as saguaro, organ pipe (*Lemaireocereus thurberi*), and cardon (*Pachycereus pringlei*), or cultivated grainfields, or both. In Arizona these bosques are riparian and are composed largely of velvet mesquite (*Prosopis juliflora*), with desert willow (*Chilopsis linearis*) and hackberry being other important arboreal constituents. Where these bosques have not been completely destroyed, the winter-deciduous salt cedar (*Tamarix chinensis*) has, since 1930, increasingly replaced mesquite and is now the single most important nesting tree for whitewings in Arizona. Arboreal species in Sonoran desert scrub such as ironwood (*Olneya tesota*), palo verde (*Cercidium floridum, C. microphyllum, Parkinsonia aculeata*), Jito (*Forchammeria watsoni*), and *Atamisquea emarginata* provide additional important nest sites. Although the riparian communities support the highest density of nesting pairs, the greater extent of desert scrub communities probably results in more doves nesting in the latter types. Some nesting also occurs in trees in communities adjacent to the Sonoran Desert, namely, coastal and interior chaparral, desert grassland, encinal woodland, and thorn scrub (Lowe 1964, Brown and Lowe 1974a,b). Mangrove swamps of *Rhizophora mangle* and

Avicennia nitada provide important nest sites adjacent to the Gulf of California in Sonora and Baja California.

Citrus groves, municipal parks, and residential areas all contribute many nest sites for western whitewing populations. Citrus in Arizona is of less importance than riparian habitats for colonial nest sites, but use of citrus is increasing as groves mature. The recent urbanization of formerly cultivated areas has resulted in many citrus areas being destroyed, so that their potential importance is difficult to ascertain.

A majority of Western whitewings winter in the tropical and subtropical woodlands of the Pacific coastal plains and foothills from southern Sinaloa to Guerrero and Oaxaca. These communities, termed "Short Tree Forest" (Gentry 1942:30-34) and Selva Baja Cauducifolia and Selva Mediana Subperennifolia by Mata et al. (1971), are composed of numerous species of drought-deciduous trees, evergreen riparian trees, and columnar cacti.

CENSUS PROCEDURES AND POPULATION TRENDS
Only the major whitewing populations hunted in Texas and Arizona are censused. The whitewing population in the Rio Grande valley of Texas is censused four times between the months of May and September.

Spring Breeding Census
A census of the population is based on the volume of noise made by a local colony (coo counts). The number of individual birds calling is not recorded on this survey; rather, the noise level produced by the colony is measured against a predetermined auditory scale. Harvest regulations are based on this census.

Production Census
Nest transects of 0.25 acre (0.1 ha) in brush and 0.50 acre (0.2 ha) in citrus are used to measure relative reproductive success of colonies in each habitat type. Information from spring breeding censuses is combined with data from production censuses to provide total post-nesting-season population estimate. The annual breeding-population estimate in the Rio Grande valley indicates a somewhat erratic and declining trend since 1964 (Table 8-1). However, the trend based on population estimates from 1951 to 1975 shows the whitewing population in the Lower Rio Grande Valley of Texas to be increasing (linear increase significant at the 99 percent level, $r = 0.78$).

Fall Flight Census
A time-area census is used to determine the number of whitewings that will be available during the hunting season. This census also determines the number of whitewings that fly into Mexico to feed and are therefore unavailable to Texas hunters. The census is taken at each of the major roosting areas (about 30 in

Table 8-1. Breeding-population trends of white-winged doves by nesting habitat types in the Rio Grande valley, 1964–73.

Year	Brush			Citrus			Total	
	Number of White-wings	Percentage of Total	Percentage Increase or Decrease	Number of White-wings	Percentage of Total	Percentage Increase or Decrease	Annual Breeding Population	Percentage Increase or Decrease
1964	302,000	48	+60	331,000	52	+276	633,000	+129
1965	354,000	59	+17	250,000	41	− 24	604,000	− 5
1966	426,000	53	+20	379,000	47	+ 52	805,000	+ 33
1967	361,000	54	−15	306,000	46	− 19	667,000	− 17
1968	293,000	56	−18	226,000	44	− 26	520,000	− 22
1969	219,000	53	−25	197,000	47	− 13	416,000	− 20
1970	276,000	43	+22	350,000	57	+ 77	618,000	+ 48
1971	183,000	35	−31	342,000	65	− 2	525,000	− 15
1972	174,000	37	− 5	301,000	63	− 12	475,000	− 10
1973	194,747	37	+12	331,149	63	+ 9	525,896	+ 10

the valley) in the morning when whitewings form flights to their feeding areas. The census is conducted for 2 minutes of each 3-minute period and lasts about 1 hour.

Aerial Census of Hunters' Cars

The aerial census of hunters' cars is related to unmanned check stations on the ground and is used to determine the number of hunters afield (hunter-days). The census also determines whitewing harvest and crippling loss through information reported on paper sacks at the check stations. Whitewing legs deposited in these sacks at unmanned check stations provide information on age ratios. The relationship between the number of cars observed in the hunting areas through aerial census is correlated with hunter success as determined from the information on the hunters' sacks, each representing one hunting party. These data indicate a widely fluctuating harvest from 1947 through 1972 (Table 8-2).

Statewide estimates of dove hunts and harvests are determined through mail questionnaires. An intensive banding program provides estimates of mortality and harvest levels.

Western breeding populations are censused in Arizona by means of 32 randomized call-count surveys conducted in conjunction with the annual mourning dove (*Zenaida macroura*) survey, in which individual calling doves are recorded. A formula considering stratification by vegetative type has been used since 1962 to compute an annual breeding-dove index. A comparison of this index with the estimated harvest for each year since 1962 is made in Table 8-3. Linear regression analysis indicates a significant relationship ($r = 0.86$) between

Table 8-2. Hunting statistics for white-winged doves in the lower Rio Grande valley, 1947–72.

Year	Number of Hunter-Days[a]	Number of Whitewings Bagged[b]	Number of Whitewings per Hunter-Day	Total Kill	Sample Size	Percentage of Immatures in Bag
1947	13,063	44,868	3.43		478	55
1948	21,657	144,362	6.67		11,975	69
1949	29,940	218,365	7.55		13,359	68
1950	28,721	203,440	7.08		33,664	52
1951	19,139	27,883	1.46		4,855	38
1952	19,735	117,324	5.94		7,481	52
1953	14,300	28,514	1.93		2,181	38
1954–56	Season Closed					
1957	14,821	115,249	7.78	172,874[c]	27,229	58
1958	16,303	83,145	5.10	104,543[d]	9,684	61
1959	15,150	104,838	6.92	125,595[d]	16,069	52
1960	9,340	21,108	2.26	26,640[d]	1,860	62
1961	10,539	49,140	4.66	59,709[d]	4,868	69
1962	16,281	114,789	7.05	131,764[d]	11,299	58
1963	Season Closed					
1964	33,972	239,097	7.04	288,528[d]	13,533	54
1965	29,477	145,108	4.92	184,911[d]	8,759	51
1966	38,544	233,735	6.06	295,833[d]	13,143	48
1967	36,012	282,134	7.83	356,325[d]	16,750	49
1968	42,050	220,692	5.25	302,429[d]	6,160	25
1969	18,140	100,693	5.69	125,731[d]	7,765	37
1970	20,066	85,311	4.25	104,727[d]	4,281	48
1971	15,136	78,586	5.18	102,130[d]	3,854	54
1972	23,097	166,029	7.16	210,232[d]	10,000	[e]

[a] A hunter-day is defined as one hunter in the field 1 day of the season.
[b] Unretrieved birds are not included.
[c] Includes unretrieved birds, estimated to be 50 percent of total birds bagged.
[d] Includes unretrieved birds as reported by hunters on questionnaires.
[e] Preliminary spurious results precluded aging of whitewing legs.

the breeding-dove index and the licensed harvest over this period (Fig. 8-4). Both the breeding-dove index for whitewings and the licensed harvest since 1968 have been generally lower than they were from 1962 to 1967.

An intensive banding program in selected areas, check stations, and boxes for collecting information on hunting provide comparative data on age ratios, recovery rates, harvests, and hunter success. As with the eastern populations, band recoveries are the only method of determining any change in status on the wintering range. A comparative summary of check station data since 1956 from Arlington, Arizona, a main concentration area for whitewing hunters, is shown in Table 8-4. The percentage of immature whitewings in the bag has generally increased and hunting success has declined in this area during the

Table 8-3. Summary of call-count and license-harvest surveys of whitewings in Arizona from 1962 to 1972.

Year	Mean Number of White-winged Doves Calling (call-count index)	Licensed Harvest[a]
1962	33.146	448,398
1963	40.200	385,249
1964	35.947	412,542
1965	43.216	549,045
1966	48.410	578,166
1967	51.471	703,157
1968	52.315	740,079
1969	41.093	664,053
1970	33.924	407,921
1971	31.297	390,016
1972	35.404	355,633

[a] Does not include crippling loss.

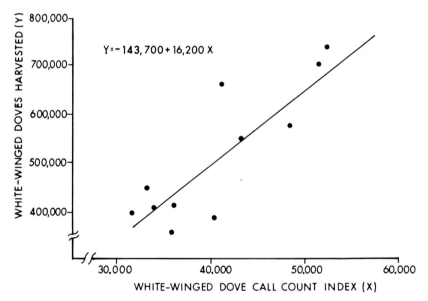

Fig. 8-4. Relationship between white-winged dove call-count index and statewide harvest in Arizona, 1962–72.

period studied. Band recoveries between 1961 and 1970 indicate mean annual adult harvest levels of around 8.2 percent and a mean annual adult mortality of 48 percent for the population around Arlington. Harvest levels and mortality rates were lower in other areas sampled. Questionnaires sent to a random sample of licensed hunters are used to estimate annual harvests. No census

Table 8-4. Information on white-winged doves collected during first 2 days of the hunting season at Arlington Check Station, Arizona.

Year	Number of Hunters	Number of Whitewings	Percentage of Whitewings in Dove Harvest	Number of Whitewings per Hunter	Percentage of Immatures in Bag
1956[a]	471	2,659	61.3	5.6	29
1957[b]	764	8,936	74.2	11.7	58
1958[c]	1,018	8,261	63.1	8.1	51
1959	552	3,967	52.9	6.4	52
1960	581	7,734	78.3	13.3	31
1961	1,069	5,886[d]	41.4[d]	5.5[d]	
1962	1,236	8,267	54.8	6.7	50
1963	1,029	3,325	35.8	3.2	52
1964	360	2,024	42.2	5.6	74
1965	500	2,344	41.2	4.7	68
1966[e]	538	1,982	32.0	3.7	55
1967	676	3,248	44.0	4.8	52
1968	1,343	5,725	41.7	4.3	57
1969	1,175	3,061	29.6	2.6	69
1970[f]	800	2,499	30.7	3.1	75
1971[f]	554	1,758	32.4	3.2	72
1972[f]	906	1,615	21.4	1.8	76

[a] Bag limit, 15.
[b] Bag limit, 25 doves, of which no more than 10 could be mourning doves.
[c] Bag limit of 25 whitewings initiated.
[d] Wing boxes used. These ratios are biased.
[e] Inclement weather.
[f] Bag limit, 10 whitewings.

efforts are regularly undertaken for whitewing populations in California, Nevada, New Mexico, trans-Pecos Texas, or any of the Mexican states including those comprising the wintering range.

CURRENT HARVEST AND HUNTING PRESSURE

Harvest estimates for the Rio Grande valley of Texas since 1968 have been from less than 80,000 to more than 220,000 annually (Table 8-2). During 1972, 23,000 hunter-days were spent harvesting 166,000 whitewings in the Rio Grande valley. It is estimated that an additional 44,000 whitewings were crippled or lost, for a total kill of approximately 210,000. The average whitewing bag was 7.2 birds per hunter-day. The crippling loss was estimated by biologists in spy blinds to be between 18 and 28 percent of the harvest. The harvest in the trans-Pecos area, where neither whitewings nor hunters are concentrated, is believed to have been less than 10,000 in 1972.

In recent years, hunting pressure has increased dramatically in northeastern Mexico at the expense of the Rio Grande valley population, which feeds extensively on domestic grains on both sides of the international boundary. The harvest in the Rio Grande valley of Mexico has on occasion been much larger than that in Texas (178,000 whitewings declared in 1970). In 1971, the open-ing of the hunting season in Mexico was changed from 1 August to 1 September so that there now is less incentive for Americans to harvest whitewings in Mexico.

No estimates of hunting pressure or harvest are available for Eastern white-wings in their wintering range in Central America. Mean annual direct-recovery rates of banded Rio Grande valley populations averaged 2.8 percent between 1951 and 1970. Mortality estimates based on banding data collected from 1940 through 1970 indicate a continuing mean annual adult mortality of just under 50 percent.

Western whitewing populations are subject to hunting in Arizona, California, Nevada, and Sonora, and in those Mexican states that host wintering popula-tions. Only in Arizona and in the states of Colima, Guerrero, and Michoacan, which comprise the major wintering range, is the harvest of potential signifi-cance to whitewing populations in the western United States. Estimates of whitewing harvest and hunting pressure from mail questionnaires are available only from Arizona. These data are available for the period from 1962 through 1972 and are summarized in Table 8-3. A licensed harvest of 355,633 white-wings was estimated for 1972. This number was the lowest harvest estimate since 1962, when this type of survey was initiated. Band recoveries, check station records, and other census data suggest that the increase in the annual harvest to over 500,000 whitewings from 1965 through 1969 was not commensurate with the decrease in acreage of good-quality nesting habitat and that local but im-portant populations may have been overharvested. Since 1970, when the daily bag limit was reduced from 25 to 10, the estimated licensed harvest has been under 500,000, and call-count surveys no longer indicate a declining population. During the 5 years from 1968 to 1972, an estimated average of 48,500 licensed hunters each spent 3.6 days to harvest 512,000 whitewings in Arizona each year. Kill estimates, which include crippling loss, unlicensed harvest, and birds taken in California, increase the mean annual kill during this period to approximately 650,000 whitewings. This figure does not take into account reporting bias, but the number of birds shot in the western United States during the last 5 years has probably been from less than 0.5 to about 0.7 million each year. Band re-coveries indicate that the harvest of banded Arizona populations in Mexico has been relatively consistent and is equivalent to from 35 to 50 percent of the Arizona harvest. Such a harvest adds an estimated mean take of between 175,000 and 250,000 birds on the wintering range each year since 1968. Although Sonoran harvests have not been monitored, it seems safe to assume that the total annual kill of Western whitewing populations exceeds 1.0 million.

The mean annual adjusted-recovery rate (harvest level) of a banded colonial population of whitewings in Arizona averaged 12.5 percent from 1961 through 1969. In comparison, statewide harvest level averaged under 4 percent. The mean annual mortality of the adult segment of this colonial population during the same period was estimated to be 48 percent and that of immatures, 85 percent (David E. Brown. 1970. Summary of whitewing dove banding and hunt information in Arizona. Arizona Game and Fish Department.)

POTENTIAL HARVEST

Approximately 95 percent of the whitewing harvest in Texas occurs in the four southernmost counties of the state — Cameron, Willacy, Hidalgo, and Starr; consequently, hunting and management efforts are concentrated in this area. Technicians believe that the available habitat there will support a breeding population of approximately 500,000 to 800,000 birds, and therefore harvest regulations are set to maintain the breeding population within this level. After increase from production and decrease from overwinter mortality are allowed for, a breeding population of this size can permit a harvest of from 200,000 to 250,000 birds. Harvest levels should be less than 25 percent of the breeding population, however. In 1967 and 1968, it is estimated that more than 25 percent of the population was shot, a proportion that was deemed excessive. The management goals are to restrict the harvest to less than 25 percent of the population except in years of unusually high production. The potential harvest depends on reproductive success and on the number of returning whitewings, factors that vary each year. The Texas Parks and Wildlife Department annually sets season dates, bag limits, and shooting hours in an attempt to restrict the harvest to the desired level. Another factor that may limit harvest quotas in the future is a continuation of increased hunting pressure in northeastern Mexico. The Mexican harvest regulations are tailored to manage a large whitewing population that is subject to very little hunting pressure nationally. In recent years, however, hunting has increased dramatically in northeastern Mexico at the expense of any surplus Texas whitewing populations drawn to Mexico to feed on such domestic grains as milo (*Sorghum durra*), sorghum (*Sorghum vulgare*), and hegari (*Sorghum* sp.). These crops are more abundant in the Rio Grande valley of Mexico than in Texas. Texas and United States officials have been in contact with Mexican officials for several years in an effort to curtail the harvest of whitewings that occurs close to the international boundary. The potential harvest of the small proportion of the total population that occurs between Laredo and El Paso is unknown. These areas may be able to provide measurably more hunting than is currently done, but both the population levels and the current harvest in this part of the state need to be determined.

The potential harvest of Western whitewings, like that of the Rio Grande valley population, is not much greater than is taken at present. In fact, it is doubtful if current harvest levels can be maintained in the face of the declining quality and quantity of colonial nesting habitat. The long term outlook is for further decrease in colonial nest sites and an attendant drop in harvests. Banding data have shown that the bulk of whitewings harvested in Arizona are produced in river bottom environments. Although citrus groves are increasing contributors to whitewing production, they are still relatively unimportant, and their future is almost as uncertain as that of the bosques. As a member of the desert avifauna, the white-winged dove has a relatively secure future. Thousands of square miles of Sonoran desert scrub assure the species continued habitat for nesting on their return from Mexico. The present and future needs of dove hunters, however, necessitate more than the production from residential and desert scrub nest sites. Maintenance of the hunting resource, even at present levels, requires the preservation of the maximum acreage of remaining colonial nesting habitat. Even if such preservation is accomplished, proper management of the present population will probably necessitate limiting the annual licensed harvest in Arizona to under 0.5 million. Harvests in Nevada, New Mexico, and, to a lesser extent, California have never been of consequence. With much, if not most, of the colonial nesting habitat in California destroyed, the potential harvest of this species in that state is no greater than the present harvest. Only in Sonora and in the Mexican states with wintering whitewings can the harvest be expected to increase. Any increase in harvest in the Mexican wintering range could affect the population returning to Arizona. Should some level of hunting mortality prove to be noncompensatory, hunting in Arizona will have to be further curtailed.

SPECIES NEEDS

Like all wildlife, white-winged doves need food, cover, and a place to reproduce. It is the last factor that now limits this species in the United States. The once magnificent subtropical riparian forest and woodland communities of the southwestern United States are now largely destroyed, and, since 1940, virtually all areas formerly used by white-winged doves for colonial nesting have been adversely altered by man's activities. Land *reclamation,* dropping water tables, flood-control projects, phreatophyte removal, burning, and *clearing* have reduced colonial nesting habitat to a fraction of its former acreage (Figs. 8-5 through 8-8). Because of these losses, the greatest need of both major whitewing populations is breeding habitat. Although both Texas and Arizona have programs for habitat acquisition, these programs largely serve only to preserve existing habitat and do not compensate for that already lost. Even when selected lands are acquired and managed by public conservation agencies, dropping water tables, burning, and condemnation for flood easement channels continue to be threats.

If most of the remaining nesting habitat were acquired by public and private conservation agencies, efforts to increase whitewing production and harvest could be accelerated. Until such acquisition is accomplished, however, the

Fig. 8-5. White-winged dove nesting habitat photographed in 1941 near the confluence of the Gila and Salt rivers, Arizona. This area, although considerably altered, still provides colonial nesting habitat. (Photo by Arizona Game & Fish Department.)

Fig. 8-6. White-winged dove nesting habitat in the Rio Grande valley, Texas, June 1973. This particular area, appropriately called the La Paloma Unit, was purchased and is managed by the World Wildlife Fund. (Photo by David E. Brown.)

Fig. 8-7. Santa Cruz River where it passes through "San Xavier Thicket," February 1970. Channel cutting and dropping water tables have resulted in the death of most of the mesquite and hackberry trees. This area was once one of the most famous riparian woodlands in Arizona. An interstate highway now bisects the thicket. (Photo by David E. Brown.)

Fig. 8-8. Heart of another famous Arizona white-wing nesting area, Komatke or New York thicket. Dropping water tables from upstream dams, diversions, and groundwater pumping are the primary — and fire the secondary — causative agents in this pitiful scene. (Photo taken in July 1972, by David E. Brown.)

populations and harvests must be monitored as closely as possible to provide maximum populations from existing resources. Determining the effects of hunting and controlling the harvest levels are, and should be for the foreseeable future, a major management effort.

Because of the mobility of the species, feeding areas and roosting sites are generally not considered as critical as nesting habitat. However, they are major areas of concern and in some cases, especially in the Rio Grande valley of Texas, may be affecting the huntable resource more than the nesting habitat. Additional areas of concern and facets of whitewing management heretofore investigated are crop depredations, mortality from pesticides, and predation. None of these, however, approaches in importance the losses of breeding sites and nest sites.

PUBLIC NEEDS

In both the eastern and the western range, the public has only one real need — more whitewings and whitewing habitat. Hunting areas are accessible feeding areas, and the whitewing season draws large numbers of resident and nonresident hunters from all parts of Texas, Arizona, and neighboring states. There are no public lands available to the whitewing hunter in the Rio Grande valley of Texas, but most landowners allow hunting on their property for nominal fees. Most hunting in Arizona takes place on private lands also; and posting, although becoming more prevalent, is still of minor consequence. Finding a place to hunt apparently is not a problem even to out-of-state hunters. In Texas, tracts of land where hunting is permitted are advertised, either in the news media or by signs erected on the properties. Harvest regulations based on the current status of the resource are prepared annually. Since the demand exceeds the supply, increasingly intensive management of the harvest is required and each year's regulations are designed to provide the maximum hunting benefits possible without endangering the resource.

Bird watchers and photographers can observe and photograph white-winged doves in many residential, desert scrub, and riparian areas. Much if not most of the remaining nesting and roosting habitat is in public or public-oriented ownership. Even though these areas may be closed to hunting, other public access is not restricted.

MANAGEMENT NEEDS

Texas and Arizona currently have programs funded by Federal Aid Projects that have management of white-winged doves as their objective. We present here a summary of those facets of these programs that should be continued or accelerated during the next 5 years. Estimates of suggested expenditures on these projects in Texas and Arizona are given in Table 8-5, which includes also estimates for California, the only other American state that has sizable populations of this species.

Habitat Acquisition

The primary management need for the white-winged dove in the United States is for public conservation agencies to acquire, improve, manage, and maintain nesting habitat. Acquisition of remaining high-density habitat is of particular importance in Texas, Arizona, and California. Research studies during the past 13 years have shown the feasibility of rehabilitating arable land in the Rio Grande valley of Texas to produce nesting habitat for white-winged doves. Water rights or irrigation facilities, or both, would have to be acquired for many woodlands in Arizona and California in areas where water tables are declining or critically low. The budget must also provide for the maintenance, management, and rehabilitation of lands already owned, including programs for fencing, posting, fire control, and enforcement of trespass laws.

Resource Inventory
Annual census activities include coo counts, nest surveys, flight counts, and the gathering of information from hunter check stations and information boxes. We include census surveys of the same types, conducted by United States personnel, of international populations in northeastern Mexico. Harvest data are obtained from questionnaires designed to elicit general information on small game hunting, and obtaining them requires no additional expenditures. All of these programs should be continued.

Banding programs provide data on mortality and harvest rates and information on wintering populations. The banding programs should be continued and expanded to sample previously unbanded populations. Present annual costs of banding, including analysis of banding data and publication of results, are estimated to be $17,000 per year.

Predator Control
Research in Texas has indicated that whitewing production in that state can be increased if numbers of boat-tailed grackles are controlled during the nesting season. Boat-tailed grackle populations can be controlled in selected high-density nesting areas of white-winged doves by shooting, poisoning, and nest destruction (Blankenship 1966, Dunks 1969, and Evans 1972).

Law Enforcement and Determination of Hunting Regulations
Hunting regulations, a necessary tool in the management of white-winged doves, should be carefully formulated and rigorously enforced. Law-enforcement activities, whether special investigations or routine patrols, are normally funded as a part of general wildlife programs. Setting of most hunting regulations and attendance at meetings and study sessions are likewise funded. Special workshops, or sessions in which representatives of the states and Mexico would disseminate current management findings relating to this species, would require special funding. Annual meetings for these purposes would be particularly desirable for helping to formulate harvest regulations for Texas and parts of Mexico.

RESEARCH NEEDS
Up to now, most white-winged dove research has focused on population dynamics and nesting-habitat requirements as matters of urgent priority. We suggest additional investigations of white-winged dove ecology, population dynamics, and present management techniques. All of the studies suggested below would provide data useful in the management of this species. We list the pro-

Table 8-5. Budget requirements for a 10-year white-winged dove management plan.

Major Program or Area for Funding	Specific Jobs Within Each Program	Research or Management (R or M)	Job Priority	Estimated Cost of Jobs for Each Fiscal Year (in thousands of dollars)										Total Cost by Job (thousands)	Continuing Job
				1	2	3	4	5	6	7	8	9	10		
Status of the Resource	Study population on winter range														
	Texas[a]	R	1	10										$ 10	No
	Arizona[b]			9										9	No
	Analyze census technique	R	1												
	Texas			3.5										3.5	No
	Arizona			0.5										0.5	No
	Study by banding (Research)	R	2												
	Texas[c]			9	9	9	9	9	9	9	9	9	9	90	Yes
	Arizona			6	6	6	6	6	6	6	6	6	6	60	Yes
	California			3	3	3	3	3	3	3	3	3	3	30	Yes
	Study limiting factors in citrus groves	R	2												
	Texas			10	10									20	No
	Arizona and California			10	10									20	No
	Study feasibility of establishing nesting colonies	R	2												
	Texas			12	12	12	12	12						60	No
	Arizona			6	6	6	6	6						30	No
	Determine density and status of unstudied populations	R	2												
	Texas			3	3	3	3	3	3	3	3	3	3	30	No
	California			3	3	3	3	3	3	3	3	3	3	30	No
	Monitor diseases and parasites	R	2												
	Texas			2	2	2	2	2	2	2	2	2	2	20	Yes
	Arizona			2	2	2	2	2	2	2	2	2	2	20	Yes

Conduct annual census	M	1											
Texas			12	12	12	12	12	12	12	12	12	120	Yes
Arizona			6	6	6	6	6	6	6	6	6	60	Yes
California			2	2	2	2	2	2	2	2	2	20	Yes
Banding (monitor populations)	M	2											
Texas			8	8	8	8	8	8	8	8	8	80	Yes
Arizona			8	8	8	8	8	8	8	8	8	80	Yes
California			2	2	2	2	2	2	2	2	2	20	
Total Cost of Program per Fiscal Year[d]			127	104	84	84	84	66	66	66	66	813	
Use of the Resource													
Study control and management of crop depredations	R	2											
Texas and Arizona			3	3	3	3	3					15	No
Maintain, manage, and rehabilitate lands now owned	M	1											
Texas			15	15	15	15	15	15	15	15	15	150	Yes
Arizona			30	30	30	30	30	30	30	30	30	300	Yes
California			5	5	5	5	5	5	5	5	5	50	Yes
Control predators	M	2											
Texas			6	6	6	6	6	6	6	6	6	60	
Conduct workshop to formulate regulations	M	1											
Texas			1	1	1	1	1	1	1	1	1	10	Yes
Arizona			0.25	0.25	0.25	0.25	0.25	0.25	0.25	0.25	0.25	2.5	Yes
California			0.25	0.25	0.25	0.25	0.25	0.25	0.25	0.25	0.25	2.5	Yes
Total Cost of Program per Fiscal Year			60.5	60.5	60.5	60.5	60.5	57.5	57.5	57.5	57.5	590.0	

(Continued)

(Table 8-5. Continued.)

Major Program or Area for Funding	Specific Jobs Within Each Program	Research or Management (R or M)	Job Priority	Estimated Cost of Jobs for Each Fiscal Year (in thousands of dollars)										Total Cost per Job (thousands)	Continuing Job
				1	2	3	4	5	6	7	8	9	10		
Grand Total Cost of All Research and Management Programs by Fiscal Year[d]				187.5	164.5	144.5	144.5	144.5	123.5	123.5	123.5	123.5	123.5	$1,403.0	
Habitat Acquisition	Acquire nesting habitat	M	1												
	Texas			50	50	50	50	50	50	50	50	50	50	500	No
	Arizona			200	200	200	200	200	200	200	200	200	200	2,000	No
	California			20	20	20	20	20	20	20	20	20	20	200	No
Total Cost of Habitat Acquisition per Fiscal Year[d]				270	270	270	270	270	270	270	270	270	270	2,700	

[a] Eastern population.
[b] Western population.
[c] Texas and Tamaulipas.
[d] Many of these programs are currently funded under Federal-Aid Project Statements.

posed projects in a rough order of priority (see also Recommendations). Unless otherwise indicated, most studies would be of approximately 3 years' duration. Estimates of the costs of making these studies are given in Table 8-5.

EVALUATION OF WINTERING HABITAT

No studies have been made of either Eastern or Western white-winged dove populations in their wintering range. The status and relative security of these wintering areas are not known, but they are of great concern. It is also not known whether any unusual or unconsidered mortality factors are operating on these populations during this period. Investigations of these matters should be conducted in the wintering ranges in Mexico and Central America by personnel from Texas, Arizona, or the federal government. The length of study would depend on findings available after an initial winter visit had determined the extent and scope of concern.

Analysis of Census Techniques

Present census techniques have yet to be proved valid for measuring population levels and trends. A critical need is to have statistically valid data on the population and harvest.

Banding Studies in Unsampled Areas

Banding and recovery data from Texas and Mexico have revealed that whitewing colonies intermingle, at least in some years. Banding data from whitewings banded in Arizona have yet to indicate anything but strong fidelity to breeding and nesting areas. There is reason to believe that small colonies of urban and desert scrub populations north of the principal areas hunted contribute little to the harvest. This evidence, however, is meager and inconclusive, and it should be determined through banding whether these colonies and individuals supplement the harvest of major colonial populations. Mortality rates and harvest levels calculated for various populations could help determine to what extent hunting mortality replaces natural mortality.

Feasibility Studies of Food Plots

A potential management tool is the manipulation of post-nesting feeding flights. Segments of particular populations are known to be anywhere from heavily harvested to virtually unhunted because of the availability to the public or location of the fields where they are feeding. Perhaps leasing fields in strategic locations and planting small grains in them could affect the migration time of these populations, or the harvest level, or both. If so, the importance to management is obvious. In Texas, the leasing of these fields could be funded with revenue from white-winged dove stamps. In Arizona, lands owned or leased by the Game and Fish Department could be planted to accomplish similar objectives. Total cost over a 2-year period is estimated at just under $120,000.

Evaluation of Citrus Orchards as Nesting Habitat
It is not known what conditions limit the productivity of citrus groves as white-wing nesting habitat. Many factors that determine which orchards are selected as colonial nest sites have yet to be ascertained. The effects on nesting success of cultural practices such as the jet-type spraying of pesticides and chemicals into citrus foliage should be determined.

Experimental Establishment of Colonies in Unoccupied Areas
Within the range of white-winged doves are unoccupied areas that appear to be potential sites for nesting colonies. It has been suggested either to trap and transplant juvenile whitewings from present high-density areas to candidate sites (Texas) or to collect white-winged dove eggs from colonial nests and deposit them in active mourning dove nests in the candidate area (Arizona).

Mapping Density and Distribution of Specific Populations
The density and status of white-winged doves in California and along the upper Rio Grande valley in Texas have not been investigated. The size of these populations is a matter of speculation, and it is recommended that their density and distribution be determined and mapped.

Studies of Diseases and Parasites
Diseases and parasites of this species remain largely uninvestigated. It is desirable to determine what diseases and parasites affect whitewings and how important they are for long-term management purposes. The effects of trichomoniasis on both individuals and populations are of particular interest.

Exploration of Methods of Controlling Crop Depredations
Because of potential or imagined damage to domestic grains by large, concentrated populations of whitewings, it is believed desirable to determine both the economic significance of losses and the methods to be used in reducing or preventing such depredations.

RECOMMENDATIONS
As we have previously stated, the pressing need of this species is the acquisition and protection of colonial nesting habitat. These subtropical environments are of importance to the sportsman and other members of the public oriented toward wildlife.

A state-issued white-winged dove stamp should be considered by the Arizona Game and Fish Department as a means of meeting the principal management objective of acquiring nesting habitat. This method has already been initiated by the Texas Parks and Wildlife Department. Latest figures from that state indicate approximately 25,000 stamps issued per year. Since each stamp costs $3, approximately $76,000 has been realized each year. Half of this revenue is earmarked for acquisition of habitat and half for research and management for the protection of white-winged doves. Therefore, both funds are accruing at a rate of approximately $38,000 each per year. Expenditures of these funds will probably qualify for federal aid reimbursements, but because such reimbursements no longer carry the original earmarks, they will not necessarily enhance the program's finances. All sources of revenue will be needed to successfully implement the total whitewing plan, but the bulk of the work could and should request funding as Pittman-Robertson projects. Such funding seems only fair because this species provides substantial hunting recreation. Research needs and priorities have already been outlined.

LITERATURE CITED

Alamia, Leticia A. 1970. Renesting activity and breeding biology of the white-winged dove (*Z. a. a.*) in the lower Rio Grande valley of Texas. M.S. Thesis. Texas A&M University, College Station. 126pp.

Blankinship, David R. 1966. The relationship of white-winged dove production to control of great-tailed grackles in the lower Rio Grande valley of Texas. Transactions North American Wildlife and Natural Resources Conference 31:45-58.

———. 1970. White-winged dove nesting colonies in northeastern Mexico. Transactions North American Wildlife and Natural Resources Conference 35:171-182.

———, James G. Teer, and William H. Kiel, Jr. 1972. Movements and mortality of white-winged doves banded in Tamaulipas, Mexico. Transactions North American Wildlife and Natural Resources Conference 37:312-325.

Brown, David E. 1973. The natural vegetative communities of Arizona. Arizona Resource Information Systems. Phoenix. Map.

———, and C. H. Lowe. 1974a. The Arizona system for natural and potential vegetation — Illustrated summary through the fifth digit for the North American southwest. Journal of the Arizona Academy of Science. 9(Supplement 3). 56pp.

———, and ———. 1974b. A digitized computer-compatible classification for natural and potential vegetation in the Southwest with particular reference to Arizona. Journal Arizona Academy Science 9 (Supplement 2). 11pp.

Cottam, Clarence, and James B. Trefethen (editors). 1968. Whitewings: The life history, status, and management of the whitewinged dove. D. Van Nostrand Co., Inc., Princeton, New Jersey. 348pp.

Cuevas, A. S. 1974. La paloma de ala blanca — 1974. Bosques y Fauna. Epoca 11(6): 9-15.

Dunks, Jim. 1969. Whitewings vs. grackles. Texas Parks & Wildlife Department 27(7):2-5.

Evans, Philip K. 1969. How the hunter can help. Texas Parks and Wildlife Department 27(8):12-14.

———. 1970. The Longoria unit of the Las Palomas Wildlife Management Area. Texas Parks & Wildlife Department 28(12):2-5.

———. 1972. Grackle control as an aid to white-winged dove management. Proceedings Southeastern Association Game & Fish Commissioners Conference 26:296-298.

Gentry, Howard S. 1942. Rio Mayo plants: A study of the flora and vegetation of the valley of the Rio Mayo, Sonora. Carnegie Institution of Washington Publication 527. 328pp.

Grimes, J. E., Thelma D. Sullivan, and J. V. Irons. 1966. Recovery of ornithosis agent from naturally infected white-winged doves. Journal Wildlife Management 38(3): 594-598.

Kufeld, Roland C. 1963. Summary and analysis of data for mourning and white-winged doves banded in Arizona. Project W-53-R-13, WP3, J2, Special Report. Arizona Game & Fish Department, Phoenix. 9pp.

Lowe, Charles H. 1964. Arizona's natural environment: Landscapes and habitats. University of Arizona Press, Tucson. 136pp.

MacMillen, Richard E., and Charles H. Trost. 1966. Water economy and salt balance in white-winged and inca doves. Auk 83(3):441-456.

Mata, G. F., J. J. Lopez, X. M. Sanchez, F. M. Ruiz, and F. T. Takaki. 1971. Tipos de vegetacion de la Republica Mexicana. Subsecretaria de Planeacion y Direccion General de Estudios; Direccion de Agrologia. Mexico. 59pp.

Mexico General Office of Wildlife. 1968. La paloma de alas blancas in Mexico. Subsecretary of Forestry and Fauna, Mexico. 19pp.

Saunders, George B. 1968. Seven new white-winged doves from Mexico, Central America, and southwestern United States. North American Fauna #65. U.S. Bureau of Sport Fisheries and Wildlife, Washington, D.C. 30pp.

Shaw, H. 1961. Influence of salt cedar on white-winged doves in the Gila valley. Special Report. Arizona Game & Fish Department, Phoenix. 8pp.

Shreve, Forrest. 1942. The desert vegetation of North America. Botanical Review 8(4):195-246.

———. 1951. Vegetation and flora of the Sonoran Desert. Vol. 1, Vegetation. Carnegie Institute, Washington, D.C. Publication 591. 192pp.

Waggerman, Gary. 1972. Brushland for whitewings. Texas Parks & Wildlife Department 30(9):2-5.

Wigal, Dennis D. 1973. A survey of the nesting habitats of the white-winged dove in Arizona. Special Report No. 2. Arizona Game & Fish Department, Phoenix. 37pp.

Williams, Louis. 1971. A renesting study of the white-winged dove (*Z. a. a.*) in the lower Rio Grande Valley of Texas. M.S. Thesis. Texas A & I University, Kingsville. 82pp.

9

Mourning Dove
(Zenaida macroura)

James E. Keeler, Chief, Game Research, Alabama Department of Conservation and Natural Resources, Montgomery, *Chairman*.

Charles C. Allin, Wildlife Biologist, Rhode Island Department of Natural Resources, Division of Fish and Wildlife Field Office, West Kingston.

John M. Anderson, Director Sanctuary Division, National Audubon Society, Sharon, Connecticut.

Steve Gallizioli, Research Chief, Arizona Game and Fish Department, Phoenix.

Kenneth E. Gamble, Migratory Bird Coordinator, United States Fish and Wildlife Service, University of Missouri, Columbia.

Don W. Hayne, Southeastern Cooperative Fish and Game Statistics Project, Institute of Statistics, North Carolina State University, Raleigh.

W. H. Kiel, Jr., Biologist, King Ranch, Inc., Kingsville, Texas.

Fant W. Martin, Director, Migratory Bird and Habitat Research Laboratory, United States Fish and Wildlife Service, Laurel, Maryland.

James L. Ruos, Wildlife Biologist, Office of Migratory Bird Management, United States Fish and Wildlife Service, Laurel, Maryland.

Kenneth C. Sadler, Research Supervisor, Wildlife Research Section, Missouri Conservation Department, Columbia.

Larry D. Soileau, Research Leader, Game Division, Louisiana Wildlife and Fisheries Commission, Opelousas.

Clait E. Braun, Wildlife Researcher and Howard D. Funk, Wildlife Research Leader, Colorado Division of Wildlife, Ft. Collins, served as alternate members.

SUMMARY

The mourning dove breeds throughout the 48 contiguous states, the southern portions of the Canadian provinces, the Greater Antilles, and Mexico. Most mourning doves winter in the southern tier of states, in Mexico, in Central America, or in the West Indies. Since the 1920's, research has been conducted on life history, population levels, production, movements, and mortality. Some of these studies have been carried out in local areas and should be expanded to cover other areas within the range of the species. Dove hunting was permitted in 31 states during the 1973–74 hunting season and involved states with approximately 73 percent of the land area and 73 percent of the breeding population. Since 1953, mourning dove populations have been monitored nationwide by means of an annual call-count survey of the breeding population. This survey provides information necessary for establishing hunting regulations. The trend in the continental breeding population from 1963 to 1973 has been downward by an average annual rate of 2 percent. The estimated annual harvest of mourning doves is 49.4 million birds. More mourning doves are harvested each year than all other migratory game birds combined. Hunting mourning doves provides an estimated 11.4 million recreational trips per year. The total out-of-pocket expenditures for mourning dove hunting is approximately $86.9 million annually in the United States and represents a total of $137 million of income forgone annually by dove hunters. The estimated annual cost of needed dove research and management for the next 10 years is $2,580,500. A list of research and management needs and costs is given in this report.

DESCRIPTION

The mourning dove, a native member of the same family as the common pigeon or rock dove (*Columba livia*), is relatively abundant throughout its range. This streamlined bird has a small head and a long, pointed tail. Its total length is from 11 to 13 inches (27.9 to 33.0 cm). Coloration is slaty blue above and reddish fawn below, with large white spots on the tail. It has a black spot behind the eye and a black bill, and the legs and feet are red. The adult male in typical plumage has a light blue crown and nape, whereas the typical adult female has a brownish crown and nape. Also, males have rosy breast feathers, whereas the breast feathers of females are usually tan or brownish. Immature doves when very young possess whitish or buffy-edged wing and back feathers and mottled breast, neck, and head feathers (Reeves and Amend 1970). The best identifying characteristics for immature doves is the white or buff-colored edging on the wing coverts. Flight is direct and rapid, and the wing beat usually produces a noticeable whistle, especially when the bird is flushed. Its call is a slow, mournful cooing that becomes lower in pitch and volume at the end.

Five subspecies of mourning doves are recognized, two of which are chiefly limited to the mainland of North America. The other three have relatively restricted insular distributions. The Eastern subspecies (*Z. m. carolinensis*) breeds throughout the eastern third of temperate North America; the slightly smaller and paler Western subspecies (*Z. m. marginella*) occupies much of the western two-thirds of North America. The line of demarcation in the United States between the two subspecies roughly coincides with the boundary between the eastern deciduous forests and the western grasslands. There is an extensive mingling of racial types during migration in the southern latitudes. Heavy concentrations of fall migrants occur in certain areas in the southern United States, Mexico, and Central America.

LIFE HISTORY

In most parts of the United States, the nesting season extends from April or May to September; in some of the southern states, however, the dove has been reported to nest throughout the year. The peak in nesting in northern and southwestern states comes during the summer months; in the Southeast the peak is reached in midspring.

Nests are flimsily constructed and are usually placed in trees or shrubs, but sometimes they are placed on the ground. The usual clutch size is two eggs, but occasionally one and rarely three eggs are laid. Incubation takes about 14 days. During incubation, the male relieves the female at the nest from about 0800 hours until late afternoon (Moore and Pearson 1941:14). Newly hatched young, called squabs, are fed *pigeon's milk,* a secretion from crop glands of the parent birds. Within a few days, pigeon's milk is supplemented with various weed seeds and grains.

The squabs develop rapidly and leave the nest in about 12 to 14 days. Including several days for nest building and egg laying, a complete nesting cycle requires approximately 30 days. As many as six broods may be fledged by one set of parents during the long nesting season.

Migration from northern areas begins in August. Most mourning doves winter in the southern tier of states, in Mexico, in Central America, or in the West Indies.

HISTORICAL REVIEW

The first modern research on mourning doves included studies by Nice in Oklahoma in the 1920's and Demeritt in Key West in the 1930's (Peters 1961), pertaining to nesting and movements, respectively. The Alabama Cooperative Wildlife Research Unit conducted one of the first banding and life-history studies from 1935 to 1941 (Moore and Pearson 1941). Another important life-history study was conducted in Iowa during the late 1930's by McClure (1943). The first dove studies under the Federal Aid (Pittman-Robertson) Act were conducted in North Carolina from 1939 to 1942 and from 1945 to 1952 (Thomas L. Quay. 1951. Mourning dove studies in North Carolina. North Carolina Wildlife Resources Commission P-R Report, Project 2-R and 26-R. 90pp.; 1954. Mourning dove populations in North Carolina. North Carolina Wildlife Resources Commission P-R Report, Project W-30-R. 46pp.)

In 1948, the Southeastern Association of Game and Fish Commissioners (1957) initiated a regional study under the Federal Aid in Wildlife Restoration Program. This study terminated in 1956, and the resulting publication, "Mourning Dove Investigations, 1948–56" also incorporated data from states outside the southeastern region. An important contribution of the 1948–56 study was the development of the call count as an annual index to status of breeding populations. This index, with refinements, is presently used by the United

States Fish and Wildlife Service in estimating the population status for setting annual hunting regulations. The numerous recoveries from the study's extensive banding program provided much-needed information about movements and mortality. The publication also listed and summarized problems to be solved before a sound management program could be implemented.

The recognized decline in the dove population in the eastern half of the United States in the early 1950's spurred an intensive study in Illinois (Hanson and Kossack 1963). This study was carried out to provide basic information for management of the species as a game bird and provided additional information pertaining to life history, distribution, mortality, and population dynamics.

A preliminary analysis of banding data collected throughout the United States (Kiel 1959) resulted in the formation of three dove management units (Fig. 9-1). Annual hunting regulations were established on a management-unit basis in 1960.

Although interest in dove research declined somewhat in the late 1950's, new studies were begun at the Missouri Cooperative Wildlife Research Unit and other agencies and schools. Important findings were that adult mourning doves return with remarkable fidelity to the areas in which they nested the year before, but that immatures are much less faithful to their natal areas (Tomlinson et al. 1960, Harris 1961). This information led to further studies in the area of dove behavior.

Foote et al. (1958) investigated the representativeness of call-count routes

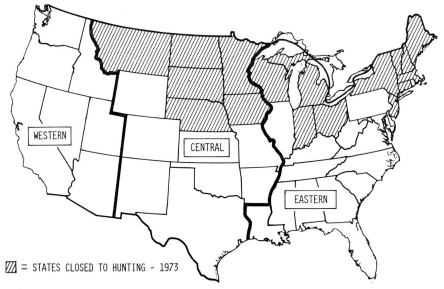

WESTERN

CENTRAL

EASTERN

▨ = STATES CLOSED TO HUNTING - 1973

Fig. 9-1. Mourning dove management units.

selected by cooperators and concluded that survey results were biased by the exercise of judgment in the selection of routes. As a result, new routes were randomly selected throughout the country.

Studies by Swank (1955) in Texas on moulting rates of pen-reared immature doves, Allen (1963) in Indiana on moulting rates of wild immature doves, and Sadler et al. (1970) in Missouri on adult moulting rates provided better ways of interpreting wing-survey data.

Blankenship et al. (1971) analyzed call-count data based on grouping of routes by areas of potential natural vegetation and concluded that information yielded by this type of analysis is more precise than information available hitherto. Research on calling behavior (Frankel and Baskett 1961, Jackson and Baskett 1964) contributed information of potential value to a better understanding of the relationship of calling doves to breeding populations.

In September 1959, the president of the International Association of Game, Fish and Conservation Commissioners appointed a Dove Technical Committee to outline a program of mourning dove research and management (Kiel 1961). Many of the objectives proposed in that plan have been reached.

Mourning dove studies are presently (1974) being conducted in many states under the Federal Aid in Wildlife Restoration Program and the Accelerated Research Program. Current regional studies include a cooperative banding program in the Central Management Unit and an extensive study in the Eastern Management Unit aimed at measuring effects of changes in regulations.

DISTRIBUTION AND DENSITY

The mourning dove breeds throughout the 48 contiguous states, the southern portions of the Canadian provinces, the Greater Antilles, and Mexico (Fig. 9-2). It occurs sporadically in the forested areas of Canada, well beyond the fringe of agriculture, and has been seen in southeastern Alaska.

During fall migration, mourning doves generally move southward from northern portions of their breeding range and occupy areas of good habitat as far south as Panama (Fig. 9-3). During August and September, migrating doves move into southern states and intermingle with local populations. The migrating doves remain in these areas and with local doves provide large concentrations of wintering doves in these latitudes.

During the late fall and winter months, when doves arrive in southern latitudes, agricultural crops such as corn (*Zea mays*), peanuts (*Arachis hypogaea*), row-crop sorghums (*Sorghum* spp.) (Fig. 9-4), millets (*Setaria* spp.), and rice (*Oryza sativa*) are beginning to mature. Mature seeds of wild grasses and weeds also provide abundant food supplies, and doves readily seek out areas that provide easily available food. Considerable shifting of flocks occurs from area to area during the winter months (Fig. 9-5).

The clearing of large areas of deciduous forests in the 1800's greatly improved

mourning dove habitat. Shelterbelts planted in the plains states have also increased nesting habitat for doves.

Dove habitat is difficult to define because the species is found throughout the
nation and adapts to numerous ecological types. Nesting habitat consists of
woods edges (Fig. 9-6), shelterbelts, church and cemetery sites, cities, farmlands, orchards, and many other types (Fig. 9-7). Doves display a tendency to

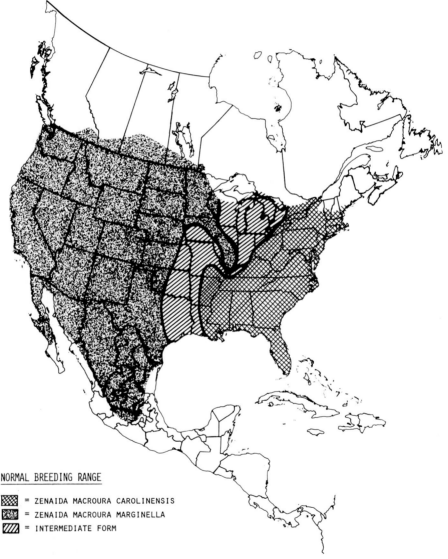

NORMAL BREEDING RANGE

▨ = ZENAIDA MACROURA CAROLINENSIS
▨ = ZENAIDA MACROURA MARGINELLA
▨ = INTERMEDIATE FORM

Fig. 9-2. Breeding range of the mourning dove.

build nests in isolated trees and sometimes place them in shade trees near dwellings. Most nests are located on horizontal limbs and are relatively free of any nearby concealing vegetation (Moore and Pearson 1941:12). In the Plains States, where trees and shrubs are scarce, considerable ground nesting occurs.

Not all habitat changes now under way are beneficial to the mourning dove (Fig. 9-8). The clearing of riparian brush in the Southwest by phreatophyte-

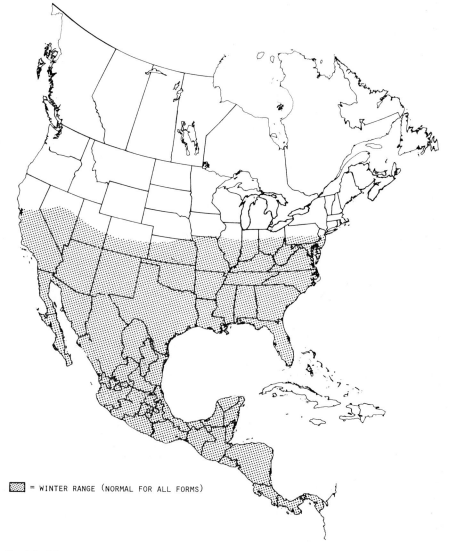

▒ = WINTER RANGE (NORMAL FOR ALL FORMS)

Fig. 9-3. Winter range of the mourning dove.

Fig. 9-4. Row-crop sorghum fields, when harvested, provide excellent fall feeding grounds for mourning doves. (Photo by Kenneth E. Gamble.)

Fig. 9-5. The flocking tendency is very strong in mourning doves. This condition exists from mid-July through February. (Photo by Texas Parks and Wildlife Department.)

Fig. 9-6. Typical mourning dove nest with two young about 10 and 11 days old. (Photo by Texas Parks and Wildlife Department.)

Fig. 9-7. Prime dove nesting cover along the Colorado River before it was cleared by bulldozers. (Photo by Dennis D. Wigal.)

Fig. 9-8. Same area as in Fig. 9-7 after clearing. (Photo by Dennis D. Wigal.)

control programs has destroyed thousands of acres of extremely valuable habitat for both the mourning dove and the white-winged dove (*Zenaida asiatica*) (Cottam and Trefethen 1968:277, 290). In the Southeast, the large-scale planting of large pine (*Pinus* spp.) plantations creates a homogeneous habitat inferior to the former complex of scattered croplands and mixed forests. In the Midwest, an increasing threat is the removal without replacement of mature or overage shelterbelts. Generally, the current trend toward intensified agriculture, as reflected by larger farms and fields, probably is detrimental to the mourning dove (Reeves 1972).

Mourning dove hunting during the 1973–74 hunting season was permitted in 31 of the 48 contiguous states, representing approximately 73 percent of the land area and 73 percent of the current breeding population. In 1973, the mean breeding-population index for the United States was 18.6 doves heard per route (Ruos 1974b:7). Relative densities of breeding mourning doves by physiographic regions in the United States from 1965 to 1973 are shown in Figure 9-9.

CENSUS PROCEDURES AND POPULATION TRENDS

Mourning dove populations have been monitored on a nationwide basis since 1953 by the call-count survey. The survey provides the best available index to relative density and total population of breeding doves. The primary purpose of the survey is to detect important year-to-year changes in breeding-population levels and to document significant long-term population trends. As the only nationwide dove survey, the call count provides information necessary for establishing appropriate hunting regulations. Call-count indices are also used by scientists as time-series indicators of both quality of dove habitat and quality of human environment.

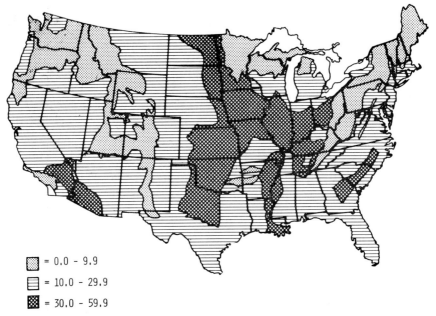

= 0.0 - 9.9

= 10.0 - 29.9

= 30.0 - 59.9

Fig. 9-9. Relative densities of breeding mourning doves by physiographic region, 1965–73. Mean number of doves heard calling per 70-stop call-count survey route.

The call-count survey is a roadside count of doves seen and heard by co-operators over 900 randomly selected routes in 48 states. The survey method was founded upon the studies of McClure (1939) and refined by Foote and Peters (1952:1–3). Numbers of doves heard at 20 different 3-minute listening stations on each route are checked once between 20 May and 10 June each year. Data comparable to those of the preceding year are grouped by physiographic regions and adjusted for differences in land area of each region within states and management units. The resultant index of breeding density is used to document year-to-year changes in the dove population and, when adjusted to a representative base value, provides long-term trend indices (Ruos 1974a). Although the call-count survey has received considerable research emphasis, the biological meaning in numbers of breeding birds actually represented by counts is poorly understood.

The trend in breeding-population indices from 1963 to 1973 is downward (linear regression, $P < 0.05$) for all management units. Annual rates of decline for the 11-year period are as follows: Eastern Unit, 1 percent; Central Unit, 2 percent; Western Unit, 4 percent; and the United States as a whole, 2 percent. Population indices for 1973 are below the preceding 10-year means by 9 percent in the Eastern Unit, 6 percent in the Central Unit, 4 percent in the Western Unit, and 6 percent in the United States as a whole (Fig. 9-10).

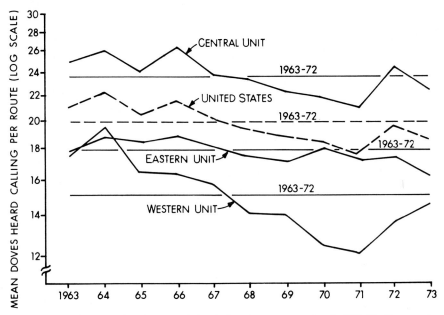

Fig. 9-10. Breeding mourning dove population indices by management unit, 1963–73. Mean number of doves heard calling per route.

CURRENT HARVEST AND HUNTING PRESSURE

In 1973–74, mourning dove hunting was permitted in 31 of the 48 contiguous states representing 73 percent of the breeding-dove population (as calculated from call counts), 73 percent of the land area, and 62 percent of the human population.

Estimates of the mourning dove kill are made by most states where dove hunting is permitted. Harvest figures for 1972 are shown in Table 9-1. These estimates are based on different harvest-survey methods in different states. State figures have been accepted where available except in those few cases where state figures are corrected for response bias, in which cases uncorrected figures are listed. The reliability of the state figures is not well known. If we make a reasonable allowance for missing information, the total annual kill is about 49.4 million birds. Total harvest for previous periods has been estimated to be more than 11 million in 1942 (McClure 1944), 15 million in 1949 (Dalrymple 1949: 161), 19 million in 1955 (Peters 1956), and 41 million in 1965 (Ruos and Tomlinson 1968:31-32).

Average numbers of dove-hunting trips, determined in the same state surveys as the harvest estimates, are also listed in Table 9-1 for states from which information is available. If an allowance is made for missing information, mourning dove hunting annually provides about 11.4 million recreational trips in the United States.

Table 9-1. Current harvest for mourning doves. State figures are 1972-73 unless otherwise specified.

State, Province, or Country (includes all where substantial numbers of doves occur)	Hunting Allowed in 1973	Estimated Number of Hunters (thousands)	Estimated Days Each Hunter Hunted	Estimated Total Hunting Days (thousands)	Harvest (thousands)
Alabama	Yes	106.6	6.8	727.2	3,334.8
Arizona	Yes	63.3	5.3	335.2	1,747.4
Arkansas[a]	Yes	[b]	[b]	[b]	1,069.1
California	Yes	226.3	4.0	902.5	3,850.5
Colorado[c]	Yes	22.0	4.6	101.4	298.8
Connecticut	No				
Delaware[c]	Yes	7.3	4.9	35.6	97.1
Florida	Yes	89.1	8.0	709.4	2,650.3
Georgia	Yes	136.2	5.2	707.5	3,590.3
Idaho	Yes	24.0	3.5	84.2	251.5
Illinois[c]	Yes	135.0	5.0	677.0	2,227.0
Indiana	No				
Iowa	No				
Kansas[c]	Yes	81.2	4.7	378.4	1,363.0
Kentucky[c]	Yes	50.0	5.6	278.0	1,264.0
Louisiana[d]	Yes	68.1	5.9	400.2	1,444.3
Maine	No				
Maryland	Yes	33.8	4.9	166.1	371.7
Massachusetts	No				
Michigan	No				
Minnesota	No				
Mississippi	Yes	90.2	4.9	443.5	2,576.4
Missouri	Yes	81.2	4.9	395.6	1,387.3
Montana	No				
Nebraska	No				
Nevada[c]	Yes	10.6	3.0	32.4	115.8
New Hampshire	No				
New Jersey	No				
New Mexico[c]	Yes	24.5	5.8	141.0	500.6
New York	No				
North Carolina	Yes	141.1	5.1	716.5	3,064.5
North Dakota	No				
Ohio	No				
Oklahoma[c]	Yes	57.7	[b]	[b]	1,293.1
Oregon	Yes	17.9	4.1	73.4	192.3
Pennsylvania[c]	Yes	113.2	5.0	565.9	1,031.1
Rhode Island[d]	Yes	[b]	[b]	[b]	5.8
South Carolina[d]	Yes	98.9	5.8	577.5	2,243.1
South Dakota[c]	No	13.8	3.7	50.5	205.4
Tennessee[d]	Yes	127.0	4.5	572.0	3,087.0
Texas	Yes	318.2	3.7	1,177.2	7,106.0
Utah	Yes	29.3	3.2	94.0	238.4
Vermont	No				
Virginia[d]	Yes	108.5	5.7	623.1	2,425.4
Washington	Yes	27.0	[b]	[b]	280.0

(Continued)

(Table 9-1. Continued.)

State, Province, or Country (includes all where substantial numbers of doves occur)	Hunting Allowed in 1973	Estimated Number of Hunters (thousands)	Estimated Days Each Hunter Hunted	Estimated Total Hunting Days (thousands)	Harvest (thousands)
West Virginia[d]	Yes	5.4	6.3	33.9	57.5
Wisconsin	No				
Wyoming	Yes				
Costa Rica[a]	Yes	[b]	[b]	[b]	6.3
Guatemala[a]	Yes	[b]	[b]	[b]	77.3
Nicaragua[a]	Yes	[b]	[b]	[b]	106.3
Salvador[a]	Yes	[b]	[b]	[b]	472.7
Mexico[a]	Yes	[b]	[b]	[b]	2,507.5
Honduras[a]	Yes	[b]	[b]	[b]	19.6
Alberta	No				
British Columbia	Yes	0.8	[b]	[b]	5.1
Manitoba	No				
Ontario	No				
Saskatchewan	No				

[a] Estimated from band recoveries: data from 1966–68 harvest from U.S. populations.
[b] Unknown.
[c] 1971–72 season.
[d] 1970–71 season or earlier.

Expenditures for Dove Hunting

If we allow $7.62 per small-game-hunting trip (United States Bureau of Sport Fisheries and Wildlife 1972), total out-of-pocket expenditures for mourning dove hunting are approximately $86.9 million annually in the United States. An allowance of $12.02 for income forgone per 4-hour small-game-hunting trip (Soileau et al. 1973:16, 23) indicates that mourning dove hunters forego $137 million of income annually. This sum may be viewed as a partial measure of the value placed by dove hunters on their sport.

POTENTIAL HARVEST

There is undoubtedly an additional potential for hunter kill of mourning doves in the continental United States, southern Canada, and Mexico; however, research carried out thus far cannot precisely designate areas for additional harvest.

States in which dove hunting is not permitted produce doves that are not vulnerable to hunting pressure until they migrate into states where hunting is allowed. Nationwide production and harvest studies are needed to provide information on dove-hunting potential. The jobs necessary to provide the needed information are listed as high-priority items in the 10-year management plan (Table 9-2).

Table 9-2. Budget requirements for a 10-year plan for mourning dove management.

Major Program or Area for Funding	Specific Jobs Within Each Program	Research or Management (R or M)	Job Priority	Estimated Cost of Jobs for Each Fiscal Year (in thousands of dollars)										Total Cost by Job (thousands)	Continuing Job
				1	2	3	4	5	6	7	8	9	10		
Population Appraisal	Evaluate call count	R	1	80	80	80	80	80						$ 400	No
	Develop production index	R	2	60	60	60	60	60						300	No
	Appraise fall and winter population	R	21				100	100	100					300	No
	Improve external age and sex criteria	R	10	30	30									60	No
	Measure seasonal sex composition	R	25				60	60	60	60	60			300	No
	Determine seasonal and annual permanency of breeding pairs	R	28								50	50	50	150	No
	Determine extent of immature breeding	R	22						20	20	20	20	20	100	No
	Determine productivity by habitat types	R	16	40	40	40	40	40						200	No
	Evaluate extent of nonmigratory segments	R	26				50	50	50					150	No
	Appraise population annually	M	3	150	150	150	150	150	150	150	150	150	150	1,500	Yes
Total Cost of Program per Fiscal Year				360	360	330	540	540	380	230	280	220	220	3,460	
Harvest and Mortality Appraisal	Determine survival rates	R	4	400	400	400								1,200	No
	Determine band-reporting rate	R	7	100	100									200	No
	Evaluate crippling loss	R	8	100	100	100								300	No
	Evaluate effects of regulations	R	11	200	200	200	200	200						1,000	No
	Develop national harvest survey	R	5	100	100	100	100	100						500	No
	Relate production and harvest areas	R	15						30	30	30	30	30	150	No
	Evaluate population weighting factors	R	27						30	30	30	30	30	150	No
	Determine importance of disease and pollutants	R	20	100	100	100	100	100	100	100	100	100	100	1,000	Yes

Program	Type	No.	FY 1	FY 2	FY 3	FY 4	FY 5	FY 6	FY 7	FY 8	FY 9	FY 10	10-Year Total	
Appraise harvest annually	M	6	150	150	150	150	150	150	150	150	150	150	1,500	Yes
Regulate harvest from production areas	M	18	50	50	50	50	50	50	50	50	50	50	500	Yes
Total Cost of Program per Fiscal Year			1,200	1,200	1,100	660	660	360	360	360	300	300	6,500	
Habitat Management														
Evaluate habitat changes on census routes	R	14	40	40	40								120	No
Determine nest densities by habitat type	R	19	80	80	80	80	80						400	No
Evaluate effects of land-use practices	R	17	100	100	100	100	100						500	No
Evaluate breeding densities and water distribution	R	29	25	25	25	25	25						125	No
Evaluate characteristics of flocking areas	R	24						40	40	40	40	40	200	No
Study value of winter food plots	R	13	150	150	150	150	150	150	150	150	150	150	1,500	Yes
Improve habitat	M	23	200	200	200	200	200	200	200	200	200	200	2,000	Yes
Total Cost of Program per Fiscal Year			595	595	595	555	555	390	390	390	390	390	4,845	
Information Program														
Institute a conservation-education program	M	12	100	100	100	100	100	100	100	100	100	100	1,000	Yes
Grand Total Cost of All Research and Management Programs by Fiscal Year for 10-Year Period			2,255	2,255	2,125	1,855	1,855	1,230	1,080	1,130	1,010	1,010	15,805	
Habitat Acquisition	M	9	1,000	1,000	1,000	1,000	1,000	1,000	1,000	1,000	1,000	1,000	10,000	No

SPECIES NEEDS

Mourning doves have shown over the long run that they are a versatile, adaptable species. They are one of the foremost game birds in the United States and have sustained an annual kill of tens of millions for many years. During the past 10 years, however, there has been a gradual decline in the breeding population as measured by the national call-count survey. Reasons for the indicated decline are unknown. The pattern is erratic: breeding populations in those states of the Central Management Unit in which dove hunting is not allowed have declined, whereas those in states where the dove is hunted have increased; the reverse is true in the Eastern Unit. No long-term kill statistics are available to correlate with population trends.

Whatever the relationship is between hunter kill and the dove breeding population, management should mean more than documenting population fluctuations and adjusting hunting regulations. Production is an important part of wildlife management and needs emphasis in dove management. Research can uncover present limitations in breeding and winter habitat. Based on such findings, recommendations can be made to enhance dove habitat on public and private land, whether it be forest, range, or agricultural land, or even an urban site. For example, development of a good livestock forage grass that would also produce a seed valuable as dove food could be an important factor in supporting higher dove populations.

Canada, as a production area, and Mexico, important as both a production and a harvest area, should be considered in a mourning dove management plan that seeks to maintain a population capable of sustaining an annual harvest by hunters and providing opportunity for enjoyment for nonhunters as well.

PUBLIC NEEDS

The goal in mourning dove management is to maintain the population in a healthy, productive state that will provide both continued good hunting and nonhunting recreation. Research is needed to delineate factors limiting population size. Once these factors are known, management programs should be developed to remove or reduce these limitations if possible. Efforts should be made to keep the dove population as widely distributed as possible so as to make it readily available for both viewing and hunting by the greatest number of people.

Research programs should be continued to estimate harvest levels that can be safely sustained by mourning doves without diminishing the long-term supply. Hunting regulations should be simple, clear, and enforceable.

The general public, and particularly urban dwellers, should be informed of the value of the dove resource through an extensive information program. Such a program should also attempt to gain acceptance of a national research and management plan for doves.

MANAGEMENT NEEDS

A budget to provide for the management needs of mourning doves is given in Table 9-3. Explanations of the various needs follow.

Population Appraisal

The status of mourning dove breeding populations is estimated from the call-count survey, which is presently the only nationwide mourning dove survey. Results of this survey are reviewed annually by wildlife management scientists and administrators for the purpose of establishing hunting regulations. Supplemental information would enhance the value of the call-count survey by permitting a more thorough population appraisal. A nationwide survey and assessment of fall and winter population distribution and abundance would satisfy this need.

Harvest Appraisal

Current management of mourning doves in the United States is primarily the regulation of hunting to achieve proper harvest and maintenance of breeding-population levels. However, no quantitative evaluation of the effects of dove regulations on kill and on breeding populations has been attempted except in the Eastern Management Unit. Additional studies are urgently needed to clarify the relationships between regulations, harvest, and population levels. Also, a reliable measure of the number of hunters and kill levels would provide information needed for monitoring population status.

Regulating Harvest from Production Areas

The quantitative relationship between dove production areas and dove harvest areas must be established if hunting regulations are to provide maximum recreational benefits consistent with optimal population levels. A continuing appraisal of banding and migration data is a high-priority need if regulatory agencies are to administer an intensive dove management program.

Table 9-3. Budget requirements to provide management needs for mourning doves.

Program	Total Cost per Year	Anticipated Total Cost for 10 Years
Population Appraisal	$ 150,000	$ 1,500,000
Harvest Appraisal	150,000	1,500,000
Regulation of Harvest from Production Areas	50,000	500,000
Habitat Improvement	200,000	2,000,000
Acquisition and Management of Key Habitat	1,000,000	10,000,000
Conservation-Education Program	100,000	1,000,000
Total	$1,650,000	$16,500,000

Habitat Improvement

Improvement of habitat for mourning doves has not been a primary management activity in the past. An increase in the recreational demand for greater opportunities to hunt and view doves will necessitate an aggressive habitat-management program to enhance production and survival. In most instances, improvement of dove habitat on both public and private lands can probably be accomplished through economically feasible modifications in existing forestry, range, landscaping, and agricultural practices, and through federal cropland-retirement programs.

Acquisition and Management of Key Habitat

Habitat destruction or deterioration in some western states is the single most important dove problem, making the need for acquisition and restoration of nesting and roosting habitat a high-priority goal. Acquisition of key dove areas, especially near metropolitan centers, to provide hunting and viewing opportunities for the public is expected to become a management need of increasing importance.

Conservation Education Program

Uniform enforcement of dove regulations throughout the nation by state and federal agencies is a continuing management objective. Legislation, where necessary, should be enacted to help in attainment of this goal. Understanding and acceptance of dove-management programs by both hunting and nonhunting segments of the public increases the effectiveness of these programs. An informed hunter is less likely than an uninformed one to violate regulations imposed both to protect the resource and to permit an equitable distribution of the harvest. Additional funds for an expanded program of conservation education are needed to help in achieving this objective.

RESEARCH NEEDS

A budget to provide for the research needs of mourning doves is given in Table 9-4. Explanations of these needs follow.

Population Appraisal

Objective 1. — Improve techniques of population appraisal to permit determination of the density and distribution of mourning doves on the continent so that the basic status of the population may be appraised periodically in relation to harvest and other uses.

Procedures: (1) Establish the ratio of calling doves to breeding pairs and production in various habitat types of the dove range, (2) develop and evaluate a production index, (3) develop a method of assessing the distribution and

Table 9-4. Budget requirements to provide research needs for mourning doves.

Objective	Job	Number of Years Required	Cost per Year	Anticipated Total Cost for 10 Years
Population Appraisal	Evaluate call count	5	$ 80,000	$ 400,000
	Develop production index	5	60,000	300,000
	Appraise fall and winter populations	3	100,000	300,000
	Improve external age and sex criteria	2	30,000	60,000
	Measure seasonal sex composition	5	60,000	300,000
	Determine seasonal and annual permanency of breeding pairs	3	50,000	150,000
	Determine extent of immature breeding	5	20,000	100,000
	Determine productivity by habitat types	5	40,000	200,000
	Determine extent of nonmigratory segments	3	50,000	150,000
Harvest and Mortality Appraisal	Determine survival rates	3	400,000	1,200,000
	Determine band-reporting rates	2	100,000	200,000
	Estimate crippling loss	3	100,000	300,000
	Evaluate effects of regulations	5	200,000	1,000,000
	Develop national harvest survey	5	100,000	500,000
	Relate production and harvest areas	5	30,000	150,000
	Evaluate population weighting factors	5	30,000	150,000
	Determine importance of disease and pollutants	10	100,000	1,000,000
Habitat Management	Evaluate habitat changes on census routes	3	40,000	120,000
	Determine nest densities by habitat type	5	80,000	400,000
	Evaluate effects of land-use practices	5	100,000	500,000
	Determine breeding densities and water distribution	5	25,000	125,000
	Study characteristics of flocking areas	5	40,000	200,000
	Study value of winter-food plots	10	150,000	1,500,000
Total Cost				$9,305,000
Mean Annual Cost			$930,500	

abundance of fall and winter populations, and (4) improve sex and age criteria to permit analysis of population structure at different seasons.

Objective 2. — Extend knowledge of population behavior to facilitate better understanding and interpretation of population censuses and relationships between density and habitat.

Procedures: (1) Measure sex composition of populations in spring and fall through trapping, collecting, and making bag checks; (2) study permanence of breeding pairs; (3) study extent of breeding by young-of-the-year; (4) study productivity of populations in different habitat types and in different parts of the continent, and evaluate contributions of different periods of the breeding season to fall populations; and (5) study the composition and extent of non-migratory segments of the population.

Harvest and Mortality Appraisal

Objective 1. — Develop techniques to aid in evaluating the effects of hunting on dove populations.

Procedures: (1) Investigate changes in band-reporting rates, and (2) estimate the rates of crippling loss.

Objective 2. — Evaluate the effects of various types of hunting regulations on the dove kill and populations.

Objective 3. — Develop a national survey of the kill of doves by hunters.

Objective 4. — Relate production and harvest areas to mortality rates so that subpopulations can be identified.

Objective 5. — Evaluate weighting factors and other procedures underlying banding analyses.

Objective 6. — Establish the importance of disease and environmental pollution as mortality factors.

Habitat Management

Objective. — Extend and refine knowledge of habitat needs.

Procedures: (1) Compare densities shown by call-count transects or other extensive surveys with characteristics of habitat shown by amount and kinds of cropland (agricultural statistics), soils, topography, natural vegetation, and broad ecologic zones; (2) delineate actual nest densities in different localized habitat types; (3) evaluate influence of agricultural and civil works and land-use practices, such as the soil bank and cover plantings for other species; (4) study relationship of breeding densities to distribution of water in intermountain and plains areas, and evaluate influence of drainage and water development; (5) study characteristics of flocking areas, including types and distribution of food, water, roosts, soils, land use, and relationship to production areas; and (6) study value of late-winter food plots in carrying birds through the winter.

RECOMMENDATIONS

In order to plan a sound mourning dove management and research program for the future, the committee reviewed vast quantities of data gathered and published in the past. It was evident from this review that, although a tremendous effort has been expended on the mourning dove, much of it has produced results that may not be applicable to the entire nationwide population. Dove management in the future will require not only the development of new techniques but also the application on a larger scale of the knowledge and techniques developed at the local level.

We are not recommending that all mourning dove research and management programs be applied throughout the nation. For instance, habitat types in the western states are remarkably different from those in other parts of the dove's range, and information obtained from eastern areas would not necessarily be applicable to western areas.

The estimated cost of needed nationwide dove research for the next 10 years is $9.3 million, and the estimated cost of dove management for the same period is $16.5 million. But the total cost of this 10-year program of essential research and management, large though it seems, is less than 3 percent of the $868 million that dove hunters will, it is estimated, spend during the next decade in pursuit of this important game species.

Recommendations for mourning dove management include an intensified program aimed at improved population and harvest appraisals, regulation of the harvest from each production area so that no breeding population is overharvested, habitat improvement, acquisition and management of key habitat areas, and a program of conservation education. The members of the committee believe that all these activities are of sufficient importance to warrant being initiated as soon as funds become available.

The research effort may be carried out by the various state agencies, by the United States Fish and Wildlife Service, and by colleges and universities under contract. Pilot projects will be needed to develop techniques for some of the programs proposed before they are implemented in all three of the dove management units. Although the proposed research jobs are ranked according to priority, members of the committee believe that all objectives are important.

It is recommended that an intensified effort be made to increase considerably funds allocated by Congress to the Accelerated Research Program. If ARP appropriations could be substantially increased, the amount allocated to dove research and management, plus money derived from other federal and state funds, would provide enough money to carry out a sound program of research and management on mourning doves. The success of our recommendations hinges on the cooperative efforts of federal, state, and private agencies.

Some states where doves are hunted are currently spending considerable sums on dove research and management, and they should be encouraged to continue. The United States Fish and Wildlife Service should allocate more money annually for work on the mourning dove. An amount equal to or even greater than the sum spent on waterfowl would seem to be warranted by the dove's importance as a game bird.

It is further recommended that the Dove Committee, as established by the International Association of Game, Fish and Conservation Commissioners, remain a viable body and that, whenever possible, future dove research and management projects be coordinated through this committee. The function of the committee would be mainly advisory.

ACKNOWLEDGMENTS

The chairman of the Mourning Dove Technical Committee extends his appreciation to the members of the committee for their assistance in developing the research and management plan for the mourning dove. Each member contributed his time and talents in a cooperative manner, resulting in a plan that, when implemented, will yield more knowledge and better management of the mourning dove throughout the United States than have heretofore been possible.

The various dove technical committees in the Eastern, Central, and Western management units also contributed to this plan. Close liaison with the National Program Planning Group made the committee's job much easier by providing a standardized format and numerous suggestions and recommendations.

A valuable side-effect came from this work. The persons involved in research on and management of mourning doves now have close working relations with one another and have gained knowledge of the problems involved in managing a migratory species distributed nationwide in diverse habitats. These two improvements should contribute immensely to the future well-being of the mourning dove.

LITERATURE CITED

Aldrich, John W., and Allen J. Duvall. 1958. Distribution and migration of races of the mourning dove. Condor 60(2):108-128.

Allen, J. M. 1963. Primary feather molt rate of wild immature doves in Indiana. Indiana Department Conservation Circular 4. 7pp.

Blankenship, Lytle H., Alan B. Humphrey, and Duncan MacDonald. 1971. A new stratification for mourning dove call-count routes. Journal Wildlife Management 35(2):319-326.

Cottam, Clarence, and James B. Trefethen (editors). 1968. Whitewings: The life history, status, and management of the whitewinged dove. D. Van Nostrand Co., Inc., Princeton, New Jersey. 348pp.

Dalrymple, Byron W. 1949. Doves and dove shooting. G. P. Putnam's Sons, New York. 243pp.

Foote, Leonard E., and Harold S. Peters. 1952. Introduction. Pages 1-3. In Investigations of methods of appraising the abundance of mourning doves. U.S. Fish and Wildlife Service. Special Scientific Report: Wildlife No. 17. 53pp.

———, ———, and Alva L. Finkner. 1958. Design tests for mourning dove call-count sampling in seven southeastern states. Journal Wildlife Management 22(4):402-408.

Frankel, Arthur I., and Thomas S. Baskett. 1961. The effect of pairing on cooing of penned mourning doves. Journal Wildlife Management 25(4):372-384.

Hanson, Harold C., and Charles W. Kossack. 1963. The mourning dove in Illinois. Illinois Department of Conservation Technical Bulletin 4. 133pp.

Harris, Stanley W. 1961. Migrational homing in mourning doves. Journal Wildlife Management 25(1):61-65.

Jackson, Gary L., and Thomas S. Baskett. 1964. Perch-cooing and other aspects of breeding behavior of mourning doves. Journal Wildlife Management 28(2):293-307.

Kiel, William H., Jr. 1959. Mourning dove management units — a progress report. U.S. Bureau Sport Fisheries and Wildlife. Special Scientific Report: Wildlife No. 42. 24pp.

————. 1961. The mourning dove program for the future. Transactions North American Wildlife and Natural Resources Conference. 26:418-435.

McClure, H. Elliott. 1939. Cooing activity and censusing of the mourning dove. Journal Wildlife Management 3(4):323-328.

————. 1943. Ecology and management of the mourning dove, *Zenaidura macroura* (Linn.), in Cass County, Iowa. Iowa Agricultural Experiment Station Research Bulletin 310:355-415.

————. 1944. Mourning dove management. Journal Wildlife Management 8(2):129-134.

Moore, George C., and Allen M. Pearson. 1941. The mourning dove in Alabama. Alabama Department Conservation Bulletin. 37pp.

Peters, Harold S. 1956. 19 million doves. Southern Outdoors 4(6):9.

————. 1961. The past status and management of the mourning dove. Transactions North American Wildlife and Natural Resources Conference 26:371-374.

Reeves, H. M. 1972. The mourning dove management program. U.S. Bureau Sport Fisheries and Wildlife Special Report to South Dakota Chapter, The Wildlife Society. 24pp.

————, and Spencer R. Amend. 1970. External age and sex determination of mourning doves during the preseason banding season. U.S. Bureau Sport Fisheries and Wildlife. 5pp.

Ruos, James L. 1974a. Mourning dove status report, 1972. U.S. Bureau Sport Fisheries and Wildlife. Special Scientific Report: Wildlife No. 176. 35pp.

————. 1974b. Mourning dove status report, 1973. U.S. Fish and Wildlife Service. Special Scientific Report: Wildlife No. 186. 36pp.

————, and Roy E. Tomlinson. 1968. Mourning dove status report, 1966. U.S. Bureau Sport Fisheries and Wildlife. Special Scientific Report: Wildlife No. 115. 49pp.

Sadler, Kenneth C., Roy E. Tomlinson, and Howard M. Wight. 1970. Progress of primary feather molt of adult mourning doves in Missouri. Journal Wildlife Management 34(4):783-788.

Soileau, Lawrence D., Kenneth C. Smith, Roger Hunter, Charles E. Knight, Daniel K. Tabberer, and Don W. Hayne. 1973. Atchafalaya basin usage study. Louisiana Wild Life and Fisheries Commission Interim Report, July 1, 1971–June 30, 1972. 49pp.

Southeastern Association of Game and Fish Commissioners. 1957. Mourning dove investigations, 1948–56. Southeastern Association Game and Fish Commissioners Technical Bulletin 1. 166pp.

Swank, Wendell G. 1955. Feather molt as an ageing technique for mourning doves. Journal Wildlife Management 19(3):412-414.

Tomlinson, Roy E., Howard M. Wight, and Thomas S. Baskett. 1960. Migrational homing, local movement, and mortality of mourning doves in Missouri. Transactions North American Wildlife and Natural Resources Conference 25:253-267.

U.S. Bureau of Sport Fisheries and Wildlife. 1972. National survey of fishing and hunting, 1970. U.S. Bureau Sport Fisheries and Wildlife. Resource Publication 95. 108pp.

10

Shorebirds

Ronald M. Jurek, Assistant Wildlife Manager–Biologist, California Department of Fish and Game, Sacramento, *Cochairman.*

Howard R. Leach, Nongame Wildlife Coordinator, California Department of Fish and Game, Sacramento, *Cochairman.*

INTRODUCTION

Shorebirds comprise the superfamily Charadrioidea in the Order Charadriiformes (American Ornithologists' Union 1957). In the United States they are those species in five families: Haematopodidae (oystercatchers), Charadriidae (plovers), Scolopacidae (sandpipers and allies), Recurvirostridae (avocets and stilts), and Phalaropodidae (phalaropes). Fifty-two species of shorebirds occur regularly in the United States (Table 10-1) with an additional 12 species of uncommon or occasional occurrence. Although the members of this group were originally classified as game birds, hunting seasons on all but common snipe and American woodcock have been closed for many years.

OBTAINING INFORMATION

A questionnaire was sent to all states in late 1973 to derive general information on shorebirds occurring in the individual states. Data were requested on seasonal occurrence, population status, habitat trends, hunting status before 1936, and realistic evaluations regarding potential for future hunting.

Additional questions were as follows: Are you conducting programs of management and research on nonhunted shorebirds? If so, what are your annual expenditures? If not, give estimates for program costs. What shorebirds, if any, are classified by your state as being endangered, rare, or threatened?

Shorebirds were categorized according to their occurrence as (1) breeding birds (a population regularly breeds in the state each year), (2) transients (the species occurs in the state only as a fall or spring migrant, or both), and (3) wintering birds (a population regularly occurs in the state throughout the winter season, that is, a wintering population is present during January and February every year).

Categories of population status were as follows: (1) C, or common (species whose population level is compatible with existing habitat and which is cur-

Table 10-1. Shorebirds occurring in the United States.

American oystercatcher	(*Haematopus palliatus*)
Black oystercatcher	(*H. bachmani*)
Lapwing	(*Vanellus vanellus*)[a]
American golden plover	(*Pluvialis dominica*)
Black-bellied plover	(*P. squatarola*)
Wilson's plover	(*Charadrius wilsonia*)
Killdeer	(*C. vociferus*)
Semipalmated plover	(*C. semipalmatus*)
Piping plover	(*C. melodus*)
Snowy plover	(*C. alexandrinus*)
Mongolian plover	(*C. mongolus*)[a]
Mountain plover	(*C. montanus*)
Dotterel	(*Eudromias morinellus*)[a]
Hudsonian godwit	(*Limosa haemastica*)
Bar-tailed godwit	(*L. lapponica*)
Marbled godwit	(*L. fedoa*)
Eskimo curlew	(*Numenius borealis*)
Whimbrel	(*N. phaeopus*)
Bristle-thighed curlew	(*N. tahitiensis*)
Long-billed curlew	(*N. americanus*)
Upland sandpiper	(*Bartramia longicauda*)
Spotted redshank	(*Tringa erythropus*)[a]
Greater yellowlegs	(*T. melanoleuca*)
Lesser yellowlegs	(*T. flavipes*)
Solitary sandpiper	(*T. solitaria*)
Wood sandpiper	(*T. glareola*)[a]
Willet	(*Catoptrophorus semipalmatus*)
Spotted sandpiper	(*Actitis macularia*)
Polynesian tattler	(*Heteroscelus brevipes*)[a]
Wandering tattler	(*H. incanus*)
Ruddy turnstone	(*Arenaria interpres*)
Black turnstone	(*A. melanocephala*)
American woodcock	(*Philohela minor* = *Scolopax minor*)
Pintail snipe	(*Gallinago stenura*)[a]
Common snipe	(*Capella gallinago* = *G. gallinago*)
Jack snipe	(*G. minima*)[a]
Short-billed dowitcher	(*Limnodromus griseus*)
Long-billed dowitcher	(*L. scolopaceus*)
Surfbird	(*Aphriza virgata*)
Great knot	(*Calidris tenuirostris*)[a]
Red knot	(*C. canutus*)
Sanderling	(*C. alba*)
Semipalmated sandpiper	(*C. pusilla*)
Western sandpiper	(*C. mauri*)
Rufous-necked sandpiper	(*C. ruficollis*)
Long-toed stint	(*C. subminuta*)[a]
Least sandpiper	(*C. minutilla*)
White-rumped sandpiper	(*C. fuscicollis*)
Baird's sandpiper	(*C. bairdii*)
Pectoral sandpiper	(*C. melanotos*)

(Continued)

(Table 10-1. Continued.)

Sharp-tailed sandpiper	(C. acuminata)
Purple sandpiper	(C. maritima)
Rock sandpiper	(C. ptilocnemis)
Dunlin	(C. alpina)
Curlew sandpiper	(C. ferruginea)[a]
Spoon-billed sandpiper	(Eurynorhynchus pygmeus)[a]
Stilt sandpiper	(Micropalama himantopus)
Buff-breasted sandpiper	(Tryngites subruficollis)
Ruff	(Philomachus pugnax)
Red phalarope	(Phalaropus fulicarius)
Northern phalarope	(P. lobatus)
Wilson's phalarope	(P. tricolor)
Black-necked stilt	(Himantopus himantopus)
American avocet	(Recurvirostra americana)

Note: Common names comply with the AOU checklist and supplements, and scientific names, except for the semipalmated plover, follow Edwards (1974). The scientific name for the semipalmated plover is from Clements (1974).

[a] Species does not occur regularly in the United States.

rently secure because essential habitats are not severely threatened by environmental degradation), (2) U, or uncommon (species or subspecies not immediately threatened with extinction but vulnerable because it exists in such small numbers or is so restricted throughout its distribution that it may become endangered if its total population declines or if environmental conditions deteriorate), (3) E, or endangered (species or subspecies whose prospects for survival or reproduction, or both, within the state are in jeopardy, or are likely to be in jeopardy within the foreseeable future), (4) P, or peripheral (species that extends into the state but is at the edge of its geographic distribution — not in danger of extinction or uncommon in its distribution as a whole), (5) I, or irregular (species that has been recorded, though a population does not regularly occur each year in the state), and (6) A, or absent (species never recorded in the state). Categories of habitat trends were (1) increasing, (2) decreasing, (3 static, and (4) unknown.

Editing of questionnaires was held to a minimum. With a few exceptions, no attempt was made to correct or omit questionable responses; however, obvious errors were not tallied on summary sheets. For purposes of the summary, habitat trend was not tallied for any species listed as being irregular in a state.

RESULTS AND DISCUSSION

The occurrence of shorebirds, their population status, and habitat trends, based on information provided by states, are summarized in Tables 10-2, 10-3, and 10-4. From the responses, it was apparent that data on the status of shorebird resources are generally incomplete and inadequate.

Table 10-2. Occurrence of shorebirds in the United States, by states.

Species	Breeding	Transients	Wintering
American oystercatcher	A Al Ca De Fl Ga Md Ms NC NJ Or SC Tx Va Wa	Cn La Md Me Mi NY Ut	A Ca Fl NC SC Va Wa
Black oystercatcher	Al Ca Or Wa	Ut	Ca Wa
Lapwing[a]		Me NY RI	
American golden plover	Al	A Ar Az Cn Co De Fl Ga Ia Id Il In Ks La M Md Me Mi Mn Mo Ms Mt Nb NC ND NH NJ Nv NY Oh Ok Or Pa RI SD Tn Tx Ut Va Vt Wa Wi WV	Ca Hi Il In Ky Wi
Black-bellied plover	Al	Ar Az Cn Co Ia Id Il In Ks Md Me Mi Mn Mo Ms Mt Nb NC ND NH NJ NM Nv NY Oh Ok Pa RI SD Tn Tx Ut Vt Wa Wi WV	A Ca De Fl Ga Hi Ky La M Or SC
Wilson's plover	A Fl Ga La M Md NC Tx Va	Cn Ka Md Pa SC	Fl
Killdeer	A Al Ar Az Ca Cn Co De Fl Ga Ia Id Il In Ks Ky La M Md Me Mi Mn Mo Ms Mt Nb NC ND NH NJ NM Nv NY Oh Ok Or Pa RI SC SD Tn Tx Ut Va Vt Wa Wi WV Wy	Md	A Ar Az Ca Co D Fl Ga Ks Ky La M Md Mo NC NM Nv NY Pa SC Tn Tx Ut Va WV
Semipalmated plover	Al	Ar Az Cn Co De Ia Id Il In Ks Ky M Md Me Mi Mn Mo Ms Mt Nb NC ND NH NJ NM Nv NY Oh Ok Or Pa RI SD Tn Ut Va Vt Wa Wi WV	A Ca Fl Ga La SC
Piping plover	De Il In Md Me Mi Mn Ms Nb ND NH NJ NY Oh RI SD Va Wi	Ar Co Cn Ia Ks Ky La Mo Mt NC Ok Pa SC Tn WV	A Fl Ga M Tx
Snowy plover	A Ca Co Fl Ks M NM Nv Ok Or Ut Wa	Az Id In Mo Mt NC	Ca Fl La Tx
Mongolian plover[a]		Al	
Mountain plover	Co Nb NM Ok Wy	Ks Mo Mt Nv SD Ut	Az Ca
Dotterel[a]			
Hudsonian godwit		Al Ar Cn Co De Fl Ia Id Il In Ks La Md Me Mi Mn Mo Ms Mt Nb NH NM NY Oh Ok Pa RI SC SD Tn Wi WV	
Bar-tailed godwit	Al		Al
Marbled godwit	Mn Mt ND SD	A Ar Az Cn Co De Ia Id Il In Ks La M Md Me Mi Mo Ms Nb NH NM Nv NY Oh Ok Or Pa RI Tn Ut Va Wa Wi Wy	Ca Fl Ga NC SC

(Continued)

(Table 10-2. Continued.)

Species	Breeding	Transients	Wintering
Eskimo curlew		Co Ok	
Whimbrel	Al	A Az Cn Co De la Il In Ks La M Md Me Mi Mn Mo Ms Nb NH NJ NM Nv NY Oh Ok Or Pa RI SD Tn Ut Va Wa Wi	Ca Ga NC Tx
Bristle-thighed curlew	Al		Hi
Long-billed curlew	Ca Co Id Ks Mt Nb ND NM Nv Or SD Tx Ut Wa	Ar Az Cn la In M Mn Mo NC NJ NY Oh Ok Va Wy	A Ca Fl La NM RI SD Tx
Upland sandpiper	Co la Id Il In Ks Ky Md Me Mi Mn Mo Ms Nb ND NH NY Oh Pa SD Wi WV	A Az Cn De Fl La M NC NM Ok Or Tn Va	
Spotted redshank[a]		RI	
Greater yellowlegs	Al Wy	Ar Cn Co De la Id Il In Ks Ky M Me Mi Mn Mo Ms Mt Nb ND NH NJ NM NY Oh Ok RI SD Tn Va Vt Wa Wi WV	A Az Ca Fl Ga La NC Nv Or Pa SC Tx Ut
Lesser yellowlegs	Al Wy	Ar Az Cn Co De la Id Il In Ks Ky M Md Me Mi Mn Mo Ms Mt Nb NC ND NH NJ NM Nv NY Oh Ok Or Pa RI SD Tn Ut Va Vt Wa Wi WV	A Ca Fl Ga La SC Tx
Solitary sandpiper	Al In Me	Ar Az Ca Cn Co De Ga la Id Il Ks Ky La M Md Mi Mn Mo Ms Nb NC ND NH NJ NM Nv NY Oh Ok Or Pa RI SC SD Tn Ut Va Vt Wa Wi WV Wy	A Fl
Wood sandpiper[a]		Al	
Willet	A Ca Co De Fl Ga Id La M Md Me Mt NC ND NJ Nv Or SC SD Tx Ut Va WY	Ar Az Cn la Il In Ks Ky Md Mn Mo Ms Nb NH NM NY Ok Pa RI Tn Wa Wi	A Ca Fl La M NC SC
Spotted sandpiper	Al Ar Az Ca Cn Co la Id Il In Ks Ky Md Me Mi Mn Mo Ms NC ND NH NJ NM Nv NY Oh Or Pa RI SD Ut Va Vt Wa Wi WV Wy	De Ga M Nb Ok Tn	A Az Ca Fl NM SD Ut
Polynesian tattler[a]		Al	
Wandering tattler	Al	Az Or Wa	Ca Hi
Ruddy turnstone	Al	Ar Az Ca Cn Co la Id Il In Ks La Md Me Mi Mn Mo Ms Mt Nb NC ND NH NJ NM Nv NY Oh Ok Or Pa RI SD Tn Ut Vt Wa Wi	A De Fl Ga Hi Ky M SC Va

(Continued)

(Table 10-2. Continued.)

Species	Breeding	Transients	Wintering
Black turnstone	Al	Az Mt	Al Ca Id Ut Wa
American woodcock	A Ar Cn De Ga Ia Il In Ky La M Md Me Mi Mn Mo Ms NC NH NJ NY Oh Pa RI SD Tn Tx Va Vt Wi WV	Co Ka Md Mt Nb ND NM Ok	A Ar Ca[b] Fl Ky La M Md NC Pa SD Tn Tx Va
Pintail snipe[a]			
Common snipe	Al Az Ca Cn Co Id In Md Mi Mn Mt ND NH Nv NY Or Pa Ut Vt Wa Wi WV Wy	De Ia Ks Md Me Ms NJ Oh Ok RI SD	A Ar Az Ca Co Fl Ga Id Il Ky La M Md Mo Nb NC NM Nv Pa SC Tn Tx Ut Va Wa WV
European jacksnipe[a]		Al	
Short-billed dowitcher	Al	Ar Az Cn Co De Ia Id Il In Ks Ky M Md Me Mi Mn Mo Ms Mt Nb ND NH NM NY Oh Ok Or Pa RI SD Tn Ut Va Vt Wa Wi	A Ca Fl La NC Nv
Long-billed dowitcher	Al	Ar Az Cn Co De Ia Id Il In Ks Ky M Md Me Mi Mn Mo Ms Mt Nb ND NH NM NY Oh Ok Or Pa RI SD Tn Ut Va Vt Wa Wi	A Ca Fl La NC Nv
Surfbird	Al		Al Ca Or Wa
Great knot[a]		Al	
Red Knot		A Az Cn Co De Fl Ia Il In Ks Ky M Md Me Mn Mo Mt ND NH NJ NM Nv NY Oh Ok Or Pa RI Tn Va Wa Wi Wy	Ca Ga Ms NC
Sanderling		Al Az Cn Co Ia Id Il In Ks Ky Md Me Mi Mn Mo Mt ND NH NM Nv Oh Ok Pa RI SD Tn Tx Ut Vt Wy	A Ca De Fl Ga Hi Il In La M Ms NC NJ NY Oh Or SC Va Wa Wi
Semipalmated sandpiper	Al	Ar Az Cn Co De Ia Id Il In Ks Ky M Md Me Mi Mn Mo Ms Mt Nb ND NH NJ NM Nv NY Oh Ok Pa RI SD Tn Ut Va Vt Wa Wi WV	A Fl Ga La NC SC
Western sandpiper	Al	Ar Az Cn Co De Ia Id Il In Ks Ky Md Me Mo NH NJ NM Nv NY Oh Or Pa RI SD Tn Ut Vt Wa Wi WV	A Ca Fl Ga La M SC Va
Rufous-necked sandpiper	Al		
Long-toed stint[a]		Al	

(Continued)

(Table 10-2. Continued.)

Species	Breeding	Transients	Wintering
Least sandpiper	Al	Cn Co De la Id Il In Ks Ky Md Me Mi Mn Mo Ms Mt Nb ND NH NJ NM Nv NY Oh Ok Pa RI SD Ut Va Vt Wa Wi WV Wy	Ar Az Ca Fl Ga La M NC Or SC Tn Tx
White-rumped sandpiper	Al	A Ar Cn Co De Fl Ga la Id Il In Ks Ky M Md Me Mi Mn Mo Ms Mt Nb NC ND NH NJ NM NY Oh Ok Pa RI SC SD Tn Va Vt Wi WV	
Baird's sandpiper	Al	A Az Ca Cn Co De Fl la Id Il In Ks Ky M Md Me Mi Mn Mo Ms Mt Nb NC ND NH NM Nv NY Oh Ok Or Pa RI SD Tn Ut Va Vt Wa Wi WV	
Pectoral sandpiper	Al	A Ar Az Ca Cn Co De Fl Ga la Id Il In Ks Ky M Md Me Mi Mn Mo Ms Mt Nb NC ND NH NJ NM Nv NY Oh Ok Or Pa RI SC SD Tn Ut Va Vt Wa Wi WV	
Sharp-tailed sandpiper		Al Az Ca Wa	
Purple sandpiper		Cn In Md Me Mo Oh Pa Tn	De Fl Ga Md Ms NC NH NJ NY RI SC Va
Rock sandpiper	Al		Ca Or Wa
Dunlin	Al	Az Cn Co la Id Il In Ks Ky Me Mi Mn Mo Mt ND NJ Nv NY Oh Ok Pa RI SC SD Vt Wi WV	A Ca De Fl Ga La M Ms NC NH NM Or Tn Va Wa
Curlew sandpiper[a]		Al De Me Pa	
Spoon-billed sandpiper[a]		Al	
Stilt sandpiper		A Al Ar Az Cn Co De Fl Ga la Id Il In Ks Ky La M Md Me Mi Mn Mo Ms Mt Nb NC ND NH NJ NM Nv NY Oh Ok Pa RI SC SD Tn Va Wa Wi WV	Ca
Buff-breasted sandpiper	Al	A Ar Co De Fl Ga la Id Il In Ks Ky La M Me Mi Mn Mo Ms Mt Nb NC ND NH NY Oh Ok Pa RI SD Tn Tx Va Wa Wi	

(Continued)

(Table 10-2. Continued.)

Species	Breeding	Transients	Wintering
Ruff		Al De Md Me Mo NY Oh Pa RI Tn Va	
Red phalarope	Al	Az Ca Cn Co Id In Ks Ky Md Me Mn Mo Ms Mt NC NH NJ NM Nv NY Oh Ok Or Pa RI Tn Wa Wi	A Fl Hi SC
Northern phalarope	Al	A Ar Az Ca Cn Co De Fl Ga Ia Id Il In Ks Ky Md Me Mn Mo Ms Mt Nb NC ND NH NJ NM Nv NY Oh Ok Or Pa RI SC SD Tn Ut Wa Wi WV	
Wilson's phalarope	Ca Co Id Ks Mn Mt Nb ND Nv Or SD Ut Wa Wi Wy	A Ar Az De Fl Ga Ia Il In Ky La M Md Me Mo Ms NC NH NJ NM NY Oh Ok Pa RI SC Tn WV	
Black-necked stilt	Az Ca De Fl Hi Id NC NM Nv Or SC Tx Ut	A Ar Co Ga Ia In Ks La M Me Mo Mt Nb NY Ok Pa RI Wa Wy	Ca Hi Tx
American avocet	Az Ca Co Id Ks Mt Nb ND NM Nv Or SD Ut Wa Wy	A Ar Cn De Ga Ia Il In Ky Md Me Mo NY Oh Ok Pa RI Tn Wi	Ca Fl La M NC NM SC Tx

[a] Species does not occur regularly in the United States.
[b] Woodcocks were experimentally introduced into California.

A	Alabama	La	Louisiana	Oh	Ohio
Al	Alaska	M	Mississippi	Ok	Oklahoma
Ar	Arkansas	Md	Maryland	Or	Oregon
Az	Arizona	Me	Maine	Pa	Pennsylvania
Ca	California	Mi	Michigan	RI	Rhode Island
Cn	Connecticut	Mn	Minnesota	SC	South Carolina
Co	Colorado	Mo	Missouri	SD	South Dakota
De	Delaware	Ms	Massachusetts	Tn	Tennessee
FL	Florida	Mt	Montana	Tx	Texas
Ga	Georgia	Nb	Nebraska	Ut	Utah
Hi	Hawaii	NC	North Carolina	Va	Virginia
Ia	Iowa	ND	North Dakota	Vt	Vermont
Id	Idaho	NH	New Hampshire	Wa	Washington
Il	Illinois	NJ	New Jersey	Wi	Wisconsin
In	Indiana	NM	New Mexico	WV	West Virginia
Ks	Kansas	Nv	Nevada	Wy	Wyoming
Ky	Kentucky	NY	New York		

Table 10-3. Population status of shorebirds in the United States, by states.

Species	Common	Uncommon	Endangered	Peripheral	Irregular
American oystercatcher	Ga Md NC NJ	Fl SC Tx Va		De La Ms NY	Ca Cn M Me NH RI
Black oystercatcher	Al Ca	Or Wa			Tx Ut
Lapwing[a]					Me NY Pa RI
American golden plover	Al De Hi Il In La M Mn Mo Nb NY RI SD Wi Wy	A Ga Ks Md Me Ms Mt NH NJ Oh Or Tx Ut Vt Wa WV		Ca Co Ky	Ar Az Cn Fl Id NC Nv Ok Pa Va
Black-bellied plover	A Al Ca Cn Co De Fl Ga Il In La M Md Me Mo Mt Nb NC NH NJ NY Oh Ok Or RI SC SD Ut Va Vt Wa Wi	Az Ks Mn Ms NM Pa WV		Hi Id Ky Nv	Ar Tx
Wilson's plover	A Fl Ga La M NC SC	Va Md		NJ	Ca Cn Ks Ms NY Pa RI Vt
Killdeer	A Ar Az Ca Cn Co De Fl Ga Ia Id Il In Ks Ky La M Md Me Mi Mn Mo Mt Nb NC ND NH NM Nv NY Oh Ok Pa RI SC SD Tn Tx Ut Va Vt Wa Wi WV Wy	Ms NJ			Al Hi
Semipalmated plover	A Al Ar Ca Cn De Fl Ga Id Il In Ks Ky La M Md Me Mo Mt Nb NC NJ NH NY Oh Pa RI SC SD Tx Va Vt Wa Wi	Az Mn Ms Nm Ut WV		Co Nv	Hi
Piping plover	A Fl Ga La M Nb ND NY RI SC	De In Ky Md Mi Ms NC NH SD Va Wi	Il Oh	Me Mn	Ar Ca Co Ks Mo Mt Ok Pa Tn Vt WV
Snowy plover	Ca Co Ka M NM	Al Az Nv Or Ut Wa		Mo Ok	Hi Id In Mt Nb Wi
Mongolian Plover[a]					Al
Mountain plover	Co NM Wy	Az Ca Id Mt		Ks Ok	Mo Nb ND Nv Or SD Ut
Dotterel[a]					Al Hi
Hudsonian godwit	Mo RI	De Il La Me Mn Ms NH SD		Tn Wi	Al Ar Cn Co Fl Id Ks Md Mt Nb NC NJ NM NY Oh Ok Pa SC Va Vt
Bar-tailed godwit	Al RI				Ca Hi Ms NC
Marbled godwit	Al Ca Co Ga La M Mt ND Nv RI SC Ut	A Az Il Md Me Ms NC NM Or SD Wa Wy		Fl Mn Mo NH Tn Va Wi	Al Ar Cn Hi Id Ks Nb NY Oh Ok Pa

(Continued)

(Table 10-3. Continued.)

Species	Common	Uncommon	Endan-gered	Periph-eral	Irregular
Eskimo curlew			Al		Co Ok
Whimbrel	Al Ca De Ga La Md NJ NY RI Va Wa	A Mn Ms NC NH Or Wi		SD	Az Cn Co Hi Il In Ks Ky M Me Mo Nb ND Nv Oh Ok Pa SD Tn Ut
Bristle-thighed curlew		Hi		Al	ND
Long-billed curlew	Ca Co Id La Mt Nb NM Or Tx Ut	Az NJ Nv SC SD Wa Wy	A Mn	ND Oh	Ar Cn Fl Ga In Ks M Me Mo NC NH NY Ok RI Va
Upland sandpiper	Co De Ia In Ks La M Mi Mn Nb ND SD	A Id Il Md NY Pa Wi WV	Ky Me Mo Ms NH Oh	Va	Az Ca Cn Fl NC Ok Or
Spotted redshank[a]				RI	
Greater yellowlegs	Al Ar Az Ca Co De Fl Ga Id Il In Ky La M Me Mo Mt Nb NH NM Nv NY Oh Ok Pa RI SC SD Ut Va Vt Wa Wi	A Cn Ks Mn Ms NC NJ WV Wy			Hi
Lesser yellowlegs	Al Ar Ca Cn Co De Fl Ga Id Il In Ks Ky La M Md Me Mn Mo Mt Nb NH NJ NM NY Oh Ok Pa RI SC SD Ut Va Vt Wa Wi	A Az Ms NC WV Wy		Nv	Hi
Solitary sandpiper	A Ar Co De Ga Id Il In Ky La M Md Me Mn Mo Nb NH NM NY Oh Pa RI SC SD Vt Wi	Az Ms NC NJ Or Ut Va Wa WV		Al Ca Nv	Cn Fl Ks Ok
Wood sandpiper[a]					Al Hi
Willet	Ar Ca De Fl Ga Id La M Md Mt Nb NC ND NJ NM Nv RI SC Tx Ut Va Wy	A Az Il In Ks Me Ms NH Or SD Wa Wi		Co Mn Mo NY	Cn Ky Mn Oh Ok Pa Tn WV
Spotted sandpiper	Al Ar Az Ca Cn Co De Fl Ga Ia Id Il In Ky La M Md Me Mi Mn Mo Nb NC ND NH NM Nv NY Oh Or Pa RI SC SD Ut Va Vt Wa Wi Wy	A Ms NJ WV		Ks	Ok
Polynesian tattler[a]				Al	Hi
Wandering tattler	Al Ca Hi Wa	Or			Az Ms
Ruddy turnstone	A Al Ca De Fl Ga Hi Il In La M Md Me NC NH NJ NY Oh RI SC Tx Va Vt Wi	Mn Ms Or SD Wa		Co Ky Mo	Ar Az Cn Id Ks Mt Nb NM Nv Ok Pa Ut

(Continued)

(Table 10-3. Continued.)

Species	Common	Uncommon	Endangered	Peripheral	Irregular
Black turnstone	Al Ca Or Wa			Mt	Az Mt Wi
American woodcock	A Ar Cn De Fl Ga Il In La M Md Me Mi Mn Mo NC NH NJ NY Oh Pa RI Tx Va Vt Wi	Ky Ms ND Ok SC		Ia Ks Nb SD WV	Co Mt Nb NM
Pintail snipe[a]					Hi
Common snipe	A Al Ar Az Ca Cn Co De Fl Ga Ia Id Il In Ks Ky La M Md Me Mi Mn Mo Mt Nb NC ND NJ NM Nv NY Oh Ok Or Pa RI SC SD Tx Ut Vt Wa Wi Wy	Ms NH		WV	Hi
European jacksnipe[a]					Al Ca
Short-billed dowitcher	A Ca De Fl Il Ky La M Md Mn Mo NC NH NJ NY Oh Or RI Va Wa Wi Wy	Al Me Ms Pa Ut Vt		Nv SD	Ar Az Cn Co Ga Hi Id Ks Mt Nb NM Ok
Long-billed dowitcher	Al Az Ca Co De Fl Id Ks M Me Mn Mo Mt Nb NM Nv Or RI SD Ut Wa Wi	A Il Md Ms SC Vt		Ky NC NH Va	Ar Cn Ga Hi La NY Ok
Surfbird	Al Ca Or Wa				
Great knot[a]					Al
Red Knot	Ca De Md Fl NH NY RI Va Wa	A Il Me Mn Ms NC NJ Wi Wy		La	Az Cn Co Ga Hi In Ks Ky M Mo Mt NM Nv Oh Ok Pa Tn
Sanderling	A Ca Cn De Fl Ga Hi Il In La M Md Me Mt NC NH NJ NY Oh Or RI SC SD Tx Va Vt Wa Wi	Az Ks Mn Ms NM Pa Ut Wy		Al Co Mo Nv	Id Ky Ok In
Semipalmated sandpiper	A Al Ar Cn Co De Fl Id Il Ks Ky La M Md Me Mn Mo Mt Nb NC NH NJ NY Oh Pa RI SC SD Ut Va Vt Wi WV	Ga Ms			Az Ca NM Nv Ok Or
Western sandpiper	A Al Ar Az Ca Co De Fl Ga Id La M Md Mo Mt Nv Or RI Ut	Il Ks Me Ms NC NH NJ NM NY Oh Vt Wi		Ky SD	Cn Hi Mn Nb Pa
Rufous-necked sandpiper					Al Mt
Long-toed stint[a]					Al Hi

(Continued)

(Table 10-3. Continued.)

Species	Common	Uncommon	Endan-gered	Periph-eral	Irregular
Least sandpiper	Al Ar Az Ca Co De Fl Ga Id Il In Ks Ky La M Md Me Mn Mo Mt Nb NC NH NJ NM Nv NY Oh Ok Or Pa RI SC SD Ut Va Vt Wa Wi WV	Cn Ms Wy			Hi
White-rumped sandpiper	Ar Co De In Ks La M Mo Nb NY RI SD	A Il Md Me Mn Ms NH NJ NM Oh SC Va Vt Wi	Ga	NC	Al Ca Cn Fl Id Ky Mt Pa
Baird's sandpiper	Al Az Co Id In M Md Mo Mt Nb NM Ok RI SD Wa	A Il Mn Ms NY Oh Or Ut Vt Wi	WV	Ca La NC NH Nv	Ar Cn De Fl Ks Ky Me NC NJ Pa Tn Va
Pectoral sandpiper	Al Ar De Fl Ga Id Il In Ks Ky La M Md Me Mn Mo Mt Nb NJ NY Oh Pa RI SC SD Va Wa Wi	A Az Cn Ms NC NH NM Or Ut Vt		Ca Co	Hi Nv Ok
Sharp-tailed sandpiper		Wa			Al Az Ca Hi Ms
Purple sandpiper	Md Me NH RI	Ga Ms NJ NY SC			Cn In Mi Mo NC Oh Pa Tn Va Vt
Rock sandpiper	Al	Wa		Ca	Vt
Dunlin	A Ca De Fl Ga Il In La M Md Mn Mo NC NH NJ NY Oh Or RI Va Vt Wa Wi	Az Me Ms Mt NM Pa SD		Al Co Ky Nv	Cn Id Ks Ok SC WV
Curlew sandpiper[a]				NY	Al Ca De Me Pa Wi
Spoon-billed sandpiper[a]					Al
Stilt sandpiper	Ar Co De Fl Il La M Md Mo Nb NY RI SD Wi	A Al Az Ks Mn Ms NC NH NJ NM Oh Va Wa WV		Ca Nv	Cn Ga Id Ky Me Mt Ok Or Pa SC Tn Vt
Buff-breasted sandpiper	Ar La RI Tx	A Al Il Mn Ms SD Wa		Mo NC NH	Ca Co De Fl Ga Id Ks Ky M Me Mt Nb NJ NY Oh Ok Or Pa SC Va Wi
Ruff				DI	A Al Ca Hi Il Md Me Mo NY Oh Pa RI Tn Va Wi
Red phalarope	A Al Ca Me Ms NY Or RI	Az NH NJ Wa		Hi Ok Va Wi	Cn Co Fl Id Il Ks Ky La Md Mi Mn Mo Mt NM Nv Oh Pa SC Tn WV

(Continued)

(Table 10-3. Continued.)

Species	Common	Uncommon	Endan-gered	Periph-eral	Irregular
Northern phalarope	Al Ca Co Id Me Ms Mt NH NM Nv NY Or RI Ut Wa Wy	A Az Il Mn NJ Oh SD Vt Wi			Ar Cn Fl Ga Hi Ks Ky Md Mi Mo Nb Ok Pa SC Tn
Wilson's phalarope	Ar Az Ca Co Id Il La Me Mt Nb ND NM Nv Ok Or RI SD Ut Wa Wi Wy	A Ks Mn Ms Oh	NJ	Mo NH NY	Fl Ga Hi Ky M Md Mi Pa SC Tn
Blacked-neck stilt	Az Ca Fl La NM Nv Or Ut Tx	A Ga Hi Id NC Wa Wy		Co De SC Va	Ar Il Ks M Me Mn Mo Ms Mt Nb ND NJ NY Ok Pa RI Tn Va Wi
American avocet	Ar Az Ca Co Id La Mt Nb ND NM Nv Or SD Tx Ut Wy	A Il Ka NC SC Wa		De Mn Mo Wi	Cn Fl Ga Ky M Md Me Mi Ms NH NJ NY Oh Ok Pa RI Vt

Note: For abbreviations of states see Table 10-2.

[a] Species does not occur regularly in the United States.

Table 10-4. Shorebird habitat trends, by states.

Species	Increasing	Decreasing	Static	Unknown
American oystercatcher		De Ms NJ NY SC Va Tx	A Fl La Md NC	Ga
Black oystercatcher		Wa	Al Ca	Or
Lapwing[a]				
American golden plover		Md Ms NH NJ NY Or Tn	A Al Ca De Hi Il Ky La M Me Mn Mo SD Tx Vt Wy	Co Ga Ia Mt Nb NM RI Ut Wa
Black-bellied plover		A Az Ca Md Ms NJ NY Pa SC Tn	Al De Fl Id Ky La M Me Mn Mo NC NH SD Ut Va Vt	Cn Co Ga Hi Ia Il Mt Nb NM Ok RI Wa
Wilson's plover		A NC SC Va	Fl La M	Ga
Killdeer	Me Mt Oh SD Va	Az Ms NH Or RI Tn	A Ca Cn De Fl Ia Id Il La M Md Mi Mn Mo NC NM NY Pa SC Tx Ut Vt Wy	Ar Co Ga Nb ND NJ Ok Wa
Semipalmated plover	Ks	Ca Ms NY Or Pa SC Tn	A Al Cn De Fl Id Il Ky La M Md Mo NC NH NJ NM SD Ut Va Vt	Ar Co Ga Ia Me Mn Mt Nb ND Ok RI Tx Wa
Piping plover	Ks	De Il Me Ms NC NH NJ NY SC Va	A Cn Fl La M	Ga Ia Mi Mn Nb ND RI SD Tx
Snowy plover	Ks	Al Ca Ky Or	La M Mo NM Ut	Co Ok Tx Wa
Mongolian plover[a]				
Mountain plover			Az Id NM Wy	Ca Co Mt Ok
Dotterel[a]				
Hudsonian godwit		Ms Tn	De La Me Mo NH SD	Ia Il Md Mn RI
Bar-tailed godwit			Al	RI
Marbled godwit		A Ca Ms Mt SC Tn Va	De Fl La M Md Me Mn Mo NC NH Wa Wy	Co Ga Ia Il NM RI Ut
Eskimo curlew			Al	
Whimbrel		A Ca Ms NJ NY Or Va	Al De La Md NC NH Wa	Ga Ia Mn RI
Bristle-thighed curlew			Al Hi	
Long-billed curlew		Al Ca Mt SC SD	Id La Nb ND Tx Ut Wa Wy	Co Ia Mn NJ NM Or
Upland sandpiper		Ia Il Ky Md Mo Ms ND NH SD Tn Va	A De Id Ks La M Me Mi Mn NY Pa	Co Nb NM
Spotted redshank[a]				
Greater yellowlegs		Ca Ms NY Or RI Tn Va	A Al Cn De Fl Id Il Ks Ky La M Me Mo Mt NC NH Pa SC SD Ut Vt Wa Wy	Ar Co Ga Ia Mn Nb NJ NM Ok

(Continued)

(Table 10-4. Continued.)

Species	Increasing	Decreasing	Static	Unknown
Lesser yellowlegs		Ca Md Ms NJ NY Or RI Tn Va	A Al Cn De Fl Id Il Ks Ky La M Me Mo Mt NC NH Pa SC SD Tx Ut Vt Wa Wy	Ar Co Ga Ia Mn Nb NM Ok
Solitary sandpiper	Va	Ms Or SC Tn	A Al De Id Ky La M Md Me Mo NC NH NY Pa SD Vt Wa Wy	Ar Co Ga Ia Il Mn Nb NJ NM RI Ut
Wood sandpiper[a]				
Willet	Ks	A Ca Mn Mt NJ NY Or SD Ut Va	De Fl Id La M Md Me Mo Ms NC ND NH SC Tx Wa Wy	Ar Co Ga Ia Il Nb NM RI
Spotted sandpiper	Va	A Ms ND SC SD Tn	Al Ca Cn De Fl Ia Id Ky La M Md Me Mi Mo NC NH NY Pa Ut Vt Wa Wy	Ar Az Co Ga Il Ks Mn Nb NJ NM Or RI
Polynesian tattler[a]			Al	
Wandering tattler			Al Ca Hi Wa	Or
Ruddy turnstone	Ks	A NC Ms NJ SC SD Tn Tx Va	Al Ca De Fl Hi Ky La M Md Me Mo NH Vt	Co Ga Ia Il Mn Or RI Wa
Black turnstone			Al Ca Id Wa	Or
American woodcock	NH Va	Ca Cn Ia Il Ky La NJ NY Oh Ok RI Tn	A Ar De Fl M Md Me Mi Mn Mo Pa SC Tx Vt WV	Ga NC SD
Pintail snipe[a]				
Common snipe	Ga NH NY Ok	A Az Ca Co Fl La Ms NJ NM Oh Or Pa RI SD Tn Va WV	Al Ar De Ia Id Ky M Md Me Mi Mn Mo Mt SC Tx Ut Vt Wa Wy	Cn Co Il NC ND
European jacksnipe[a]				
Short-billed dowitcher		A Ca Ms NJ NY Or Pa Tn Va	Al De Fl Ky La M Md Me Mo NC NH SD Vt Wa Wy	Ia Il Mn RI Ut
Long-billed dowitcher		A Ca Ms Or Tn Va	Al De Fl Id Ks M Md Me Mo NC NH SC SD Vt Wa	Co Ia Il Ky Mn Mt Nb NM RI Ut
Surfbird			Al Ca	Wa
Great knot[a]				
Red knot		A Ca Md Ms NC NJ NY Or Va	De Fl La Md Me Ms NH Wa Wy	Ia Il Mn RI
Sanderling	SD Va	A Ms NC Pa	Al Ca Cn De Fl Hi Ks La M Md Me Mo NH NJ NY Or SC Tx Vt Wa Wy	Ga Ia Il Mn Mt NM Ok RI Ut

(Continued)

(Table 10-4. Continued.)

Species	Increasing	Decreasing	Static	Unknown
Semipalmated sandpiper		A Ms NJ Pa SC Tn Va	Al De Fl Id Il Ks Ky La M Md Me Mo NC NH NY SD Vt Wa	Ar Co Ga Ia Mn Mt Nb RI Ut
Western sandpiper		A Ca Ms NJ NY Or SC Tn Va	Al Cn De Fl Id Il Ks Ky La M Md Me Mo NC NH SD Vt Wa	Ar Co Ga Ia Mt NM RI Ut
Rufous-necked sandpiper				
Long-toed stint[a]				
Least sandpiper	Ks	Ca NC Or Pa SC Tn Va	A Al Cn De Fl Id Il Ky La M Md Me Mo Ms NH NJ NY SD Tx Vt Wa Wy	Ar Co Ga Ia Mn Mt Nb NM Ok RI Ut
White-rumped sandpiper		Ks NY SC Tn Va	A De La M Md Me Mo Ms NH SD Vt	Ar Co Ga Ia Il Mn Nb NC NJ NM RI
Baird's sandpiper		Ca NY Or	A Al Id Il La M Md Ms Mo NH SD Vt Wa	Co Ia Mn Mt Nb NM Ok RI Ut
Pectoral sandpiper		Ca Fl Or Pa SC Tn Va	A Al Cn De Id Il Ks Ky La M Md Me Mo Ms NH NY SD Vt Wa	Ar Co Ga Ia Mn Mt Nb NC NJ NM RI Ut
Sharp-tailed sandpiper			Wa	
Purple sandpiper	NC NJ	SC Tn	De Me NH NY	Ga Ms RI
Rock sandpiper			Al Ca	Or Wa
Dunlin		A Ca Il Ms NC NJ Or Pa Tn Va	Al De Fl Ky La M Md Me Mo NH NY Vt Wa	Ga Ia Mn Mt NM Ok RI SD
Curlew sandpiper[a]				
Spoon-billed sandpiper[a]				
Stilt sandpiper		A Ms NY Va	Al Ca De Fl Ks La M Md Mo NC NH SD Vt Wa	Ar Co Ia Il Mn Nb NJ NM RI
Buff-breasted sandpiper		A Ms NH Tn	Al La Mo Wa	Ar Ia Il Mn NC RI
Ruff			De	Md
Red phalarope		A	Al Ca Me Ms NC NH NY Or Wa	Hi Md NJ Ok Ri
Northern phalarope		Ca	A Al De Id Me Ms NC NH NM NY Or SD Vt Wa Wy	Co Ia Il Md Mn Mt NJ RI Ut
Wilson's phalarope		A Ca Ms Or Ut	De Id Ks La Me Mo Mt NC NH NM NY Wa Wy	Ar Co Ia Il Md Mn Nb ND Ok RI
Black-necked stilt		A Ca Fl Hi Or Ut Va	De Id La NC NM SC Tx Wa Wy	Co Ga Ia
American avocet	Ka	A Ca Mn Or Ut	De Id Il Mo Mt Nb NC NM SC Tx Wy	Ar Co Ia Md ND Wa

Note: For abbreviations of states see Table 10-2.
[a] Species does not occur regularly in the United States.

Nearly every species was listed as having been legally hunted in one or more states in the past. Several states commented that all species were once hunted. Shorebirds listed most frequently as having been hunted were the following, in order of decreasing frequency: common snipe, American woodcock, black-bellied plover (Fig. 10-1D), long-billed curlew, greater yellowlegs (Fig. 10-1E), lesser yellowlegs, American golden plover, whimbrel, upland sandpiper, and willet (Fig. 10-1C).

Fig. 10-1. A. Nest of snowy plover, San Francisco Bay, California. (Photo by Robert Gill, California Department of Fish and Game.)

Fig. 10-1. B. Sanderlings. J. N. "Ding" Darling National Wildlife Refuge. (Photo by Ronald M. Jurek.)

Fig. 10-1. C. Willets. J. N. "Ding" Darling National Wildlife Refuge. (Photo by Ronald M. Jurek.)

Fig. 10-1. D. Black-bellied plover. Naples, Florida. (Photo by Ronald M. Jurek.)

Fig. 10-1. E. American avocets and greater yellowlegs. Woodland, California. (Photo by Ronald M. Jurek.)

Fig. 10-1. F. Least and western sandpipers. Morro Bay, California. (Photo by Ronald M. Jurek.)

Although several states expressed optimism that some nonhunted shorebirds could be hunted in the future, 42 states indicated that, except for snipe and woodcock, there is no realistic potential for shorebird hunting.

Eighteen shorebirds not now hunted were listed by eight states as having potential for hunting. Common snipe and American woodcock already are hunted in some areas but have potential for additional utilization. Other species suggested as having consumptive use potential include the killdeer, American golden plover, black-bellied plover, ruddy turnstone, long-billed curlew, upland sandpiper, spotted sandpiper, solitary sandpiper, willet, greater yellowlegs, lesser yellowlegs, pectoral sandpiper, least sandpiper (Fig. 10-1F), semipalmated sandpiper, long-billed dowitcher, American avocet (Fig. 10-1E), black-necked stilt, and Wilson's phalarope. The preceding list includes those species that are believed by some states to have sporting qualities and some potential for sport hunting. It is expressly noted here, however, that the Steering Committee of the National Program Planning Group for Migratory Shore and Upland Birds, The Planning Group, and the International Association of Fish and Wildlife Agencies do not propose or support placing any of these species on the sport-hunting list under current conditions.

Several states reported that they have programs of research or management for nonhunted species. Those conducting management programs include Colorado, Hawaii, Illinois, and Maryland. States conducting research programs include California, Colorado, Illinois, Nevada, and Texas. A research program in Maryland was scheduled to begin 1 July 1975. Limited response to the question on this subject likely resulted from lack of clarification. As increased interest and emphasis are given to nongame wildlife species, many states are becoming directly or indirectly involved in research and management programs on nongame species, including shorebirds.

Expenditures that have been made for shorebird research and management are summarized in Table 10-5. Some of the estimated needs are indicated also. Estimated needs are typically listed in the range of $15,000 to $25,000 per year per state.

Ten species of shorebirds have been classified by 15 states as being rare, threatened, endangered, or uncertain status (Table 10-6). The status of these species has been based on local conditions rather than on the rangewide status.

LITERATURE CITED

American Ornithologists' Union. 1957. Check-list of North American birds. 5th ed. The Lord Baltimore Press, Inc., Baltimore. 691pp.

Clements, James T. 1974. Birds of the world: A check list. Two Continents Publishing Group, Ltd., New York. 524pp.

Edwards, Ernest P. 1974. A coded list of birds of the world. Ernest P. Edwards, Sweet Briar, Va. 174pp.

Table 10-5. Expenditures made and estimated needed expenditures for shorebird research and management.

	Major Program or Area for Funding	Annual Amount	Years	Source
EXPENDITURES				
California	Population survey and banding	$ 12,000	1970–73	ARP
		6,650	1968–74	P-R
Colorado	Snipe project	15,000[a]	1973–74	ARP
Hawaii	Maintenance of 140-acre sanctuary	2,000		
	Population survey of Hawaiian stilt	3,000		
Nevada	Limited survey work	3,000		
Texas		ca 5,000		
NEEDS				
Alabama		40,000	2 years	
Alaska	Eskimo curlew research or survey	50,000		
Arizona		15,000-25,000		
Colorado	Inventory of species, habitat, and relative abundance and trends	150,000[b]	10 years	
Connecticut		4,000		
Florida	Annual inventory of all species	2,000		
Idaho		20,000[c]		
Maine	[d]	NA	1975–	
Maryland	Research and management	25,000[c]	10 years	
New Jersey	Research and management	100,000[f]		State Legislature
New Mexico		12,000[c]		
Oregon		25,000[g]		
Rhode Island	No need at present[h]			
Vermont		8,000		
Wisconsin		25,000[f]		

[a] No specific funds have been allocated for these species except for snipe, for which there is an ARP project. The total nongame budget is $15,000, but $149,000 is requested for 1974–75.
[b] Total for 10 years or about $4,000 per species for 10 years.
[c] Per project.
[d] Species plans are being developed for nongame species and any programs that are necessary will arise from these plans. The plans were to be implemented in July 1975; cost estimates were not available when this table was prepared.
[e] Minimum.
[f] A nongame program is in the planning stage. It is presently not funded, but there is a $10,000 request in the state legislature.
[g] Initially.
[h] If done, probably restricted to woodcock at $10,000 to $15,000 per year.

Table 10-6. Shorebirds classified by states as rare (R), threatened (T), endangered (E), or of uncertain status (?).

State	Species	Status
Alabama	American oystercatcher	R
	Snowy plover	R
	Long-billed curlew	E
Alaska	Eskimo curlew	E
Delaware	Piping plover	E
Georgia	White-rumped sandpiper	E
Illinois	Upland sandpiper	?
	Piping plover	E
	Wilson's phalarope	?[a]
Kentucky	Upland sandpiper	?[a]
Maine	Upland sandpiper	E
Minnesota	Long-billed curlew	E
Missouri	Upland sandpiper	E
New Hampshire	Piping plover	E
	Upland sandpiper	E
New Jersey	Wilson's phalarope	E
Ohio	Upland sandpiper	?
	Piping plover	?
Oklahoma	Eskimo curlew	?
	Whimbrel	?
Oregon	Snowy plover	T
West Virginia	Baird's sandpiper	E

[a] As a breeding species.

11

The Resources and Their Values

Steering Committee of the National Program Planning Group for Migratory Shore and Upland Game Birds

Wayne W. Sandfort, Assistant Director, Resources, Colorado Division of Wildlife, Denver, *Chairman.*

Spencer R. Amend, Energy Activities Leader, Office of Biological Services, U.S. Fish and Wildlife Service, Portland, Oregon.

George A. Ammann, Former Wildlife Biologist, Michigan Department of Natural Resources, Lansing.

John M. Anderson, Director Sanctuary Department, National Audubon Society, Sharon, Connecticut.

Harold T. Harper, Upland Game Coordinator, California Department of Fish and Game, Sacramento.

Fant W. Martin, Director, Migratory Bird and Habitat Research Laboratory, U.S. Fish and Wildlife Service, Laurel, Maryland.

James M. Ruckel, Assistant Chief, In Charge of Game Management, Division of Wildlife Resources, West Virginia Department of Natural Resources, Charleston.

Kenneth C. Sadler, Research Supervisor, Wildlife Research Section, Missouri Department of Conservation, Columbia.

DISTRIBUTION AND ABUNDANCE
James M. Ruckel and **Kenneth C. Sadler**

Geographically, migratory shore and upland game birds are found throughout the North American continent. Some species are common and widely distributed, others are highly localized and extremely rare. The mourning dove (*Zenaida macroura*) and the common snipe (*Capella gallinago = Gallinago gallinago* of Edwards 1974) occur in all, or nearly all, of the 48 contiguous states, Alaska, and Canada. Band-tailed pigeons (*Columba fasciata*) are located along the West Coast, and an interior flock occurs in Mexico and in the states of Arizona, Colorado, New Mexico, and Utah. Woodcock (*Philohela minor = Scolopax minor* of Edwards 1974) are found mostly in forested areas east of the Great Plains. As though to equalize further the distribution of these resources, the white-winged dove (*Z. asiatica*) is confined to the subtropical, largely arid regions of the southwestern states and Mexico, and the common (*Gallinula chloropus*) and purple (*Porphyrula martinica*) gallinules are found principally in wetland areas of the eastern and southeastern states.

The six species of rails [king (*Rallus elegans*), clapper (*R. longirostris*), Virginia (*R. limicola*), sora (*Porzana carolina*), yellow (*Coturnicops noveboracensis*), and black (*Laterallus jamaicensis*)] and the American coot (*Fulica americana*) are found, seasonally, throughout the continent where suitable lowland habitat exists. At least one species of rail occurs in every state. The breeding range of the coot is largely confined to the glaciated region of the northern plains. This species winters along the Gulf of Mexico, in the Central Valley of California, in the South Atlantic coastal region, and into Mexico.

Of the six subspecies of sandhill cranes, three are migratory [the lesser (*Grus c. canadensis*), the greater (*G. c. tabida*), and the Canadian (*G. c. rowani*)] and three are nonmigratory [the Florida (*G. c. pratensis*), the Cuban (*G. c. nesiotes*), and the Mississippi (*G. c. pulla*)]. The migratory species nest in the higher latitudes and elevations in the United States north through the tundra region and winter in the southern United States and Mexico.

The shorebirds — that is, the oystercatchers (*Haematopus palliatus, H. bachmani*), plovers (*Pluvialis dominica, P. squatarola, Charadrius* spp.), sandpipers (many genera and species), avocets (*Recurvirostra americana*), and phalaropes (*Phalaropus fulicarius, P. lobatus, P. tricolor*) — are also an extremely well distributed and interesting group, all belonging to the Order Charadriiformes. This order includes some species that make spectacular migrations — nesting in the northern limits of North America and wintering in the southern part of South America. It is perhaps for this reason that the shorebirds have always held a special fascination for bird watchers, photographers, and nature-study enthusiasts.

Not all shorebirds, by any means, migrate between Alaska and Patagonia. Others in the group remain within the continental United States. Killdeer (*Charadrius vociferus*) reportedly nest in all of the 48 contiguous states and in Alaska. Significant nesting populations of spotted sandpipers (*Actitis macularia*), willets (*Catoptrophorus semipalmatus*), black-necked stilts (*Himantopus himantopus*), piping plovers (*Charadrius melodus*), long-billed curlews (*Numenius americanus*), upland sandpipers (*Bartramia longicauda*), Wilson's phalaropes (*Phalaropus tricolor*), and others also occur in the United States. In addition to the many coastal wintering populations of shorebirds, a few species, notably golden plovers (*Pluvialis dominica*), spotted sandpipers, greater yellowlegs (*Tringa melanoleuca*), black turnstones (*Arenaria melanocephala*), sanderlings (*Calidris alba*), and least sandpipers (*C. minutilla*), also occur in noncoastal states.

As the reader has learned from the previous sections of this book, precise data relating to the sizes of breeding populations, nest success, and production of all the migratory shore and upland birds are not available. Lacking this information, it is virtually impossible to determine accurately the number of birds that make up the fall flights. Using indirect methods, such as band recovery rates, harvest estimates, assumptions based on data from life tables, and long-term observations, it has been possible to develop some estimates of population sizes. It is apparent that some species within this group of birds are extremely abundant and others are limited in numbers and distribution. For instance, from a variety of evidence, biologists believe the fall flight of mourning doves numbers in the hundreds of millions. Woodcock continue to attract an increasing number of hunters, and, despite this increase in hunting pressure, indices of hunting success and of breeding populations have remained relatively stable.

The fact that common snipe are frequently encountered over a wide geographic range suggests that they, too, are abundant, although present techniques for gathering population data on snipe are inadequate to permit annual population estimates. The continental population is believed to have been relatively stable during recent years.

The annual breeding populations and fall harvests of white-winged doves have varied widely during the past 10 years. Breeding populations in the Rio Grande Valley in Texas have been estimated as high as 805,000 (1966) and, after 3 successive years of decline, reached a low of 416,000 in 1969. The latest population estimate of breeding birds in the Lower Rio Grande Valley (1975) is above the average of the past 10 years. The average breeding population is about 580,000. The Western whitewing population is equivalent to, or larger than, the Eastern (Rio Grande) population. The abundance of this species is in jeopardy from habitat clearing. Periodic damage to citrus groves from freezing also depresses levels of the Eastern population, at least temporarily. The major concerns for both Eastern and Western populations, however, are flood control, channelization, and groundwater-pumping programs that are causing serious losses of nesting habitat. Cessation of these programs and the establishment or replacement of colonial nesting habitats, or both, are essential to the future well-being of this resource in the United States.

Sandhill crane populations vary widely among the several subspecies. Some are abundant and others are scarce. It is estimated that there are 220,000 lesser and Canadian sandhill cranes, about 25,000 greater sandhills, and approximately 5,000 of the Florida subspecies. The Mississippi subspecies, listed as endangered, is represented by fewer than 50 birds, and the Cuban sandhill cranes occur in small, but unknown, numbers.

Coots are well distributed, with good nest densities in the northern prairie pothole region and in western marshes. Dynamic nesting environments with adequate water levels are essential for good annual production and the maintenance of traditionally large fall flights. Surveys in the northern prairies of the United States and Canada between 1955 and 1971 indicate that coots are the eighth most abundant "waterfowl" in that region — less abundant than mallards (*Anas platyrhynchos*) and scaups (*Aythya affinis, A. marila*), but more abundant than American wigeon (*Anas americana*), canvasbacks (*Aythya valisineria*), and American green-winged teal (*Anas crecca carolinensis*). The latest data on nesting populations of coots (from sample areas only) are slightly below the average for the past 10 years, although large concentrations continue to occur in migration and winter areas.

Two distinct populations of band-tailed pigeons occur in the United States — a Coastal subspecies that extends from British Columbia south to Baja California and an Interior subspecies that generally occurs in Mexico and in the states of Arizona, Colorado, New Mexico, Texas, and Utah. Population estimates for both the Coastal and Interior segments have thus far been related to harvest and banding data and to an overall appraisal of trends in populations. Portions of the Interior population appear to be relatively stable, whereas others seem to fluctuate in response to the availability of the food supply. In the coastal region, varying habitats within the range of the band-tailed pigeon make comprehensive censuses and appraisal of densities difficult. It is hoped that research planned for the future will provide refined population estimates for both races.

Of the smaller rails — the Virginia, sora, black, and yellow — the sora is the most numerous and has the widest distribution. This species is found during at least some period of the year in most freshwater and saltwater marshes between Panama and the permafrost. It is unfortunate that even gross estimates of the magnitude of this resource are lacking. In view of the common occurrence and wide distribution of this species, the sora rail population is believed to be sizable.

Virginia rails have far more restricted breeding and wintering ranges than soras, remaining largely within the continental United States, and are doubtlessly much less numerous than soras. Systematic census data are lacking, and data on population trends are therefore not available for either species.

Difficult as it is to obtain data on population trends for Virginia and sora rails, yellow and black rails present an even greater problem because of the difficulty in obtaining observational data. These latter two species are extremely secretive. As a result, the status of yellow and black rails is unknown. A subspecies of the black rail, the California black rail (*L. j. coturniculus*), is officially listed as threatened. The United States Department of the Interior has not allowed the hunting of black and yellow rails in recent years. Optimists will be encouraged by the fact that because of their secretive nature these two small rails may be more abundant than is commonly supposed. Pessimists will be discouraged by the continuing loss of marsh habitat — a loss that must be detrimental to all marsh birds. Until rangewide studies that will yield data on population trends are begun, the status of these rails will remain clouded.

The breeding range of king rails extends over most of the eastern half of the United States, with the wintering range largely confined to the coastal marshes of the South Atlantic and Gulf States. Some additional wintering of king rails is known to occur in freshwater marshes in the lower Mississippi River valley. Further destruction of inland marshes and, to a lesser extent, degradation of coastal marshes will doubtlessly have a depressing effect on king rail populations.

Clapper rails are divided into eight subspecies, most of which occupy coastal saltwater marshes from southern Maine to Florida and along the Gulf Coast, and the coastal marshes of southern California and Baja California. Estimates of population trends based on observational data indicate that Atlantic coastal populations of clapper rails appear to be fairly stable. The remaining subspecies appear to be declining. Two of the subspecies, the Yuma (*Rallus longirostris yumanensis*) and the light-footed (*R. l. levipes*) clapper rails, have a very limited distribution in Arizona, California, and northern Mexico. The three remnant populations in the southwestern United States have declined to the point where they are now officially listed as endangered.

The breeding range of the common gallinule encompasses most of the United States east of the Great Plains. Additional nesting territories are located in the western and southwestern United States and in Mexico. Wintering range is confined to the southern margins of the United States and the coastal areas of northern Mexico. Common gallinules do not occur in large concentrations and they are secretive. As a result of this combination of factors, data on range-wide population trends are difficult to obtain. Loss of habitat is believed to have a depressing effect on the size of the population.

Purple gallinules are not as widely distributed in the United States as their drab cousins, although their range extends from the southeastern United States into Central and South America. They are also transient visitors over a considerable part of the eastern United States and southeastern Canada. This species shares some habitats and behavioral characteristics with the common gallinule and both are difficult to census. The purple gallinule population in the United States, like that of the common gallinule, may be declining. This decline is conjectural, because systematically gathered census data are not available.

It is difficult to imagine a group of birds with a wider geographical and ecological distribution than the migratory shore and upland game birds. From the Arctic to the Antarctic and from the arid southwestern United States to the spruce bogs of Labrador one or more of the migratory shore and upland game birds and their allies occupy virtually every habitat type in North America.

MANAGEMENT APPROACHES AND BENEFITS
Harold T. Harper and Kenneth C. Sadler

Individually and as a group, these widely distributed and diverse species are extremely valuable members of our avifauna — from the viewpoints of both hunting and nonhunting recreational use.

Before discussing the hunting of these shore and upland game birds, it might be well to clarify their "game" status. Historically, many shorebirds have been hunted for food and for the market. However, many of these birds now have greater values for nonconsumptive uses — for example, bird watching, photography, and nature study — than for hunting. To our knowledge, there is no attempt being made to extend game status to species not presently hunted. Furthermore, should evidence indicate that hunting is having an adverse effect on the status of *any* species, immediate steps would be taken to restrict or eliminate the harvest. However, because many of these birds have traditionally been hunted and because they possess outstanding sporting qualities and the ability to produce an annual surplus that can be safely harvested, we feel strongly that the present harvests are consistent with the welfare of the species. There is, in fact, evidence that several species, or in some cases subpopulations of species, can support greater hunting opportunities. It is this subject — the present magnitude of these resources and their current and potential uses — that will occupy the remainder of this section.

Management Approaches

For the most part, current management of migratory shore and upland game birds is directed toward annual appraisals of the population status of some species, together with an evaluation of proposed regulations to permit harvest of selected species by sport hunting, a traditional and highly important form of outdoor recreation for millions of Americans. The objective of the management program is to permit the optimal recreational opportunity that is consistent with the continuing well-being and abundance of the resource. Population evaluations are made by the United States Fish and Wildlife Service, the Canadian Wildlife Service, and cooperating state and provincial agencies, and regulatory decisions are reached, through statutory authority, by the Secretary, United States Department of the Interior, after careful consideration and in consultation with representatives from state conservation deparments, private organizations, other groups, and the general public. The procedures followed are described in the recent environmental statement on sport hunting of migratory game birds (U.S. Department of the Interior 1975).

A wide variety of information — including evaluations of population levels, harvest estimates, recruitment estimates, and measurements of shooting pressure determined from recovery rates of banded samples — is collected each year as a means of assessing the status of the different populations. Specific methods vary among the different birds, as is apparent in the species accounts in this book. However, most population data that are gathered by the federal and state agencies represent indices and are used to measure trends in abundance rather than absolute numbers. Even if actual numbers of birds could be determined with a high degree of accuracy, it would not be possible to maintain the birds at a given level of abundance solely through regulation of harvest. The abundance of migratory shore and upland game birds, as well as other kinds of wildlife, usually is determined by habitat conditions that alter the carrying capacity of the land. These conditions do not remain static. Thus, if suitable habitat declines, numbers of birds will also decline, whether or not they are hunted. Like other wild animals, migratory game birds usually will produce at a rate higher than is needed to maintain their numbers at a given level. They generally will continue to produce at such a rate until they have reached the limit at which the habitat meets their needs. When the carrying capacity of the habitat is reached, reproduction or survival declines, or both may occur. Sport hunting thus provides a means of harvesting a fraction of the population without lasting detriment to the resource. Although protection from hunting will not insure the maintenance of a population indefinitely, excessive harvest will surely cause a decline. Therefore, effective management involves providing suitable habitat and regulating the harvest wisely. A later section in this chapter focuses on the major endeavors that are required to insure that this priceless resource will continue to flourish and be enjoyed by future generations of citizens.

Benefits

It is an understatement to say simply that these shore and upland game birds provide important hunting opportunities for North American sportsmen. It is estimated that the mourning dove alone attracts 3.5 million hunters, who participate in over 11 million hunting trips and spend 224 million dollars each year (Table 11-1). The harvest of mourning doves is presently estimated at about 50 million birds annually. Accordingly, the mourning dove is not only the most important of the migratory shore and upland game bird group but also probably the single most important game bird of any type in North America. Although mourning doves are found in sufficient numbers in virtually all states to permit hunting, traditionally they have been hunted in only 31 states. During recent years, several nonhunting states have attempted to place the mourning dove on their game lists. These efforts have, in general, met with little success. Opening the season in any or all of these states would probably have little effect on either the state or the continental populations of doves. As mentioned previously, although the current dove harvest is estimated to be about 50 million birds annually, band recovery data indicate that this enormous harvest probably represents no more than 10 percent of the total dove population. It seems doubtful that the extension of hunting into northern states, which lack the tradition of dove hunting, would produce a discernible impact on the continental dove population. Liberalizing the regulations in states with established traditions of dove hunting and heavy hunting pressure may, in time, have an adverse effect on the continental population but such an effect is by no

Table 11-1. Hunting activity and the approximate annual harvest of migratory shore and upland game birds in the United States.

Species	States Hunted	Number of Hunters	Hunter Days	Annual Harvest	Expenditures by Hunters[c]
Sora rail	36	15,500[a]	77,000[b]	82,150[a]	1,512,280
Virginia, king & clapper rails	36, 15, 15	40,000[a]	200,000[b]	305,000[a]	3,928,000
Gallinules	42	10,000[a]	50,000	62,000[a]	982,000
Sandhill cranes	8	8,000	23,000	10,400	451,720
Coots	49	136,500	436,800	906,600	8,578,750
Woodcock	34	500,000	2,750,000	1,500,000	54,010,000
Snipe	47	175,000	875,000[b]	1,000,000[a]	17,185,000
Band-tailed pigeon	7	77,300	386,500[b]	525,000	7,590,860
White-winged dove	5	60,000	150,000	900,000	2,946,000
Mourning Dove	31	2,300,000	11,400,000	50,000,000	223,896,000
Total		3,322,300	16,348,300	55,291,150	321,080,610

[a] Estimate based on data from U.S. Fish and Wildlife Service (1975).
[b] Based on five trips per hunter per season.
[c] Based on $19.64 daily expenditures and income foregone by mourning dove hunters (U.S. Bureau of Sport Fisheries and Wildlife 1972, Soileau et al. 1973).

means certain. Unfortunately, since present programs do not permit the gathering of national harvest data, the relationship between regulatory changes and harvest will remain speculative until a national harvest survey can be established.

Hunting traditions have also long been associated with band-tailed pigeons, rails, gallinules, coots, common snipe, and woodcock. The lesser sandhill crane has recently been reestablished as a hunted species. The harvest of cranes is confined to all or portions of nine states — Alaska, New Mexico, Texas, Colorado, Oklahoma, North and South Dakota, Montana, and Wyoming. In view of recently announced plans to channelize portions of the Platte River in Nebraska, there is a likelihood of massive habitat damage to vital sandhill crane staging areas in that state. This project places the future status of this subpopulation in serious jeopardy and is another of the many examples of man's role as a competitor for space. In this case, man's competition with cranes for habitat could have an extremely deleterious effect. Man's role as a predator (hunter), on the other hand, has no lasting impact because the hunter's take is limited to a portion of annual productivity. The annual harvest of cranes in the United States at the present time is 8,000 to 10,000 birds. In this case, countless hours of enjoyment for bird watchers and photographers can be supplemented by the limited but important recreational opportunity afforded by the fall hunting season.

In terms of hunting opportunity and annual harvest, the woodcock ranks as the second most important member of the group of migratory shore and upland game birds. Woodcock are often taken incidentally while grouse (*Bonasa umbellus*) hunting in the Lake States and New England and while quail

(*Colinus virginianus*) hunting in southern states. However, this excellent game bird attracts devoted followers who consider all other game birds to be decidedly distant second choices. The sporting qualities of this interesting and secretive bird are especially esteemed in the northeastern and north central states and the maritime provinces of Canada. Present surveys place the annual harvest in the United States at 1.5 million woodcock taken by about 500,000 hunters. Although the number of woodcock hunters has increased rapidly during recent years, singing ground counts and harvest success have remained fairly stable. This species would profit immensely from a harvest survey based on a national sampling frame. A survey of this type would more accurately assess the impact of harvest changes on populations.

Although snipe are well distributed and there has been a tradition of snipe hunting in a few areas, this species is lightly hunted. At the present time, snipe are legally taken in 47 of the 48 contiguous states and in Alaska. The annual harvest in the United States is estimated to be about a million birds. The limited information that is available (band recoveries have averaged about 2 percent) suggests that this species could sustain an increased harvest.

In some respects the white-winged dove is the opposite of the common snipe. Unlike the snipe, which occurs in wetland areas throughout much of the United States and Canada and supports a relatively long (65-day) season, the whitewing occupies a restricted range in subtropical areas of the Southwest and attracts, in Texas, at least, a large number of hunters during a short (usually 4-day) season. The future prospects for this species appear to be closely tied to the maintenance or reestablishment, or both, of colonial nesting habitats.

Band-tailed pigeons have been hunted in Washington, Oregon, and California for a number of years. This Coastal population yields an average harvest of about 500,000 pigeons annually. Hunters number about 75,000. The Interior population of Arizona, Utah, New Mexico, and Colorado sustains an average annual harvest, in the United States, of between 5,000 and 10,000 birds. The impact of a continued or an expanded harvest of bandtails might depress these populations, and harvest restrictions may be needed in the future. It seems doubtful that either the Coastal or the Interior populations of band-tailed pigeons can sustain a large increase in hunting mortality.

The yellow rail and the black rail are very small, highly secretive birds. Federal regulations do not permit hunting of either species. The remaining four species are either slightly larger (Virginia and sora rails) or much larger birds (king and clapper rails) and are hunted to some extent. The clapper rail occurs in great numbers in some coastal brackish or saltwater marshes and sustains the most hunting pressure. The sora is the most abundant rail and could provide considerably more hunting opportunity. The present annual sora harvest is estimated to be 75,000, with a band recovery rate of less than 2 percent.

Although it is abundant, widely distributed, and has sporting qualities, the

American coot is comparatively lightly hunted and could provide greater hunting opportunity. The present annual harvest is about 800,000 birds. The band recovery rate for coots is about 5 percent. The coot seems to suffer from a poor public image, but if the waterfowl populations, especially the ducks, continue to decline, coots will probably absorb some increased hunting pressure.

Like the American coot, the common and purple gallinules presently attract little hunter interest and it seems doubtful that they ever will. Despite the shrinking habitat for all marsh-dwelling species, annual population surpluses will continue to be available. Unless precipitous population declines occur, it is probable that these annual surpluses can be safely harvested. As a group, the rails and gallinules have been the least studied and, consequently, are the least known of all the migratory shore and upland game birds. As mentioned elsewhere, information on population density and trends, harvest estimates, and even basic life history is largely unavailable for these species. Until better population estimates and trend data are available, conservative approaches to harvest seem in order. The present harvest of gallinules is believed to be about 60,000 birds annually.

In summary, these migratory shore and upland birds are immensely valuable now, and it is hoped that their overall value for hunting and nonhunting recreation will increase. Some species appear to be harvested at, or near, the maximum limit; these include the Coastal band-tailed pigeons, white-winged doves, and perhaps woodcock. Other species, such as the sandhill cranes and the Interior band-tailed pigeons might support additional hunting pressure on some subpopulations. Some species, such as the mourning dove, American coot, sora rail, and the common snipe appear capable of supporting more hunting pressure. A national harvest survey for all species is essential if we are to understand the relationships between harvest and population status. Finally, the tradition of hunting species such as the yellow and black rails, plover, curlews, godwits, and sandpipers no longer exists, and they may never be hunted again.

The last column in Table 11-1 shows a gross estimate of the annual expenditures by hunters (about $321,000,000) in pursuit of this group of birds. In a study recently completed in the southeastern United States, bird watching, photography, and similar activities were engaged in 6.5 times more frequently than hunting. Although these nonconsumptive activities may represent a smaller investment per trip than the costs related to hunting, the addition of this nonhunting recreational use makes the value of the migratory shore and upland game birds truly staggering.

MANAGEMENT NEEDS — NOW AND IN THE FUTURE
George A. Ammann and Fant W. Martin

The preceding text has described the management needs of various migratory shore and upland game birds and has outlined specific research that will be required to meet these needs. The species in this group differ widely in their distribution, abundance, habits, and popularity as game birds. Collectively, they represent a renewable resource of enormous economic and esthetic value.

The purpose of this section is to focus on the management needs of these species and to outline examples of high priority. It is important to realize that the information base needed for effective management is the same for all species, even though the methods used to gather requisite information will differ. Furthermore, there is a more critical need for management action for some species than for others.

The major endeavors required may logically be divided into two parts: (1) development and improvement of methods to measure and monitor population status and (2) identification, monitoring, acquisition, and management of habitats. These two general needs are discussed in this section.

Species and Populations

An ideal program to collect the data needed to measure the annual population status of migratory shore and upland game birds would include five types of information: (1) a measure of or index to size of the breeding population, (2) a measure of recruitment, (3) estimates of size of harvest, (4) estimates of rate of harvest or the proportion of the population retrieved by hunters, and (5) estimates of annual survival rates for various population components. This five-point program would make it possible not only to determine the population status each year but also to identify the cause of any marked change in abundance. For example, if the rate of harvest remained consistent but the numbers of breeding birds decreased, then a decline in reproduction or annual survival, or both, would be responsible. If recruitment remained unchanged from previous years, then the only possible explanation for reduced numbers would be increased natural mortality, a conclusion that would be confirmed by reduced annual survival measured by banded samples. On the other hand, if the numbers of birds declined but the survival and harvest rates remained unchanged, then poor reproductive success would account for the decline. Again, this conclusion would be supported by information collected concerning recruitment rates.

It is clear that this data-collection program would provide the means for optimalizing the harvest and evaluating the status of species and population segments. These objectives can be accomplished generally by means of population indices comparable to those now being used in management, although knowledge of absolute numbers would be valuable. It is unfortunate that at our current levels of funding and knowledge, a comprehensive data-collection program is not feasible. Consequently, alternative procedures must be developed and employed. The need for information is much greater for heavily hunted species than for abundant but lightly harvested birds. Nevertheless, measurements of harvest and of population size or rates of harvest, or both, are required for monitoring the status of all hunted species in order to insure their continued well-being and to provide optimal benefits to the hunting and nonhunting public.

One of the greatest challenges facing us is to obtain valid indices and to develop practical and reliable surveys and other procedures that can be used in population management. There is a pressing need for such action now. This need will soon become critical because of rapidly increasing pressures upon the resource and its habitats. We must also develop an effective program to monitor the status of nonhunted shore and upland birds. This large and varied group is an important part of the resource and provides many benefits to the public.

Habitat

The development and improvement of census, harvest, and other survey techniques is essential in order to monitor population status, evaluate the effects of environmental pollutants — such as pesticides — on populations, and properly regulate the harvest. Effective management is not possible without the capability to assess continually the importance of shooting and other factors on migratory shore and upland birds. Nevertheless, population evaluations alone are not adequate to conserve these species. Habitat plays a key role in regulating the distribution and abundance of migratory shore and upland birds as well as other forms of wildlife. No amount of protection from shooting will maintain a wildlife population if its essential habitat needs are not met.

The various species accounts vividly document the fact that habitat needs are not being fulfilled for all hunted species in this group. In many instances, the extent of the problem is not known because habitat trends are poorly understood and the actual habitat requirements of some species are not fully known. Therefore, it is of paramount importance to determine the habitat requirements of hunted and nonhunted shore and upland species, monitor habitat trends, and acquire or manage, or both, critically needed habitats.

Research and Management Priorities

The previous discussions in this section have addressed the major general needs for effective long-range management of migratory shore and upland birds, particularly the hunted species. These needs include both population and habitat management. The following discussion briefly outlines ways of developing a program to meet these needs. The outline is not complete but stresses the most important areas requiring attention and is based upon a general synthesis of the material included in the different species accounts. These needs cannot realistically be arranged in order of priority because the required research should be conducted simultaneously on various problems involving different objectives. For instance, habitat research should not be postponed until population census methods are developed or improved. Both jobs are too important to delay. Implementation of research findings should similarly be integrated into a comprehensive management program. A list of important needs follows:

1. *Initiation of nationwide harvest survey*
There is no standardized survey by which the annual harvest of different species of migratory shore and upland game birds can be measured throughout the United States because there is no way presently available to obtain information from a completely representative sample of hunters. Such surveys are being made in Canada. Some type of hunting permit or other sampling frame, with names and addresses, is badly needed in the United States to provide a means of monitoring the harvests of doves, woodcock, and the more lightly hunted species of birds. Estimates of harvest levels of different species are currently obtained from a variety of sources including state harvest surveys, telephone surveys, and the waterfowl harvest survey of the U.S. Fish and Wildlife Service. The reliability of nationwide estimates from these surveys is not known but is probably poor because of the impossibility of including representative numbers of hunters in survey samples and the widely different survey procedures among the states. When these estimates are used in conjunction with actual or index values on size of breeding populations, or with information on annual rates of harvest determined from banded samples of the prehunting season population, the population status of the different hunted species can be monitored. When a harvest survey also includes a parts-collection survey to measure the fraction of the harvest consisting of young birds, it is possible to obtain an index of reproductive success during the past breeding season.

2. *Development and improvement of census techniques, methods of measuring recruitment, and other aspects of population surveys*
The development of techniques for evaluating the status of the population for most species of shore and upland game birds is in its infancy. Even the operational call-count surveys used to measure comparative abundance of mourning doves and woodcock have not been appraised. Continued study will be required to refine and resolve the accuracy of existing methods, to determine the extent to which such surveys represent the female segment of the breeding population, and to assess their value in predicting the production of young birds.

With some species — such as snipe — rangewide population censuses are impracticable; many of the birds breed and winter in inaccessible habitats such as northern bogs and tundras and southern marshes. In such cases, alternative methods of assessing the status of populations should be developed and implemented. For example, it may be possible to monitor snipe adequately by means of a harvest survey (to measure harvest size) and winter banding (to measure harvest rates of important population units). Foresight and ingenuity are needed to select alternative economical methods, which can be used to assess the status of different species. The same techniques will not be equally useful for each species. Major efforts should be directed toward those species that are most likely to be affected now or in the near future by shooting, habitat deterioration, and environmental pollutants such as pesticides and heavy metals.

3. *Evaluation of impact of shooting on population status, effects of hunting regulations, and potential for increased harvest*

The impact of shooting on migratory game birds is poorly known, even though this factor is of fundamental importance in management. For example, if popular and more heavily hunted species such as the mourning dove can sustain increased rates of hunting kill without adverse effects upon population levels, the present strict regulations of the harvest could be relaxed. Regulations could then be optimized and stabilized, population status would be monitored, and major efforts would be directed toward habitat management. On the other hand, if research demonstrates that shooting is an important factor that determines abundance of different species of migratory shore and upland game birds, the harvest should be carefully measured and regulated.

Hunting pressure is steadily increasing on most shore and upland species. Consequently, there will be an increasing need to monitor sizes of populations and rates of harvest. Some species should be monitored annually; others may need to be appraised only at intervals of several years. The potential for increased hunting recreation and harvest should be determined for the species that are more lightly hunted at present. Some of these species may provide opportunities for increased harvest, thus permitting a shift in shooting pressure from species that should not be exposed to increased hunting kill.

There is also a need to identify discrete population units of hunted species as a means of optimalizing harvest. It may be necessary to restrict the harvest of some populations whereas other populations within the same species could provide increased hunting recreation. Identification of such populations and their management by harvest units may be an increasingly important management tool.

4. *Improvement in our basic knowledge of different species*

There are important gaps in our basic knowledge of most migratory shore and upland birds. This lack of knowledge is especially evident for nonhunted species; but there are also many unanswered questions concerning hunted birds with respect to taxonomy, life history, age and sex determination, vital statistics, habitat requirements, and adaptability to habitat changes. A comprehensive knowledge of such topics is essential for any management program to be truly effective. Consequently, basic research is needed on a wide variety of subjects to facilitate development and improvement of techniques and their application to management.

5. *Assessment of habitat trends, impact of land use, and habitat acquisition and management*

We have a limited understanding of general trends in habitat quality and quantity, even for those species for which habitat needs are generally known. Such information is vital in long-term planning for wise management of the resource. In some cases, species and populations are clearly being adversely affected by habitat deterioration, but we are deficient in general knowledge of the effect of habitat decline upon migratory shore and upland game and nongame birds. There is a special need, then, to develop the capability of assessing the abundance of different habitats required by the various species and to monitor changes in habitat abundance.

Generally it is not economically feasible to manage habitats on such a large scale that species abundance would be affected on a nationwide or regional basis. Consequently, abundance of shore and upland game and nongame birds will rise and fall in response to major uses of the land. Nevertheless, there is a serious need to investigate ways in which land-use practices may be modified to benefit key species of birds as well as other kinds of wildlife. Such information will be useful to public agencies and to major forestry and other land-holding companies. In addition, many private landowners would undertake a large number of habitat management practices if techniques were known and made available to them. Finally, there is a serious need to identify habitats that may be limited in present abundance and that may be of critical importance to certain species on a local or even regional basis. The importance and locations of such habitats should be documented, and land-use practices should be monitored to ensure that these habitats are not destroyed. In many cases, it will be necessary to protect them through environmental assessments or acquisition.

FINANCING — PAST, PRESENT, AND FUTURE

Spencer R. Amend, Fant W. Martin, and Wayne W. Sandfort

The annual selection and funding of migratory bird projects have historically resulted in lack of full consideration for migratory shore and upland game birds. Whatever the reason for this neglect, there have never been adequate funds to develop the types of studies and programs necessary to meet our responsibilities to the migratory shore and upland bird resource. Specific needs and shortcomings relate to population surveys and enhancement of property, harvest and hunter estimates, and habitat management programs. Research to support each of these functions has been generally lacking or inadequate.

Past

Efforts initiated in the late 1950's to gain support for this group of migratory birds resulted in the establishment of the Accelerated Research Program (ARP) for shore and upland migratory game birds. In 1967, $250,000 was appropriated for research to establish surveys and gather basic data needed for scientific management. The proposal establishing the ARP called for annual increases during the program's first 3 years until an annual level of $1,296,000 has been reached. Only the initial level of $250,000 has been achieved — an amount little more than half of the $450,000 requested for the initial year.

Of the initial amount requested ($450,000), $250,000 was to have been contracted to states on a 100 percent reimbursable basis, and $200,000 was to have been used to increase support activities and special long-range studies of the United States Fish and Wildlife Service. Of the $250,000 appropriated, $175,000 annually has gone to the states for contract studies, and $75,000 has been utilized by the United States Fish and Wildlife Service for special studies and contract administration.

Since the initial appropriation of $250,000 under the ARP program, effective 1 July 1967, a total of $2,000,000 has been appropriated in the budget of the United States Fish and Wildlife Service for accelerated research on migratory shore and upland game birds through 30 June 1975. A summary of the use of these funds is as follows:

STATE CONTRACTS

Total funds obligated:

$175,000 × 8 years = $1,400,000
Less   12,000 For committee meetings and preparation of species
                                   plan.
Less   7,000 For initiation of contract for printing the species plan.
   Total $1,381,000

ARP money has been received by 40 states. The 67 projects, which were initiated between FY 68 and FY 75 are listed in Table 11-2. Twenty-one projects under way as of 1 July 1975 are listed in Table 11-3.

The eight species that have been studied under ARP are the band-tailed pigeon, clapper rail, mourning dove, sandhill crane, common snipe, white-winged dove, woodcock, and coot. One additional study was made of the total shorebird resource in California. Accelerated research allotments by species and state are shown in Table 11-4.

Ten types of studies have been conducted with ARP funds to date. These include:

Banding
Randomization of census routes
Population dynamics
Movement and ecology
Harvest and abundance
Call-count evaluation
Habitat evaluation
Breeding biology
Parasites
General census and inventory

Table 11-2. Contracts awarded for studies of migratory shore and upland game birds during the 8-year history of ARP, 1968–75.

Fiscal Year	State	Contract Number	Contract Title	Fiscal Years Funded	Total ARP Allocation
68	Arizona	933	Evaluate the importance of various vegetation types as nesting habitat for white-winged doves	68–72	$ 87,000
	Florida	928	Ascertain the distribution, effects of harvest regulations, mortality rates, and habitats of common snipe	68–74	31,100
	Georgia	931	Determine the effects of zoning regulations as a mourning dove management tool in Georgia	68–71	66,000
	Illinois	947	Ascertain the distribution, effects of harvest regulations, mortality rates, and habitats of mourning doves	68–70	10,500
	Indiana	963	Ascertain the distribution, effects of harvest regulations, mortality rates, and habitats of woodcock	68–69, 71	13,500
	Louisiana	944	Ascertain the distribution, effects of harvest regulations, mortality rates, and habitats of common snipe	68–73	26,400
	Maine	945	Ascertain the distribution, effects of harvest regulations, mortality rates, and habitats of woodcock	68–72, 74–75	41,050
	Massachusetts	962	Ascertain the distribution, effects of harvest regulations, mortality rates, and habitats of mourning doves	68–73	21,000
	Michigan	926	Banding mourning doves in Michigan as a means of contributing to the knowledge of migration, production, and population dynamics of the species	68–72	21,000
	Minnesota	965[a]	Ascertain the distribution, effects of harvest regulations, mortality rates, and habitats of woodcock	68–69	8,800
	New York	952	Ascertain the distribution, effects of harvest regulations, mortality rates, and habitats of woodcock and mourning doves	68–74	63,250
	New Jersey	937	Ascertain the distribution, effects of harvest regulations, mortality rates, and habitats of clapper rail and mourning doves	68–73	77,000
	North Carolina	946	Ascertain the distribution, effects of harvest regulations, mortality rates, and habitats of woodcock	68–69	8,800

(Continued)

(Table 11-2. Continued.)

Fiscal Year	State	Contract Number	Contract Title	Fiscal Years Funded	Total ARP Allocation
	Ohio	935	Ascertain the distribution, effects of harvest regulations, mortality rates, and habitats of mourning doves	68–72	21,000
	Pennsylvania	969	Ascertain the distribution, effects of harvest regulations, mortality rates, and habitats of woodcock and mourning doves	68–74	58,900
	Texas	934	Ascertain the distribution, effects of harvest regulations, mortality rates, and habitats of common snipe	68–74	30,000
	Washington	941	Ascertain the distribution, effects of harvest regulations, mortality rates, and habitats of band-tailed pigeons	68–70	40,500
	West Virginia	932	Ascertain the distribution, effects of harvest regulations, mortality rates, and habitats of woodcock	68–75	49,550
	Wisconsin	925	Ascertain the distribution, effects of harvest regulations, mortality rates, and habitats of woodcock and mourning doves	68–72	56,050
	Subtotal				731,400
69	Vermont	994	Ascertain the distribution, effects of harvest regulations, mortality rates, and habitats of woodcock	69–70	3,500
	New Hampshire	995	Ascertain the distribution, effects of harvest regulations, mortality rates, and habitats of woodcock	69–70	3,500
	Subtotal				7,000
70	Massachusetts	538	Conduct research studies on woodcock in Massachusetts	70–71, 73	7,200
	Minnesota	527	Radio telemetry studies in woodcock behavior and activities	70–72	42,000
	Minnesota	539	Woodcock habitat evaluation study in Minnesota	70–71	2,900
	Missouri	537	Mourning dove coo-call count evaluation	70	5,000
	Ohio	542	Establishing randomized woodcock singing survey in Ohio	70–71	4,800
	Subtotal				61,900
71	California	586	Accelerated research on migratory upland game birds	71–73	37,000
	Iowa	575	Ascertain the distribution, effects of hunting regulations, mortality rates, and habitats of mourning doves	71–75	25,000

(Continued)

(Table 11-2. Continued.)

Fiscal Year	State	Contract Number	Contract Title	Fiscal Years Funded	Total ARP Allocation
	Minnesota	576	Ascertain the distribution, effects of harvest regulations, mortality rates, and habitats of mourning doves	71–74	14,000
	Montana	577	Ascertain the distribution, effects of harvest regulations, mortality rates, and habitats of mourning doves	71–75	25,000
	Nebraska	578	Ascertain the distribution, effects of harvest regulations, mortality rates, and habitats of mourning doves	71–75	17,500
	New Mexico	587	Study of populations of the interior band-tailed pigeon	71–75	23,500
	North Dakota	580	Ascertain the distribution, effects of harvest regulations, mortality rates, and habitats of mourning doves	71–75	21,000
	Oklahoma	581	Ascertain the distribution, effects of harvest regulations, mortality rates, and habitats of mourning doves	71–74	14,000
	South Dakota	582	Ascertain the distribution, effects of harvest regulations, mortality rates, and habitats of mourning doves	71–75	17,500
	Utah	588	Four-corners cooperative band-tailed pigeon investigation	71–73	12,000
	New Mexico	579	Ascertain the distribution, effects of harvest regulations, mortality rates, and habitats of mourning doves	71–75	15,500
	West Virginia	585	Investigations of American woodcock parasite fauna	71–73	18,000
	Wyoming	583	Ascertain the distribution, effects of harvest regulations, mortality rates, and habitats of mourning doves	71–75	17,500
	Subtotal				257,500
72	Colorado	626	Band-tailed pigeon investigations	72–73	14,000
	Connecticut	630	Research studies on Connecticut woodcock populations	72–74	7,200
	Michigan	628	Research studies on Michigan woodcock populations	72–74	11,400
	Missouri	625	Research studies to evaluate the mourning dove call-count survey	72–75[b]	31,800
	Subtotal				64,400
73	Louisiana[c]	693	Research on clapper rail ecology along the Gulf Coast	73–75[d]	15,000

(Continued)

(Table 11-2. Continued.)

Fiscal Year	State	Contract Number	Contract Title	Fiscal Years Funded	Total ARP Allocation
	New Mexico	692	Research studies on population dynamics of the sandhill crane in New Mexico	73	3,200
	New York	695	Research studies on ecology and behavior of nesting female woodcock and their broods	73–75	14,550
	Oklahoma	694	Research on overwintering mourning doves in Oklahoma	73–75	13,000
	Washington	690	Band-tailed pigeon research	73–75[d]	37,900
	Wisconsin	691	Research studies on woodcock banding and breeding biology in Wisconsin	73–75	46,500
	Subtotal				130,150
74	Alabama	793	Clapper rail nesting and winter population survey in Alabama	74–75[e]	6,700
	California	794	Pacific states band-tailed pigeon investigations	74–75[e]	20,900
	Colorado	792	Research investigations of snipe in Colorado	74–75	7,000
	Georgia	789	Research studies on woodcock and clapper rail banding in Georgia	74–75[e]	7,000
	Kentucky	798	Research studies on origins of doves shot in Kentucky	74–75	4,000
	North Carolina	797	Research studies on crippling losses to dove populations in North Carolina	74–75	12,000
	Oregon	790	Research study of band-tailed investigations in Oregon	74–75[e]	20,900
	Pennsylvania	791	Characteristics of fall migration routes of woodcock banded in Pennsylvania	74–75	8,800
	Virginia	796	Research on mourning dove movement for Virginia use	74	2,500
	Subtotal				89,800
75	Kansas	881	Research studies on the status of Kansas rail populations	75[f]	5,000
	North Carolina	882	Research studies on the status of woodcock in North Carolina	75[g]	5,000
	Oklahoma	878	Research studies on the status and potential of woodcock in Oklahoma	75[f]	5,000
	Vermont	880	Research studies on woodcock banding and habitat use (Vermont)	75[f]	6,000
	Virginia	883	Research studies on the life history of woodcock in Virginia	75[f]	3,500

(Continued)

(Table 11-2. Continued.)

Fiscal Year	State	Contract Number	Contract Title	Fiscal Years Funded	Total ARP Allocation
	Virginia	884	Research studies on the Virginia clapper rail	75[h]	1,500
	Wisconsin	877	Research studies on abundance, harvest, and ecology of the American coot	75[h]	4,000
	Missouri	1,134	Calling performance of mourning doves in relation to the call-count survey	75[i]	6,350
	Michigan	898	Research study on evaluation of effects on woodcock of large-scale habitat manipulation	75[i]	2,500
	Subtotal				38,850
	Total — All Years				$1,381,000

[a] Replaces 943.
[b] 5-year study, to be funded through FY 76.
[c] Changed to 1097 in FY 74.
[d] 4-year study, to be funded through FY 76.
[e] 3-year study, to be funded through FY 76.
[f] 2-year study, to be funded through FY 76.
[g] 4-year study, to be funded through FY 78.
[h] 3-year study, to be funded through FY 77.
[i] Ongoing U.S. Fish and Wildlife Service contracts supported in part by ARP funds.

Table 11-3. Accelerated Research Program for shore and upland migratory game birds — projects receiving fiscal year 1976 funds.

State	Project Description	Appropriation
Alabama	Clapper Rail Census & Banding	$ 3,350
California	Band-tailed Pigeon Census & Banding	10,450
Colorado	Investigations of Rails	4,500
Georgia	Woodcock and Clapper Rail Banding	3,500
Kansas	Rail Study	5,000
Louisiana	Clapper Rail Movement and Ecology	5,000
Maine	Effect of Timber Harvest on Woodcock	5,800
Missouri	Mourning Dove Call Count Survey Evaluation	8,100
North Carolina	Woodcock Banding and Habitat Evaluation	5,000
North Carolina	Mourning Dove Population Dynamics — Eastern Management Unit	8,000
Oklahoma	Woodcock Distribution and Status	5,000
Oklahoma	Spring Census of Sandhill Cranes	2,000
Oregon	Band-tailed Pigeon Census and Banding	10,450
Oregon	Data Analysis of Mourning Doves — Western Management Unit	7,200
Texas	Electronic Censusing of White-winged Doves	6,000
Vermont	Woodcock Banding	6,000
Virginia	Woodcock Banding and Habitat Evaluation	3,500
Virginia	Clapper Rail Banding Study	1,500
Washington	Band-tailed Pigeon Census and Banding	10,450
Wisconsin	Abundance, Harvest, and Ecology of the Coot	4,000
Wisconsin	Woodcock Population Biology and Habitat	22,000
Total		$136,800

Note: $38,200 was reserved for publication of the Species Management book and related expenses.

Table 11-4. Total ARP allocations by species and state for fiscal years 1968 through 1975.

BAND-TAILED PIGEON		**MOURNING DOVE**	
Washington	$ 78,400	Georgia	$ 66,000
New Mexico	23,500	Illinois	10,500
Utah	12,000	Massachusetts	21,000
Colorado	14,000	Michigan	21,000
California	20,900	Ohio	21,000
Oregon	20,900	Missouri	43,150
	$169,700	Iowa	25,000
		Minnesota	14,000
RAILS		Montana	25,000
Louisiana	$ 15,000	Nebraska	17,500
Alabama	6,700	North Dakota	21,000
Kansas	5,000	Oklahoma	27,000
Virginia	1,500	South Dakota	17,500
	$ 28,200	New Mexico	15,500
		Wyoming	17,500
SHOREBIRDS		Kentucky	4,000
California	$ 37,000	North Carolina	12,000
		Virginia	2,500
SANDHILL CRANE			$381,150
New Mexico	$ 3,200		
		WOODCOCK	
COOT		Virginia	$ 3,500
Wisconsin	$ 4,000	Indiana	13,500
		North Carolina	13,800
WHITE-WINGED DOVE		Maine	41,050
Arizona	$ 87,000	Michigan	13,900
		Minnesota	53,700
SNIPE		New York	14,550
Florida	$ 31,100	Wisconsin	46,500
Louisiana	26,400	West Virginia	67,550
Texas	30,000	Pennsylvania	8,800
Colorado	7,000	Vermont	9,500
	$ 94,500	Oklahoma	5,000
		New Hampshire	3,500
		Massachusetts	7,200
CLAPPER RAIL AND MOURNING DOVE		Ohio	4,800
New Jersey	$ 77,000	Connecticut	7,200
			$314,050
WOODCOCK AND MOURNING DOVE			
New York	$ 63,250	**WOODCOCK AND CLAPPER RAIL**	
Pennsylvania	58,900	Georgia	$ 7,000
Wisconsin	56,050		
	$178,200		
Total			$1,381,000

FISH AND WILDLIFE SPECIAL STUDIES AND ADMINISTRATION

The amount spent on projects was $50,000 annually for 8 years for a total of $400,000. These projects included population and habitat studies of mourning doves and woodcock at field stations in South Carolina and in Maine. Total administrative costs for ARP have been $25,000 annually for 8 years (total, $200,000). Editorial services for this book required an initial expenditure of $10,000 from the administrative fund, leaving $190,000 as direct administrative costs for ARP since its initiation.

SPECIAL PURPOSE FUNDS (development of this book)

$12,000 For committee meetings and preparation of species plans.
 7,000 For initiation of contract for printing.
 10,000 For editorial services on the species plans and the book.
$29,000 Total as of 6 January 1975.

Additional funds were reserved in FY 76 to complete publication of the book.

TOTAL — ALL EXPENDITURES

$1,381,000 State contract funds.
 400,000 Fish and Wildlife Service research.
 190,000 ARP administration.
 29,000 Special purpose.
$2,000,000 Total expenditures of ARP funds to date.

In addition to the expenditure of ARP money, considerable amounts of Federal Aid funds under the Pittman-Robertson program have been utilized in state programs. Annual expenditures of these funds during recent years have probably approached $500,000. Expenditures from state wildlife cash funds by state conservation agencies and funding of miscellaneous projects by colleges and universities, private organizations, and individuals cannot be accurately accounted for; collectively, however, they have provided an additional substantial contribution toward improved management of migratory shore and upland game birds.

Present (FY 75)

Funding of the ARP by the United States Fish and Wildlife Service for FY 75 has amounted to $250,000. Budget requests for FY 76 carry an equivalent amount for ARP.

ARP funds directed toward migratory shore and upland game bird research and management are augmented by an estimated $550,000 of Federal Aid funds, plus $137,500 contributed by the states. As in the past, states programs and the efforts of private organizations and individuals are providing a significant contribution toward management of the resource. United States Fish and Wildlife Service funds, other than those of the ARP, are directed toward migratory shore and upland bird management in the areas of overall administration, analysis of band recoveries, development of hunting regulations, and law enforcement.

Future

The total expenditure of $2,000,000 of ARP funds during an 8-year period and an even greater amount expended through Pittman-Robertson Federal Aid projects, state-supported programs, and private endeavors may seem to be adequate. However, when one considers the many species involved, their continent-wide distribution, and the nearly inconceivable complexity of the problems attending their welfare and management, serious funding problems become apparent. As an example, requests for ARP money, backed by well-designed project plans, amounted to approximately $335,000 in 1971. These needs were additional to projects already under way. Only $96,200 was available that year to accomplish a job requiring a third of a million dollars.

It is estimated that the funds needed for migratory shore and upland game birds during a 10-year period total more than $58 million. This figure is based on the species plans for research and management, including habitat improvement and acquisition. Specific needs vary by species and are summarized in Table 11-5. Greatest financial needs are indicated for the mourning dove and rails and gallinules. Next in point of need are woodcock, common snipe, sandhill crane, white-winged dove, band-tailed pigeon, and coot. As shown in Table 11-5, the estimated funds required for habitat acquisition total more than 26 million dollars in the next 10 years. These estimates exceed the total estimated funding needed for either research or management and emphasize the importance of maintaining and providing suitable habitat.

Personnel responsible for budget preparation may at first question the estimated financial needs outlined here by the specialists for the various species. Suggestions for yearly expenditures for these species, however, amount to approximately $5.8 million annually or less than $400,000 per species involved. These funds, expended now, would probably be considerably more efficacious in assuring the welfare of migratory shore and upland game birds than future attempts to improve their status in unfavorable environments and with insufficient information upon which to base management programs.

From the standpoint of time, some decrease in the annual expenditure requirements would result from spreading the program over a longer period. We also know that expenditures for some types of development for one species will benefit other species. This overlap in benefits could lower the collective estimates of expenditures.

Pending development of detailed plans for research and management projects, further evaluation of funding requirements is premature. This analysis, however, is intended to portray the financial obligations that lie ahead. Details of needs outlined in individual species plans will provide guidance in the establishment of priorities for allocation of available money.

It is not the purpose of this book to suggest a specific means to achieve funding. The provision of funds is appropriately a prerogative of administrators in various agencies and organizations with the interest in, and responsibility for, management of the resource. However, because of detailed study given to funding needs and to approaches for meeting them, it seems appropriate to point out several alternatives that could be used in seeking funds.

Perhaps the most obvious and dependable source of funds for needed programs in the immediate future is additional Congressional appropriation. Financial support for the Accelerated Research Program has been obtained in this manner. Since this approach permits development of a uniform national program that can be applied to all areas and to all species, based on needs, it is recommended among the first options or priorities for funding sources. Substantial increases, however, are required to meet the recognized needs. Of major importance is the fact that management problems related to clarification of use of different species would not be solved by additions to the ARP funding base. While notable progress has been made under the 8-year Accelerated Research Program, failure to gain sufficient increases in these appropriations to accomplish the tasks at hand indicate that this approach is inadequate. The total job is not being done.

Although limited funds are much better than none, an alternative that insures a substantial increase in annual revenues is certainly desirable or worthy of exploration. Since one of the major deterrents to improved management of the migratory shore and upland bird resource is lack of a uniform method for determining hunter participation and consumptive use, it seems logical that the procurement of additional funds should be tied in some way to a national framework that would enable us to determine consumptive and nonconsumptive uses for individual species.

The need for additional funds *in conjunction with a sampling framework* would probably preclude the following approaches to funding if they are the sole revenue source: (1) additional appropriations in the budget of the United States Fish and Wildlife Service, (2) use of the existing migratory bird stamp as a vehicle for funding and sampling, (3) donations and gifts, and (4) any other approach that does not provide additional money related to a framework for determining consumptive and nonconsumptive use.

What is needed is a national requirement that users of each species in this resource identify themselves, thus enabling us to make surveys to determine the nature, extent, and location of use. Since both consumptive and nonconsumptive uses are involved, both types of users should be identified insofar as is possible. Likewise, the additional funds should logically come from both types of users — the hunters and the nonhunters (photographers, birds watchers, and the like).

Table 11-5. Budget recommendations for a 10-year plan for migratory shore and upland bird management as taken from species management plans (cost in thousands of dollars per year).

Species	Type of Funding Need	Years										All Years
		1	2	3	4	5	6	7	8	9	10	
Sandhill Crane	R[a]	64.5	64.5	29.0	29.0	15.0	90.0	90.0	115.0	132.0	132.0	$ 761.0
	M[a]	90.0	125.0	167.5	142.5	107.5	130.0	125.0	105.0	120.0	105.0	1,217.5
	HA[a]	500.0	500.0	200.0	500.0	500.0	500.0	250.0				2,950.0
Subtotal												4,928.5
Rails and Gallinules	R	250.0	250.0	140.0	90.0	90.0	70.0	70.0	70.0	90.0	90.0	1,030.0
	M	185.0	185.0	185.0	185.0	185.0	155.0	155.0	155.0			1,570.0
	HA	500.0	500.0	500.0	500.0	500	500.0	500.0	500.0	500.0	500.0	5,000.0
Subtotal												7,600.0
Coot	R	70.0	70.0	75.0	65.0	75.0	45.0	25.0	25.0	25.0	25.0	500.0
	M	15.0	15.0	15.0	30.0	30.0	30.0	15.0	15.0	15.0	15.0	195.0
	HA											
Subtotal												695.0
Woodcock	R	265.0	265.0	715.0	715.0	705.0	425.0	390.0	90.0	90.0	90.0	3,750.0
	M	70.0	45.0	40.0	40.0	40.0	140.0	140.0	190.0	190.0	190.0	1,085.0
	HA			100.0	300.0	300.0	300.0	300.0	300.0	300.0	300.0	2,200.0
Subtotal												7,035.0

											Total
Common Snipe R	250.0	250.0	250.0	250.0	250.0	200.0					1,450.0
Common Snipe M	150.0	150.0	150.0	150.0	150.0	50.0	50.0	50.0	50.0	50.0	1,000.0
Common Snipe HA	300.0	300.0	300.0	300.0	300.0	300.0	300.0	300.0	300.0	300.0	3,000.0
Subtotal											5,450.0
Band-tailed Pigeon R	96.0	80.0	83.0	76.0	86.0	117.0	97.0	79.0	62.0	16.0	792.0
Band-tailed Pigeon M	103.0	123.0	156.0	221.0	160.0	129.0	98.0	128.0	128.0	128.0	1,374.0
Band-tailed Pigeon HA	64.0	128.0	255.0	128.0	63.0						638.0
Subtotal											2,804.0
White-winged Dove R	92.0	69.0	49.0	49.0	49.0	28.0	28.0	28.0	28.0	28.0	448.0
White-winged Dove M	95.5	95.5	95.5	95.5	95.5	95.5	95.5	95.5	95.5	95.5	955.0
White-winged Dove HA	270.0	270.0	270.0	270.0	270.0	270.0	270.0	270.0	270.0	270.0	2,700.0
Subtotal											4,103.0
Mourning Dove R	1,605.0	1,605.0	1,475.0	1,205.0	1,205.0	580.0	430.0	480.0	360.0	360.0	9,305.0
Mourning Dove M	650.0	650.0	650.0	650.0	650.0	650.0	650.0	650.0	650.0	650.0	6,500.0
Mourning Dove HA	1,000.0	1,000.0	1,000.0	1,000.0	1,000.0	1,000.0	1,000.0	1,000.0	1,000.0	1,000.0	10,000.0
Subtotal											25,805.0
All Species R	2,692.5	2,653.5	2,816.0	2,479.0	2,475.0	1,555.0	1,130.0	887.0	697.0	651.0	18,036.0
All Species M	1,358.5	1,388.5	1,459.0	1,514.0	1,418.0	1,379.5	1,328.5	1,388.5	1,338.5	1,323.5	13,896.5
All Species HA	2,634.0	2,698.0	2,625.0	2,998.0	2,933.0	2,870.0	2,620.0	2,370.0	2,370.0	2,370.0	26,488.0
Grand Total	6,685.0	6,740.0	6,900.0	6,991.0	6,826.0	5,804.5	5,078.5	4,645.5	4,405.5	4,344.5	58,420.5

[a] R = research, M = management, HA = habitat acquisition.

For the reasons outlined, it appears that funding from several sources is most appropriate. Administration of the program, including identification of users, however, must be mandatory and uniformly applied to be effective.

In summary, research and management needs for migratory shore and upland birds are substantially more than can be met with funds now available. We urge administrators on federal and state levels to work cooperatively in the development of new approaches for an adequate funding base to do the job as outlined in this book.

LITERATURE CITED

Edwards, Ernest P. 1974. A coded list of birds of the world. Ernest P. Edwards, Sweet Briar, Va. 174pp.

Soileau, Lawrence C., Kenneth C. Smith, Roger Hunter, Charles E. Knight, Daniel K. Tabberer, and Don W. Hayne. 1973. Atchafalaya Basin usage study. Louisiana Wild Life and Fisheries Commission Interim Report, July 1, 1971–June 30, 1972. 49pp.

U.S. Bureau of Sport Fisheries and Wildlife. 1972. National survey of fishing and hunting, 1970. U.S. Bureau Sport Fisheries and Wildlife Resource Publication 95. 108pp.

U.S. Fish and Wildlife Service. 1975. Final environmental statement for the issuance of annual regulations permitting the sport hunting of migratory birds FES 75-54. Department of the Interior, Washington, D.C. 710pp. + Appendices.

Index

Abies
  balsamea, 166
  concolor, 223
  lasiocarpa, 223
Acacia
  berlandieri, 254
  farnesiana, 252
Accelerated research program, 1, 337-350
Acer macrophyllum, 222
Actitis macularaia, 302, 324
Adenostoma fasciculatus, 223
Alder, 151
  red, 222
Alfalfa, 153
Allin, Charles C., 275
Alloniscus mirabilis, 73
Alnus, 151
  rubra, 222
Amend, Spencer R., *x,* 3, 323, 337
American
  avocet, see avocet, American
  coot, see coot, American
  golden plover, see plover, American
    golden
  Oystercatcher, see oystercatcher,
    American
  wigeon, see wigeon, American
  woodcock, see woodcock, American
Ammann, George A., *x,* 3, 323, 332
Anaqua, 252
Anas
  acuta, 136
  americana, 136, 326
  clypeata, 136
  crecca carolinensis, 326
  discors, 136
  platyrhynchos, 136, 326
  strepera, 138
Anderson, John M., *x,* 45, 66, 123, 149,
  275, 323
Aphriza virgata, 302
Arachis hypogaea, 279
Arbutus menziesii, 222
Archibald, George W., 5
Arctostaphylos spp., 223
Arenaria
  interpres, 302
  melanocephala, 302, 324
Arizona white-winged dove, see dove,
  Arizona white-winged
Arnold, Keith A., 189
Artmann, Joheph W., 149
Arundinaria tecta, 159

Atamisquea emarginata, 254
Avicennis nitada, 255
Avocet, American, 300-301, 303, 308, 313,
  316-317, 324
Aythya
  affinis, 136
  americana, 138
  collaris, 138
  marila, 136
  valisineri, 138, 326

Bachman's warbler, see warbler, Bach-
  man's
Baird's sandpiper, see sandpiper, Baird's
Bald eagle, see eagle, bald
Band-tailed pigeon, see pigeon, band-
  tailed
Barley, 11
Bar-tailed godwit, see godwit, bar-tailed
Bartramia longicauda, 302, 324
Bateman, Hugh A., Jr., 45, 93
Betula spp., 158
Biotelemetry, 79
Birch, 158
Black-bellied plover, see plover,
  black-bellied
Black crake, see rail, black
Black-necked stilt, see stilt, black-necked
Black oystercatcher, see oystercatcher,
  black
Black rail, see rail, black
Black turnstone, see turnstone, black
Blankinship, David R., 247
Blue-winged teal, see teal, blue-winged
Bobwhite, 93, 330
Bonasa umbellus, 172, 330
Bowing-cooing pursuit, 213
Branta canadensis, 32
Braun, Clait E., 211, 275
Brazil, 252
Bristle-thighed curlew, see curlew,
  bristle-thighed
Brogla crane, see crane, Brogla
Brown, David E., 211, 247
Bubo virginianus, 130
Bucephala
  clangula, 138
  islandica, 138
Buckrush, 223
Buff-breasted sandpiper, see sandpiper,
  buff-breasted
Bulrush, 125
  three-square, 72, 76, 113

Cactus,
  giant, 250, 254
  prickly-pear, 254
Calidris
  acuminata, 303
  alba, 302, 324
  alpina, 303
  bairdii, 302
  canutus, 302
  ferruginea, 303
  fuscicollis, 302
  maritima, 303
  mauri, 302
  melanotos, 302
  minutilla, 302, 324
  ptilocnemis, 303
  pusilla, 302
  ruficollis, 302
  subminuta, 302
  tenuirostris, 302
California black rail, see rail, black
California clapper rail, see rail, California
    clapper
Campephilus principalis, 78
Canada goose, see goose, Canada
Canadian crane, see crane, Canadian
Cane, switch, 159
Cannon-net trapping, 235
Canvasback, 138, 326
Capella gallinago, 1, 150, 188-209, 302,
    323
Cardon, 254
Carex, 46, 113
Carolina rail, see rail, sora
Carthamus tinctoris, 250
Carya illinoensis, 254
Cascara, 222
Cassidix mexicanus, 251
Catoptrophorus semipalmatus, 302, 324
Cattail, 22, 46, 125
Ceanothus spp. 223
Cedar,
  incense, 223
  Port Orford, 222
  red, 222
  salt, 254
Celtis
  pallida, 252
  reticulata, 253
Cercidium
  floridum, 254
  microphyllum, 254
Cereus giganteus, 250
Chamaecyparis lawsoniana, 222
Chamise, 223
Charadrius
  alexandrinus, 302

  melodus, 302, 324
  mongolus, 302
  montanus, 302
  semipalmatus, 302
  spp., 324
  vociferus, 302, 324
  wilsonia, 302
Cherry, wild, 222
Chilopsis linearis, 254
Cladium sp., 22
Clapper rail, see rail, clapper
Clark, Eldon R., 149
Coffeeberry, 223
Colima, 252
Colinus virginianus, 93, 331
Columba
  fasciata, 1, 210-245, 323
  fasciata fasciata, 211
  fasciata monilis, 211
  livia, 212, 276
Common gallinule, see gallinule, common
Common snipe, see snipe, common
Condalia obovata, 252
Coot, American, 1, 2, 111, 113, 122-147,
    324, 326, 330, 343-344, 348
Cordgrass, 84-85
Corn, 250, 279
Cornus nuttallii, 222
Corvus spp., 86
Cotton, 131
Cottonwood, 223
Coturnicops noveboracensis, 66-70, 324
Crab, fiddler, 85
Crake, black, see rail, black
Crane,
  brogla, 33
  Canadian, 15, 324
  Cuban, 23, 324
  Florida, 22, 324
  greater sandhill, 9, 324
  lesser sandhill, 15, 324
  Mississippi, 23, 324
  sandhill, 1, 2, 4-43, 330, 342-343, 348
  whooping, 27
Crow, 86
Cuban crane, see crane, Cuban
Curlew,
  bristle-thighed, 302, 305, 310, 314
  Eskimo, 302, 305, 310, 314, 320
  long-billed, 302, 305, 310, 314, 320, 324
  sandpiper, see sandpiper, curlew

Deer, white-tailed, 167, 172
Dilworth, Timothy G., 149
Dogwood, western flowering, 222
Dotterel, 302, 304, 309, 314

Dove,
　Arizona white-winged, 248
　eastern white-winged, see dove, Texas
　　white-winged
　Mexican highland white-winged, 248
　mourning, 2, 214, 256, 274-298, 323,
　　330, 339-344, 349
　rock, see pigeon, domestic
　Texas white-winged, 248
　upper Big Bend white-winged, 248
　western white-winged, see dove, Arizona
　　white-winged
　white-winged, 2, 246-272, 283, 323, 330,
　　339, 343, 349
　white-winged, state-issued stamp, 270
Dowitcher, 203
　long-billed, 302, 306, 311, 315
　short-billed, 302, 306, 311, 315
Drewien, Roderick C., 5
Duck, ring-necked, 138
Duckweed, 106
Dunlin, 303, 307, 312, 316

Eagle, bald, 130
Eastern meadowlark, see meadowlark,
　eastern
Eastern white-winged dove, see dove,
　Texas white-winged
Ebony, 252
Echinochola crusgalli, 106
Ectopistes migratorius, 193, 216
Ehretia anacua, 252
Elderberry, 222, 241
Elm, winged, 253
Eskimo curlew, see curlew, Eskimo
Eudromias morinellus, 302
Eurasian woodcock, see woodcock,
　Eurasian
Eurynorhynchus pygmeus, 303

Farallon rail, see rail, black
Fiddler crab, see crab, fiddler
Fir,
　alpine, 223
　Douglas, 222, 223
　white, 223
Florida clapper rail, see rail, Florida
　clapper
Florida crane, see crane, Florida
Flowering dogwood, see dogwood,
　flowering
Fogarty, Michael J., 189
Forchammeria watsoni, 254
Forestiera acuminata, 159
Four Corners States Cooperative Pigeon
　Study, 219

Fraxinus sp., 253
Fredrickson, Leigh H., 123
Frith, Charles R., 5
Fulica americana, 1, 122-147, 324
Funk, Howard D., 275

Gadwall, 138
Gallinago
　gallinago, see *Capella gallinago*
　minima, 302
　stenura, 302
Gallinula chloropus, 105, 110-117, 323
Gallinule, 118-121, 330, 348
　common, 44, 105, 110-117, 323, 327
　purple, 105-109, 324, 327
Gallizioli, Steve, 275
Glycine max, 168
Godwit,
　bar-tailed, 302, 304, 309, 314
　Hudsonian, 302, 304, 309, 314
　marbled, 302, 304, 309, 314
Goldeneye, 138
Golden plover, see plover, American
　golden
Goose, Canada, 32
Gossypium spp., 131
Grackle, great-tailed, 251
Granjeno, 252
Grass,
　salt, 15
　salt-marsh, 46
　saw, 22
　wire, 67
Greater sandhill crane, see crane, greater
　sandhill
Greater yellowlegs, see yellowlegs, greater
Great horned owl, see owl, great horned
Great knot, see knot, great
Great-tailed grackle, see grackle, great-
　tailed
Greenbrier, 160
Green-winged teal, see teal, American
　green-winged
Gregg, Larry E., 149
Grouse, ruffled, 172, 330
Grus
　americana, 27
　canadensis, 1, 4-43
　　canadensis, 5, 324
　　nesiotes, 5, 324
　　pratensis, 5, 324
　　pulla, 5, 324
　　rowani, 5, 324
　　tabida, 5, 324
　rubicunda, 33
Guajillo, 254
Gull, 86

Hackberry, 253
Haematopus
  bachmani, 302, 324
  palliatus, 302, 324
Haliaeetus leucocephalus, 130
Halladay, D. Ray, 211
Harper, Harold T., *xi,* 2, 323, 327
Hayne, Don W., 275
Hegari, 261
Hemlock, western, 222
Herpestes javanicus, 76
Heteroscelus
  brevipes, 302
  incanus, 302
Himantopus himantopus, 303, 324
Holliman, Dan C., 45, 105, 118
Holly, 159
Honeysuckle, 159
Hordeum spp., 11
Howard, Paul M., 211
Huckleberry, 222
Hudsonian godwit, see godwit, Hudsonian
Huisache, 252

Ilex spp., 159
Incense cedar, see cedar, incense
International Association of Fish and
    Wildlife Agencies, *vii, ix,* 1, 2
Ironwood, 254
Ivory-billed woodpecker, see woodpecker,
    ivory-billed

Jack snipe, 306, 311, 315
Jeffrey, Robert G., 211
Jito, 254
Juncus sp., 84
Juniper, California, 223
Juniperus californica, 223
Jurek, Ronald M., 301

Kebbe, Chester E., 211
Keeler, James E., 275
Kiel, William H., Jr., 247, 275
Killdeer, 302, 304, 309, 314, 324
King rail, see rail, king
Klataske, Ronald D., 5
Knot,
  great, 302, 306, 311, 315
  red, 302, 306, 311, 315
Kozlik, Frank M., 123

Lapwing, 302, 304, 309, 314
Larch, 158
Larix laricina, 158
Larus spp., 86
Laterallus jamaicensis, 71-83, 119, 324

coturniculus, 79, 326
jamaicensis, 76, 79
Leach, Howard R., 301
Least sandpiper, see sandpiper, least
Lemaireocereus thurberi, 254
Lemna sp., 106
Lesser sandhill crane, see crane, lesser
    sandhill
Lesser yellowlegs, see yellowlegs, lesser
Lewis, James C., 5
Libocedrus decurrens, 223
Light-footed clapper rail, see rail, light-
    footed clapper
Limnodromus
  griseus, 302
  scolopaceus, 302
Limosa
  fedoa, 302
  haemastica, 302
  lapponica, 302
Little black rail, see rail, black
Littlefield, Carroll D., 5
Lobipes lobatus, 204
Long-billed curlew, see curlew, long-billed
Long-billed dowitcher, see dowitcher,
    long-billed
Long-toed stint, see stint, long-toed
Lonicera spp., 159
Louisiana clapper rail, see rail, Louisiana
    clapper

Madrone, Pacific, 222-223
Maize, see corn
Mallard, 136, 138, 325
Mangold, Robert E., 45, 84
Mangrove, 254
Mangrove clapper rail, see rail, mangrove
    clapper
Manzanita, 223
Maple, broadleaf, 222
Marbled godwit, see godwit, marbled
Martin, Fant W., *ix, xi,* 3, 149, 275, 323,
    332, 337
McKibben, Larry, 189
Meadowlark, eastern, 72
Medicago sativa, 153
Melanitta
  deglandi, 136
  nigra, 136
  perspicillata, 136
Mesquite,
  Texas honey, 252
  velvet, 254
Mexican highland white-winged dove,
    see dove, Mexican highland white-
    winged

Micropalama himantopus, 303
Millet, wild, 106, 279
Milo, 261
Mineral-spring, 228, 230
Mississippi crane, see crane, Mississippi
Mist netting, 73
Mongolian plover, see plover, Mongolian
Mongoose, 76
Mountain plover, see plover, Mountain
Mourning dove, see dove, mourning
Muskrat, 111

National Program Planning Committee
    for Migratory Shore and Upland
    Game Birds, *vii, x*
Needlerush, 84
Nelumbo, sp., 106
Newsom, John D., 149
Nish, Darrell H., 211
Northern clapper rail, see rail, northern
    clapper
Northern phalarope, see phalarope,
    northern
Numenius
    americanus, 302, 324
    borealis, 302
    phaeopus, 302
    tahitiensis, 302
Nymphae sp., 106

Oak,
    black, 223, 241
    blue, 223
    Gambel, 223
    huckleberry, 223
    interior live, 223
    Oregon, 223
    scrub, 223
Odocoileus virginianus, 167
Odom, Ron R., 45, 57
Olneya tesota, 254
Ondatra zibethicus, 111
Opuntia spp., 254
Oryza sativa, 113, 125, 279
Owen, Ray B., Jr., 149
Owl, great horned, 130
Oystercatcher, 301, 324
    American, 302, 304, 309, 314, 320
    black, 302, 304, 309, 314

Pachycereus pringlei, 254
Palo verde, 254
Parkinsonia aculeata, 254
Passenger pigeon, see pigeon, passenger
Peanuts, 279

Pecan, 254
Pectoral sandpiper, see sandpiper, pectoral
Phalarope, 301, 324
    northern, 303, 308, 313, 316
    red, 303, 308, 312, 316
    Wilson's, 303, 308, 313, 316, 320, 324
Phalaropus
    fulicarius, 204, 303, 324
    lobatus, 303, 324
    tricolor, 303, 324
Philohela minor, 1, 93, 148-186, 193, 302,
    323
Philomachus pugnax, 303
Phragmites, 113
Phreatophyte-control, 281
Picea
    engelmanni, 223
    sitchensis, 222
    spp. 166
Pickleweed, 72
Pigeon,
    band-tailed, 1, 2, 210-245, 323, 326, 330,
        340-342, 344, 349
    common, see pigeon, domestic
    domestic, 212, 276
    passenger, 193, 216
Pine, 159, 283
    digger, 223
    limber, 223
    lodgepole, 223
    longleaf, 23
    -oak, woodland, 211
    pinon, 223
    ponderosa, 223
    slash, 23
Pinon-juniper woodland, 223
Pintail, 138
    snipe, see snipe, pintail
Pinus
    caribaea, 23
    contorta, 223
    edulis, 223
    flexilis, 223
    palustris, 23
    ponderosa, 223
    sabiniana, 223
    spp., 159, 283
Pipe organ, 254
Piping plover, see plover, piping
Pithecellobium flexicaule, 252
Plover, 301, 324
    American golden, 193, 302, 304, 309,
        314, 324
    black-bellied, 302, 304, 309, 314, 317
    golden, see plover, American golden
    Mongolian, 302, 304, 309, 314

mountain, 302, 304, 309, 314
piping, 302, 304, 309, 314, 320, 324
semipalmated, 302, 304, 309, 314
snowy, 302, 304, 309, 314, 317, 320
Wilson's, 302, 304, 309, 314
Pluvialis
    dominica, 193, 302, 324
    squatarola, 302, 324
Polynesian tattler, see tattler, Polynesian
Populus tremuloides, 223
Porphyrula martinica, 105-109, 324
Port Orford cedar, see cedar, Port Orford
Porzana carolina, 46, 56-65, 324
Pospichal, Leo B., 189
Power lines, 130
Privet, swamp, 159
Procyon lotor, 86
Prosopis
    glandulosa, 252
    juliflora, 254
Prunus spp., 222
Pseudotsuga menziesii, 222
Purple gallinule, see gallinule, purple
Purple sandpiper, see sandpiper, purple
Pursglove, Samuel R., Jr., 149

Quail, see bobwhite
Quercus
    douglasii, 223
    dumosa, 223
    gambelii, 223
    garryana, 223
    kelloggii, 223
    vaccinifolia, 223
    velutina, 241
    wislizenii, 223

Raccoon, 86
Rail, 118-121, 344, 348
    black, 71-83, 119, 324, 326
    California black, see rail, black
    California clapper, 86-87, 119
    Carolina, see rail, sora
    clapper, *xiv,* 84-92, 94-95, 108, 119, 324,
        330, 339, 341, 343, 344
    farallon, see rail, black
    Florida clapper, 86-87
    king, 46, 93-104, 324, 330
    light-footed clapper, 86-87, 119, 327
    little black, see rail, black
    Louisiana clapper, 86-87
    mangrove clapper, 86-87
    northern clapper, 86-87
    sora, 56-65, 324, 326, 330
    Virginia, 46-56, 95, 324, 326, 330

Wayne clapper, 86-87
yellow, 66-70, 324, 326
Yuma clapper, 86-87, 119, 327
Rallus
    elegans, 46, 93-104, 324
        elegans, 95
        ramsdeni, 95
        tenuirostris, 95
    limicola, 45-56, 95
        limicola, 46, 324
    longirostris, 84-92, 94, 108, 119, 324
        crepitans, 86-87
        insularum, 86-87
        levipes, 86-87, 119, 327
        obsoletus, 86-87, 119
        saturatus, 86-87
        scottii, 86-87
        waynei, 86-87
        yumanensis, 86-87, 119, 327
Recurvirostra americana, 303, 324
Red cedar, see cedar, red
Redhead, 138
Red knot, see knot, red
Red phalarope, see phalarope, red
Redshank, spotted, 302, 305, 310, 314
Redwood, 222
Rhamnus
    californica, 223
    purshiana, 222
Rhizophora mangle, 254
Rice, 113, 125, 279
    wild, 106
Rock dove, see pigeon, domestic
Rock sandpiper, see sandpiper, rock
Ruckel, James M., *xi,* 2, 323
Ruddy turnstone, see turnstone, ruddy
Ruff, 303, 308, 312, 316
Ruffed grouse, see grouse, ruffed
Rufous-necked sandpiper, see sandpiper,
    rufous-necked
Ruos, James L., 275
Ryder, Ronald A., 123

Sadler, Kenneth C., *xi,* 2, 275, 323, 327
Safflower, 250
Saguaro, see cactus, giant
Salicornia spp., 72
Salt
    cedar, see cedar, salt
    grass, see grass, salt
    -hay, 72
Sambucus
    callicarpa, 241
    spp., 222
Sanderling, 302, 306, 311, 315, 317, 324

Sandfort, Wayne W., *x*, 1, 3, 323, 337
Sandhill crane, see crane, sandhill
Sandpiper, 301
    Baird's, 302, 307, 312, 316, 320
    buff-breasted, 303, 307, 312, 316
    curlew, 303, 307, 312, 316
    least, 302, 307, 312, 316, 317, 324
    pectoral, 302, 307, 312, 316
    purple, 303, 307, 312, 316
    rock, 303, 307, 312, 316
    rufous-necked, 302, 306, 311, 316
    semipalmated, 302, 306, 311, 316
    sharp-tailed, 303, 307, 312, 316
    stolitary, 302, 305, 310, 315
    spoon-billed, 303, 307, 312, 316
    spotted, 302, 305, 310, 315, 324
    stilt, 303, 307, 312, 316
    upland, 302, 305, 310, 314, 320, 324
    western, 302, 306, 311, 316, 317
    white-rumped, 302, 307, 312, 316, 320
    wood, 302, 305, 310, 315
Sands, James, 5
Saw grass, see grass, saw
Scaup, 136, 138, 326
Scirpus
    americanus, 72
    sp., 125
Scolopacidae, 150
Scolopax
    minor, see *Philohela minor*
    rusticola, 150
Scoter, 136, 138
Semipalmated plover, see plover, semi-
    palmated
Semipalmated sandpiper, see sandpiper,
    semipalmated
Sequoia sempervirens, 222
Setaria spp., 279
Sharp-tailed sandpiper, see sandpiper,
    sharp-tailed
Shorebirds, 301-320, 344
Short-billed dowitcher, see dowitcher,
    short-billed
Shoveler, 136, 138
Smilax spp., 160
Smith, Walton A., 211
Snipe,
    common, 1, 2, 150, 188-209, 302, 306,
    311, 315, 323, 330-331, 335, 339-340,
    342, 344, 349
    pintail, 302, 306, 311, 315
Snowy plover, see plover, snowy
Soileau, Larry D., 275
Solitary sandpiper, see sandpiper, solitary
Sora, see rail, sora

Sorghum, 261, 279
Sorghum
    durra, 261
    spp., 261, 279
    vulgare, 261
Southeastern Association of Game and
    Fish Commissioners, 1
Soybean, 168
Sparganium, 113
Spartina
    alterniflora, 45
    patens, 67, 72
    sp., 84
Species committees, *vii*
Sphaeridiotrema globulus, 129
Spoon-billed sandpiper, see sandpiper,
    spoon-billed
Spotted redshank, see redshank, spotted
Spotted sandpiper, see sandpiper, spotted
Spruce,
    Engelmann, 223
    Sitka, 222
Stamp, state-issued white-winged dove,
    270
Steganopus tricolor, 204
Stephen, W. J. D., 5
Stilt, 301
    black-necked, 303, 308, 313, 316, 324
    sandpiper, see sandpiper, stilt
Stint, long-toed, 302, 306, 311, 316
Strohmeyer, David L., 45, 110
Sturnella magna, 72
Surfbird, 302, 306, 311, 315

Tamarisk, 254
Tamarix chinensis, 254
Tattler,
    Polynesian, 302, 305, 310, 315
    wandering, 302, 305, 310, 315
Teal,
    American green-winged, 138, 326
    blue-winged, 136, 138
Texas white-winged dove, see dove, Texas
    white-winged
Thuja plicata, 222
Todd, Richard L., 45, 71
Trichomonas, 216
Tringa
    erythropus, 302
    flavipes, 302
    glareola, 302
    melanoleuca, 302, 324
    solitaria, 302
Triticum aestivum, 131
Tryngites subruficollis, 303

Tsuga heterophylla, 222
Tully, Robert J., 189
Turnstone,
   black, 302, 306, 311, 315, 324
   ruddy, 3, 302, 305, 310, 315
Typha, 22, 46, 125

Uca, sp., 85
Upland sandpiper, see sandpiper, upland

Vaccinium spp., 222
Vanellus vanellus, 302
Vermivora bachmanii, 78
Varginia rail, see rail, Virginia

Waggerman, Gary L., 247
Wandering tattler, see tattler, wandering
Warbler, Bachman's, 78
Western sandpiper, see sandpiper, western
Western white-winged dove, see dove,
   Arizona white-winged
Wheat, 131
Whimbrel, 302, 305, 310, 314, 320, 322
White-rumped sandpiper, see sandpiper,
   white-rumped
White-tailed deer, see deer, white-tailed
White-winged dove, see dove, white-
   winged
Whooping crane, see crane, whooping
Wigeon, American, 136, 138, 326
Willet, 302, 305, 310, 315, 317, 324
Williams, Lovett E., Jr., 5
Willow, desert, 254

Wilson's phalarope, see phalarope,
   Wilson's
Wilson's plover, see plover, Wilson's
Winkler, Charles K., 247
Wire grass, see grass, wire
Woodcock,
   American, 1, 2, 93, 148-186, 193, 302,
   306, 311, 315, 323, 330-331, 339-344,
   348
   Eurasian, 150
Woodpecker, ivory-billed, 78
Wood sandpiper, see sandpiper, wood

Yellowlegs,
   greater, 302, 305, 310, 314, 317, 324
   lesser, 302, 305, 310, 315
Yellow rail, see rail, yellow
Yuma clapper rail, see rail, Yuma clapper

Zanthoxylum fagara, 252
Zapatka, Thomas P., 211
Zea mays, 250, 259
Zenaida
   asiatica, 1, 246-272, 283, 323
      asiatica, 248-249
      grandis, 248-249
      mearnsi, 248-249
      monticola, 248-249
   macroura, 1, 214, 256, 274-298, 323
      carolinensis, 276
      marginella, 276
Zimmerman, John L., 45-46
Zizania aquatica, 106